Nonbelief
& EVIL

two arguments
for the
nonexistence
of God

Nonbelief & EVIL

THEODORE M. DRANGE

 Prometheus Books
59 John Glenn Drive
Amherst, New York 14228-2197

Published 1998 by Prometheus Books

02 01 00 99 98   5 4 3 2 1

Library of Congress Cataloging-in-Publication Data

Drange, Theodore M.
    Nonbelief & evil : two arguments for the nonexistence of God / Theodore M. Drange.
        p.   cm.
    Includes bibliographical references and index.
    ISBN 1–57392–228–5 (alk. paper)
    1. God—Controversial literature. 2. God—Proof—Controversial literature. 3. Theodicy—Controversial literature. I. Title.
BL2775.2.D73   1998
212'.1—dc21   98–24173
                                                     CIP

To E. Haldeman-Julius,

who helped us break free

Contents

Part II: The God of Evangelical Christianity

Part III: Other Concepts of God and an Assessment

Appendices   297

List of Abbreviations

Argument Abbreviations

ADE = The Afterlife Defense as applied to AE

ADN = The Afterlife Defense as applied to ANB

AE = The Argument from Evil

ANB = The Argument from Nonbelief

FDE = The Free-will Defense as applied to AE

FDN = The Free-will Defense as applied to ANB

TDE = The Testing Defense as applied to AE

TDN = The Testing Defense as applied to ANB

UDE = The Unknown-purpose Defense as applied to AE

UDN = The Unknown-purpose Defense as applied to ANB

Other Abbreviations

AEH = The anti-evangelical (or anti-theistic) worldview as applied to the problem of evil

UEH = The unknown-purpose worldview as applied to the problem of evil

ANH = The anti-evangelical (or anti-theistic) worldview as applied to the problem of nonbelief

UNH = The unknown-purpose worldview as applied to the problem of non-belief

Situation L = The situation of there being less evil in the world than there actually is at present

Situation S = The situation of there being less nonbelief of a certain sort in the world than there actually is at present

Set P = A certain set of propositions that God wants people to believe

AEers, ANBers, FDEers, FDNers, UDEers, UDNers = advocates of AE, ANB, FDE, FDN, UDE, and UDN, respectively

OC = The situation of optimal opportunity for experiencing contrast between good and evil

OM = The situation of optimal opportunity for the development of moral virtues

OFW = The situation of optimal opportunity for the exercise of genuine free will

B = the Brute-fact Hypothesis

F = the Fine-tuners Hypothesis

G = the God Hypothesis

KJV = The King James Version of the Bible

NIV = The New International Version of the Bible

RSV = The Revised Standard Version of the Bible

Preface

We will be discussing, among other things, the problem of evil. In theology that is usually posed as the question "Why does God permit evil?" but in the philosophy of religion it is more often taken to be the question "Does the evil in the world provide good reason to deny the existence of God?" In this book the problem will be taken in the latter way.

The book is mostly a consideration of several arguments, which I take to be sets of propositions proceeding from premises to a conclusion. There are two basic arguments for God's nonexistence discussed throughout the book, called the Argument from Evil and the Argument from Nonbelief. Then there are defenses of God's existence against those two. Each defense is itself an argument. There are twelve defenses taken up, seven of them against the Argument from Evil and five of them against the Argument from Nonbelief. Finally, against each of the defenses there are several objections (each of which is still another argument), producing altogether dozens of objections. The basic subject matter of the book is a close consideration and assessment of all those many objections. Although not all the objections are sound, I think most of them are. My overall aim is to show that each of the twelve defenses is refuted by at least one good objection. Thus, I regard both the Argument from Evil and the Argument from Nonbelief to be forceful and cogent attacks on the popular belief that God exists. This expresses my basic outlook, though it needs to be qualified by considerations pertaining to the many different concepts of God (or definitions of the word "God") discussed in the book, and that is done in chapters 12–15.

I hold the "proper-name theory" according to which the word "God" is either a proper name or a special term very much like a proper name. However, to speak of "concepts of God" or "definitions of 'God,'" as I do in the book, is to depart somewhat from the theory, for proper names are not normally spoken of in that way. Expressions such as "concept of Bill Clinton" or "definition of 'Bill Clinton' " would sound odd in ordinary language. Despite that, I use such expressions in connection with the word "God" as a matter of convenience and continue to regard "God" as a kind of proper name. In the background is the assumption that, given sufficient time and space, all such linguistic niceties could be adequately taken care of.

When the word is pluralized or has an indefinite article in front of it, then I regard it to be a common noun (synonymous with "deity") and do not capitalize it but instead use the lower-case "g." Thus, I write "gods" and "a god." In my view, the word is also a common noun when it is preceded by the definite article, but, following common practice, I there capitalize it. For example, I write "the God of Christianity," though I regard that expression to be equivalent to "the deity of Christianity," and so the lower-case "g" would be more correct. In other words, the expression "the god of Christianity" would be more correct than the usual expression ("the God of Christianity") that, bowing to common practice, I use in the book. When I say this, there is no disrespect intended, nor is there intended any connotation that more than one god might exist. An alternate expression would be "God as conceived of within Christianity." As for pronouns which have "God" as their antecedent, I write them in lower-case letters. Again, there is no disrespect intended, but I regard the capitalization of such pronouns as a religious practice and I am not in any way religious.

This is a lengthy book with many strands of thought, addressed to many different kinds of readers. One dichotomy within the readership is that between evangelical Christians and everyone else. Another dichotomy is that between professional philosophers and laypersons. This book aims to have material of interest to all these different groups. I have tried to hold everything together by three devices: a fairly detailed table of contents, an extended index at the end, and the division of the book into three parts, followed by a lengthy set of appendices. It is recommended that readers first skim through various parts to try to get a handle on the book's overall structure before digging into chapter 1. Also, readers should be prepared to skip certain chapters, especially ones, if any, that they find to express points which they regard to be obviously true.

The appendices in the back of the book go into topics that are relevant, though somewhat tangential, to the main thread of argument that runs through the book. Some of those topics, though dealt with only sketchily in the given appendix, are suitable for book-length treatments of their own. My goal is not to provide anything close to a complete analysis, but only to express a few ideas on the subject. In some of the appendices, my thinking has not led to any definite results, but I include it anyway. Even where conclusions are rather indefinite and tentative, I think the reasoning that leads up to them is worth presenting and considering. In the last appendix, in the spirit of "applied philosophy," I make a few suggestions about applications of the central topic to various matters, including a few issues of public policy. However, the reader has my permission to take those suggestions "with a grain of salt." The main focus of the book is not public policy but a presentation and defense of the Argument from Nonbelief as an important issue in the philosophy of religion.

The book can be used as a text in any course titled Philosophy of Religion or Metaphysics, or even Introduction to Philosophy, provided that its emphasis is philosophical reasoning. Some parts of the book would be more appropriate than others for the treatment of specific issues. I leave it up to the instructor what to include and what to exclude. The table of contents and the index should be helpful guides regarding the various topics.

My work was aided by the helpful comments of many persons, particularly the following: Mark Aronszajn, Don Turner, Ned Markosian, Richard M. Gale, David E. Schrader, and Chip Keating. I thank them for their assistance and encouragement. Most of the writing of the book was done in 1995–96 during a sabbatical leave granted to me by West Virginia University, for which I am very grateful. I hope readers get out of it as much as I tried to put into it.

Part I

The Project

1

Introduction

1.1. Atheological Arguments

Atheological arguments are arguments for the conclusion that God does not exist. The specific subject matter of this book will be a certain pair of them called the Argument from Evil, to be abbreviated AE, and the Argument from Nonbelief, to be abbreviated ANB.

Some atheological arguments are based on alleged incompatible properties within the very concept of God. For example, God is sometimes said to possess the properties of being a perfect being and also of having deliberately created the universe. But to deliberately create anything, so it is claimed, requires having some sort of *lack*, and that is incompatible with being a perfect being. Therefore, if God is defined as possessing both properties, it becomes logically impossible for God to exist. Another pair of incompatible properties is that of being all-merciful and being all-just with regard to deserts. An all-merciful being would treat all offenders with *less* severity than they deserve, whereas an all-just being would treat them in a way incompatible with that, viz., with *exactly* the severity they deserve. Since no being can have both properties, it is impossible for God, thus defined, to exist.

Other alleged incompatibilities are between God being immutable (or unchangeable) vs. God having created the universe, and between God being immutable vs. God being omniscient. These two incompatibilities are the basis of what Richard M. Gale calls "the Creation-immutability Argument" and "the Omniscience-immutability Argument."[1] The idea behind the first is that it is logically impossible for God to deliberately create the

21

universe without changing in some way (e.g., from not willing the creation to willing it). And the idea behind the second is that it is logically impossible for God to be omniscient without changing in some way (e.g., with respect to an event E that occurs at time t, from knowing before t that E has not yet occurred to knowing after t that E has occurred). So if God is defined as immutable and also as having created the universe or as being omniscient, then it is logically impossible for God to exist. A similar point might be made with regard to God interacting with the world, for it is logically impossible to interact with the world without in some way being affected by it. Hence, if God is defined as an immutable being who interacts with the world, then God cannot possibly exist.

There are several arguments of the above type, which may be called "incompatible-properties arguments." In some cases they may be applied specifically to the God of the Bible, and that topic will be explored below in section 3.2. Although such arguments are interesting and important, they will not be the focus of the present book. Rather, its focus will be on another type of atheological argument in which God's existence is claimed to be incompatible with some actual feature of the world. An example would be the Argument from Evil (or AE), which maintains that God's existence is incompatible with the sort and/or quantity of evil that actually exists. Such arguments may be called "God-vs.-world arguments."

Another example of a God-vs.-world argument is what I call the Argument from Nonbelief (or ANB). It maintains that God's existence is incompatible with the quantity of *nonbelief* of a certain sort that exists in the world. In the simplest version, the sort of nonbelief is nontheism itself. That is, there are a certain number of nontheists in the world (i.e., persons familiar with the proposition that God exists but who do not believe it) and ANB claims that *that* fact is incompatible with God's existence. If God really did exist, then he would have very much wanted people generally to believe in him. (For economy, I shall take the expression "believe in God" as short for "believe that God exists.") So God would have done something to prevent people from being nontheists. The fact that there are nontheists, especially so many of them, is therefore a reason to deny God's existence. An alternate version, put forward by J. L. Schellenberg,[2] appeals to the existence of *reasonable* nontheism in the world. We will consider these and other versions of ANB as we go along.

One way to express the two arguments is by means of a *modus tollens* form (i.e., the form "if P then Q, not-Q, therefore not-P"), as follows:

AE: (1) If God were to exist, then there would be no unjustifiable evil in the world.

(2) But there is unjustifiable evil in the world.

(3) Therefore, God does not exist.

ANB: (1) If God were to exist, then there would be no avoidable non-theism in the world.

(2) But there is avoidable nontheism in the world.

(3) Therefore, God does not exist.

Here the expression "unjustifiable evil" could be tentatively taken to refer to whatever evil there is beyond the minimum needed to achieve the greatest possible good (assuming that the concept of the "greatest possible good" can be sufficiently understood). And the expression "avoidable non-theism" means the absence of belief in God among people who are familiar with the concept of God and who could in one way or another have been caused to have such belief. Although the modus tollens forms given here may be very simple, they are somewhat vague. More precise formulations will be presented and discussed later.

1.2. Deduction vs. Induction

Some writers draw a distinction between a so-called "deductive problem of evil" and an "inductive problem of evil," but in my opinion that is not the best terminology to use here. Let us look at the distinction more closely. Some versions of AE make use of the concept of probability. For example, consider the following formulation:

(1) If God were to exist, then there would be no unjustifiable evil in the world.

(2) But probably there is unjustifiable evil in the world.

(3) Therefore, probably God does not exist.

This is clearly a deductive argument, despite the occurrence of the word "probably" within it. One change that would make it inductive would be the addition of preliminary premises in support of step (2). If step (2) were inductively inferred from such prior premises, then, although the rest of the argument would still be deductive, that inductive component would suffice to make the extended (or overall) argument inductive in character. But without such an inductive component, the argument should be regarded as deductive.

Since the argument as it stands is deductive, the question might be raised whether it is valid. Let us consider that briefly. The relevant logical form is:

If p then not-q.
Probably q.
Therefore, probably not-p.

I think this form is definitely valid, given a suitable interpretation of the "if-then." But note that material implication may not be a suitable interpretation, for consider the argument:

> If snow is white then the (unexamined) dice came up twelve.
> Probably the (unexamined) dice did not come up twelve.
> Therefore, probably snow is not white.

If the "if-then" in the first premise were taken to express material implication and if the dice happened to come up twelve, then under a certain interpretation of this argument it might be argued to have true premises and a false conclusion. So let us take the "if-then" in our argument form to express a stronger connection than mere material implication.

One might still try to refute the form as follows. Suppose that Joe is in Alaska but all the members of his family think he is in the Yukon, which they all mistakenly believe to be in Alaska. From the postmarks on his letters, they have good evidence that Joe is in Alaska. In one sense, that would also be good evidence that Joe is not in the Yukon, but let us assume here that evidence requires awareness; so, given the beliefs of Joe's family, there is no good evidence that Joe is not in the Yukon, at least so far as they are concerned. In this situation, the following argument might be maintained to have true premises and a false conclusion:

> If Joe is in the Yukon, then he is not in Alaska.
> Probably Joe is in Alaska.
> Hence, probably Joe is not in the Yukon.

The first premise would be true even though Joe's family is unaware of it, and the conclusion would be false from their (mistaken) point of view. If it is assumed that in some sense evidence requires awareness and that probability is tied to evidence in that sense, then it might be claimed that this argument has true premises and a false conclusion, which would prove the invalidity of the argument form in question. To avoid this result, let us understand probability in such a way that it is based on all the relevant evidence that there is, rather than on some restricted subset of the evidence. Since the totality of the evidence includes the facts that Joe is in Alaska and that whoever is in Alaska is not in the Yukon, our understanding of probability would make the conclusion of the given argument true rather than false.

With this understanding of "if-then" and probability, let us look again at the probabilistic version of AE given above. Its premise (2) asserts that probably there exists unjustifiable evil in the world, where "unjustifiable evil" could be defined as evil beyond the minimum needed to achieve the greatest possible good (assuming that that concept can be adequately understood). Why believe that premise? It might be suggested that we can think of various evils that serve no apparent purpose in relation to the greatest good. Perhaps an example would be the widespread famine that occurs in parts of Africa and Asia resulting in many deaths, including the deaths of millions of children. How could such famine and death possibly maximize the good in the world seeing that when children die there is a net loss of such benefits as learning and development of moral virtues? Some theologians or theistic philosophers might try to construct what is called a theodicy, which is a general theistic explanation and justification of all the evil in the world. Others might be inclined simply to say, "We know that God exists, so there must be some answer, but we do not as yet know what it is: God has some justifying purpose that we may find out about later." I call that the "Unknown-purpose Defense." Let us postpone such issues to later in the book.

It seems that one inevitably gets into such issues whether one is trying to solve a so-called "deductive problem of evil" or an "inductive problem of evil." It is the issues themselves that are important and not the way the overall problem is structured. For example, if AE were formulated as the deductive "probabilistic" version given above, then the focus would be on the truth of its premises, especially step (2). But suppose that AE were instead formulated as an inductive argument, as follows:

(1)   If God were to exist, then there would be no unjustifiable evil in the world.
(2a)   There has occurred widespread famine in parts of Africa and Asia, resulting in the deaths of millions of children, which is evil.
(2b)   Possible justification for such evil has been sought for a long time by some of the world's brightest people.
(2c)   No one has ever succeeded in coming up with such justification.
(2d)   So, probably the given evil is unjustifiable. [from (2b) & (2c)]
(2e)   Hence, probably there is unjustifiable evil in the world.
(3)   Therefore, probably God does not exist. [from (1) & (2e)]

The focus here might still be on the truth of a premise. For example, someone with a theodicy to expound might attack step (2c). Alternatively, the focus might be on the strength of the inference from (2b) and (2c) to (2d). For example, it might be said that the inference is weak because we lack data pertaining to God's purposes, which I think would be an implicit use of the Unknown-purpose Defense. But in either case, whether AE is formulated as a deductive argument or as an inductive argument, the *same* issues will emerge in the ensuing debate. We would still be debating the adequacy of some theodicy or the force of the Unknown-purpose Defense. And it is *those* issues that are the important consideration. I conclude that it matters very little whether AE and ANB are formulated as deductive arguments or as inductive arguments.

Thus, the distinction should be not between "deductive" and "inductive," but between "conclusive" and "nonconclusive," that is, between arguments that purport to conclusively establish their conclusions and arguments that don't. How should the latter type be labeled? The term "nonconclusive" is misleading, for it might be associated with "inconclusive," which connotes weakness, and that is not the intention here. Another term that might be used is "probabilistic," but that is a bit too narrow. Not all arguments that attempt to prove God's nonexistence in a nonconclusive way make appeal to probabilities. An expression suggested by Frank B. Dilley is "non-fool-proof."[3] But that strikes me as too cumbersome. Let us use the more common term "evidential" to represent arguments which aim to provide grounds for a conclusion that are strong but not conclusive. We could say, then, that all the versions of AE and ANB to be later presented and discussed in the present book will be evidential arguments or evidential versions of those arguments.

Instead of talking of "the deductive problem of evil" vs. "the inductive problem of evil," which we have seen to be misleading, we should distinguish the following two issues:

(1) Is there any version of AE which conclusively establishes its conclusion?

(2) Is there any evidential version of AE which is a strong argument?

My answers to these two questions are no and yes, respectively. And I would answer the same way for the analogous questions asked about ANB. Later I shall explain why I answer question (1) negatively. The main focus of the book will be question (2), applied to both AE and ANB. In the old (misleading) way of speaking, it could be said of me that I address "the inductive problem of evil" and "the inductive problem of nonbelief." But the terminology that I prefer would instead use the expressions "the Evidential Argument from Evil" and "The Evidential Argument from Nonbelief."

1.3. Good and Evil

In the title of this book, the terms "nonbelief" and "evil" are being used in a somewhat different way from each other in the following respect. Whereas "evil" means the same thing throughout the book, the term "nonbelief" means different things depending on context. For example, in chapters 2–11 "nonbelief" is taken to mean an absence of belief in the basic message of evangelical Christianity (the so-called "gospel message"), but in chapters 12–14 other meanings for "nonbelief" are considered. On the other hand, in every chapter and appendix the term "evil" is taken in the same way, and that is to refer just to suffering and premature death.

It is not my claim that such a naturalistic concept (suffering and premature death) is what the word "evil" means in ordinary language. Exactly what it does mean there is not completely clear, though it no doubt refers to other features of our world. For example, it might include unfairness and dishonesty, even where no suffering or death results from them. However, to formulate AE in the strongest possible way, it seems to me that it would suffice to take "evil" to refer just to suffering and premature death. Such an interpretation would have various advantages, one of which is avoiding complicated issues of ethics and meta-ethics. In the interest of usefulness and economy, then, the term "evil" will be taken in that naturalistic way. My goal is to formulate AE without the use of moral or evaluative concepts. I shall take "doing evil" to mean "causing suffering or premature death" and I shall take "experiencing evil" to mean simply "suffering or dying prematurely."

By a "premature" death I mean to exclude the sort of death that my parents had. Both of them lived to a very advanced age, and being frail and suffering various ailments, they both expressed a readiness to die. They said that they had lived a full life and were satisfied with that. If people die long before reaching such a stage in life, then I would say that they die prematurely and that that is something evil. I realize that this is an exceedingly vague definition and that someone who aims to avoid moral and evaluative concepts should present something clearer. For a full treatment, certainly more is needed, not only regarding the concept of "premature death" but also regarding the concept of "suffering." There are a number of borderline cases that need to be addressed. However, I shall bypass all that and simply assume that it is possible to solve such definitional problems while conceding that the expressions in question are vague. In the way that AE comes to be formulated later in the book, such vagueness will not present any insurmountable difficulty.

It might be objected that death is not evil at all, for no one ever regrets having died. Nor does one ever experience death, for no one ever remembers it, even fleetingly. But a person who dies prematurely is deprived of whatever good there may have been in continuing to live. And to be deprived of a good might reasonably be taken to be a type of evil. Certainly most people fear death, which in itself might be said to make death evil. You would probably dread the news that you have a terminal disease. People are also greatly saddened by the premature death of others, especially ones close to them, not only because of their own loss, but for the sakes of those who died. They say things like, "It is very sad that so-and-so died because of the great potential that s/he had." In other words, there is evil in death beyond the suffering that it causes among the living. The Bible also regards death as evil (Rom. 6:23, 1 Cor. 15:54–57). To be consistent and to be true to their faith, Christians and Jews need to regard the matter in that way.

Just as there is a certain unclarity in the term "evil," so also there is unclarity, to an even greater extent, in the words "good" and "perfect" as applied to God. I have great difficulty comprehending what they might mean in that context. My understanding of "good" and "perfect" in ordinary language is that their meaning is context-dependent, and related to standards of grading. In one context they might mean one thing, being related to one particular standard of grading, whereas in another context they might mean something quite different, being related to a quite different standard. This is a view that was expressed by Charles Crittenden.[4] We apply the words "good" and "perfect" to various things, such as apples, ball point pens, swan dives, safecrackers, etc., and it is apparent that quite different standards of grading are referred to in these various contexts. But we have no clear idea of how God might be graded. According to William J. Wainwright: "If God is maximally perfect, then (1) every possible reality can be compared with God in *some* respect and (2) no possible reality is better than God in *any* respect."[5] It is condition (1) that I do not understand here. In what respect might a ball point pen be compared with God? Suppose I have three pens and I declare, "This one is the best and it couldn't be better." How might God come in here for comparison with the best pen? Wainwright's criterion for absolute (nonrelative) perfection is unclear.

Even when the terms are narrowed to "morally good" and "morally perfect," it is unclear what they might mean in connection with God. There would presumably then be some reference to conformity with moral rules or moral standards, for that is what we mean by the adverb "morally" in ordinary language. A morally perfect person is one who (among other things) never violates a moral rule except to avoid violating a still more important moral rule. But to what rules or standards must God conform in order to be "morally perfect"? Are they the same rules or standards as apply to humans? No one, so far as I know, has ever listed them specifically for God. Do they include such rules as "Do that act which produces the greatest balance of pleasure over pain in the long run"? And how are they to be ranked? Which ones outweigh or outrank others? This gets into some complicated issues of ethics and meta-ethics. After discussing the debate between deontologists and consequentialists, David and Randall Basinger say the following:

> It should not be surprising, accordingly, that even among those theists who believe that God is perfectly good, there is no single, straightforward response to . . . the contention that a perfectly good being would never desire (seek to bring about) the occurrence of evil.[6]

In other words, different theists interpret "perfectly good" in different ways, depending on what their overall ethical theory may be. Many philosophers and theologians have called God "morally good" or "morally perfect," but none, so far as I can see, has ever explained in a precise and unambiguous way what that might mean. Most of them would deny that it involves God conforming to humanity's moral rules or standards. But they do not explain in a clear way just what it does involve.

Within Christianity, one prominent outlook is that God himself is the criterion of good. Patterson Brown says the following:

> Not only would we withhold the name 'God' from any being who was imperfect by Christian standards; in addition, the appellation 'God' is reserved for that particular being who is the ultimate Christian *criterion* of the good. The saint is good because he follows God's will; but God is good because he is the standard of goodness. . . . 'God is the ultimate standard of the good' is true by definition, and this entails that 'God is good' is trivially true.[7]

I find this to be a very confusing way to view the relation of God to goodness. It may make the statement "God is good" trivially true, but it does not really clarify what that statement is supposed to mean.

The problem of evil has been discussed for centuries by nontheists as well as theists using such terms as "good," "evil," and "perfect." For example, J. L. Mackie, who was a nontheist, wrote the following:

> [G]ood is opposed to evil in such a way that a being who is wholly good eliminates evil as far as he can. . . . A wholly good omnipotent being would eliminate evil completely; if there really are evils, then there cannot be any such being.[8]

I have two problems with this formulation of AE. One of them has to do with the conclusion "there cannot be any such being," which is a separate matter and which will be discussed later. But the problem relevant to this section is my great difficulty in comprehending what "a being who is wholly good" might mean. It seems to make the argument exceedingly obscure. I want to steer clear of such formulations of AE because of their unclarity.

Another writer on the topic, one who is a theist, is Bruce R. Reichenbach. He wrote the following:

> Goodness refers to the superb degree to which one has the perfection of ontological qualities and attributes. . . . It is in this sense that goodness is predicated of God in virtue of his nature.[9]

Again, I find the term "goodness" as used here to be obscure. Reichenbach appears to be saying that God is good in that he is omnipotent and omniscient, etc., but surely that is not what he intends. God's goodness is usually thought to be a separate quality, independent of God's power and knowledge and other qualities. But just what that separate quality amounts to is unclear. I do not wish to try to defend any version of AE that makes reference to "God's goodness."

As I view the topic, to call God "good," "perfect," "morally good," or "morally perfect" in the absence of any specific context or interpretation makes no clear sense, so I shall not use any of those terms in formulating AE. According to Edward H. Madden and Peter H. Hare, if the expression "God is infinitely good" is not clearly meaningful, then there would be no problem of evil.[10] And Mark T. Nelson says the following:

> [I]t may be worth reconsidering the possibility that a version of the argument from evil could be offered which neither contains, nor depends on, any premises which are moral judgments. Still, it is difficult to imagine how it would even begin, since if the aim of the argument from evil is to show that an all-good all-powerful God does not exist, the argument seems indelibly moral or evaluative from the outset.[11]

I think these authors are mistaken. The nonevaluative term "all-loving" could be put in place of "infinitely good" or "all-good." Thus, AE could (and should) instead be formulated in a way that conceives of God as a being who is omnipotent, omniscient, and *all-loving*, where to be "all-loving" is simply to love everyone maximally. The argument would be that such a being cannot (or probably does not) exist, in light of the fact that there is so much suffering and premature death in the world. The expressions "all-loving" and "suffering and premature death," unlike ethical terms such as "good," "perfect," "evil," etc., can be understood apart from specific contexts and interpretations.

According to Robert M. Adams, God could be omnipotent and perfect and yet not create a perfect world.[12] I cannot easily assess that proposition for I lack a clear sense of what the term "perfect" might mean in either of its occurrences in the given sentence. As explained above, it makes little or no sense to call God "perfect," for we lack any system of standards in relation to which such a use of the term could derive meaning. We have no way to grade God. And the expression "perfect world" (or "best of all possible worlds") is also unclear. It might be suggested that it is simply a world that contains no unjustified suffering and no unjustified premature death. That, at least, is something I can understand, but there would be problems with such a suggestion. One problem is that there are no doubt many (perhaps an infinite number of) such worlds, so it would not permit reference to "*the* perfect world." And another problem is that those who speak of a "perfect world" usually mean something more, something referring to certain positive qualities that it contains. But just what those positive qualities might be is hard to comprehend. Furthermore, there are reasons to prefer a world that contains a little bit of suffering to one that contains none at all, and that complicates matters a bit when it comes to describing "the perfect world." Such reasons will be discussed later.

The main problem is that of relativity. ("One man's meat is another man's poison.") A young man, for example, might prefer a world full of adventure, complexity, change, variety, discord, risk, and potential excitement, and so he would like there to be many of the features of our present world: violent weather, dangerous situations, large cities, and perhaps even some political turmoil, that is, circumstances that for the most part make our world unpredictable. He is one who feels that freedom is more valuable than contentment. On the other hand, a much older man might prefer a world that is full of peace, simplicity, stability, security, harmony, and serenity, and so he might *dislike* features of our present world that make it unpredictable. He is one who feels that contentment is more valuable than freedom. Since the world cannot be both predictable and unpredictable, the perfect world to one of these persons could not be the perfect world to the other, nor would there be any way to prove one right and the other wrong. There would be no fact of the matter here. Nor would there be any fact of the matter regarding the issue whether or not freedom is more valuable than contentment. That is why I find talk of the one "perfect world" in some absolute sense to be very obscure.

Another way to bring out the relativity of perfection would be by means of a competitive game. Suppose A and B are both master chess players. When we ask A what the perfect world would be like, he replies, "It is one in which I always defeat B and all the other great chess players of the world." And when we ask B what the perfect world would be like, he replies, "It is one in which I always defeat A and all the other great chess players of the world." Obviously, no world could be perfect for both A and B, nor would we have much hope of understanding what the "really perfect world" might be, in some absolute sense. There will always be competing interests and no way to satisfy all of them.

Relativity also affects the concept of a "wholly good" being. Suppose such a being were to judge an offender O who deserves punishment of severity S. Would the "wholly good" judge have O punished to degree of severity S, which would be just and fair, or would he have O punished to a degree less than S, which would be merciful? Some theists would give the one answer and others would give the other answer. I say there is no fact of the matter here, which implies that we have no clear, objective concept of a "wholly good" being.

The problem of evil, as I understand it, need make no reference to either "the perfect (or wholly good) being" or "the perfect world." Rather, it could simply be formulated as the question how an omnipotent, omniscient, and all-loving being, who rules the world, could permit it to contain suffering and premature death of the sort and/or quantity that it actually does. And AE, as interpreted and formulated in the present book, is the argument that God, conceived as such an omnipotent, omniscient, and all-loving ruler, probably does not exist, in light of the sort and/or quantity of suffering and premature death that there actually is.

One objection that might be raised against putting "all-loving" in place of "perfect" or "wholly good" is that only a perfect or wholly good being is worthy of unqualified worship, devotion, and adoration, which are the actions and attitudes that properly relate creatures to their Creator. By referring to God as merely "all-loving," we would be failing to capture that special relationship. But this objection misses the force of AE. The problem of evil need not be taken to confront unqualified worship, etc., only theistic belief. So long as God is defined as, among other things, all-loving, and so long as AE refutes the existence of such a being, AE has done its job. The fact that additional predicates (such as "perfect" and "wholly good," whatever they might mean) are commonly ascribed to that nonexistent being is irrelevant to the evaluation of AE.

It might be objected that the term "all-loving" is itself vague or unclear. Consider again our example of the judge. Suppose an all-loving judge were to administer punishment to the offender, O, who deserves punishment of severity S. Would the judge (being perfectly just) administer punishment to O that is exactly equal to S (which is what O's victims and other onlookers demand) or would he (being merciful) instead administer punishment that is less severe than degree S (which is what O and O's supporters desire)? What is the "more loving" course of action here, seeing that the judge obviously cannot please everyone? I grant that this presents a puzzle, but, as pointed out above, it applies at least as much to the concept of a "perfect" or "wholly good" judge as it does to the concept of one who is "all-loving." Those who call God "perfect" or "wholly good" do not have any better way to solve the "justice vs. mercy" problem. Some evangelical Christians emphasize God's justice (warning people of future judgment), while others emphasize God's mercy (bringing to people the "good-news" message of undeserved salvation). Most Christians seem not to appreciate the incompatibility between the two concepts. Hence, although I grant the relevant vagueness or unclarity of the term "all-loving," I do not see that as a fatal objection. To call God "all-loving" instead of "perfect" or "wholly good" may not help solve the "justice vs. mercy" problem, but at least it does not exacerbate it.

Another objection to my revised form of AE, which appeals to "unjustifiable suffering and premature death," is that it is inferior to the alternate version of AE that appeals to "unjustifiable evil." We can compare the following two principles:

(1) If X loves Y, then X would not cause or permit Y to endure unjustifiable evil.

(2) If X loves Y, then X would not cause or permit Y to endure unjustifiable suffering or premature death.

The objection is that principle (1) is stronger and more forceful than principle (2), so when AE is formulated using (2) instead of (1), that weakens the force of AE. My main reply to this is simply to deny that (1) is stronger and more forceful than (2). I see no good reason to believe that. Furthermore, principle (2) expresses part of our criterion for love, which makes it sufficiently forceful for the purposes of AE. We would not say that X loves Y if X causes or knowingly permits Y to endure unjustifiable suffering or premature death. As for (1), we need to know what more there is to endured "evil" than what is given in (2). I do not see that theodicists have ever made that clear. Thus, in the remainder of the book, I shall construe the problem of evil as simply the problem of suffering and premature death, which, for the sake of brevity, I shall often abbreviate just by the term "suffering."

1.4. Unjustifiability vs. Great Quantity

Even when one is working strictly with the Evidential Argument from Evil, there are many different ways to formulate the argument. Bruce Russell divides them first into those versions that proceed from our *inability to justify* certain types or amounts of suffering and those that proceed from the mere *existence* of certain types or amounts of suffering.[13] He then divides each of those kinds into those versions that are based on sampling and those that are inferences to the best explanation. My own preference, using Russell's classification system, is for a version that proceeds from the mere existence of certain types or amounts of suffering and aims at the best explanation for them. Within that category, there are basically two different ways to formulate AE, which may be referred to as the "Unjustifiability Version" and the "Great-quantity Version." They are as follows:

The Unjustifiability Version of AE

(1) If God were to exist, then he would not permit the occurrence of any unjustifiable suffering.

(2) But unjustifiable suffering does occur.

(3) Therefore, God does not exist.

(Some other words that philosophers have used in place of "unjustifiable" are "pointless" and "gratuitous." I regard all three terms to be equivalent in this context.)

The Great-quantity Version of AE

(1) If God were to exist, then he would not permit the occurrence of such a great quantity of suffering as actually occurs.

(2) But the quantity of suffering that actually occurs does occur.

(3) Therefore, God does not exist.

It should be noted that premise (2) in the second argument, though true, *could* be false. It should be understood in such a way as to be only a contingent fact about the world. To help the reader comprehend this point, here is an analogy. Suppose I put three pieces of chalk on a table. Then the statement "there are not fewer than three pieces of chalk on the table" would be only a contingent truth. But another way of expressing it would be to say, "there are not fewer pieces of chalk on the table than the number that there actually is at present." Although there is indeed a way to interpret the latter statement which would make it a necessary truth, it need not be taken that way. It could instead be taken to mean simply "there are not fewer than three pieces of chalk on the table," which would make it merely contingent. (That is, it is to be given a *de re* interpretation, referring to something understood apart from language, rather than a *de dicto* interpretation, which refers only via the specific terms used.) Similarly, premise (2) of the Great-quantity Version, above, is to be interpreted in the way that makes it merely contingent. The expression "the quantity of suffering that actually occurs" is to be taken to refer only to a certain specific amount, just as "the number that there actually is at present" in the chalk analogy could be just a way of referring to the number three.

Each of the two versions of AE has a drawback. We need to consider which drawback is the less serious one. In the case of the Unjustifiability Version, it is the unclarity surrounding the term "unjustifiable." Earlier, it was suggested that suffering might be justified by showing how it is needed to achieve the greatest possible good (whatever that means). But in section 1.3, it was argued that the concept of the "greatest possible good" is obscure, mainly because goodness is relative to individuals and to standards of grading. There is the problem of ascertaining in an objective way how suffering is to be justified at all. I can imagine scenarios in which person A claims that result R justifies suffering S but person B (who agrees with A on all the facts surrounding the case) claims that R does not justify S. How are we to decide who is right and who is wrong? A and B might have quite different sets of preferences and systems of value. There is a kind of relativity surrounding this issue which constitutes a drawback to the first argument.

It would help if "unjustifiable" were not defined in terms of "the greatest possible good" but simply in terms of the standards of morality.

Although there would still be a problem of relativity here, it would be less formidable. Suppose there were an instance of suffering which, given all known data relevant to the case, no one could justify by any ethical system known to humanity. It would be reasonable to classify such a case as "unjustifiable." Since there do indeed occur such events, premise (2) of the Unjustifiability Version of AE should be regarded as true beyond all reasonable doubt. In other words, although there may occur instances of suffering the justifiability of which is unclear, especially if different ethical systems are involved, we can simply disregard such cases. Just the occurrence of *some* other clear cases is enough to adequately support premise (2). Of course, there may still be some debate about premise (1), though I shall disregard that. Premise (2) is usually the more controversial one and most theists would concede that establishing *that* premise would suffice to show the soundness of the argument.

In the case of the Great-quantity Version of AE, the drawback has to do with a certain regress that is involved in premise (1). Suppose people were to state the argument and, in response, God were to reduce the suffering in the world but not eliminate it completely. Then the world's inhabitants would still complain about the suffering that remains and the Great-quantity Version of AE could again be stated. In response, God could again reduce the suffering but not eliminate it completely. People would still complain, and the process could go on and on, indefinitely. Let us look at two possible reasons why people would still complain even though God reduces the suffering.

The first reason is that suffering is relative. Whatever may be the greatest amount of suffering that a person experiences, even if it is rather slight compared to what we are used to, the person will perceive the suffering to be utterly dreadful. For example, suppose the worst thing that ever happens to Mr. X is that he occasionally bites his tongue. Then Mr. X will utterly dread such occurrences and perhaps even blame God for permitting them. No matter how little Mr. X suffers, he would blame God for permitting whatever suffering he endures in life.

Possibly another reason why people would still complain is that in addition to decreasing their suffering, God could also make the world better by making them brighter people. This is a suggestion made by George Schlesinger.[14] He says that such a regress would be infinite. That is, God would make Mr. X brighter, but X might not be satisfied; X could complain that God could have made him brighter still. And there would be no maximal state there: it would be an infinite regress. I think that this point, though interesting, is not relevant to the Great-quantity Version of AE as it is formulated above. The argument is not that if God were to exist then he would have maximized people's intelligence and set their level of suffering at some ideal state. It is only that if God were to exist then he would not have permitted as much suffering as there actually is. Schlesinger's point may apply against some other version of AE, but it does not apply against the version put forward in this book.

However, the first reason still applies. People would still complain, even if God were to reduce the amount of suffering in the world. This could be called the Regress Objection. We would like to know at what point such a sequence might end and the world be in such a state that the Great-quantity Version of AE would no longer be applicable to it. Without some understanding of what such a state might be like, we find premise (1) of the Great-quantity Version to be obscure.

It would not do to say that God should simply eliminate *all* suffering, for there is definitely some suffering that makes the world better than it would otherwise be. Many examples could be cited here, but it would suffice to point out that some suffering is needed just for the sake of *contrast*. Otherwise, people's lives would be too bland to be enjoyable. It seems that the ideal world (by any system of values whatever) needs to contain some minimal amount of suffering. The problem comes in describing exactly what that minimal amount would be like. It would need to be an amount such that if the world were to contain just that amount then any reduction in suffering would make the world worse. The Regress Objection is that such a description is impossible and that the concept of an ideal world is hopelessly obscure. No matter how God changes the world, there would always be room for further improvement.

One reply to the Regress Objection is that it misconstrues the force of premise (1). The idea is not that there is some possible world or situation that would definitely obtain if God were to exist, but that there is some definite situation (namely, our world) that would probably *not* obtain if God were to exist. It can simply be granted that there is no definite world to which the advocate of AE might refer and say "if God were to exist then this is how it would be."

Another reply that might be made is one which grants that there *is* some definite world that would obtain if God were to exist, but then points out that we are unable to describe it fully. I do not find it hopelessly obscure to try to envision a world in which the amount of suffering it contains is just right: so that any increase or decrease in suffering would make the world worse than it was. It would be hard to describe such a world in precise terms, but it would not be impossible. At least we can know some things about it, and in particular, that our world is *not* it, even though there are also many other things about it that we do not know. By analogy, if I have proof that Jones is not in Florida, say, because I know it is very snowy where he is, then I can know that he is not in Miami, even if I do not know exactly where he is.

This conception of our situation (the "partial knowledge" idea) provides a framework within which AE can be put forward. We can know that if God were to exist then the world would not be the way ours is even if we cannot specify exactly how the world would be in that case. In other words, even if the description of the ideal world has not been given, it is still possible for us to know that our present world is far from the ideal. I can know that I have too much or too little of something even if I do not know exactly what the perfect amount would be. For example, I can know that my food is too salty even if I do not know exactly how much salt would be ideal. I can know that I put too much air into a balloon (because it burst) even if I do not know just what the perfect amount would have been. I can know that my neighbor is playing his music too loudly even if I do not know exactly what the ideal volume should be. And so on. In a similar way, we can know that our present world contains too much suffering even if we cannot describe in detail just what the ideal amount of suffering should be.

Imagine the Regress Objection applied to my neighbor's music. I complain to him that it is too loud and he argues as follows:

> If I turn the volume down slightly, you would still complain. Since you are not insisting that I turn the music off completely, you need to tell me exactly what the right volume should be, to the nearest decibel. But you cannot tell me that. Therefore, it seems you would still complain no matter what I do. Hence, there is no point in my turning down the volume even a little.

It is clear that there is something wrong with this argument. My neighbor ought to turn down the volume of his music even if I am unable to specify exactly what the ideal volume setting would be. In a similar way, God ought to have prevented or reduced some of the suffering that occurs in our world even if we are unable to specify exactly what the ideal amount of suffering may be.

In a response to the above-mentioned essay by Bruce Russell, Peter van Inwagen has pressed the Regress Objection by using the analogy of a sinking island with one thousand men still on it. The captain of the rescue ship must choose how many men he can take on board. Each man taken on board reduces the chances of a safe arrival at the mainland by 0.1 percent. So if he takes them all, then the ship would certainly sink. Van Inwagen says: "[N]one of the following is morally acceptable: to take none of the refugees; to take only a handful of them; to leave none of them behind; to leave only a handful of them behind."[15] Thus, wherever the captain draws the line, he would need to leave behind "someone whose admission would not significantly decrease the ship's chances of reaching the mainland safely." Van Inwagen thinks that God may be in such a situation. He cannot prevent suffering completely and has already done a lot in the way of suffering-prevention. He *could* do more without any significantly adverse effects. But a line *must* be drawn somewhere, as in the case of the ship captain, and it may be the case that our world is right there at the line.

I find that van Inwagen's analogy is no good because it is clear that we are nowhere near the line described. It is as if the ship captain had taken only, say, two refugees on board and left the remaining 998 men on the island to drown. Van Inwagen himself maintained that that would not be morally acceptable. But I would not use the ship example to try to illustrate the situation of suffering in our world, for it contains too much precision. I prefer the example of the neighbor who is playing his music much too loudly. Even if the neighbor were to say that he has already turned down the volume a bit and has "drawn the cutoff line" at the present volume, we could still readily ascertain that the volume is still way too loud. As far as situation L is concerned, there is (still) far too much suffering (and premature death) in the world for it to be morally acceptable for God to declare, "I have already drawn the line," and to refuse to bring about situation L. I readily grant that it would be difficult to describe a world which contains the maximum level of suffering that is "morally acceptable" or which a loving deity would permit. However, it is readily apparent that our world is nowhere near that level.

To my way of thinking, although both versions of AE are excellent, the drawback to the second is slightly less serious than the drawback to the first. It seems to me, then, that the Great-quantity Version of AE is preferable to the Unjustifiability Version, though only slightly so. For that reason (among others), when I present a more precise formulation of AE in the next chapter I shall construct it along the lines of the Great-quantity Version.

1.5. Divine Hiddenness

Let me turn now to a consideration of the Argument from Nonbelief. The claim is sometimes made that there is no good argument or evidence for God's existence. An alternate way of expressing the point is to say, "God is hidden" or "the world is ambiguous (as between being governed by God or being totally natural)." Whether the claim is made in terms of "hiddenness" or "ambiguity," it runs counter to St. Paul's (general-revelation) idea that "God's invisible qualities—his eternal power and divine nature—have been clearly seen, being understood from what has been made" (Rom. 1:20). So if it is a claim made by Christian writers at all, they would not be Calvinists or evangelical Christians but rather Christians of a more liberal persuasion.

One example of such a writer is John Hick. After putting forward what he takes to be opposing considerations that are equal or balanced, Hick concludes as follows:

It seems, then, that the universe maintains its inscrutable ambiguity. In some aspects it invites whilst in others it repels a religious response. It permits both a religious and a naturalistic faith, but haunted in each case by a contrary possibility that can never be exorcised. Any realistic analysis of religious belief and experience, and any realistic defence of the rationality of religious conviction, must therefore start from this situation of systematic ambiguity.[16]

Although Hick in effect acknowledges God's hiddenness, he never views that fact as a grave problem for theism itself. Hick thinks that if God were to exist, then for certain reasons it would be only natural and expected for him to be hidden from humanity. But other writers do not see the matter that way.

The "hiddenness problem" has been around for a long time. The idea of divine hiddenness appears in Scripture (Ps. 44:24, Isa. 45:15) and has been recognized as posing a problem for theism by various writers down through the centuries, including Blaise Pascal and Sören Kierkegaard.[17] One of the earlier writers of recent times to mention it is Ronald Hepburn, who in 1963 wrote:

One might be tempted to see in that ambivalence a vindication of atheism. For how could such an ambiguous universe be the work of perfect love and perfect power? Could this be a way to love and express love, to leave the loved one in bewildering uncertainty over the very existence of the allegedly loving God? Would we not have here a refined weapon of psychological torture? That is: if the situation is ambivalent, it is *not* ambivalent; since its ambivalence is a conclusive argument against the existence of the Christian God.[18]

Another writer who has seen God's hiddenness as a problem for theism is Terence Penelhum, who says:

Theologians should . . . welcome, not discourage, attempts to provide intellectual support for belief in God. If they conclude, in the face of the long record of failures, that they have to agree with those philosophers who dismiss such attempts as hopeless, they should judge this result to be what it is—a great pity, and a significant theological *problem*. For what reason could there be for unbelievers always to have reasonable grounds for their hesitations?[19]

In a later work, Penelhum pins the problem down a bit more, for he applies it to faiths which appeal to "a God who wishes us to respond to him":

If the world really is ambiguous, there are some faiths for which this is a *problem*. Put simply, how can it be that a God who wishes us to respond to him reveals his reality only in ways that it is possible conscientiously not to recognize? If one or more of the theistic faiths is true, why is it not *unambiguously* true? This problem may well have adequate answers within those traditions where it can arise, but it is not an inconsiderable one, especially if the advocate of such a tradition rejects appeals to evidence or any other form of natural theology. (Original italics)[20]

Two other writers who have wrestled with the "hiddenness problem," and who use the term "hiddenness" instead of "ambiguity," are Thomas Morris[21] and Robert McKim. McKim says the following:

Part of the cost of divine hiddenness is uncertainty and profound disagreement about the existence and nature of God. Another important part . . . is this. God, if God exists, is worthy of adoration and worship. A worshipful and respectful attitude is appropriate towards a morally good and wise creator. . . . But if many creatures are in the dark about the existence and nature of the creator, then the appropriate human responses are, at least, made more difficult than they otherwise might be. So another part of the cost of divine hiddenness is its contribution to the large-scale failure of human beings to respond to God in the right way. It inhibits the fulfillment of many duties. And there are further costs. The profound disagreements about God, and more broadly the profound disagreements between religious groups, sometimes play a role in promoting social conflict. . . . And the mystery surrounding God provides opportunities for charlatans and frauds to pose as experts on the nature and activities of God, and for religious authorities to acquire and exercise power and control over others.[22]

Despite the recognition by these writers that there is a grave "hiddenness problem," none of them declares the problem insoluble or employs it in an attempt to construct a sound (or strong) atheological argument.

So far as I know, the first writer to approach the topic in the latter way is J. L. Schellenberg, who says:

Why, we may ask, would God be hidden from us? Surely a morally perfect being—good, just, loving—would show himself more clearly. Hence the weakness of our evidence for God is not a sign that God is hidden; it is a revelation that God does not exist.[23]

When the matter is put in this way, then the problem should not be called "the problem of God's hiddenness," which would normally be taken to presuppose God's existence, but "the problem of the lack of good evidence for God's existence." However, this way of putting the matter still differs significantly from ANB, mentioned above in sections 1.1 and 1.2, for, among other things, it appeals, as its basic datum, not to the fact of nonbelief, but to the alleged fact of "the weakness of our evidence for God." I myself certainly agree that that is a fact, but it is not a fact which can be established by simply taking a survey. Furthermore, it is a debatable issue: there are many theists, perhaps the majority of them, who claim to have strong evidence for God's existence. So in that respect, Schellenberg's formulation can be attacked in a way not applicable to ANB.

It is important to clearly distinguish ANB from this other (God-vs.-world, atheological) argument, which may be called the "Lack-of-evidence Argument." (I do not mean to imply that this other argument is the main one in Schellenberg's book, only that it is suggested by the passage quoted above.) One way of formulating the Lack-of-evidence Argument is as follows:

(A) Probably, if God were to exist, then there would be good objective evidence for his existence.
(B) But there is no good objective evidence for God's existence.
(C) Therefore, probably God does not exist.

Despite the dissent from many theists, let us here assume that premise (B) is true. Then we need to focus attention on premise (A). Why believe it? The reasons can be divided into two sorts. First, there is the idea that may be expressed as ANB: if God were to exist, then he would probably cause people to believe in him. However, that in itself does not yield premise (A), for there are other ways for God to bring about belief than by means of good objective evidence. One way, for example, would be by the direct implantation of belief in people's minds. Another way, emphasized by Schellenberg, is for God to reveal himself to people by means of religious experiences. In order for premise (A) to be established, it would need to be shown that if God were to exist and were to cause people to believe in him, then he would probably do so by means of good objective evidence rather than by any other method. It seems to me that would be very hard to show, which is certainly a weakness in the given line of reasoning. In other words, to try to support premise (A) by appeal to ANB would not be at all promising.

The second sort of reason that might be given for premise (A) is one that makes no appeal to ANB. It is that there are specific divine attributes, apart from any desire on the part of God to reveal himself to humanity, which imply the existence of the type of evidence in question. To put it metaphorically, God is the kind of being that would "leave clear tracks." Well, what divine attributes might they be? Perhaps the attribute of "being the ruler of the universe" would be a possible candidate. It might be claimed that if A is a ruler over B, then B would probably be aware of it. This is a debatable matter that I shall not go into here. Simply let it be noted that there are problems with both premise (A) and, as mentioned previously, premise (B). Since those problems do not arise for ANB, this is a reason to prefer ANB to the Lack-of-evidence Argument. I would say that to view our lack of evidence for God's existence as direct support for atheism might be a reasonable approach to the topic, but it is definitely a line of thought different from (and in my opinion, inferior to) that pursued in this book.

With regard to ANB, the "nontheist" version of it, formulated above, may not seem plausible, for there is no very obvious reason why God, should he exist, would want people to believe in him. Schellenberg suggests that if God were "perfectly loving," then he would necessarily do something to bring about such belief:

> A being who did not seek to relate himself to us explicitly in this life—who elected to remain elusive, distant, hidden, even in the absence of any culpable activity on our part—would not properly be viewed as perfectly loving.[24]

It is a controversial matter whether an elusive or hidden deity might still possibly be "perfectly loving." Furthermore, it is certainly doubtful whether God, when understood in a general way, quite apart from any particular religion, has to be "perfectly loving" toward humanity. Both of these issues will be addressed in chapter 14, where I shall try to show that neither ANB nor the atheological argument that Schellenberg expounds and defends in his book clearly establishes the nonexistence of God in general, taken in a totally unrestricted way.

1.6. Applying AE and ANB to Christianity

A more plausible version of ANB is produced when the type of nonbelief to which it appeals is nonbelief in specifically Christian doctrines and the argument is directed at proving the nonexistence, not of God in general, but specifically the God of Christianity. That is the version I employed in a recent article.[25] It makes ANB more plausible because there is more reason to maintain that the God of Christianity, should he exist, would want people to believe certain specific Christian doctrines than that God in general, should he exist, would want people simply to believe that he exists. A closely related point having to do with the problem of evil is raised by David and Randall Basinger, who say the following:

> [T]he philosophical community would be better served if it concerned itself primarily with the relationship between evil and the actual characterizations of evil and God's omnipotence and goodness that exist within *specific* theological systems. (Original italics)[26]

I agree fully with this point, and I think that it can be made with regard to the problem of nonbelief as well as the problem of evil. It is a point that expresses the basic theme of the present book.

To see the connection between ANB and Christianity, consider the strong desire on the part of the Christian God for a kind of fellowship with a special group of his creatures. Those creatures have somehow gone astray and he wants to redeem them. But such redemption requires a kind of acceptance of that particular God by the creatures, which in turn calls for them to believe that certain Christian doctrines are true. Among the doctrines would be the propositions that God exists, that he has a son, and that the son was sent to be the savior of humanity. It was because of such a requirement on the part of the creatures that St. Paul was inspired to say of God that he "wants all men to be saved and to come to a knowledge of the truth" (1 Tim. 2:4).

Another reason for claiming that the God of Christianity very much wants people generally to believe the above-mentioned Christian doctrines is that, according to the Bible, he directed missionaries to go forth to all nations and "spread the word." In the last two verses of the book of Matthew there is given what is called the Great Commission: "go and make disciples of all nations, ...teaching them to obey everything I have commanded you." A similar thought is expressed in the long ending of the book of Mark: "Go into all the world and preach the good news to all creation. Whoever believes and is baptized will be saved, but whoever does not believe will be condemned" (Mark 16:15–16). The "good news" referred to here includes the idea that God's son was sent to be the savior of humanity. There is some doubt about the origin of the long ending of Mark, in which the given passage appears, but the idea that might be inferred from it, that God at least wants people to be aware of what he has done for them, is central to Christianity.

When ANB is directed at the God of Christianity, it is the argument that *that* God does not exist, for if he did exist, then by now he would have in one way or another made the world aware of the truth of the basic doctrines of Christianity. But that obviously has *not* happened, since far more than half the people in the world either have never heard of those doctrines or have heard of them but do not believe them. ANB is a "God-vs.-world argument" because it appeals to a certain feature of our planet, the absence of belief of a certain sort among the people inhabiting it, to try to show that that feature is incompatible with the existence of God, when God is assigned certain divine attributes. When ANB is applied to Christianity, the given type of belief is specifically awareness of the so-called "gospel message," and the divine attributes include a strong desire on God's part that people generally have such belief.

Christianity takes different forms, only some of which emphasize the importance of "spreading the word." The main form with such an emphasis is what is called "evangelical." As a working definition, I shall take evangelical Christianity to be that form of Christianity which maintains that the Bible, and no other book or source, is the "word of God" and that the Bible (by way of the Great Commission of Matt. 28:19–20 and other passages) shows that God wants people generally to be aware of the truth of certain basic Christian doctrines, in particular, the "gospel message," such awareness usually being taken to be required for eventual salvation in the afterlife. Later in the present book the definition will be further refined. The hallmark of evangelical Christianity is missionary work: the spreading of the gospel message in the belief that such work was commanded by God and is regarded by God as vital, not only to the transformation of people's earthly lives but also to their salvation in the afterlife as well. The paradigm example of an "evangelical Christian" as I shall use that expression is the well-known evangelist Billy Graham. I am not restricting the expression to fundamentalists and could still count people as "evangelical" even if they were to deny the doctrine of strict biblical inerrancy. I would include Jehovah's Witnesses as evangelical Christians, though not Mormons (since the Mormons have scriptures other than the Bible). Some readers may use the expression "evangelical Christianity" still more broadly than my working definition. If they therefore balk at my use of the expression, I would suggest that they simply regard it as shorthand for some lengthier description. The important point is that there are *many* Christians who would fit my working definition of "evangelical" and it is to them that ANB will be addressed.

In addition to missionary work, evangelical Christianity emphasizes the doctrine that God greatly loves humanity and wants humanity to reciprocate that love. It echoes the Judaic idea, expressed in the Old Testament (Deut. 6:5), that the first and foremost commandment given to humanity by God is that people love God maximally. (For the expression of that idea in the New Testament, see Matt. 22:37–38 and Mark 12:29–30.) The fact that God has given people such a commandment implies that he wants them to be aware not only of his existence but also of what he has done for them.

Evangelical Christianity's emphasis upon God's great love of humanity also makes it a target for AE. We want to know how and why a god who loves humanity to the extent claimed by evangelical Christians would permit people to experience so much suffering and premature death in this earthly life as actually occurs. Prima facie, at least, the facts regarding the amount of evil in our world do seem to make it highly improbable that such a god exists, which is the essence of AE.

Since evangelical Christianity describes God in ways that readily give rise to both AE and ANB, most of the present book, and in particular chapters 2–11, will be devoted to a study of the two arguments applied specifically to *that* God. So, wherever the word "God" is used in those chapters, it is intended to refer specifically to the God of evangelical Christianity. Some other ways of conceiving of God are considered later on in chapters 12-15.

1.7. Is ANB a Species of AE?

When the two arguments are constructed within the framework of Christianity, it might be suggested that ANB is not a totally separate argument from AE, but is, rather, merely a species of it. This is suggested by a remark made by William P. Alston:

> There is, from within any particular religion, a theological problem. In a theistic religion this will take the form: why does God allow such a diversity of incompatible systems of belief about Himself? This is allied to the more general question: why doesn't He make at least the main outlines of the truth about these matters clear to everyone? And both are simply particular versions of the familiar problem of evil.[27]

It appears that Alston would claim that the problem of widespread nonbelief in Christianity's gospel message is "simply a particular version of the familiar problem of evil," which would in effect make ANB a species of AE.

But why believe that? Is it that people's nonbelief in the gospel message is itself a type of evil? If it is, so it might be argued, then ANB could be regarded as merely a special version of AE, for its conclusion that God does not exist would in that case be simply inferred from a special kind of evil. Instead of arguing for God's nonexistence by appeal to the usual reasons (e.g., the claim that he wouldn't permit so much famine and disease in the world), one might instead be arguing that God does not exist because if he did then he wouldn't permit the sort of suffering that occurs as a result of people's nonbelief in the gospel message. James A. Keller has put the matter as follows:

> Because some human suffering arises from a failure to have faith in God—or so theists usually allege—and from lack of knowledge of God's will, the hiddenness of God is part of the problem of evil; that is, if God is as many theists have claimed, we might find it inexplicable that God remains hidden, since that hiddenness causes suffering.[28]

Instead of speaking of God's hiddenness, which presupposes God's existence, I prefer to speak of people's nonbelief in God or nonbelief in the gospel message. Certainly it is possible that such nonbelief causes suffering, whether or not God exists. And if it should be the case, as most evangelical Christians claim, that nonbelievers will be eternally punished in the afterlife, then their nonbelief would, in retrospect, turn out to be quite a calamity. That aspect of the matter has been called "the Soteriological Problem of Evil."[29]

Certainly there is some merit to this suggestion, but it becomes a little puzzling when one inquires whether the calamity of nonbelief is a form of moral evil or a form of natural evil. Moral evil, as I understand it, is suffering that is a consequence of deliberate actions. Most crimes would be examples of moral evil in that sense. Natural evil, on the other hand, is suffering that is *not* a consequence of any deliberate actions. The usual examples are natural disasters (storms, earthquakes, volcanic eruptions, etc.) and disease. So here is the question: into which category of evil, moral or natural, should the relevant type of nonbelief be placed?

Some might say that it is a form of moral evil because people have control over their beliefs, and when they fail to believe the gospel message it is only because they have deliberately chosen not to believe it and so are culpable for their nonbelief. This brings up the issue of doxastic voluntarism, the view that belief is directly subject to the will. Many philosophers reject the idea that people ever have direct control over their beliefs. I discuss the matter below in appendix C.

Even if belief were directly subject to the will, it seems unfair to hold people responsible for their lack of belief in doctrines with which they are totally unfamiliar. There are hundreds of millions of heathens in the world with no awareness of Christianity's gospel message. So if *their* nonbelief is a moral evil, then the responsibility for it must fall on others, not the nonbelievers themselves. But that may not be a problem, for many evangelical Christians do indeed view the matter in just that way. They say that the heathens' lack of belief in the gospel message is a moral evil for which Christians themselves are responsible. God will not only reward missionaries (Dan. 12:3) but will also punish or at least chastise most Christians for not doing enough missionary work, in effect, for disobeying the Great Commission (Ezek. 33:8). However, the moral evil of disobeying the Great Commission is one thing and the alleged effect of it, the damnation of nonbelievers, is something else. We want to know how anyone might *deserve* to be damned, but let us postpone that issue to later.

It might be maintained that even if nonbelievers do not automatically end up damned, their lack of belief could still be a kind of evil if the belief in question were *true*. For if Christianity were true, then non-Christians would go through life with a kind of *ignorance* about basic and important matters. Of course it can be questioned whether such ignorance is always bad, for there seem to be many perfectly happy non-Christians around the world. People need not believe the gospel message to gain enjoyment and self-fulfillment from this earthly life, even if that message were true. (One is reminded of the maxim "Where ignorance is bliss, 'tis folly to be wise.") But even if we were to assume that ignorance of the truth is always bad, the question is whether *that* badness is of a moral sort or of a natural sort. The alleged moral evil of Christians' failure to adequately spread the gospel message could be brought in here, but let us disregard it. Not all Christians view the matter in those terms.

An alternate view is that there is moral evil involved but it is the work of the devil. In 2 Cor. 4:4, St. Paul says: "The god of this age has blinded the minds of unbelievers, so that they cannot see the light of the gospel." This is a reference to Satan. (In John 12:31, he is referred to as "the prince of this world.") In 1 John 5:19 it says, "the whole world is under the control of the evil one." Evangelical Christians do not usually pursue this line of thought, since it seems to release nonbelievers from any culpability for their nonbelief. Evangelicals are instead inclined to view heathens as largely culpable for their own nonbelief, especially if they reject the gospel message after it has been presented to them by a missionary. But this comes back to the matter of doxastic voluntarism and other issues, which we will take up later.

Assuming that people's nonbelief in the gospel message is something bad, perhaps it is not a moral evil of any sort but just a kind of *natural* evil that has befallen them. It is bad in the way that ignorance in general is bad. Some ignorance can have terrible consequences. People sometimes make very big mistakes, and not through any fault of their own. The availability of knowledge is often a matter of luck. Person A, being by chance at a certain place at a certain time, learns the truth of proposition P, which leads to A's good fortune. Person B, on the other hand, being by chance at a different time or place, comes to believe not-P, which has disastrous results in B's life. Was B's nonbelief then a form of natural evil? If it could be chalked up purely to bad luck, then the obvious answer would be Yes.

In the case of *some* people, their nonbelief might contribute to their immorality. It is unclear how many are like that, but probably there are at least some. They are people such that if they were to come to strongly believe the gospel message, then they would come to behave more morally than they do, and that would be of benefit to everyone involved. Even mere conversion to theism might incline some people toward greater morality, at least with respect to their behavior. In the case of people like that, their nonbelief would be a kind of evil related to morality, but that in itself would not make it a form of moral evil. It could still be a form of natural evil, for their nonbelief could very well be a result of chance.

Perhaps a mixed view could be held according to which some people's nonbelief in the gospel message is their own fault, perhaps through a kind of investigative negligence, and thereby possibly a moral evil, whereas other people's nonbelief is not their own fault but just a natural evil that has befallen them. As I see the matter, if nonbelief is an evil at all, being a kind of ignorance which will eventually cause suffering, then it is surely just a form of natural evil.

J. L. Schellenberg makes a comment about this issue which would be worth considering, even though his focus is not on the God of evangelical Christianity or on nonbelief in the gospel message but rather God in general and the reasonableness of nonbelief in theism. He says the following:

> I seem to be in a position to claim that the problem of reasonable nonbe-
> lief is a problem of evil. However, the "evil" to which it refers is, as we
> have seen, not of the ordinary sort (for it does not consist in pain or suf-
> fering or any other commonly recognized evil, nor would its removal be a
> great good unless personal relationship with God is possible); and so, to
> mark this difference, it may be appropriate to refer to it as a *special
> instance* of the problem of evil.[30]

When nonbelief is "reasonable," on Schellenberg's view, if it is evil at all,
it seems that it would be a form of natural evil rather than moral evil, for
those who have it would not be in any way culpable for having it. And that
would apply even if the nonbelief in question were specifically nonbelief in
the gospel message instead of nonbelief in theism. However, it is highly
debatable whether the sort of nonbelief that Schellenberg is discussing, i.e.,
nontheism (or nonbelief in God in general) is evil at all in my sense of
"evil," that is, as causing suffering or premature death. Let us here disregard the possibility that being a nontheist might cause a person to behave
immorally or that it might eventually get someone damned in the afterlife.
There are many nontheists in the world who, to all outward appearances,
seem not to suffer at all for believing the way they do. Even if we assume
that they are ignorant regarding the fundamental nature of reality, they (like
the lower animals) seem not to be any the worse off because of such ignorance. Of course, their nonbelief may very well be an evil from God's point
of view, since it deprives God of what he wants from them (love, adoration,
glory, worship, prayer, rituals, etc.), but it seems not to be an evil from their
own point of view. This in itself is a reason for denying that nonbelief in
theism is any form of evil. It is certainly not an evil in the way that natural
disasters, disease, crime, and so on are evil. But let us postpone further discussion of general nontheism to chapter 14.

Another writer who comments on our present topic is Thomas V. Morris,
who says:

> It seems commonly to be thought that the problem of evil is the single
> greatest intellectual problem for religious belief. How could a benevolent,
> loving, and all-powerful God allow his creation to contain so much pain
> and suffering? The problem of the hiddenness of God may be at least as
> great a problem, if not a greater problem, for theism. Of course there are
> close ties between the two issues. The problem of the hiddenness of God
> can be viewed as a limited version of the problem of evil. . . . Our lack of
> a clear vision of deity could be seen as just one more widely suffered form
> of evil. On the other hand, and, I think, more insightfully, the problem of
> evil can be seen as a subcategory of the problem of the hiddenness of God.
> . . . As many philosophers have realized, the problem of evil alone can be
> taken to generate no more than an argument to the conclusion that if there

is a personal creator and sustainer of the world, then he is evil, or at the least, in the words of Woody Allen, "an underachiever." The general problem of the hiddenness of God can be taken much more directly to support an atheistic denial that there is any personal creator and sustainer of the world of any kind.[31]

I agree with Morris's idea that the problem of the hiddenness of God is separate from the problem of evil and that it is at least as great a problem for theism as is the problem of evil. However, I do not agree that there is no move regarding the hiddenness problem that would correspond to the "God is evil or God is an underachiever" move in the problem of evil. The corresponding move in the hiddenness problem would be "God does not care about people's awareness of his existence." Also, I see no point to Morris's suggestion that the problem of evil can be seen as a subcategory of the problem of the hiddenness of God. That suggestion eludes me.

To return to the context of evangelical Christianity, even if we grant that people's nonbelief in the gospel message is a kind of evil, that does not in itself make ANB a species of AE. The thrust of ANB is not "how could God let such a bad thing happen?" but rather "how could God let happen something which he clearly does not want to happen?" Even if nonbelief were something good, something for which people eventually reap huge rewards, the given atheological argument (ANB) could still go through. Good or bad, nonbelief in the gospel message is something which the Bible shows is contrary to God's desires. *That* is the force of ANB: if God exists then nothing that is contrary to his (ultimate) desires could exist in the world. But nonbelief in the gospel message, which is contrary to God's (ultimate) desires, does exist (in great quantity!); therefore God does not exist. This is clearly *not* a special instance of AE.

We can see, then, that the issue of whether or not nonbelief is in any way evil, though interesting in itself and worth pursuing, is in the end irrelevant to our question in this section, for God's reason(s) for wanting people to believe the gospel message may have nothing to do with any benefits of such belief or with any bad consequences of nonbelief for *them*. Assuming that the Christian God exists, there are many other reasons that he might have. Let us consider a few.

First, God may want people to believe simply because he wants them to worship and glorify him. Why did he want people to sacrifice animals to him and to perform the other rituals described in the Book of Leviticus? Such adoration pleased him. God said of himself that he is jealous (Exod. 20:5, 34:14) and would not tolerate the worship of any other deity. The idea that he strongly desires worship from people all over the world, which is something he will eventually bring about, is a recurrent theme throughout the Old Testament.[32] Apparently God very much enjoys being worshiped, so, even apart from people making him jealous by worshiping other deities, he must feel bad about people totally ignoring him, as nontheists do. This in itself is a reason for God to want people to be aware of the truth of the gospel message, quite apart from any benefit that such awareness might have for them. Whoever comes to believe the gospel message will acquire a strong inclination to glorify the Christian God, which is precisely what that deity most desires from humans.

Alternatively, God may simply want people to be aware of the truth for its own sake, perhaps because of the intrinsic value of knowledge, especially knowledge about the ultimate nature of reality. Even if some people may not regard knowledge of ultimate truths to be intrinsically good, God may so regard it. And it is God's values that are at issue here. Note that the intrinsic value of knowledge does not make lack of it an evil in my sense of "evil." There may be forms of goodness other than an absence of suffering, and there may be ways in which goodness might be absent without any suffering present. Thus, even if belief in the gospel message were intrinsically good within God's system of values, that would not make nonbelief in the gospel message evil in the sense of "evil" used in the present book. Here again, God's desire that nonbelief be eliminated or reduced may have nothing to do with any "evil" that it possesses.

Finally, God may have some unknown reason having to do with divine priorities of which humans are totally unaware. Just as Job was unaware of God's "bet" with Satan regarding Job's future behavior, so also humans may be unaware of just what role or significance their belief in the gospel message might have in God's scheme of things. The key premise in ANB is just that God (strongly) desires that people believe the gospel message, whatever reason there may be behind that desire, whether it be to receive glory from them or to have them learn the truth for its own sake or some other (unknown) reason. On that basis, I maintain that the problems of religious plurality and widespread nonbelief in Christianity's gospel message are *not* simply particular versions of the problem of evil. ANB is *not* merely a species or special instance of AE but is a genuine atheological argument in its own right. In the present book, the two arguments will be treated as presenting different, though for the most part parallel, problems in the philosophy of religion.

Let us proceed in the next chapter to a consideration of how the two arguments might be expressed in a more precise way.

Notes

1. Richard M. Gale, *On the Nature and Existence of God* (Cambridge: Cambridge University Press, 1991), chapters 2 and 3.

2. J. L. Schellenberg, *Divine Hiddenness and Human Reason* (Ithaca, N.Y.: Cornell University Press, 1993).

3. Frank B. Dilley, "Fool-Proof Proofs of God?" *International Journal for Philosophy of Religion* 8 (1977): 18–35.

4. Charles Crittenden, "The Argument from Perfection to Existence," *Religious Studies* 4 (1968): 124.

5. William J. Wainwright, *Philosophy of Religion* (Belmont, Calif.: Wadsworth, 1988), p. 7.

6. David and Randall Basinger, "The Problem with the 'Problem of Evil,' " *Religious Studies* 30 (1994): 93.

7. Patterson Brown, "Religious Morality," *Mind* 72 (1963): 239. See also replies to the Brown article by Antony Flew and Keith Campbell in *Mind* 74 (1965): 578–84.

8. J. L. Mackie, *The Miracle of Theism* (Oxford: Oxford University Press, 1982), p. 150.

9. Bruce R. Reichenbach, *Evil and a Good God* (New York: Fordham University Press, 1982), p. 148.

10. Edward H. Madden and Peter H. Hare, *Evil and the Concept of God* (Springfield, Ill.: Thomas, 1968), pp. 96–97.

11. Mark T. Nelson, "Naturalistic Ethics and the Argument from Evil," *Faith and Philosophy* 8 (1991): 376.

12. Robert M. Adams, "Must God Create the Best?" *Philosophical Review* 81 (1972): 317–22; reprinted in *The Problem of Evil: Selected Readings*, edited by Michael L. Peterson (Notre Dame, Ind.: University of Notre Dame Press, 1992), pp. 275–88.

13. Bruce Russell, "Defenseless," in Daniel Howard-Snyder, ed., *The Evidential Argument from Evil* (Bloomington and Indianapolis: Indiana University Press, 1996), pp. 193–194.

14. George Schlesinger, *Religion and Scientific Method* (Dordrecht: Reidel, 1977), chapters 9 and 10.

15. Peter van Inwagen, "Reflections on the Chapters by Draper, Russell, and Gale," Daniel Howard-Snyder, ed., *The Evidential Argument from Evil*, p. 234.

16. John Hick, *An Interpretation of Religion* (New Haven, Conn.: Yale University Press, 1989), p. 124.

17. For an excellent discussion of Pascal's and Kierkegaard's treatments of the hiddenness problem, see Schellenberg, *Divine Hiddenness*, chapter 6.

18. R. W. Hepburn, "From World to God," *Mind* 72 (1963): 50; reprinted in Basil Mitchell, ed., *The Philosophy of Religion* (Oxford: Oxford University Press, 1971), p. 178.

19. Terence Penelhum, God and Skepticism (Dordrecht: Reidel, 1983), p. 158.

20. Terence Penelhum, *Reason and Religious Faith* (Boulder, Colo.: Westview Press, 1995), p. 132.

21. Thomas V. Morris, "The Hidden God," *Philosophical Topics*, 16 (1988): 5–11; revised and reprinted as chapter 6 of *Making Sense of It All* (Grand Rapids, Mich.: Eerdmans, 1992), pp. 85–108.

22. Robert McKim, "The Hiddenness of God," *Religious Studies* 26 (1990): 142.

23. Schellenberg, *Divine Hiddenness*, p. 1.

24. Ibid., pp. 28–29.

25. Theodore M. Drange, "The Argument from Non-belief," *Religious Studies* 29 (1993): 417–32.

26. David and Randall Basinger, "The Problem with the 'Problem of Evil,'" p. 97.

27. William P. Alston, "Religious Diversity and Perceptual Knowledge of God," *Faith and Philosophy* 5 (1988): 445.

28. James A. Keller, "The Hiddenness of God and the Problem of Evil," *International Journal for Philosophy of Religion* 37 (1995): 14.

29. See, e.g., William Lane Craig, " 'No Other Name': A Middle Knowledge Perspective on the Exclusivity of Salvation through Christ," *Faith and Philosophy* 6 (1989): 179.

30. Schellenberg, *Divine Hiddenness*, p. 7.

31. Morris, *Making Sense of It All*, pp. 89–90.

32. There are hundreds of such verses and here are just a handful of them: Exod. 7:5, 14:4,18; 1 Sam. 17:46; 1 Kings 8:42–43; 2 Kings 19:19; Ps. 22:27, 46:10, 57:5,11, 64:9, 65:8, 66:4, 67:2–5, 86:9, 98:2–3, 99:2–3; Isa. 45:23, 66:23; Ezek. 20:41, 28:25, 36:23; Hab. 2:14; Mal. 1:11.

2

Precise Formulations and Comments

We will consider versions of AE and ANB that apply just to the God of evangelical Christianity. However, the way the arguments were expressed in chapter 1 was too vague. Let us proceed to formulations more conducive to analytical scrutiny.

2.1. The Argument from Evil (AE) Formulated

We first define an expression that will be used in the argument:

Situation L = the situation (or situation-type) of the amount of suffering and premature death that is experienced by humans in the world at the present time being significantly *less* than what it actually is at present. (In other words, if the actual amount, at present, is, say, a total of n units of suffering and premature death, then in situation L that amount would be, at present, significantly *less* than n units.)

Then AE, making reference to situation L, can be expressed as follows:

(A) If the God of evangelical Christianity were to exist, then he would possess all of the following four properties (among others):
   (1) *being able* to bring about situation L, all things considered;
   (2) *wanting* to bring about situation L, i.e., having it among his desires;
   (3) *not wanting* anything else that necessarily conflicts with his desire to bring about situation L, as strongly as he wants to bring about situation L;

53

(4) *being rational* (which implies always acting in accord with his own highest purposes).

(B)   If there were to exist a being who has all four properties listed above, then situation L would have to obtain.

(C)   But situation L does *not* obtain. The amount of suffering and premature death in the world at the present time is *not* significantly less than what it actually is at present.

(D)   Therefore [from (B) & (C)], there does not exist a being who has all four properties listed in premise (A).

(E)   Hence [from (A) & (D)], the God of evangelical Christianity does not exist.

(The reader who is planning to study the discussion of AE in the next section and in later chapters is urged to insert a bookmark at this page so as to be able to refer back to the precise formulation of the argument given here.)

2.2. Comments on AE

It should first be noted that this is the Great-quantity Version of AE that was discussed above in section 1.4. One reason for expressing AE in this way, apart from the considerations raised there, is to place the pressure of the debate on premise (A) rather than premise (C), thereby making AE more akin to ANB (which will be discussed below) than it would otherwise have been. Consider, for example, the effect of defining "situation L" as "the situation of the world at the present time containing no unjustifiable suffering or premature death." Although that change would no doubt make AE's premise (A) more plausible, it would have an adverse effect on premise (C), which maintains that situation L does not obtain. I think that premise (C) would still be defensible, that is, a reasonable case could be made that the world does indeed contain unjustifiable suffering. However, there would be a certain doubt surrounding it. Its truth could not then be simply declared as an obvious fact. So a large part of the discussion of AE would revolve around that premise. I want to avoid such a result because premise (C) in ANB is totally noncontroversial and one of my aims is to show how AE and ANB can be expressed in a way that makes them parallel or analogous to each other.

In both AE and ANB, (A) functions as a kind of collective premise, with (A1), (A2), etc. being subpremises. However, for simplicity, I shall ignore such niceties and refer to (A) itself as well as each of its parts as "premises." We could say that AE has six premises, from (A1) through (C). Note that the "if" clause of (A) is to appear in each of its four parts. Thus, the full formulation of premise (A1) is as follows: "If the God of evangelical

Christianity were to exist, then he would be able to bring about situation L, all things considered."

One other general point should be noted. Behind AE's premise (A) there is a partial reportive definition of "the God of evangelical Christianity." It is partial because not all of that deity's defining properties are appealed to within the premise, which uses the parenthetical phrase "among others" to indicate that there are other properties not mentioned. And it is a reportive definition because it is my intention to unpack the actual concept of God that evangelical Christians have. To reject any part of premise (A) is in effect to say that the "report" is mistaken, that evangelical Christians do not conceive of God in the given way. This same consideration applies equally to ANB, below.

The expression "being able, all things considered" in AE's premise (A1) is there taken very literally. It means that there is absolutely nothing to prevent the action, not even chance. Consider, for example, a boy who has on past days done twenty consecutive pushups. Today the issue is raised whether he is able to do merely five consecutive pushups. The obvious answer is yes. If he has done twenty, then, refreshed, he is certainly able to do five. But suppose that, just as he is about to perform the fifth pushup, he is struck by lightning, which prevents him from completing it. We should say of the boy, in retrospect, that he was able to do the five pushups, but he was not able to do them *all things considered*. When his being struck by lightning is considered, then we must say that under those conditions the boy was *not* able. Thus, in premise (A1), when God is said to be able to bring about a situation, all things considered, that means that if he were to try to bring it about then there is absolutely nothing which might prevent him from doing it. In other words, if he tries to do the given action, then, necessarily, he does it.

Understood in the above way, AE's premise (A1) is supported by the Bible's repeated claim that God is all-powerful.[1] Since evangelical Christianity identifies its God with God as described in the Bible, with the descriptions taken as literally true, it follows that if *that* God were to exist, then, being all-powerful, he would have been able to bring about situation L, all things considered, as claimed in premise (A1). There are many ways in which God might have brought about situation L. One of them was for him to have made the earth a calmer and more stable planet, with fewer storms, earthquakes, and volcanic eruptions. Then there would not occur so much suffering and premature death as a consequence of such natural catastrophes.

Another way would have been for God to make people hardier and more resistant to germs and other afflictions. Then there would not occur so much suffering and premature death as a consequence of disease and infirmities. It might be objected that a significant reduction in premature deaths would soon lead to overpopulation and even worse problems. But, being all-powerful, God could have done things to prevent overpopulation in a humane way. For example, while making humans less subject to premature death, he could also have given them genes that make women increasingly less fertile the more times they give birth, thereby preventing very large families. That would bring about situation L in a way that would not introduce additional problems down the road.

Another way for God to have brought about situation L would have been for him to make humans smarter than they are. That would have given them a better means for coping with evil than they presently have. In addition, God could have made people more altruistic than they are. Had he done that, there would be much less crime and cruelty in the world than there is. (The topic of altruism will be discussed in chapter 4, below.) Still another way for God to have brought about situation L would have been to reveal to humanity (in a clearer way than has been done, if it has been done at all) that he exists and what exactly he wants people to do. One of the benefits of such revelation would have been the prevention of harmful divisions among people regarding religion. It is clear that there are many ways in which God could have improved the world, which makes AE's premise (A1) clearly true.

Something should be said about the bifurcation of premise (A) into (A2) and (A3). The main reason for it lies in a certain ambiguity in the expression "X wants Y." It could mean merely that Y is among X's wants or it could mean, further, that Y is X's "all-things-considered" desire, i.e., X's "resultant desire" after all of X's conflicting desires are taken into account. I find that the issues can be made clearer if the expression is taken in the former (simpler) way, so that is how I take it in this book. "X wants Y" could be true in that sense even if it is not true in the latter sense. People can have conflicting desires one of which outweighs another, so they can want something in the simple sense without thereby wanting it in the "all-things-considered" (or "resultant") sense or thereby having to try to attain it. For example, I might desire to eat a large piece of chocolate cake but also desire to keep my daily calorie intake under a certain amount. Those two desires may conflict. If they do and if the calorie-restriction desire wins out, then I might refrain from eating the cake even though I want to eat it. Another example is the mother who takes her son to the dentist to have a filling put in. She wants him to experience no pain, but she also has a conflicting and overriding desire that his tooth be fixed. So she has him endure some pain despite her desire that he not experience any. If God can have conflicting desires, then AE's premise (A3) could be false even if (A2) were true. It is to allow for that possibility that the argument is constructed in the way that it is.

It might be objected that since God is omnipotent, he cannot have conflicting desires. The phrase "necessarily conflicts" in premise (A3) conveys the idea that it would have been impossible even for God to satisfy both desires simultaneously. But for God, nothing is impossible. Hence, he cannot have such conflicting desires, which makes premise (A3) automatically true.

One defect in this argument is that it paradoxically claims both that God cannot have conflicting desires and that for God nothing is impossible, which seems to be a contradiction. But the more basic defect in the argument is that it interprets "for God, nothing is impossible" in an unrestricted way. Most theologians and philosophers of religion recognize that omnipotence needs to be restricted to what is logically and conceptually possible and to what is consistent with God's other defining properties. Even the Bible (Titus 1:2, Heb. 6:18) says that it is impossible for God to lie. Presumably, if it is part of the very definition of "God" that God never does anything wrong, then it follows that there are actions, namely, wrong ones, which God cannot perform. Thus, God might very well have two desires that logically or conceptually conflict. If it is logically impossible for both desires to be satisfied, then even a being who is omnipotent (defined in the appropriate way) would be unable to satisfy both of them. And that is how the phrase "necessarily conflicts" in premise (A3) is to be taken.

Premise (A2) might be supported in various ways. First of all, evangelical Christianity regards Jesus of Nazareth as having the same attitudes as God, and Jesus is described in the Bible as feeling compassion for the multitudes he encountered with regard to their earthly suffering.[2] So if God exists, then he, too, must feel such compassion, which entails that God must want situation L. Secondly, according to Psalm 145:9, "The Lord is good to all; he has compassion on all he has made," and according to James 5:11, "The Lord is full of compassion and mercy." Third, God loves humanity (John 3:16, 1 John 4:8–16), and the sacrifice of Jesus was supposed to exhibit maximal love (John 15:13). Evangelical Christianity often describes its God as being "all-loving," which means that God loves everyone and everything maximally. But part of the concept of love is wanting the best for whoever or whatever the object of love may be. Thus, the God of evangelical Christianity must want situation L, at least in the minimal sense that situation L is among his desires. (In chapters 8 and 10 we will take a closer look at this mode of reasoning.)

But there is a problem here. AE's premise (A2) maintains not just that God wants situation L itself, but that he wants to bring it about. Someone could want something which he is able to bring about and yet not want to bring it about himself. For example, I may want my study to be clean and yet not want to clean it myself, since, out of laziness, I want someone else to clean it. Or, alternatively, my wife may want my study to be clean and yet not want to clean it herself. She may instead want *me* to clean the room because she thinks that for me to do that would help develop my character. Thus, simply to show that God as described in the Bible wants situation L would not in itself establish AE's premise (A2). I shall try to address this problem.

First of all, given human nature and the state of the world, it is not clear that there was any way for situation L to come to obtain other than for God to bring it about. However, even if there were such a possibility, if indeed God does not want to bring about situation L himself, then there must be some other desire on his part that overrides a desire to bring about situation L. But AE could then be refuted on the basis of its premise (A3). In that case it would not matter much whether we say that (A2) is false as well. On the other hand, if there is no such overriding desire, then there is little difference between God wanting situation L and God wanting to bring about situation L himself. There is reason to say that, with God, the one entails the other. That is, assuming God has no desire that overrides a desire to bring about situation L, since he is not lazy and since his all-loving nature fills him with zeal directed at the object of his love, for God to want situation L is essentially the same as for him to want to bring it about. In that case, any arguments showing that God has situation L among his desires would indeed suffice to support AE's premise (A2) as well.

Given the bifurcation of AE's premise (A) into (A2) and (A3), and given our understanding of omnipotence as being restricted at least by logic, it becomes clear that premise (A3) is the most problematic one of the bunch. Whether there is any good reason to either accept it or doubt it will be discussed below, especially in chapters 4, 6, 7, and 10.

Premise (A4) claims that God is rational. The point here is that God would not simply abandon one of his goals for no reason. Rather, he would perform whatever actions are called for by a goal that is not overridden by any other goal. The idea that God is rational in this sense is implied throughout Scripture. It is implied by those biblical verses that declare him to have infinite understanding (Ps. 147:5) and to have created the universe through his wisdom and understanding (Prov. 3:19). It is also implied by those biblical verses that say of God that he does what he wants and nothing ever prevents from happening those things that he wants to happen (Isa. 46:9–11; Eph. 1:11). The Bible is largely the story of a ruler of the universe who is eminently rational in having goals and performing actions to bring them about. AE's premise (A4) therefore receives excellent biblical support. There are ways to try to cast doubt on the premise, especially by appeal to verses that seem to show God "being of two minds" about various matters. However, that cannot be done within the framework of evangelical Christianity, which views God as eminently sane and rational. Christianity has no doubt about the truth of (A4). More will be said about that premise in section 2.4.

Premise (B) should not be controversial and is here being taken to be an analytic truth. Anyone who doubts it is probably not understanding it properly. If God is rational and has it among his top (nonoverridden) priorities to bring about a certain situation, and is able to bring it about, all things considered, in the sense discussed above, then there is no way for him not to bring it about. Since all conceivable alternatives have been eliminated, it becomes necessary that God bring about the given situation. Another way to put the matter is to say that part of what it means to be "rational" is that if X is rational and X is able to do Y, all things considered, and X wants to do Y without that desire being overridden by any other desire, then X *does* Y. Thus, given a full explication of the concept of rationality, premise (B) becomes true by definition.

As was pointed out in section 1.4, above, premise (C), though true, *could* be false. It is only a contingent fact about the world. The chalk analogy could again be used to show that. AE's premise (C) is to be interpreted in the way that makes it merely contingent. The expression "the amount of suffering that there actually is at present" is to be taken to refer only to a certain specific amount, just as "the number that there actually is at present" in the chalk analogy of section 1.4 could be just a way of referring to the number three.

Steps (D) and (E) are conclusions. They follow logically from the preceding steps from which they are derived. Since the argument is valid, it might be thought to be addressing the so-called "deductive problem of evil." However, the support given for the various parts of premise (A) is not intended to be deductive. Consider premise (A2), for example. Certain passages of the Bible are cited as evidence that the God of evangelical Christianity wants something. The inference from "this is how God is described in the Bible" to "this is what the God of evangelical Christianity wants" is not intended to be deductive, but rather, inductive. It depends on certain assumptions about evangelical Christianity's acceptance of the Bible and its interpretation of specific biblical verses, both of which make the reasoning evidential in character, rather than conclusive or even putatively conclusive. If the support for premise (A) were incorporated into the argument itself, then it would be an inductive argument. Thus, the present version of AE should be thought of as addressing the so-called "inductive (or evidential) problem of evil."

2.3. The Argument from Nonbelief (ANB) Formulated

To formulate ANB more precisely, I put forward, first, these two definitions:

The gospel message = the following three propositions:
   (a) There exists a being who rules the entire universe.
   (b) That being has a son.
   (c) The ruler of the universe sent his son to be the savior of humanity.

Situation S = the situation (or situation-type) of all, or almost all, humans
                since the time of Jesus of Nazareth coming to believe all the
                propositions of the gospel message by the time of their phys-
                ical death.

Using the above definitions, ANB may be expressed as follows:

(A) If the God of evangelical Christianity were to exist, then he would pos-
     sess all of the following four properties (among others):
     (1) *being able* to bring about situation S, all things considered;
     (2) *wanting* to bring about situation S, i.e., having it among his
         desires;
     (3) *not wanting* anything else that necessarily conflicts with his desire
         to bring about situation S, as strongly as he wants to bring about
         situation S;
     (4) *being rational* (which implies always acting in accord with his own
         highest purposes).
(B) If there were to exist a being who has all four properties listed above,
     then situation S would have to obtain.
(C) But situation S does *not* obtain. It is *not* the case that all, or almost all,
     humans since the time of Jesus of Nazareth have come to believe all
     the propositions of the gospel message by the time of their physical
     death.
(D) Therefore [from (B) & (C)], there does not exist a being who has all four
     properties listed in premise (A).
(E) Hence [from (A) & (D)], the God of evangelical Christianity does not
     exist.

(As with AE, the reader is urged to insert a bookmark at this page so as to
facilitate referring back to the precise formulation of ANB given here. In
addition to the next section, later chapters will contain discussions of this
particular version of the argument, especially chapters 5, 7, 9, and 11.)

2.4. Comments on ANB

It might be objected that there is far more to the gospel message than just
the set of three propositions given. But that is something I am happy to
grant. The more there is to it, the stronger ANB's premise (C) becomes. In
the interest of economy, it will be useful to regard the gospel message as
just the "bare-bones" set of three propositions stated above. That will not
affect the truth of any of the premises of ANB and it will simplify our discussion of various issues that surround the argument.

Note that situation S does not call for *every* person, without exception, to believe the gospel message. Because of the expression "or almost all" (which is to be understood in a loose way), S allows the possibility that special circumstances may prevent such belief. By "special circumstances" I do not mean to refer to the case of severely retarded persons who, even as adults, are unable to comprehend the propositions in question. God might still *want* such people to believe, even if they are incapable of it. Rather, I have no particular exceptions in mind, but I want to leave the door open to such exceptions, should there be any. Some have claimed that when the Bible uses expressions such as "all men," they should not be taken in a rigid sense. For that reason, it seems preferable to formulate ANB in a less rigid and more flexible manner, that being quite adequate for its purpose. The qualification ("or almost all") inserted in the definition of situation S is one that, in itself, loosens the claim expressed by premise (A) and thereby helps make (A) true.

The general comments made in section 2.2 about the structure of AE apply also to ANB. As with AE, the God of evangelical Christianity can be understood, at least initially, to be God as described in the Bible. So, dividing (A) into four premises, we should inquire of each of them whether it receives any biblical support. Premise (A1), as in the case of AE, is supported by the Bible's repeated claim that God is all-powerful. It is clear that he could have brought about situation S, even all things considered. Let us consider some of the ways by which God might have done that, assuming he exists.

One way would have been direct implantation of the given beliefs into people's minds. (A possible biblical example of belief-implantation is the case of Adam and Eve.) Closely related to that method would have been the creation of "belief genes" which are passed on from one generation to the next. Infants could be born with the tendency to automatically form a belief in the gospel message as their minds develop. The process could perhaps be aided by the influence of the Holy Spirit within each person.

Schellenberg emphasizes the use of religious experience as a way for God to reveal himself to people. However, it is unclear to me just what form the experiences might take. Would people hear inner voices or see visions (like Paul on the road to Damascus)? Or would it be just a kind of feeling that overcomes them? One main problem with appeal to a feeling is that it seems incapable of delivering thoughts with as much specific content as the gospel message. Appeal to inner voices would be more effective in that regard. Schellenberg describes the experience as follows:

> This experience, let us say, is nonsensory—an intense apparent aware-
> ness of a reality at once ultimate and loving which (1) produces the belief
> that God is lovingly present (and ipso facto, that God exists), (2) continues

indefinitely in stronger or weaker forms and minimally as a "background awareness" in those who do not resist it, and (3) takes more particular forms in the lives of those who respond to the beliefs to which it gives rise in religiously appropriate ways.[3]

It is unclear to me whether Schellenberg would include inner voices as a "nonsensory" religious experience. It is also unclear whether he would even want to appeal to religious experience at all as the best way for God to reveal such detailed ideas as the gospel message. His book is directed only at the problem of nonbelief in God's existence, not the quite separate problem of nonbelief in the gospel message. How such a detailed message might be transmitted by means of religious experiences remains unclear.

Perhaps a more promising way for God to have gotten the message across would have been by the performance of spectacular miracles. For example, God could have spoken to people in a thunderous voice from the sky or used spectacular skywriting to proclaim the gospel message world-wide. In addition, back in the days of Jesus, events could have occurred differently. Instead of appearing only to his followers, the resurrected Christ could have appeared to millions of people, including Pontius Pilate and even the emperor Tiberius and others in Rome. He could thereby have made such a definite place for himself in history that it would have enlightened billions of people coming later about the truth of the gospel message. It might be objected that the use of spectacular miracles would be too intimidating. That does not seem to me to be the case, but I shall postpone discussion of the issue to chapter 5.

God could also have brought about situation S without resort to spectacular miracles. He could have done it through nonspectacular, behind-the-scenes actions. For example, he could have sent out millions of angels, disguised as humans, to preach to people in all nations in such a persuasive manner as to get them to believe the gospel message. Another useful action would have been to protect the Bible itself from defects. The writing, copying, and translating of Scripture could have been so carefully guided (say, by angels) that it would today contain no vagueness or ambiguity and no contradictions or errors of any sort. Also, it could have contained a large number of very clear and precise prophecies that then become amazingly fulfilled, with that information noted by neutral observers and widely disseminated. People reading it would have been much more likely to infer that everything in it is true, including the gospel message. If all that had been done, then situation S would probably now obtain. Certainly the way God is depicted in the Bible, he is able to accomplish such things (whether spectacular or not), all things considered, which makes ANB's premise (A1) true.

One last way worth mentioning for God to bring about situation S is the following. God could have postponed sending his son to save the world to (what we would call) the year 2000 A.D. (or C.E.), a year firmly within "the Information Age." He could then make use of the Internet to advertise the event both before and after its occurrence. Those who browse the World Wide Web could regularly receive the gospel message, perhaps even if they try to avoid it. God could also "flame" all and only nonbelievers who are sitting at their computers by warning them of future judgment. CDs could also fall from the sky (for use by those with CD-ROM drives) containing the gospel message, delivered in spectacular colors and sounds. Of course all this could also take place even if the saving of the world by God's son had occurred when it was supposed to have occurred, long ago, but in that case other methods would have been needed to enlighten those who lived before the Information Age. In either case, modern technology has made it relatively easy for God to get his message out to the world, so much so that we can declare ANB's premise (A1) to be obviously true. Unlike the problem of evil, the problem of nonbelief is one regarding a certain lack of information, and it is even more easily solvable today than it would have been in the distant past.

James A. Keller has suggested that it might be beyond God's power to transmit information of the relevant sort to humanity.[4] But certainly if that were so, then God would indeed be a limited deity, and a far cry from the Almighty who is worshiped by evangelical Christians. No one who puts much store in the Bible would attack ANB at its premise (A1). A much more likely target would be its premise (A2) or (A3).

Premise (A2) states that if God were to exist then he would *want* to bring about situation S, where that is to be understood in a kind of minimal way, meaning only that the bringing about of situation S is among God's desires. So, it is a desire that might be overridden by some other desire, which creates a need for premise (A3). The same relation exists here between premises (A2) and (A3) as was pointed out, above, in connection with AE. There is the issue of whether God might want situation S without wanting to bring it about himself. I would say that if there is some desire on God's part that overrides a desire to bring about situation S, then ANB's premise (A3), and ANB along with it, could be thereby refuted. In that case, the issue would be moot: it would matter very little whether or not we declare ANB's premise (A2) also false. On the other hand, if there is no such overriding desire, then one might very well say that for God to want situation S would be essentially the same as God wanting to bring about situation S. Since God is not lazy and is highly motivated, there would in that case be no reason for him not to want to bring it about. In other words, as with AE and situation L, if there is no counterexample to premise (A3), then there is no reason for God to want situation S but not want to bring it about himself.

I shall proceed for the time being on the assumption that there is no overriding desire on God's part that would suffice to refute ANB's premise

(A3). Given that assumption, all that would be needed in order to support premise (A2) would be arguments to the effect that the God of evangelical Christianity, whom I take here to be God as described in the Bible, has situation S among his desires. There are at least seven different arguments to show that. Let us label them arguments (1)–(7).

Argument (1)

The Bible says that God has commanded people to "believe in the name of his son Jesus Christ" (1 John 3:23). The way it is usually interpreted, "believing in the name of the son" requires at least awareness of what God's son has done for humanity, which in turn calls for awareness of the truth of the gospel message. It follows that, having issued the command, God must want people at least to believe those propositions, which means that he wants situation S. And that makes ANB's premise (A2) true.

Argument (2)

There is another biblical commandment to the effect that people love God maximally (Matt. 22:37, Mark 12:30). But loving God maximally (i.e., to an extent that could not possibly be increased) requires that one be aware of *all* the good that God has done for humanity, including his sending of his son to save the world. If someone were to love God but not be aware of all the good that God has done, then it would be possible for such a person to be made aware of all that good and thereby come to love God still more. And being aware of all the good, in turn, requires belief in the gospel message. Hence, again, having issued the given command, God must want people to believe that message, which makes ANB's premise (A2) true.

Argument (3)

A third argument has to do with the missions of Jesus of Nazareth and John the Baptist. According to John 18:37, Jesus declared: "for this reason I was born, and for this I came into the world, to testify to the truth." Presumably the truth here referred to includes the gospel message as an important component. (We may infer this despite the fact that Jesus' words gave rise to Pontius Pilate's famous query "What is truth?") It follows that an important part of the mission of Jesus was to testify to the truth of the gospel message. And, according to St. Paul, it was God who was working through Christ to reconcile the world to himself (2 Cor. 5:19). God, then, must want people to believe the message, and not just the local people to whom Jesus spoke directly, but people all over the world. This may be gathered from the previous chapter in which Jesus indicated that he has sent his disciples into the world (John 17:18) and that the purpose is to make the world aware of the gospel message. In his prayer to his Father, Jesus said, "May they also be in us so that the world may believe that you have sent me" (verse 21) and "May they be brought to complete unity to let the world know that you sent me" (verse 23). Thus, since God wants his son to testify to the truth of the message and wants it to get out to the whole world, ANB's premise (A2) must be true. As a subsidiary point connected with this argument, the mission of John the Baptist is also relevant. It says in John 1:6–7: "There came a man who was sent from God; his name was John. He came as a witness to testify concerning that light [Jesus], so that through him all men might believe." It is understood that at least part of the object of the belief here referred to is the gospel message. This, then, further supports the claim that God wants all humans to believe the gospel message.

Argument (4)

This argument is based on the Great Commission, according to which God (via his son) directed missionaries to preach the gospel message to all nations (Matt. 28:19–20) and to all creation (Mark 16:15–16 NIV). Thus, God must have wanted people to believe the gospel message. And he not only wanted the message preached to all nations, but expected that to happen (as shown by such verses as Mark 13:10; Luke 24:47; Acts 1:8, 13:47, 28:28). Furthermore, according to the Book of Acts,[5] God went so far as to empower some of the apostles to perform miracles which would help convince listeners of the truth of the message. Since miracles are works of God, we could say that, in effect, God himself was indirectly starting to bring about situation S. So, getting people to believe the gospel message must have been a high priority for him. This is very strong evidence that ANB's premise (A2) is true.

Argument (5)

According to St. Paul, God "wants all men to be saved and to come to a knowledge of the truth" (1 Tim. 2:4 NIV). As with argument (3), a good case could be made here that the "truth" referred to includes the gospel message. Certainly evangelical Christianity takes it that way. And interpreting it that way, the verse is in effect telling the reader very directly that God wants (among other things) *all* humans to come to believe the gospel message. He must then want at least situation S, which does not even call for universal belief (but nearly universal belief). So the inference from that verse to the truth of ANB's premise (A2) is very direct.

Argument (6)

The next argument for (A2) is more controversial. One of its premises is the claim that, according to the Bible, God wants all humans to be saved. There are indeed verses, like the one quoted in argument (5), above, that either state it directly or else point in that direction.[6] But in order for people to be saved they must believe in God's son,[7] which is usually taken to include accepting him as the savior of the world. Hence, God must want people to believe in his son in that sense (accepting him as the savior of the world), which entails believing all the propositions of the gospel message. It follows that (A2) must be true.

There are two main objections to this argument. One of them, sometimes raised by Calvinists, is that some verses in the Bible indicate that God does *not* want all humans to be saved.[8] The other, sometimes raised by inclusivists, is that the Bible is not perfectly clear about the requirements for salvation and some verses suggest that charitable behavior might be sufficient,[9] in which case belief in God's son would *not* be a necessary condition after all. It appears, then, that the premises of this argument for (A2) leave some room for doubt.

In defense of argument (6), it could be pointed out that biblical scholars disagree about how to interpret the alleged contrary verses, and some of their interpretations favor the argument. Furthermore, most evangelical Christians support those interpretations which favor argument (6). They reject the Calvinist ("double predestination") idea that God has preselected some people for salvation and others for damnation. On the contrary, they regard God as a loving and merciful being who wants *all* to be saved, at least in the minimal sense of having that as one of his desires. As John Hick put it, the Calvinist idea that God created beings whom he does not want to attain salvation is "diametrically at variance with the dominant spirit of the gospels."[10] I shall make it part of my working definition of "evangelical Christians" that they conceive of God as desiring universal salvation. A more precise definition will be supplied in section 8.3, below. In addition, most evangelicals are exclusivists and accept the doctrine that belief in God's son in the relevant sense is an absolute requirement for salvation (though I shall not include this in the definition of "evangelical Christians").

My conclusion regarding this matter is that, although there are other forms of biblical Christianity based on other interpretations of the verses cited above, evangelical Christianity (that form which fosters belief in the deity referred to in the version of ANB presently under consideration) would for the most part accept the premises of argument (6). That then allows argument (6) to provide further biblical support for premise (A2) of ANB as applied to the God of evangelical Christianity. I concede, though, that argument (6) remains controversial (and will discuss the issue further in section 5.3). Nevertheless, it should be noted that even if that argument were rejected, other arguments should suffice to establish premise (A2). It might be said, then, that with or without argument (6), (A2), like ANB's premise (A1), receives excellent biblical support.

Argument (7)

Finally, I want to put forward an argument for ANB's premise (A2) that makes no reference to the Bible. Evangelical Christians regard God as a being who loves humanity, who wants that love to be reciprocated, and, in connection with that, who wants people to be aware of the gospel message. People's awareness of the gospel message would help them to reciprocate God's love for them. In the case of *some*, it might incline them toward greater morality, at least in regard to their behavior. Certainly it would provide people with comfort and hope for the future, and since God loves people, he must want them to attain such a benefit. It might be argued, then, that the proposition that God wants humanity to be aware of the truth of the gospel message fits in well with evangelical Christianity's overall worldview and would therefore be affirmed and assented to by evangelical Christians. On that basis, we may infer that God, conceived of in the given way, wants all, or almost all, humans to be aware of the truth of the gospel message, which in turn makes ANB's premise (A2) true.

When it comes to ANB's next premise, (A3), the situation is somewhat different. There are no biblical verses that support it directly. If (A3) is to receive any support at all from the Bible, it would need to be of an indirect nature. There are two arguments for it that I would like to consider. The first, to be labeled "argument (8)," is that argument (6), which is sound, appeals to the matter of people's eternal destiny. Since there can be nothing regarding humanity of a "weightier" nature than that,[11] it follows that God can have no wants regarding humanity that outweigh his desire for its redemption and eventual salvation, which (on the exclusivist assumptions of most evangelical Christians) calls for situation S. And since God wants everyone to be saved and to come to a knowledge of the truth, as shown in argument (5), we may infer that there is no want on God's part that would override his desire for situation S. This, then, provides some indirect support for ANB's premise (A3). One objection to this line of reasoning is that it presupposes the soundness of argument (6), which has to do with controversial issues regarding salvation (a topic to be discussed at greater length in section 5.3, below).

There is another kind of indirect support for ANB's premise (A3) that does not get involved in such issues, which brings us to the second argument for that premise. Call it "argument (9)." It appeals to the *force* of earlier arguments, in particular, arguments (1)–(4), which made no appeal to the concept of salvation. Looking back at argument (1), we note that, according to the Bible, God has *commanded* people to believe in his son, which is quite forceful. Although that may not prove it, it does suggest that God's desire for situation S is not overridden by any other desire. As for argument (2), according to the Bible, God's commandment that people love him maximally is described as the *greatest* of all the commandments (Matt. 22:38, Mark 12:29). That, too, suggests that God wants people to be aware of what he has done for them, which calls for them to believe the gospel message, and that this is not a matter overridden by other considerations. Further, argument (3) has to do with the mission of God's son to the planet earth, indicating that a large part of that mission was to get the gospel message out to the whole world. It is hard to see how God could have any purpose regarding humanity that might override his son's mission to the planet earth. Evangelical Christians regard Jesus' mission as the key to human existence and the meaning of life, so it does not seem they could view it as overridden by something else. Finally, as pointed out in argument (4), according to the book of Acts, God not only sent out missionaries to spread the gospel worldwide, but also provided some of them with miraculous powers in order to help get their listeners to accept the message. That suggests that situation S must have been such a high priority in God's mind as not to be overridden by anything else. In summary, argument (9) is the argument that premise (A3), though not directly expressed in the Bible, is nevertheless implied by several biblical passages, particularly in the very forceful way that premise (A2) is scripturally supported.

Argument (9) is admittedly something less than a conclusive proof, especially since premise (A3) receives no direct explicit support from Scripture. On the other hand, this weakness may not be fatal, first of all because any support, even of an indirect nature, is better than none, and secondly because (A3) is put forward not just as a claim but also as a challenge. It says that if God were to exist, then he would *not* have a certain type of desire, one which both necessarily conflicts with and also outweighs his desire for situation S. It is certainly a challenge even to conceive of possible candidates for such a specialized desire, for it is hard to understand what God might want from humans as much as their belief in the gospel message, on which depends their love and worship of him and his son, and possibly even their own salvation. There is absolutely nothing in the Bible to imply that God might have such a desire. To deny its existence, then, appears not to be such a terribly bold claim. It should be taken as a challenge by anyone who wishes to attack ANB's premise (A3) to describe a plausible candidate for the specialized desire called for in it.

There is a further challenge involved here. If indeed God were to have the sort of specialized desire called for, one which overrides his desire for situation S, then certain things would need to be explained, as brought out in arguments (1)–(4), above. In particular, we would need answers to the following questions:

1. Why did God issue to people a command to "believe in the name of his son Jesus Christ," a command which, if universally obeyed, would result in situation S?

2. Why did God issue to people a command, referring to it as his "greatest commandment," to love him maximally, which, again, if universally obeyed, would result in situation S (since, arguably, only those who believe the gospel message could love God maximally)?

3. Why did God send his son Jesus (and John the Baptist) to (among other things) "testify to the truth" (where the "truth" includes the gospel message), an action which helps bring about situation S?

4. Why did God issue the Great Commission, even empowering some of his missionaries to perform miracles as an aid to convincing their listeners, which, in effect, is a way of commencing the bringing about of situation S?

Certainly it is a great challenge for the opponent of ANB's premise (A3) to answer these questions under the assumption that the premise is false. If that challenge is not met, then there is a prima facie case for the truth of the premise. The issue of whether or not ANB's (A3) is true will be taken up further in chapters 5, 7, and 11.

ANB's premise (A4) is exactly the same as AE's premise (A4). It is the only step, aside from the conclusion, that both arguments share. As was pointed out in the discussion of AE, premise (A4) receives excellent biblical support and to deny it would be totally outside the conceptual framework of evangelical Christianity.

The need for premise (A4) within AE and ANB may not be fully grasped, so let us dwell on it a bit more. Thomas Talbott has written the following:

> I assume . . . that the following is necessarily true: If it is God's redemptive purpose to reconcile all sinners to himself and it is within his power to accomplish that purpose, then he will indeed reconcile all sinners to himself.[12]

Two objections to Talbott's claim occur to me. The first is that although God might have the given redemptive purpose for mankind, it might be overridden by some higher purpose, which would make Talbott's alleged necessary truth possibly false. That is, God might indeed have the purpose and yet for some reason (a higher purpose) not follow through on it, which would make the antecedent of Talbott's statement true but its consequent false. Presumably Talbott intends to give "have a purpose" a strong interpretation in which it means that not only does God want to reconcile all sinners to himself but, in addition, he does not have any other purpose which overrides that one. (That corresponds to what I referred to, above, as the "all-things-considered" or "resultant" sense of the expression "X wants Y.") I concede that that is a possible interpretation for "have a purpose," so my objection here is just that some clarification of the given point should have been made.

It is my second objection which I regard to be more telling and which relates to premise (A4) of AE and ANB. Talbott's alleged necessary truth is really not necessarily true, even given the strong interpretation of "have a purpose," because it is possible that God is irrational and does not follow through on his own highest purposes. That is, God might very well be able to carry out the redemption of all sinners and have that as one of his highest purposes, not overridden by anything else, and yet not follow through on it. Maybe he has some mental defect which prevents such action or maybe he is quirky and impulsive. In one form or another, the assumption that God is not like that, that he really always does follow through on his highest purposes, is needed in order for the inference to go through deductively. It is only if the antecedent of Talbott's alleged necessary truth were to contain a clause to the effect that God is rational in the relevant sense that the whole statement would indeed be a necessary truth. This brings out the need for AE's and ANB's premise (A4).

Let us now consider the other steps of ANB. For reasons analogous to those given in connection with AE, premise (B) is an analytic truth (one which, when analyzed, is true simply in virtue of its logical form) and should not be controversial. It is based on the idea that if there is no way whatever for situation S not to obtain then S must obtain. And, given that there exists a being who possesses all four properties listed in premise (A), every possible way for situation S not to obtain has been ruled out, so situation S would *have to* obtain. Another way to view the matter is in terms of the definition of "rational" as it appears in premise (A4). As pointed out earlier in connection with AE and as brought out in the discussion of premise (A4), above, given the truth of all of premise (A), premise (B) comes to be true just in virtue of the definition of "rational" as used in premise (A4). That is, for a being who has all four properties cited in premise (A) not to bring about situation S would exhibit irrationality on his part, which would contradict (A4), so that is logically impossible. Premise (B) functions in ANB in somewhat like the way that Talbott's alleged necessary truth, quoted above, was intended to function in his line of reasoning. However, premise (B) really is a necessary truth and is actually an *analytic* truth. Whoever doubts it is just not understanding it properly.

Like AE's premise (C), ANB's premise (C) is an empirical fact about our world. Christianity may be the most widespread religion, but it still claims a minority of the earth's people (only 33.5 percent according to the 1996 *World Almanac*), which suffices to make (C) true. Premise (C) is the proposition from which ANB derives its name. Note that the Argument from

Nonbelief is also an argument *for* nonbelief in that it aims to prove the nonexistence of God. Thus, it is both "from nonbelief" and also "for nonbelief," which may suggest circularity. However, the circularity evaporates when the matter is more precisely specified. The argument proceeds from the fact that a certain type of nonbelief is widespread, as one of its premises, to a proposition which expresses a certain type of nonbelief, as its conclusion. There is no circularity there. In our present version of ANB, the two types of nonbelief in question are different, but there would still have been no circularity even if they had been the same.

Step (D) is the first conclusion in the argument. As in the case of AE, it follows logically from premises (B) and (C) by *modus tollens*. The final conclusion, step (E), also follows logically. As with AE, premise (A) entails the proposition that if God exists, then there would exist a being who has all four properties (1)–(4). And that proposition, together with (D), logically entails the final conclusion, (E), by *modus tollens*.

As with AE, when all the support for all the premises is included, ANB needs to be classified as an inductive argument. If a distinction were drawn between a "deductive problem of nonbelief" and an "inductive problem of nonbelief," then ANB would be addressing the latter, not the former. It is an evidential argument, not intended to be conclusive, since the support for its premises is of an inductive or evidential sort. However, ANB itself, disregarding the support for its premises, is a deductive argument, and in my opinion, sound.

Since the conclusions of ANB follow logically from its premises, the only way to attack it would be at one or more of the premises. Dividing (A) into four, there are a total of six premises to be considered: (A1), (A2), (A3), (A4), (B), and (C). Of these, I hope to have shown above that only (A2) and (A3) leave room for debate. And of those two, (A2) strikes me as the one that is more clearly true, being extremely well supported within the Bible. Still, there may be some opposition to it, and that is a matter we will take up in chapter 9. But it is premise (A3) to which the greatest attention will be devoted, beginning with chapter 5. I think that if (A3) could be adequately defended, then ANB would pose a most formidable threat to rational belief in the God of evangelical Christianity.

2.5. The Project of this Book

As indicated in the preface, my goal is to formulate and assess three groups of arguments:

(1) AE and ANB,
(2) defenses of God's existence against AE and ANB,
(3) objections to the defenses.

One of my theses is that almost all the objections are sound and that each of the defenses is refuted by at least one objection. I regard both AE and ANB to be forceful and cogent attacks on the popular belief that God exists, though this needs to be qualified by considerations related to the many different concepts of God (or definitions of "God") that there are. For some (less common) concepts of God, AE and ANB are not at all forceful. That is a matter to be discussed later, in chapters 14 and 15.

At any rate, one main thesis of this book is that AE is not the only important atheological argument around. Even when the incompatible-properties arguments are disregarded and only God-vs.-world arguments are considered, there is another contender to take on God's existence and that is ANB. But I shall try to show in the book that both arguments are very strong, especially in the context of evangelical Christianity. The main theme of the book, suggested by its title, is that the problem of nonbelief and the problem of evil are *parallel* problems in the philosophy of religion and should receive parallel treatment within it.

Another main thesis is that the problem of nonbelief is an even greater difficulty for evangelical Christianity than is the problem of evil. In other words, when AE and ANB are applied specifically to the God of evangelical Christianity, ANB is a stronger, more forceful, and more cogent argument for their conclusion (that *that* god does not exist) than is AE. The reason why it is more forceful is the following. There is biblical evidence that if the God of evangelical Christianity were to exist then he would have a great concern about humanity's widespread lack of belief in the gospel message. There is also biblical evidence that if that deity were to exist then he would have a great concern about humanity's earthly suffering. But the former evidence is stronger than the latter evidence. Hence, the widespread absence of such belief among humans is a better reason to deny the existence of *that* god than is the widespread earthly suffering among humans. I take the main project of this book to be that of supporting these two main theses.

A secondary project will be the examination and evaluation of both AE and ANB, with particular emphasis on the latter. In the case of AE, due to space restrictions, my treatment will need to be somewhat cursory. There is an extensive literature on the subject which I shall not delve into. Other works supply hundreds of good references.[13] I think, though, that, despite the brief treatment, I shall supply enough to warrant my position that AE is a strong argument. Most of the above will be carried out in part II of the book, which is comprised of chapters 4–11.

Finally, in part III (chapters 12–15), I shall consider the force of both AE-type and ANB-type arguments when they are applied to other concepts of God, in particular the God of Orthodox Judaism, the God of liberal Christianity, and God in general. In the latter two contexts, AE may be more widely applicable than ANB, though that is a debatable issue. Nevertheless, it will also be part of my project to show that, there as well, ANB is a more forceful and cogent argument than AE. My various assessments will be summarized in chapter 15.

It is important to understand what my project is *not*. It is *not* a survey of all the various types of atheological argument around. One large category that I do not get into, except briefly in chapter 3, is that of incompatible-properties arguments for God's nonexistence. They are definitely the subject matter for a separate book. Furthermore, there are also several God-vs.-world arguments that I do not explore. One of them, the Lack-of-evidence Argument, which is mentioned above in section 1.5, resembles ANB in some ways, but is a distinct argument. My project in this book is strictly confined to the discussion, and particularly the assessment, of the two atheological arguments AE and ANB, with special attention to ANB.

As mentioned in the preface, part of my aim is to address a wider audience than usual. It is to be expected, then, that some readers will find some parts of the book of lesser interest than others, given their particular outlook. My hope is that all readers, regardless of outlook, will find parts that are definitely "up their alley."

Notes

1. Gen. 17:1, 35:11; Jer. 32:17,27; Matt. 19:26; Mark 10:27; Luke 1:37; Rev. 1:8, 19:6. Unless otherwise specified, all biblical references in the present book are to *The NIV Study Bible: New International Version* (Grand Rapids, Mich.: Zondervan, 1985). One reason for choosing that translation is that it is highly regarded by most evangelical Christians.

2. Matt. 9:36, 14:14, 15:32; Mark 6:34, 8:2.

3. Schellenberg, *Divine Hiddenness*, p. 49.

4. Keller, "The Hiddenness of God and the Problem of Evil," pp. 22–23.

5. Acts 3:6–18, 5:12–16, 9:33–42, 13:7–12, 14:1–11, 28:3–6.

6. Matt. 18:12–14; John 12:32; Rom. 5:18, 11:32; 1 Cor. 15:22; Col. 1:20; 1 Tim. 2:4,6; 2 Peter 3:9.

7. Mark 16:15–16; John 3:18,36, 8:21–25, 14:6; Acts 4:10–12; 1 John 5:12.

8. Prov. 16:4; John 12:40; Rom. 9: 18; 2 Thess. 2:11–12. Also, Jesus spoke in parables so that not everyone would understand him and thereby get saved (Matt. 13:10–15; Mark 4:11–12; Luke 8:10).

9. Matt. 25:34–40,46; Luke 10:25–37, 18:18–22; John 5:28–29; Rom. 2:5–7,10; James 2:24–26.

10. John Hick, *Evil and the God of Love* (New York: Harper & Row, 1966), p. 379.

11. Matt. 10:28, 16:26; Mark 8:36–37; Luke 12:15–21.

12. Thomas Talbott, "Three Pictures of God in Western Theology," *Faith and Philosophy* 12 (1995): 79.

13. For example, 545 good references are listed on pp. 367–91 of *The Problem of Evil: Selected Readings*, edited by Michael L. Peterson.

3

Objections from the Left

This chapter is mainly written for the benefit of those readers who are non-theists, professional philosophers, or students in philosophy courses. All other readers are encouraged to skip it and to go on to chapter 4. There would not be any great loss of continuity in so doing.

3.1. The Noncognitivity Objection

I take theism to be the claim that God exists and atheism to be the claim that God does not exist. Some writers call the latter view "positive atheism" in contrast with "negative atheism," which is simply the absence of belief in God or the refraining from making the theistic claim. Although some people use the term "atheism" to mean negative atheism, I think most use it, as I do, to mean positive atheism. In this book I shall use "atheism" to mean "positive atheism" and "nontheism" to mean "negative atheism." All atheists are nontheists, but not vice versa. Some nontheists are agnostics, withholding judgment one way or another on God's existence, possibly maintaining that neither judgment can be supported. Some other nontheists make the more forceful claim that both theism and atheism are mistaken or misguided regarding the nature of discourse about God. I shall call such discourse "God-talk" (with apologies to those who find the expression unappealing). Theists and atheists both take God-talk to be cognitive, i.e., to express propositions which are true or false and capable of being supported or even known. The objection, which I shall call "the Noncognitivity Objection," is that that is a mistake: God-talk is instead noncognitive in nature. That is, it does not express propositions and it cannot be supported

74

or known, at least not in the usual sense of those terms. Hence, it is a mistake to try to prove God's nonexistence, for no argument about God could possibly be sound. Nontheists who put forward this objection to theism and atheism could be called "noncognitivists with respect to God-talk." For the sake of simplicity, I shall just refer to them as "noncognitivists."

Noncognitivists can be divided into two groups depending on whether or not they regard God-talk to be meaningless (or unintelligible). In the first category (claiming that God-talk is meaningless) would be such philosophers as A. J. Ayer, Antony Flew, Paul Edwards, and Kai Nielsen. In the second category (claiming that God-talk is noncognitive but not meaningless) would be such philosophers as R. B. Braithwaite, Ludwig Wittgenstein, and D. Z. Phillips. Although perhaps some in the second category might call themselves "theists," I regard them as nontheists. I understand theists not only to claim that God exists but also to regard that claim as a true proposition, whereas people in the second category do not do that.

Many of those in the first category espouse the verifiability theory of meaningfulness, arguing that nonanalytic sentences need to be in principle empirically verifiable or falsifiable (or at least confirmable or disconfirmable) in order to be meaningful and that all God-talk fails this test. I disagree with that view both because I have misgivings about the verifiability theory of meaningfulness itself (which I shall not go into here) and because I think that some God-talk is in principle empirically confirmable anyway. In the previous chapter I gave examples of ways in which God might bring about situation S. I think that some of those events would also constitute empirical evidence for God's existence. For example, if the gospel message were to become exceedingly prevalent on the Internet in an unsolicited form, perhaps even showing up on the screens of all and only non-Christian computer buffs, even when their computers are turned off, then that would be some evidence that God exists (though no doubt still better evidence than that could be easily described). However, I do not want to pursue this issue. Instead of attacking each individual version of the Noncognitivity Objection, I shall attack the argument in a wholesale fashion.

The Noncognitivity Objection is an "objection from the left" to the project of this book. It is the objection that the project is hopelessly misguided, or at least of no interest, since the atheistic conclusion of every version of AE and ANB is either meaningless or somehow linguistically spurious. Both the sentence "God exists" and the sentence "God does not exist" are noncognitive, which makes them inaccessible to reasoning or argumentation. In other words, no version of AE or ANB could possibly be sound for the reason that the argument lacks a true conclusion. Since the sentence "God does not exist" is either meaningless or in some other way noncognitive, it is thereby disqualified from any possible role in argumentation. In defending the soundness of AE and ANB, I find myself in a kind of middle position between theism (to the right), which accepts the cognitivity of the arguments' conclusion but rejects its truth, and noncognitivism (to the left), which denies even the cognitivity of that conclusion.

There is still another position on the matter which remains neutral on the issue not only of whether or not God exists but also of whether or not "God exists" is meaningful. Richard R. La Croix calls the position "metatheism":

> For the metatheist the problem of knowing the meaning of the sentence 'God exists' is prior to the problem of making a judgment about the truth value of that sentence. From the metatheistic point of view theism, atheism, and agnosticism are equally untenable doctrines because they all rest on a highly problematic assumption about the meaning of the sentence 'God exists.' ... [T]he meaning ... needs to be stated and explicated and not simply assumed. ... But theists, atheists, and agnostics never do in fact state explicitly and completely what the sentence 'God exists' means and it is not at all clear that they all mean the same thing.[1]

La Croix is not here claiming that "God exists" is meaningless, only that those who discuss the issue of its truth or falsity should first discuss what it means and make sure that they all mean the same thing by it. I am highly sympathetic to this outlook. I think that many of the main questions in the philosophy of religion lie in the attempt to explicate the meaning of "God exists." However, La Croix seems to think it essential that that meaning be *completely* explicated before any case can be made for atheism, and that is something I would deny. Further on, I shall argue that a good case can be made for God's nonexistence simply on the basis of a partial understanding of what God is supposed to be.

It is important to grant that if God-talk is noncognitive, then atheism is an incorrect view. One writer who has neglected to bring this point out in a clear way is Michael Martin, who says the following:

> The sentence "God exists" is not factually meaningful; that is, it is neither true nor false. Negative atheism is justified, since one can only believe that God exists if the sentence "God exists" is either true or false. Hence negative atheists are justified in not believing in God. However, positive atheism is not justified, since the sentence "God does not exist" is also factually meaningless; that is, it is neither true nor false. Hence positive atheists are not justified in believing God does not exist.
>
> However, there are two reasons why more needs to be said and why the argument cannot stop here. The thesis that the sentences "God exists" and "God does not exist" are factually meaningless is only prima facie justified. This is so because a commonly accepted and fully developed theory of meaning is not yet available. Until one is, we must rest content with a partial theory and a partial justification. This consideration tells strongly against negative atheists' relying exclusively on the verifiability

theory to support their case. In addition, even this partial justification could be undermined. Negative atheists who use the verifiability theory to support their view would be wise to have a fall-back position in case their arguments for the theory are shown to be mistaken.[2]

I understand and sympathize with Martin's appeal to a backup (or "fall-back") position. I did that in chapter 2 with arguments (1)–(7) in support of ANB's premise (A2), since if argument (6) should prove to be a failure, at least the other arguments could be relied upon to establish the conclusion. I shall also do similar things in later parts of the book. For example, although I lean toward the view that the very concept of an afterlife is incoherent (appendix E), in chapter 9 I assume that it is coherent.

The use of atheism as a backup position for noncognitivism is similar to my treatment of the afterlife issue, since noncognitivism declares atheism to be in a way incoherent. But in the quotation above, Martin comes right out and says he agrees with the view that "God does not exist" is meaningless in the sense of being neither true nor false. He later says that in the rest of his book he will disregard that and proceed as though the sentence were meaningful. How can a meaningless sentence be treated as though it were meaningful? That is, how can a sentence which cannot be used in arguments be used in arguments? Some further clarification is needed on this matter.

One thing that Martin could have done to make his position clearer would have been to take a more neutral stance on the issue whether or not the sentence "God does not exist" is meaningful. He could have said that he "leans toward" the view that the sentence is meaningless but had not as yet made up his mind on the matter. That would be similar to my position regarding afterlife-talk. Then, in that neutral situation, it would have made more sense for him to assume the sentence to be meaningful and within that context go on to argue that it expresses a true proposition.

Another approach that Martin could have taken, which I regard as still more promising, would have been to divide God-talk into two categories, the cognitive and the noncognitive (or sentences containing the term "God" which *can* be used in arguments, as opposed to those which *cannot* be used in arguments). Then he could have advocated atheism with regard to the first category and noncognitivism with regard to the second. He even suggested such an approach when he wrote: "I conclude that a case can be made that religious language is unverifiable and hence factually meaningless when it is used in a sophisticated and nonanthropomorphic way."[3] This suggests that although there is God-talk that is sophisticated and nonanthropomorphic and all or most of that kind is noncognitive, nevertheless there is also such a thing as God-talk that is unsophisticated and anthropomorphic and at least some of that kind can be cognitive. I tend to agree with that suggestion.

When mystics, for example, say that God is such an ineffable being that the very term "God" is totally indefinable, then I must agree that at least God-talk in that context is noncognitive and there just is no proposition there. The proper stance to take would be noncognitivism rather than atheism. However, with regard to the unsophisticated and anthropomorphic type of God-talk, atheism is defensible and the sort of atheological arguments discussed in the present book can be used in its support.

Sometimes a distinction is drawn between "the God of the philosophers" and "the God of the people," where the latter is presumably a concept of God that is "unsophisticated and anthropomorphic," to use Martin's terminology. I rather like that distinction and I shall say here that my book is not intended to relate to "the God of the philosophers," only to "the God of the people." I believe that there are many philosophers who understand the distinction and who have a strong interest in the *latter* notion. This book is for them! More will be said about the matter in chapters 13 and 14.

I grant that the word "God" may be used in ways quite different from, and even incompatible with, its use in AE and ANB. Some of those uses are indeed noncognitive, unlike the cognitive use of "God" in AE and ANB whereby it appears in sentences that purport to express propositions. It may very well be that most, or at least many, religious uses of the word are noncognitive. However, there are other occasions in which it is used cognitively. For example, many people, both religious and nonreligious, have claimed that there are good arguments or reasons that support the belief that God exists. When they make such a claim, they are apparently using the word "God" in a sentence that purports to express a proposition (which is the way that it is being used in AE and ANB), for one cannot use a sentence as the conclusion of an argument unless one regards it to be cognitive. Thus, the very fact that people sometimes try to support theism rationally or at least discuss the issue of God's existence provides a linguistic framework (namely, "cognitive discourse") within which atheological arguments may also be constructed. Even if such arguments were never used except to rebut those who think theism can be rationally supported, there would be at least *some* place for them to evade the Noncognitivity Objection. Although this book is not relevant to noncognitive uses of the word "God," it is relevant to cognitive uses, which I maintain are fairly common.

To see how common they may be, consider the use of the word "God" in the Bible, for example in its first verse: "In the beginning God created the heaven and the earth" (KJV). From the way the term "God" is used throughout the Book of Genesis (e.g., as referring to a being who has plans and performs actions), it can be seen that certainly that first sentence expresses a proposition if it is taken literally. But even if it is taken symbolically rather than literally, it could still express a proposition, for many people would still take it to express a *truth*. The use of symbolism does not preclude the expression of propositions. Most interpretations of biblical references to God take them cognitively even when the interpretation is symbolic rather than literal. Let us say, for the time being at least, that the word "God" in AE and ANB is to be used in the same way as it is used in the Bible, which is a cognitive use.

It may be objected that such an employment of the word "God" unduly restricts it to the God of the Bible, making the project of the book very narrow. I do consider nonbiblical concepts of God later on (chapters 13–15), but even where the focus is on the God of the Bible, I disagree with the charge of "narrowness" for various reasons. First, almost all English-speaking people learned to use the word "God" in childhood in connection with the Bible (whether from the Old Testament alone or from both Testaments). And this applies also to many people who speak other languages which have a term synonymous with the English word "God." Many of them, too, learned the given word in connection with the translation of the Bible into their language. So the biblical use of the word "God" is a quite familiar one, which would prevent the project of my book from being unduly narrow.

Second, there are hundreds of millions of people around the world who regard the Bible, with its frequent uses of the words "God" and "the Lord" (or equivalent terms in their language), to be their guide to life and to be totally, or almost totally, true. The United States has a particularly high percentage of people with such an outlook. Even if the project of this book were restricted to *those* people, it could not properly be called "narrow," simply because of the large numbers involved.

Finally, there is not so much of a difference between the God of the Bible and other conceptions of God in theology, philosophy, and everyday life. The various conceptions often share common characteristics, including such divine attributes as omnipotence, omniscience, omnibenevolence (or being all-loving), being eternal, and being the creator and ruler of the universe. Although the word "God" is exceedingly vague and has multitudinous nuances of meaning, I should think that just about everyone who uses the word (or an equivalent term) would have an interest in an argument for the nonexistence of the God of the Bible.

The main project of the book is directed at uses of the word "God" that are either biblical or very closely related to the biblical use. In chapters 4–11, we will consider AE and ANB as applied specifically to the God of evangelical Christianity. Then in chapter 12, another closely related conception of God (that of Orthodox Judaism) will be considered. By tying the project of the book to the God of the Bible, I hope to sidestep the Noncognitivity Objection. Statements cannot be noncognitive if, for example, they are about situations that can be described in stories or depicted on film. And many biblical stories about God have indeed been depicted on film. For example, in the movie *The Ten Commandments* God is portrayed as a mighty being who knows what is happening everywhere, who speaks to people in a deep male voice, and who brings about spectacular miracles, apparently through some process akin to telekinesis. Thus, in taking the conclusion of AE and ANB to be referring to *that* being, I guarantee that the sentence which expresses it is at least a cognitive one.

It might be objected that the concept of God at which most of this book is directed is a rather unsophisticated and anthropomorphic concept, and one not shared by the majority of theistic philosophers. But that is all right as far as I am concerned. As indicated above, my main interest is in the so-called "God of the people," not "the God of the philosophers." It is an important philosophical question whether or not a strong case can be made for the nonexistence of the "God of the people." Among other things, it has applications within the area of public policy, some of which are described in appendix G at the end of the book. Even philosophers of religion who themselves more often appeal to a different concept of God should have a strong interest in *that* question.

3.2. The Biblical-inconsistency Objection

A somewhat different objection might be put forward by appeal to incompatible-properties arguments. If the Bible assigns incompatible properties to God, then even though propositions might be expressed, the propositions would be self-contradictory and thereby, in an important sense, incoherent. And the Bible does indeed contradict itself regarding the divine attributes, so it is argued. For example, in some parts the biblical God is said to be invisible (Col. 1:15; 1 Tim. 1:17, 6:16) or a being who has never been seen (John 1:18; 1 John 4:12). Elsewhere God is supposed to have said, "you cannot see my face, for no one may see me and live" (Exod. 33:20). But Jacob declared, "I saw God face to face and yet my life was spared" (Gen. 32:30). It is said that God appeared to Abraham, Isaac, and Jacob (Gen. 12:7, 26:2; Exod. 6:3) and that the leaders of Israel saw him (Exod. 24:9–11) and that Moses saw him (Exod. 33:11,23).[4] It does indeed seem logically impossible (and to that extent incoherent) for God as described in the Bible to exist.

There are many such incompatible properties of the God of the Bible that might be cited. He is described in some parts of the Bible as merciful,[5] while in other parts he lacks mercy.[6] He has been said to be a being who sometimes repents or changes his mind[7] and also a being who never repents or changes his mind,[8] one who sometimes deceives or causes confusion or evil[9] and one who never does so,[10] one who sometimes punishes children for their parents' sins[11] and one who never does so.[12]

A special case is that of whether or not God became incarnate in a human being, Jesus of Nazareth. There are verses in which Jesus is called "God" or which imply that he is God,[13] which imply that Jesus created the world,[14] which seem to identify the Son with the Father,[15] which refer to both God and Jesus as "the first and the last,"[16] and which say that only God can be mankind's savior while other verses say that Jesus is mankind's savior.[17] Also, Jesus did suggest (somewhat cryptically) that he is God (John 8:58) and he did not correct Thomas when Thomas called him "my God" (John 20:28); and others thought that Jesus considered himself to be God (John 10:33). Even God called Jesus "God" (Heb. 1:8), despite the oddity of that.

On the other hand, Jesus also implied that he is not God by saying, "Why call me good? Only God is good,"[18] and by referring to "my God."[19] And God himself said repeatedly that Jesus was his (God's) son,[20] which implies that Jesus is not God. Other verses imply that Jesus had an origin in time,[21] which prevents him from being eternal. It is also implied that the Son was inferior to the Father (John 14:28) and subservient to him, not only while he was on earth,[22] but even at the end when the Son is finally victorious (1 Cor. 15:27–28); obviously God could not be inferior or subservient to himself. Furthermore, Jesus was *with* God (John 1:2); *mediated* between God and man (1 Tim. 2:5); was raised from the dead by God, his Father;[23] and presently sits at the right hand of God.[24] All that implies that Jesus is not God.

As for whether Jesus was omnipotent, Mark 6:5 implies that he wasn't, though Matt. 28:18 implies that Jesus came to be, which suggests that he became God. And as for whether he was omniscient, Mark 13:32 implies that he wasn't, though other verses imply that he was (John 16:30, 21:17). It seems, then, that the Bible contradicts itself on whether or not God became incarnate as Jesus. It follows, so the objection goes, that it would be logically impossible for the God of the Bible to exist, and so either all references to such a being, including those in God-vs.-world arguments, are in a certain way incoherent or else the issue of God's existence is moot.

I agree with most of those incompatible-properties arguments, but I deny the implication that if they are sound then all God-vs.-world arguments are rendered either incoherent or moot by means of them. Even if incompatible-properties arguments are sound, they are aiming at the very *same* conclusion that God-vs.-world arguments aim at. And so they are merely *other* ways to obtain that conclusion. An argument is not rendered incoherent, or even moot or negligible, simply because its conclusion can be established in other ways. For one thing, the other ways may turn out to contain weaknesses of one sort or another, in which case the given argument would then be shown to be needed or important.

As an analogy, consider the giant in the story "Jack and the Beanstalk." Suppose that the story were to contradict itself on the giant's properties, describing him in one place as, say, bearded at a given time, but in another passage as clean-shaven at that same time. And suppose that the giant is also described as an enormous man who lives on top of a cloud. There might then be two separate arguments for the nonexistence of the giant of "Jack and the Beanstalk," one argument based on the necessary truth that no man can be both bearded and clean-shaven at the same time, and the other argument based on the empirical observation that no man lives on top of a cloud. The first would be an incompatible-properties argument and the second would be a "giant-vs.-world" argument. It is hard to say which of the two arguments would be the more forceful. The incompatible-properties argument would have the greater logical force, since it does not rely on any contingent step other than the description (or definition) of the giant. On the other hand, the property appealed to in the "giant-vs.-world" argument may be more essential to the giant or to the story and for that reason be more resistant to any sort of hermeneutical meddling with the text, which would make that argument the more forceful one. In a similar way, the critical properties of God that are appealed to in AE and ANB may be more essential to the God of the Bible as he is commonly conceived than are the ones appealed to in the various incompatible-properties arguments. For example, people may be more inclined to say of God that he is all-loving and desirous of our belief in his son (which are appealed to in AE and ANB) than that he never changes his mind or sometimes deceives people, etc. (which are appealed to in some of the incompatible-properties arguments). Thus, people would be less likely to try to reinterpret biblical passages used to support AE and ANB than some of the biblical passages used to support incompatible-properties arguments.

Atheists should be armed with both types of atheological argument, perhaps deploying incompatible-properties arguments first and then God-vs.-world arguments as a backup should the first type fail. This book can be taken to address the issue of whether or not two of those backup arguments are sound or cogent and how forceful they are. Certainly each argument deserves consideration on its own merits, and it is in that spirit that the project of my book is undertaken.

3.3. The Unintelligible-predicates Objection

Finally, a somewhat different objection may be raised. It is not that God-talk is intentionally noncognitive or that it involves explicit contradictions, but that certain predicates or sets of predicates ascribed to God, even the God of the Bible, are just flat-out meaningless. One possible example of such a predicate is "being transcendent," which I take to designate the property of being outside space and time. It might make sense to say that numbers and other abstract entities are outside space and time, but to speak of a personal being who is outside space and time is always to talk nonsense, so the objection goes, and that includes presenting arguments which purport to establish the nonexistence of such a being. It would be as if the giant in "Jack and the Beanstalk" were described as, say, "a being that is brightly large." Then all "giant-talk" would be meaningless and that would include any argument for the giant's nonexistence. So if "God" is defined as, among other things, "a transcendent personal being," then any conclusion to the effect that such a being does not exist is unintelligible. It would make no more sense to say "there are no transcendent personal beings" than it would to say "there are no brightly large beings." If you have no idea what a "transcendent personal being" is supposed to be, then it would be irrational for you to assert that they don't exist. Hence, according to the Unintelligible-predicates Objection, the project of this book is hopelessly misguided and atheism is itself an incoherent claim.

There are various ways in which atheists might try to deal with this objection. They might deny that transcendence is a meaningless notion, perhaps on the grounds that contemporary astronomers and cosmologists sometimes suggest something analogous to that idea when they describe the universe as consisting of a hyperspace that has many higher dimensions. Although the higher dimensions are not totally outside space and time, they are at least beyond our ordinary ways of conceiving space and time. So the fact that transcendence is also beyond our ken should not deter us in appealing to the concept. Or, alternatively, atheists might try to show that there is a contradiction or inconsistency within the very idea of transcendence, at least applied to a personal being. In that case, the idea would not be altogether unintelligible but just self-contradictory, which would allow something like our reply to the Incompatible-properties Objection to become relevant. (Granted, self-contradictory predicates are in a certain sense unintelligible, but there would at least be another way of dealing with them, one which allows sentences containing such predicates to play a role in arguments.) Still another approach would be to declare the expression "transcendent person" to be a kind of type crossing, which I shall comment on below. Finally, atheists might argue that, although philosophers and theologians may refer to God as "transcendent," such a predicate is not part of God-talk in ordinary language. Hence, AE and ANB could still be put forward with regard to the ordinary concept of God.

There is some merit in each of these approaches, though none of them is totally satisfactory. I really do find the notion of a personal being who is outside space and time to be in a certain sense unintelligible, despite recent work in astronomy and cosmology and the appeal to higher dimensions. It is certainly a notion that I find myself totally unable to entertain in thought.

On the other hand, the expression "personal being who is outside space and time" is not unintelligible in the same way that "brightly large" is unintelligible. It is clearly a grammatically correct expression, whereas that is not so for "brightly large," so that analogy appears to be misguided. Nevertheless, the expression may very well be a type crossing or involve sortal incorrectness.[25] That is, the sentence "God, a transcendent person, exists" may be like the sentence "Blue theories exist," containing an expression which says of one type of thing something that has application only to a different type of thing. On the other hand, even if the sentence were to be a type crossing or involve sortal incorrectness, that need not preclude its use in arguments. Long ago, A. C. Ewing said the following:

> [The sentence] "quadratic equations do not go to race meetings" is entailed by "quadratic equations do not move in space" and entails "quadratic equations do not watch the Newmarket horse-races"; but if it is capable of entailing and being entailed, surely it must be a proposition and not a mere meaningless set of words.[26]

Also long ago, A. N. Prior defended the claim that the negations of type crossings are true: "My proof that virtue is not square is a simple syllogism—what is square has some shape, but virtue has no shape, therefore virtue is not square."[27] If the statement "virtue is not square" can be true, then it would seem that the statement "no personal beings are outside space and time" can also be true, given that the latter (like the former) is the negation of a type crossing. So I do not find it totally misguided for someone to try to argue that it is simply false that there is a personal being who is outside space and time. For the atheist simply to deny that divine transcendence is a totally unintelligible notion would be a possible defense against the Unintelligible-predicates Objection.

As for showing that the notion is in itself contradictory or inconsistent, I do not offhand see any clear way to do that, though I would certainly like to see it done if it could be done. Possibly there is some way to do it along the lines suggested above by A. N. Prior, though I would deny that type crossings are self-contradictory.[28] On the other hand, perhaps it could be shown that the expression "personal being who is outside space and time" is not a type crossing but does involve a contradiction in terms. For example, maybe "being outside space and time" could be shown to entail "being unchangeable," whereas "being a personal being" entails "being changeable." In that case, an incompatible-properties argument could be constructed for the nonexistence of God, understood as a transcendent person. I would not rule out such a possibility, though I am not prepared to defend such an argument here.

Finally, the approach which simply denies that God-talk in ordinary language makes any appeal to God's transcendence strikes me as contrary to the facts. If ordinary theists were asked whether or not God is "outside space and time," probably most of them would say yes. On the other hand,

I grant that it is not among the usual properties that are commonly attributed to God. I have never seen it appealed to either in a dictionary definition of the term "God" or in any popular argument for God's existence. Thus, each of the suggested approaches to the Unintelligible-predicates Objection mentioned above has some merit, though each also has some drawback(s).

It would be hard to refute the objection if the conception of God that is appealed to by the atheist were to *explicitly* contain some unintelligible predicate. Some theists have a tendency to utter meaningless sentences as part of their God-talk and it is certainly hard for an atheist to deal with that. Perhaps in such a context one should instead go with noncognitivism and abandon atheism and any attempt to reason about God. To put forward AE or ANB requires that one regard the concept of God as intelligible at least in the sense of capable of being reasoned about. One possible move would be to insist that the term "God" which appears in the conclusion of an atheological argument be somehow definable but *not* be explicitly defined in a way which assigns to God any totally unintelligible predicate. However, there may be other ways to deal with the given objection.

Note that premise (A) of AE and premise (A) of ANB together assign *seven* properties to God. There are seven because subpremises (A1), (A2), and (A3), referring to two different situations, L and S, assign six different properties, and then (A4) in each argument assigns the same property. None of those seven properties assigned to God is expressed by an unintelligible predicate. However, each of those premises makes use of the parenthetical phrase "among others" in order to indicate that God has *other* properties than the ones listed. The question might be raised whether or not those "other" properties include ones (like transcendence) which are obscure (or designated by an unintelligible predicate). If they do, so it may be objected, then the argument is indeed misguided, for one of the terms in it ("God") would be meaningless. Let us look at this matter in greater detail.

A distinction is sometimes drawn between a thing's essential properties and its accidental properties. For example, gold is said to be a metal and to be yellow. The former property is said to be essential to gold, one that it possesses necessarily, whereas the latter property is only an accidental one, which it possesses only contingently. Perhaps such a distinction could be drawn in connection with the word "God," though that is a polemical issue. Let us say that, although the word "God" is a proper name or very much like a proper name, nevertheless there is some definite description which can be put in place of it. The description has the form "that being which has the properties of omnipotence, omniscience, being eternal, being the creator of the universe, etc.," where the properties mentioned are essential ones and a complete list of God's other essential properties is put in place of the "etc." Then when the atheist tries to prove that God does not exist, he could be

taken to be trying to prove the nonexistence of a being having those properties specified in the given definite description. But for the atheist's purposes,
it usually suffices that only a subset of the given properties be considered.
For example, in our version of AE, it is enough to consider just those four
properties mentioned in AE's premise (A). The other essential properties of
God are irrelevant so far as the argument is concerned.

What effect would it have on AE if it should be shown that among the
other essential properties of God (i.e., those contained within the definite
description that is substitutable for the word "God") there is at least one
which is obscure (or referred to by an unintelligible predicate)? Should we
say that that would make AE itself unintelligible? Certainly AE would
become unintelligible if the substitution (of the definite description for the
word "God") were to be carried out, for then the unintelligible predicate
would appear within AE itself. But what if the substitution were not carried
out, but AE were simply formulated using the word "God"? Why not say,
then, that AE would remain intelligible under those circumstances? We
could think of words that express very complex concepts as having "partial
meanings." Then AE might be construed as an argument for God's nonexistence based on merely a partial meaning of the word "God." The full
meaning might call for listing a dozen different properties, but AE says, in
effect, "Just on the basis of these four properties, God's nonexistence can
be established." The other properties are disregarded so far as the argument is concerned.

It is clear that so long as the properties (or predicates) alluded to in
both AE and ANB by means of the parenthetical phrase "among others"
which appears in premise (A) are all intelligible, the Unintelligible-predicates Objection would not arise. But what if nothing is said one way or the
other about what those "other" properties (or predicates) might be and
whether or not they are intelligible? What if the issue is left completely
open? It seems to me that there, too, the Unintelligible-predicates Objection should not arise. It should arise only if the context of discussion is one
in which unintelligible predicates have been explicitly ascribed to God.
Perhaps in that case atheological arguments would be out of place, for "God
does not exist" would then be a meaningless sentence. But that is not the
context of this book. Nowhere in it is it assumed or implied that the "other"
predicates ascribed to God include any that are unintelligible. Thus, so far
as the context of discussion within this book is concerned, the Unintelligible-predicates Objection should not arise.

Consider, again, the analogy of the giant described in the story "Jack
and the Beanstalk." Let us refer to that being as GJB. The question might
be raised whether GJB could be proven not to exist if the story were to
ascribe to him a meaningless predicate. Suppose the story were to contain
the following passage:

When Jack reached the top of the beanstalk, he saw a giant in the distance, one who lived on a cloud. The giant was a clean-shaven man who was brightly large and who weighed ten tons. Suddenly, the giant appeared puzzled. He rubbed his bushy beard and said, "Fee-fi-fo-fum, I smell the blood of an Englishman." As soon as Jack heard that, he scooted down the beanstalk.

Despite the ascription of the meaningless predicate "brightly large" to the giant, I think it would still be legitimate to argue for his nonexistence. An incompatible-properties argument could be constructed:

If GJB were to exist, then he would be a clean-shaven man who has a bushy beard.

But it is logically impossible for a clean-shaven man to have a bushy beard.

Hence it is logically impossible for GJB to exist.

Or, alternatively, a "giant-vs.-world" argument could be constructed:

If GJB were to exist, then he would be a man weighing ten tons who lives on a cloud.

But there is no man weighing ten tons who lives on a cloud.

Hence, GJB does not exist.

Both arguments disregard the part of the story that says of the giant that he was "brightly large." The question is whether they should be considered intelligible (and even sound) in light of the ascription of that meaningless predicate to the giant in the story. I think they should be, provided that they are worded as above. In general, I see nothing wrong with attempting to prove the nonexistence of something just on the basis of a *partial* understanding of what it is. After reading the story, it would make sense for someone to say, "I do not know completely what GJB is supposed to be, but from my partial understanding I can ascertain that GJB definitely does not exist." I would use this example to refute La Croix's view that one must have a *complete* understanding of what "God exists" means in order to make any good case for atheism.

However, if a definite description were to be put in place of "GJB" in each of the above arguments and if the description were to contain the meaningless predicate in question, then I would have to classify the arguments as themselves unintelligible. And the same sort of consideration would apply to such a substitution in the case of AE or ANB. An argument would itself be meaningless if it were to explicitly contain a meaningless term, though I deny that that applies to any version of any atheological argument formulated in this book.

But does AE at least *presuppose* that the "other" properties of God do *not* include ones that are obscure (or referred to by unintelligible predicates)? There is some unclarity regarding this point, and I am not sure how to reply. Suppose AE does presuppose that. What then? Advocates of AE would then be presupposing that the term "God" which appears in their argument is not defined in a way that makes use of, say, the predicate "being a transcendent person" (which we are assuming for the sake of argument to be unintelligible) or any other unintelligible predicate.

At this point, the force or relevance of atheological arguments might again be called into question. If people mean by "God" a transcendent person, but atheological arguments presuppose that God does not have any such (obscure) attribute, then how do such arguments attack people's belief in God? There are several things that might be said here.

First, if a theist were to keep insisting that God be described as a transcendent person or keep ascribing to God some other predicate or set of predicates which is definitely unintelligible, then I must concede that it would probably be misguided to present such a person with atheological arguments. It is not clear exactly what approach should be used to discuss the topic of God with such a person. The issues would seem to continually return to, and get hung up on, those unintelligible predicates. It appears that atheism might be the wrong approach there and, instead, noncognitivism should be put forward. Within the context of such a discussion, since I could not assent to "God exists," I would at least have to regard myself to be a nontheist. But whether I would also try to espouse atheism would depend on the circumstances of the discussion and whether or not a partial definition of "God" could eventually be agreed upon by both parties within it.

Second, only thinkable propositions are the objects of belief. If a sentence is unintelligible, then either it does not express any proposition at all or else it expresses a proposition that is inconsistent or in some other way unthinkable. Therefore, it does not express anyone's belief. If people go around saying, "I believe there is a personal being who is outside space and time," then my reaction is to deny that they really believe *that*. Rather, such people are apparently mistaken about their own beliefs. To have a belief requires more than just the disposition to assert (and/or assent to) given sentences. It is also required that there be some thinkable set of ideas to serve as the object of the belief. But if a sentence is unintelligible, then it does not express any such set of ideas. It cannot express anything which anyone could entertain in thought and which could thereby be the object of a belief. So, no, people do *not* really believe that there is a personal being who is outside space and time, even if they say they do. What has happened, I think, is that such people have been trained to recite the sentence in question, or something equivalent, and also to claim that the sentence expresses a belief of theirs, when there is in fact no belief there. There is only the sentence and the claim that it expresses a belief, together with a certain misconception about what is going on. (This might be called the "mumbo-jumbo theory" of some forms of religious language.) I would say that if someone really does have a *belief* that God exists, then atheological arguments do indeed attack that belief.

Third, it is not clear that the Bible ascribes to God any unintelligible predicates. The word "transcendent" does not appear in the Bible, nor do I know of any place where it says that God is "outside space" or "outside time." Throughout the Bible, God is depicted as performing actions that are within space and time, which is presumably not an available alternative to a being that is not himself within space and time, even an omnipotent one. (As argued previously, omnipotence needs to be restricted in certain ways.) Therefore, I shall simply deny that God is described anywhere in the Bible as being transcendent or being outside space and time.

Let us look a little further for possible unintelligible predicates ascribed to the God of the Bible. What about "being triune"? God is sometimes said to be triune, meaning that he is composed of three distinct persons each of which is numerically identical to him. (This is best expressed in the Athanasian Creed.) Well, the issue is a somewhat controversial one, but I would take the position (accepted by most biblical scholars) that there is no expression of the Doctrine of the Trinity within the Bible. It is a doctrine that came to be formulated only many centuries later. Even the related Doctrine of the Incarnation is not clearly expressed in the Bible. As was pointed out in section 3.2, above, some biblical passages suggest that Jesus was God Incarnate, but other passages imply that he wasn't. So, I would deny that the predicate "being triune" is ascribed to God in the Bible.

Furthermore, it might be argued that "being triune" is not so much unintelligible as self-contradictory, given the rules of identity logic. If A is triune, then there would exist three distinct beings, B, C, and D, each of which is numerically identical to A, and that of course entails a contradiction. A Trinitarian might insist that God is somehow "beyond" the rules of identity logic or else satisfies them in a way beyond our comprehension, but that sort of reply would be applicable to all the alleged incompatible properties. Instead of treating triunity as merely an unintelligible predicate, I am inclined to put it in the category of incompatible (pairs of) properties, like being both all-merciful and all-just with regard to deserts. There is a sense in which they are "unintelligible," but, unlike the situation with predicates that are totally meaningless, reasonable proofs could be constructed to the effect that no being possesses the given property or pair of properties.

Another candidate for an unintelligible predicate ascribed to the God of the Bible is that of being a spirit (e.g., John 4:24). Possibly that is unintelligible, but it need not be. Maybe a spirit is a kind of invisible, intangible entity about which some sort of theory might be constructed. If so, then perhaps some sense might be given to the term even if it should remain exceedingly vague. Ghosts have been depicted on film as a kind of human-shaped transparent mist. I suspect that something like that is what people have in mind when they use the term "spirit." So long as they have something in mind, the term is not altogether unintelligible.

Nevertheless, there is a definite problem here regarding God's composition. Suppose God is declared to be nonphysical (or nonmaterial) and yet to perform actions. Does that make sense? I do not have a definite view on this matter. Some nontheists say yes and others say no. J. L. Mackie says the following:

> Although all the persons we are acquainted with have bodies, there is no great difficulty in conceiving what it would be for there to be a person without a body: for example, one can imagine oneself surviving without a body, and while at present one can act and produce results only by using one's limbs or one's speech organs, one can *imagine* having one's intentions fulfilled directly, without such physical means.[29]

I disagree with Mackie about the degree of difficulty in imagining such things, for I myself have very great difficulty imagining them. A view contrary to Mackie's is expressed by Kai Nielsen:

> [W]e have no understanding of 'a person' without 'a body' and it is only persons that in the last analysis can act or do things. We have no understanding of 'disembodied action' or 'bodiless doing' and thus no understanding of 'a loving but bodiless being'.[30]

It is Nielsen's outlook which is "to the left" of mine and against which I am trying to defend my position in this chapter. However, I am unsure whether to do so in something like Mackie's way or in some other way. More will be said about the intelligibility of surviving without a body in appendix E, below.

Still another property sometimes ascribed to God is that of omnipresence. What that means is that for any spatial location, God is there in that place. (Presumably omnipresence is incompatible with transcendence!) Like the predicate "being a spirit," "being omnipresent" is a predicate that is not clearly intelligible. If something is at a certain place, then how can there be anything else at that place? If no two things can exist in the same place, and God is everywhere, then it would seem that no spatial object other than God can possibly exist. For God's omnipresence to make sense, some intelligible theory would need to be developed that would make sense of the idea of two different things simultaneously existing at the same place. Perhaps God could be regarded as akin to a gravitational field. Whether that is supposed to be a good analogy I cannot say. Immediately following the passage quoted above, Mackie goes on to declare: "Knowing what it is to be present in one place, we can form the concept of a spirit who is present everywhere." I find I have great difficulty forming such a concept, but I am not as yet ready to give up on it completely.

Furthermore, I do not find the idea of God's omnipresence clearly expressed in the Bible. It does say that God can see you wherever you may try to hide,[31] but that is related to omniscience rather than omnipresence. In Jer. 23:24 it is suggested that God "fills" heaven and earth, and in Psalm 139:8 it says "if I make my bed in the depths, you [God] are there." But in the context of each passage, that may be just a metaphor for God knowing about whatever happens anywhere. It strikes me as problematic whether a good case could be made for the claim that omnipresence is an unintelligible predicate ascribed to the God of the Bible or that the Bible ascribes to God any unintelligible predicates whatever. The issue remains unsettled.

I am willing to grant that some God-talk that occurs in ordinary language is unintelligible. But not all of it is. There are theists who do not ascribe to God, as essential attributes, the property of being a transcendent person or any of the other questionable properties mentioned above. Well, what, then, do they mean by the word "God"? Many of them have in mind some large, ghostly, anthropomorphic (or "personal") being who created the universe and now somehow rules it. That ruler is eternal in the sense of being everlasting (as opposed to being "timeless"). He is all-powerful in the sense of being able to perform any conceivable act compatible with his other essential characteristics. He is also all-knowing in the sense of having all and only true propositions as beliefs. And, although he is capable of feeling anger or disappointment, he is also all-loving in the sense of loving everyone maximally. Although the matter is debated among philosophers of religion, I find all that to be intelligible. I am aware that philosophers have argued that some of the individual properties such as omnipotence and omniscience are problematic, perhaps even incoherent, quite apart from their conjunction with other divine attributes. Attempts to define them in a precise way have been shown to be confronted by great difficulties. However, I am inclined to say that all such difficulties can be in one way or another gotten around, though I lack the space to defend that claim here. At any rate, many if not most theists have in mind some such intelligible, albeit admittedly unsophisticated and anthropomorphic, conception when they say they believe in God.

The issue comes down to the relevance of the present book to the concept of God of most evangelical Christians. My position is that their concept is indeed the unsophisticated and anthropomorphic one which Michael Martin suggests is cognitive, and which does not load the "other properties" mentioned in AE and ANB with any unintelligible elements. It is the main concept with regard to which arguments for theism are constructed and the one appealed to in the Bible. Most arguments for theism do not ascribe to

God any unintelligible divine predicates, and, in my view, the Bible does not do so either, though that is admittedly a debatable point. Thus, it is my view that at least within such a framework (either that within which arguments for theism are constructed or a biblical framework) atheological arguments are intelligible.

Even if unintelligible predicates were to be ascribed to God in the Bible and in some theists' descriptions of God, it seems to me possible to ignore (or "bracket off") those predicates and to discuss the issue of God's existence with such theists simply on the basis of other predicates. Even if that were considered just a "partial understanding" of "God," it seems to me to be adequate for atheological purposes. Just as the nonexistence of the giant in "Jack and the Beanstalk" could be proven using only some portions of the story and ignoring others, so also the nonexistence of the God of the Bible might be proven using only some portions of the Bible and ignoring others. I see nothing wrong with that. Thus, taking a middle position between theism (to the right) and noncognitivism (to the left), I shall proceed on the assumption that there is indeed some framework within which AE and ANB are both coherent and relevant.

Notes

1. Richard R. La Croix, *What Is God?*, essays edited by Kenneth G. Lucey (Amherst, N.Y.: Prometheus Books, 1993), p. 181.

2. Michael Martin, *Atheism: A Philosophical Justification* (Philadelphia: Temple University Press, 1990), pp. 77–78.

3. Ibid., p. 77.

4. See also Job 42:5; Isa. 6:1,5; Amos 9:1; John 12:45, 14:9.

5. Ps. 86:5, 100:5, 103:8, 106:1, 136:2, 145:8–9; Joel 2:13; Mic. 7:18; James 5:11.

6. Deut. 7:2,16, 20:16–17; Josh. 6:21, 10:11,19,40, 11:6–20; 1 Sam. 6:19, 15:3; Nah. 1:2; Jer. 13:14; Matt. 8:12, 13:42,50, 25:30,41,46; Mark 3:29; 2 Thess. 1:8–9; Rev. 14:9–11, 21:8.

7. Gen. 6:6; Ex. 32:14; 1 Sam. 2:30–31, 15:11,35; 2 Sam. 24:16; 2 Kings 20:1–6; Ps. 106:45; Jer. 42:10; Amos 7:3; Jon. 3:10.

8. Num. 23:19; 1 Sam. 15:29; Ezek. 24:14; Mal. 3:6; James 1:17.

9. Gen. 11:7; Judg. 9:23; 1 Sam. 16:14; Lam. 3:38; 1 Kings 22:22–23; Isa. 45:7; Amos 3:6; Jer. 18:11, 20:7; Ezek. 20:25; 2 Thess. 2:11.

10. Deut. 32:4; Ps. 25:8, 100:5, 145:9; 1 Cor. 14:33.

11. Gen. 9:22–25; Exod. 20:5, 34:7; Num. 14:18; Deut. 5:9; 2 Sam. 12:14; Isa. 14:21, 65:6–7.

12. Deut. 24:16; 2 Chron. 25:4; Ezek. 18:20.

13. John 1:1; Acts 20:28; Rom. 9:5; Col. 2:9; Titus 2:13; 2 Pet. 1:1.

14. John 1:3,10; Col. 1:16; Heb. 1:2,10.

15. John 10:30,38, 12:45, 14:9, 17:11,21–22.

16. God called "the first and the last": Isa. 41:4, 48:12; Rev. 1:8, 21:6–7. Jesus called "the first and the last": Rev. 1:17–18, 2:8, 22:12.

17. Only God can be mankind's savior: Isa. 43:3,11, 60:16; 1 Tim. 4:10. Jesus is mankind's savior: Matt. 1:21; Luke 2:11; John 4:42; Titus 2:13, 3:6; Heb. 5:9.

18. Matt. 19:17; Mark 10:18; Luke 18:19.

19. Matt. 27:46; Mark 15:34; John 20:17. In this connection, see also 1 Pet. 1:3.

20. Matt. 3:17, 17:5; Mark 1:11, 9:7; Luke 3:22, 9:35; Rom. 1:3–4; 2 Pet. 1: 17–18.

21. Acts 13:33; Col. 1:15; Heb. 1:5–6, 5:5; Rev. 3:14.

22. Matt. 26:39; Mark 10:40; John 5: 19,30, 7:16; 1 Cor. 11:3.

23. Acts 2:24,32, 3:15,26, 4:10, 5:30; Rom. 10:9; Eph. 1:20; 1 Thess. 1:10; 1 Pet. 1:21. Nowhere in Scripture does it say or imply that Jesus raised himself from the dead.

24. Rom. 8:34; Eph. 1:20; Col. 3:1; Heb. 1:3, 8:1, 10:12, 12:2; 1 Pet. 3:22.

25. For a treatment of what is sometimes called "sortal incorrectness" or "category mistakes," see Theodore M. Drange, *Type Crossings* (The Hague: Mouton & Co., 1966).

26. A. C. Ewing, "Meaninglessness," *Mind*, 46 (1937): 360.

27. A. N. Prior, "Entities," *The Australasian Journal of Philosophy* 32 (1954): 159. For additional arguments of the same sort, see Drange, *Type Crossings*, pp. 24–25.

28. Drange, *Type Crossings*, pp. 26–36.

29. Mackie, *The Miracle of Theism*, pp. 1–2.

30. Kai Nielsen, An *Introduction to the Philosophy of Religion* (New York: St. Martin's Press, 1982), p. 36.

31. 2 Chron. 16:9; Job 34:21; Ps. 139:7–10; Prov. 5:21, 15:3; Jer. 16:17, 23:24.

Part II

The God of Evangelical Christianity

4

The Free-Will Defense
Applied to AE (FDE)

In this and chapters 5–11, we will consider "objections from the right," which in the present context refer to attempts by evangelical Christians to defend their God's existence against AE and ANB. One of the oldest such attempts, as applied to AE, is known as "the Free-will Defense" (abbreviated "FDE"). The basic idea behind FDE is that God permits people to endure suffering (taken here to include premature death) in order either to make free will possible or else somehow to optimize the amount of it in the world, particularly free will as exercised in a choice between doing good and doing evil, that being regarded as something of great value.

The Free-will Defense can also be applied to ANB and I shall label that argument "FDN." Its basic idea is that God permits many people to go through life without awareness of the gospel message, again, in order to make free will possible or somehow to optimize the amount of it in the world. According to the Free-will Defense, if God were to prevent or reduce human suffering or people's nonbelief in the gospel message, then that would in some way interfere with (the optimization of) their free will, which would be an even greater evil than the suffering or nonbelief that is eliminated. In the present chapter, we will consider FDE as applied to the specific version of AE given above in section 2.1. In the next chapter we will consider FDN.

4.1. Free Will and Moral Freedom

The issue of what free will is and whether or not it is compatible with determinism is complex and highly polemical. Let us, first of all, equate free will

97

with the ability to make real choices. The compatibilist-incompatibilist issue can then be formulated in terms of the definition of "real choices." Compatibilists maintain that the expression should be defined in a way which allows people to make real choices even if determinism were true (i.e., even if all choices were totally determined by past events and conditions), whereas incompatibilists maintain that the expression should be defined in such a way that if determinism were true then it would be impossible for people to make real choices. In the present chapter, I shall assume that incompatibilism is right and that free will is contracausal free will, that is, the ability to make choices among options all of which are avoidable, given the agent's (or chooser's) complete background. That is supposed to rule out choices that are totally determined by past events and conditions, such as the agent's past experiences and heredity. Such totally determined choices would not be avoidable, because, given the agent's complete background together with relevant laws of nature, it would always be theoretically possible to deduce (or infallibly predict) that the agent would make the choice that s/he actually made. A choice that can be infallibly predicted would be unavoidable. According to incompatibilism, such choices, if they could be called that at all, would not be "real choices." We will consider the adequacy of this definition and the truth of incompatibilism in appendix A, below. For the purposes of the present chapter, I shall simply assume that the incompatibilist conception of free will and real choices, which seems invariably presupposed by advocates of all versions of the Free-will Defense, is correct. Thus, the expressions "free will" and "real choices" will be used in that sense.

By "moral freedom" is meant the ability to make real choices between doing good and doing evil. My preferred understanding of the expression "doing evil," as indicated in section 1.3, is "unjustifiably causing others to suffer." This is not, of course, intended to be an exact translation. I shall assume, for the sake of discussion, that philosophers who advocate the Free-will Defense as applied to AE, whom I shall refer to as "FDEers," would be willing to go along with my (inexact) translation. It does not seem that anything of significance turns on this concession. Moral freedom, then, can be defined as a certain type of (contracausal) free will: the ability to make real choices between causing others to suffer unjustifiably and not doing so.

The question arises whether people can have free will without having moral freedom. The answer seems to be clearly yes. People could live in a world in which their only choices are between such options as eating vanilla ice cream and eating chocolate ice cream or between going on a picnic and going to a ballgame. There need not be the option of causing others to suffer. It might be a world in which people are all impervious to harm, as the fictional Superman would be if he were not susceptible to kryptonite. If someone were caught in an avalanche or earthquake, he would simply dig his way out. If a big flood were to threaten his house, he would simply divert it. Or, alternatively, such Superman-like people would be powerful enough to initially construct their environments (or remodel the planet itself) so that they could not be threatened by any physical harm.

Let us imagine such beings as having a far better defense than offense. That is, person A would be unable to harm person B even if A were disposed to do so. And, further, the superhumans would be rather "cold-hearted," not needing affection from one another, so they could not even be harmed psychologically. Thus, if A were to ignore or withhold affection from B, then that would never cause B any distress. To be like that may not be particularly appealing, but I see no reason why such people could not have free will. They would still need to make daily decisions about how to spend their time, and there is no reason to deny either that such decisions would be real choices or that the people making them would have free will.

The world described would need to be devoid of any lower animals that the people might unjustifiably harm (thereby "doing evil"). Or, alternatively, we could imagine lower animals to exist but to be also impervious to harm. In addition, something should be said about plants, since chopping trees down for sport might be regarded as a form of "doing evil." Let us simply assume for the sake of argument that the world is so set up that all such ways of causing suffering or harm are unavailable to the agents within it. That could be a world with free will but no moral freedom.

It might be suggested that people who are unable to harm one another, even psychologically, would lack certain moral qualities such as kindness and compassion. By the principle of predicative contrast, you can't treat someone kindly if it is impossible for you to treat the person unkindly. There is some truth to this, but it is a digression. The issue is free will, not moral virtues. One can have the former without the latter. We will take up the Moral-virtues Defense in chapter 6. So far as free will and FDE are concerned, it seems quite clear that one can have free will without having moral freedom. This will affect the way FDE is formulated, for it requires that the argument be posed in terms of moral freedom rather than in terms of free will.

4.2. FDE Formulated

Here is a formulation of FDE, with premises labeled as "P" and conclusions labeled as "C":

(P1): For God to have made people altruistic would necessarily prevent them from having moral freedom.

(P2): The only possible way for God to bring about situation L (as mentioned in AE) would be to have made people altruistic.

(C1): So, the only possible way for God to bring about situation L would necessarily prevent people from having moral freedom.

[from (P1) & (P2)]

(C2): Therefore, for people to have moral freedom necessarily conflicts with God bringing about situation L.   [from (C1)]

(P3): Although God wants to bring about situation L, he wants even more strongly that people have moral freedom.

(C3): Thus, there is something (namely, people having moral freedom) which necessarily conflicts with God bringing about situation L and which God wants even more strongly than it.   [from (C2) & (P3)]

(C4): Hence, AE's premise (A3) is false and AE is thereby unsound.

[from (C3)]

To assess FDE's final conclusion, (C4), it is necessary to consider AE's premise (A3), which was formulated in section 2.1, above, and which reads as follows:

> If God were to exist, then he would possess the property of not wanting anything that necessarily conflicts with his desire to bring about situation L as strongly as he wants to bring about situation L.

(C4) might be challenged on the grounds that the given premise is actually a conditional proposition with "God exists" as its antecedent, so to prove it false requires proving that its antecedent is true, which FDE has not done. But that is too strong a requirement. We can understand AE's premise (A3) as claiming that, necessarily, if God were to exist, then he would have a certain property (the one specified). So to refute (A3) it would suffice merely to show the possibility that God exists without possessing the given property. And that is something that FDE can be taken to do, provided all its premises are true. In the following three sections, each of those premises will be critically examined.

The proposition that people actually have moral freedom is not explicitly stated in FDE and indeed the conclusion could be obtained without it. Even if people do not have moral freedom, it could be something that both conflicts with situation L and which God wants for them even more than he wants to bring about situation L. That would be enough to refute AE's premise (A3) and thereby AE itself. God could theoretically have still higher priorities that prevent him from actually granting moral freedom to people, at least at the present time, priorities which are not relevant to AE or its refutation by FDE. However, that would be a very peculiar situation, and it is not one that FDEers ever envision. The way FDE is always presented and understood, either it explicitly states that people have moral freedom or it at least contains that as a background assumption. Certainly its premise (P3) would be hard to support or defend if that assumption were false. The assumption provides a framework within which God's motives are more understandable than they would otherwise be. So there is a point to considering whether or not it is true, that is, whether anyone really does possess moral freedom (or contracausal free will). The issue has been postponed to appendix B. Although it is important to the question of the overall force of FDE, it is not directly relevant to the battle between FDE and AE's premise (A3), to which I now turn.

4.3. Premise (P1): The Altruism Objection

If we were not assuming incompatibilism to be true and defining "moral freedom" as a kind of contracausal free will, then one way to attack FDE's premise (P1) would be to reject its background assumption of incompatibilism. But aside from that issue, another way to attack the given premise is through a consideration of altruism, to which it refers. Let us first consider the rationale behind (P1). It seems to be the idea that people can't have a real choice between doing good and doing evil if they have somehow been forced to be altruists (people who try to do good all the time). God could have made altruists of people in either of two ways, by genetic engineering or by operant conditioning. He could have created an "altruism gene" which inclines people toward cooperative and unselfish behavior. (Maybe some people actually have such a gene.) And then he could have seen to it that *all* people have that gene in them from the moment of conception. The other way would have been for God to have instituted a system of swift and sure punishment for doing evil. Every (or nearly every) time someone commits a deliberate misdeed, God could administer to the culprit an electric shock. Given human nature and especially mankind's ability to learn, that would be quite effective. People would come to see that they cannot get away with immoral conduct and so they would eventually give it up. They would come at least to *behave* altruistically even if they did not simultaneously become "motivational altruists." Perhaps the altruistic behavior would eventually lead to altruistic motivations down the road, though even if it didn't, people could still be regarded as "altruists." The idea behind FDE's premise (P1) is that if God were to make altruists of people in either of these ways (genetic engineering or operant conditioning), then that would necessarily infringe upon their free will and thereby their moral freedom. Instead of people having a real choice between doing good and doing evil, the genes or the conditioning would force them to always try to do good. So there would not be any real choice in that case.

But on the contrary, I shall argue that for God to make altruists of people need not interfere with their free will. Consider the analogy of an aversion. Just about everyone has an aversion toward, say, drinking (tincture of) iodine, and yet, despite that, it is possible for people to do it. Their option not to drink iodine is an avoidable one (i.e., they are able to drink it) even though they have within their natures a strong aversion toward drinking it. People's choice not to drink iodine, then, is still a "real choice," despite the aversion. By analogy, it might be said that altruism is an aversion toward unjustifiably harming others. Someone could have such an aversion and still (unjustifiably) harm others in spite of it, whether the aversion were produced by genetic engineering or by operant conditioning. Since the aversion only influences and does not totally determine behavior, it only decreases the probability that a person will do something. It does not make the probability zero. It follows that FDE's premise (P1) is false: God could have made people altruistic without interfering with their free will. They could still make real choices between causing others happiness and causing others unjustifiable suffering, for the simple reason that their altruistic natures would not have completely determined their choices, but would only have influenced them. Since it is possible for one to have an aversion toward causing others to suffer and still choose in a way contrary to the aversion, trying to do good would be avoidable, even for altruists. Hence, even those made altruists by God could have a real choice between doing good and doing evil. Let us call this the "Altruism Objection" to FDE's premise (P1).

The objection is well formulated and defended by Evan Fales.[1] He goes on to argue that God could also have made people a lot smarter, and that, too, would have improved the world without interfering with human free will. In fact, as Fales points out, making people smarter would actually enhance their free will. I shall not here pursue the point about increasing people's intelligence, but I do want to press the Altruism Objection. It is also expressed by William Alston, who says the following:

> If we allow that my altered desires, tendencies, and attitudes influence my volitions without strictly determining them, just as with my previous tendencies, then no negative consequences with respect to human free will ensue. After all, even the most convinced libertarian recognizes that human motivational structure results, for the most part, from factors other than the individual's own free voluntary acts and, indeed, from factors that were, to a large extent, not under any sort of voluntary control.[2]

All people have motivations which were at least partially determined by things which happened to them in the past. So if people can have free will (in the incompatibilists' sense) despite that, then there seems to be no reason why they could not be made into altruists by God (thereby having altruistic motivations) and still retain their free will.

Another way to pose the objection is in terms of an actual person. An example often cited is Mother Teresa, the altruistic nun who helped poor people in India. (Let us assume that she did as much good as has been claimed.) Her altruism did not at all interfere with her free will. God could have made many other people, perhaps even everyone, to be like her with regard to altruism, that is, to have a character and an inclination to follow a set of moral rules or principles similar to hers. Then people would be much more inclined toward helping rather than harming one another. Since such altruism did not interfere with free will in Mother Teresa's case, it need not interfere with free will in the case of anyone else, which makes (P1) a false premise.

It might even be argued that, instead of reducing the amount of free will in the world, for God to make altruists of people would actually increase it. People would have less fear of crime and their behavior would accordingly be less restricted. Our own criminal justice system is intended to make criminals "go straight," which is a way of making altruists (or quasi-altruists) out of them. It is generally acknowledged that if the system were to work perfectly, then crime would be eliminated. Citizens would be more free to do what they want without having to take precautions, and that would increase their options and thereby their free will. It seems ridiculous to charge our criminal justice system with having the effect of eliminating or reducing criminals' free will by making altruists out of them. On the contrary, the system, if made ideal, would generally increase the amount of free will in the world, and in a similar way God would generally increase the amount of free will by making altruists of people.

One type of response to what I call the Altruism Objection is associated with the work of Alvin Plantinga.[3] Let us call it the "Bad-luck Response." It goes as follows. For each of the possible worlds containing situation L, there may be some person X who "goes wrong" in it. What "going wrong" means in this context is that there is some action that X is somehow supposed to do in the given world, but X instead freely chooses not to do it. So, if God were to try to actualize the given world, he would fail through bad luck, because it was supposed to be a world in which X does a certain act, but X instead chooses not to do that act. Hence, it is possible that, so long as God respects his creatures' free will, he would be unable to bring about situation L.

A natural objection to this response is that if God merely wished to produce situation L, then he would not first select an exact world that contains L and then set out to actualize that particular world. Instead, he could aim at a huge set of possible worlds almost all of which contain situation L in virtue of the altruistic behavior that occurs in them, and then do something, such as make altruists of everyone, that would actualize a member, any member, of that set. It would then be highly likely that situation L would come to obtain. An analogy might be warding off mosquitoes with insect repellent. Having been bitten twenty times on a given occasion, I could say in retrospect that if I had spread the repellent on myself, I would have been bitten many fewer times. I could have spread it on myself with the aim of producing any member whatever of a set of worlds in each of which I am bitten by mosquitoes significantly fewer times than I actually was (without the repellent), namely, twenty. It would be bizarre to argue that, assuming the mosquitoes had free will, such use of the insect repellent might have been ineffective since, for whichever one of those worlds I am aiming at, there may be a group of mosquitoes that "go wrong" and bite me twenty times anyway, despite the repellent. The reply could be that, had I used the repellent, I would not have been aiming at one specific world but at any of a large number of possible worlds. And even if there were possible worlds in which I am bitten twenty times despite the repellent, nevertheless it is highly unlikely, given the normal efficacy of the repellent, that such a world would have been actualized by my action.

An advocate of the Bad-luck Response could reply that it is at least *logically* possible that God could not bring about situation L because, through bad luck, *every* member of the set of worlds that he aimed for happened to contain people who, despite having been made altruists, nevertheless "go wrong" to such an extent that there is at least as much suffering in the given world as there is in our actual world. Situation L, then, would not obtain, no matter which member of the set of possible worlds God were to actualize. The idea is that, when free will is involved, God could be exceedingly unlucky in his creative endeavors. In the insect example, it is logically possible that, even if I had used the repellent, through bad luck I may still have been bitten by mosquitoes twenty times (assuming that they had free will). In a similar way, it could be that our actual world is one in which God tried to bring about situation L by making everyone altruistic, but by sheer bad luck on his part, just about everyone has "gone wrong," and so situation L did not come to obtain after all.

Since I am here assuming the incompatibilist conception of free will, I must admit the *logical* possibility of such bad luck on God's part. He might have made everyone altruists and yet they have all "gone wrong," for being an altruist only inclines one toward doing good; it does not totally determine such behavior. I believe that Plantinga himself only aimed at the conclusion that it is logically possible that God could not produce situation L because of the bad free choices of his creatures. That is a conclusion with which I agree. However, it is not directed at my version of AE or any evidential version of the problem of evil, but a different atheological argument entirely (one which purports to be conclusive). Although it is *logically* possible that all the billions of altruists should happen to "go wrong," the probability of that actually happening is so slight that it is negligible. Thus, the suggestion that our actual world is one that came about through God's bad luck, despite his having made altruists of everyone, is too far-fetched. Logically possible, yes, but a reasonable reply to the Altruism Objection, no. AE only tries to establish God's nonexistence beyond a reasonable doubt, and the Bad-luck Response has failed to introduce such a doubt.

The Altruism Objection appeals to the idea of a world that is supposed to be better than ours (with regard to the amount of suffering, etc.), yet not perfect. In other words, a world full of altruists would presumably be one with a lot less crime in it than ours, and thereby a lot less suffering, but it need not be a world with no crime at all. Altruists only have an aversion toward harming others, and are not absolutely prevented from doing it. One problem that might be raised with this conception is that it is open to something like the Regress Objection considered in section 1.4, above. Suppose the described world containing situation L were to be actualized. It would still not be a perfect world. The people in it could imagine another world with still less crime and that would be another "situation L" in relation to their world. How, then, could AE prove God's nonexistence by appeal to an alternate world under those conditions? The people in the imagined world could still appeal to AE and a different "situation L," and so could mount the very same argument against God's existence. For every "situation L" that is achieved, there would be another one that could be appealed to. In other words, you can't legitimately say "if God were to exist then this is how it would be" if the people in the imagined world could still appeal to AE (and some other "situation L") to prove God's nonexistence.

The same sort of reply could be made to this objection as before. AE does not attempt to describe some definite world or situation that would obtain if God were to exist. It only says that there is some definite situation (namely, our actual world) that would probably *not* obtain if God were to exist. That is, he would have instead actualized any one of a great number of possible worlds, each of them a great improvement over our own. One of them would have been a world in which everyone has been made into an altruist, which need not have interfered with anyone's free will. The "regress" problem is a general one, and we will have occasion to comment on it again in this book. It does not save FDE's premise (P1) from refutation by the Altruism Objection.

In order for FDEers to deal with the Altruism Objection, they would need to revise FDE slightly. A new expression could be introduced: "being staunchly altruistic." People are staunchly altruistic if and only if their altruistic nature completely determines their choices. Such altruism would be more than a mere aversion toward harming others, it would be an absolute block toward it. It would make the probability that a staunch altruist deliberately harm someone else (without justification) equal to zero. For staunch altruists to aim at doing good would be unavoidable, so their choice to do good would not be a real choice, and thus they could not have free will. Using this new concept, FDE's premise (P1) could be revised as follows:

(P1): For God to have made people staunchly altruistic would necessarily prevent them from having moral freedom.

That would make the premise true by definition. Although there might still be the incompatibilism issue to deal with, at least the Altruism Objection would have been disposed of.

The trouble with this appeal to "staunch altruism" is that, once the change in (P1) is made, a further change in FDE would be needed in order for it to retain its deductive validity. In particular, its premise (P2) would need to be changed to the following:

(P2): The only possible way for God to bring about situation L (as mentioned in AE) would be to have made people staunchly altruistic.

This would be an atrocious result. The original premise (P2) is bad enough, as we will see in section 4.4, below, but this change in it would make it even worse. Obviously God does not need to create people to be staunchly altruistic in order to reduce the suffering in the world. For one thing, all he need do is to make people altruistic in the ordinary sense, that is, as having a strong aversion toward harming others unjustifiably. That would suffice, because it would eliminate most crime, which would greatly reduce the suffering in the world, thereby producing situation L. When premise (P2) is changed in the required way, it becomes obviously false. So this move on the part of FDEers would be of no use in defending their argument. My conclusion, then, is that FDE is hopeless: the Altruism Objection refutes its premise (P1) as it is presently worded, and if the wording were changed as suggested to get around that objection, then that would only give rise to still another refuting objection.

4.4. Premise (P2): The Natural-evils Objection

Situation L is that of there being significantly less suffering in the world than there actually happens to be. FDE's premise (P2) is the claim that the only possible way for God to bring about situation L would be to have made people altruistic. It seems that would be true only if all, or almost all, the suffering that actually occurs in our world were the result of what people do. It is only then that making people altruistic (i.e., inclined to avoid causing unjustifiable suffering) would significantly reduce the amount of suffering that occurs.

One objection to the given claim is obvious. A vast amount of suffering that occurs in our world is not at all the result of what people do. It is, rather, the outcome of so-called "natural evils," which include such events as earthquakes, volcanic eruptions, storms, floods, droughts, and a huge variety of diseases, genetic disorders, and impairments, at least those that are not at all the result of human agency. Premise (P2) is simply false because God could bring about situation L without doing anything with human nature. All he need do is to eliminate or greatly reduce natural evils. Let us call this the Natural-evils Objection.

One attack sometimes raised against the Natural-evils Objection is that it seems to require that the world be a "hedonic utopia" and such a world would need to be "massively irregular." This terminology is used by Peter van Inwagen.[4] The criticism here is that "massively irregular" worlds are inferior. However, this attack is not relevant to my version of AE, which calls only for God to bring about situation L, not to create a "hedonic utopia." It seems obvious that in order for God merely to reduce natural evils in our world it is *not* necessary that he make the world "massively irregular." The question here is whether for God to bring about such a reduction would require much ongoing tampering with the laws of nature. According to Bruce Reichenbach: "[I]nsofar as humans (or any personal agents) are natural beings it seems contingently true that any set of natural laws and conditions will be such as to affect them at times adversely."[5] If Reichenbach means that there has to be so much suffering simply to have natural laws at all, then that is simply not so. For one thing, God could have kept the laws the same but merely have altered the initial conditions on our planet, for example, make it calmer and more stable and less subject to catastrophes. After all, he is supposed to be an omnipotent being. Alternatively, starting out with slightly different natural laws, God could have made humans hardier, with better immune systems, and so on. That too would have produced a much better environment for his creatures. He could then have kept those laws; there would have been no need whatever for him to continually meddle with them. (As a separate point, even for God to occasionally meddle with the laws is not so bad if the overall result is highly beneficial.) Reichenbach's attempt to defend against the Natural-evils Objection by appeal to laws of nature is decisively refuted by Michael Martin,[6] so we need not say more about it here. In order for FDE's premise (P2) to be true, there can't be many natural evils, so it is argued. But it is obvious that there *are* many natural evils. Hence, (P2) must be false.

The Natural-evils Objection is even more devastating than may at first seem. It contains a secondary objection to FDE that has not been duly noted in the literature. It could be called "the Impediment Objection." Many of the natural evils in our world not only cause enormous suffering but are also an impediment to free will. This is especially obvious in the case of premature death. When children die, they lose all opportunity to exercise free will. It also applies to other forms of suffering, especially injuries and diseases that are greatly incapacitating. People who are so incapacitated have less opportunity to exercise free will than those who lead relatively normal lives. Thus, if God really has human free will as a higher priority than the prevention of suffering, as claimed in FDE's premise (P3), then it would have behooved him to create a world in which considerably more people come to exercise it in their lives. The fact that God (if he exists) permits so much premature death and greatly incapacitating afflictions to occur to people (especially children), thereby depriving them of the future exercise of their free will, counts against the claim that God gives human free will such a high priority. Thus, the Natural-evils Objection can be used to attack FDE's premise (P3) as well as its premise (P2).

Aside from the appeal to natural laws, there are three main defenses against the Natural-evils Objection, which may be called the "Education Defense," the "Devil Defense," and the "Moral-evils Defense." They will be discussed below.

4.41. The Education Defense

The argument is that the natural evils of our world are needed for the purpose of education. Richard Swinburne puts the matter as follows:

> [A]gents [need] to have the *knowledge* of how to bring about evil or prevent its occurrence, knowledge which they must have if they are to have a genuine choice between bringing about evil and bringing about good.[7]

It is possession of that "genuine choice" that ultimately justifies all the natural evil in the world, for, through a process of education, the evil is needed as a means to the choice.

There are of course other ways for agents to acquire knowledge of the good and bad consequences of actions than through the suffering that people presently endure. For example, they could read about those consequences in books. But Swinburne argues, in effect, that "experience is the best teacher" and that the other ways of acquiring the knowledge in question are less effective or have some other drawbacks. I think that his point about the inferiority of the other modes of knowledge acquisition can be attacked, but in the present work I shall simply accept his point and raise objections of a different sort. There is some overlap between my treatment of the Education Defense and that of Michael Martin, who also attacks Swinburne's argument.[8]

The Education Defense could be appealed to as a theodicy-related defense in its own right. That is, one might claim that God lets us suffer simply in order to educate us. However, I shall regard it only as a defense of FDE. The main thrust of it seems to relate to the origin and preservation of moral freedom. Knowledge of consequences may have some intrinsic value, but clearly not enough to justify the great amount of suffering that occurs. It is the instrumental value of such knowledge, in particular in making possible the effective use of free will and the preservation of that use, according to Swinburne, that justifies God's permitting the suffering that it requires.

Many objections could be raised against the Education Defense. One is that there occur natural evils in our world that fail to be justified by it. Consider cancer, for example. Swinburne might say that by learning about cancer, people become able to exercise free will in the search for a cure or for ways to prevent the disease. And the disease needs to have terrible consequences in order for the researchers to be highly motivated. But this approach runs afoul of relative value considerations. How valuable is it, in the long run, that medical researchers exercise their free will in relation to cancer? How could that value outweigh (or justify permitting) the great suffering that is caused by the disease? Wouldn't it be a far better world if humans and other animals were immune to cancer, all else being the same, even if medical researchers would then need to exercise their free will in other ways (e.g., seeking a cure for the common cold)?

This point is brought out very neatly by Eleonore Stump through the use of an analogy:

> If God had not allowed rabies in the world—or earthquakes or hurricanes or congenital malformations of infants, and so on—there would be no point in having knowledge of such things. If you conceal traps in my front yard, then my repeated attempts to get from my front door to my car parked at the curb will produce in me knowledge about the consequences of my movements. And this knowledge will be useful to me, if I live long enough to acquire it, because it will enable me to avoid traps in the future. So this knowledge is good, it is gained from experience of the evil which you have introduced into my yard, and without this knowledge I could not avoid the evils of the traps. But *you* are not morally justified in setting traps in my front yard—no matter how good or useful the knowledge about the consequences of my actions may be and no matter how dependent that knowledge is on my experiencing the jaws of the trap.[9]

This shows that even if all that Swinburne says about the need for natural evils were true, that still would not morally justify God in creating and permitting those evils.

The objection pertaining to cancer is particularly severe because cancer (e.g., leukemia) afflicts children in great numbers. (Other childhood diseases could also be used as an example here.) For each researcher exercising free will in seeking a cure for cancer, there are thousands of children who die from the disease and thereby lose out completely in their future exercise of free will. It seems that if God had wanted to increase the amount of free will that gets exercised by people, then he would have long ago eliminated cancer (and every other fatal childhood disease) from the earth. Or alternatively, he could have made people totally immune to it in their youth, with the immunity gradually lost as they reach advanced age. Either scenario would produce a far better world than ours, even emphasizing the high value that is to be assigned to free will. What this shows is that the Education Defense of FDE is a failure as a response to the Natural-evils Objection.

Stump argues further, against the Education Defense, that *all* natural evils could be eliminated without interfering with human free will:

> Belsen was entirely the work of man's hand, and evils of that magnitude with the serious choices they entail are still possible even if God were to prevent all hurricanes, earthquakes, mental retardation, birth defects, and so on. As an argument defending God's failure to prevent all major evils, it seems to me to have some force. But God could fail to prevent all major evils, thus leaving man serious choices and a serious choice of destiny, simply by failing to prevent all major man-made evils, those for which man rather than God is responsible. And so it is not necessary for God to allow natural evils to occur in order to give man serious choices.[10]

The idea here, I gather, is that God could have created a world such that if any natural evils at all occur in it, they would be only minor ones, whereas moral evils could still be major ones, as in our present world. The beings would not have the great Superman-like defenses against one another described in section 4.1, but would be able to harm one another. Yet they would have such defenses against nature. (Maybe they could only harm one another using kryptonite, which is an artificial substance, not found in nature.) As Stump shows, such a world need not contain less opportunity for the exercise of moral freedom than ours does. I would argue, further, that, with many more children surviving to adulthood, it would contain significantly *more*. It would also clearly be a better world than ours with regard to the amount of suffering that occurs in it, and would thus actualize situation L. This seems to refute FDE's premise (P2), and the Education Defense fails to prevent that refutation.

Swinburne might reply that in the great-defenses world, there would indeed be less opportunity for the exercise of moral freedom, for the number of ways that its inhabitants could harm one another would be limited. Only artificial means could be used, for the beings would be immune to natural evils. He could maintain that our actual world, with its mix of possible means, both natural and artificial, by which people might harm one another contains the *optimal* opportunity for moral freedom and so is the best of all possible worlds. In other worlds, if any natural evils at all were to be removed from it, that would correspondingly reduce the opportunity for moral freedom, and thereby make it an inferior world.

Several objections could be raised against this suggestion. First of all, there could be many artificial ways of harming others (not just kryptonite), so many in fact that there would be no benefit whatever in also having the use of additional natural evils. Secondly, our actual world could still not contain the optimal opportunity for moral freedom, since a world in which all, or almost all, children survived to adulthood would contain a still better opportunity. Third, it seems perverse to suggest that the removal of natural evils makes our world worse (by reducing the opportunity for moral freedom). That would imply that modern medicine, which tries to reduce the natural evils of disease, and modern agriculture, which tries to reduce the natural evils of plant pestilence, are (unknowingly) making the world worse, especially for future generations. Such a suggestion is counterintuitive. Swinburne might say that medicine and agriculture benefit the world by providing avenues of opportunity for the exercise of free will and that cancels out the negative impact they have by eliminating natural evils. But it is still counterintuitive to view their elimination of natural evils as a negative impact.

Still another objection is one based on Scripture. The suggestion implies that the removal of any natural evils would make the world worse. But what about all the cures and resurrections performed in the Bible? Jesus cured blindness, deafness, palsy, dropsy, leprosy, a withered hand, bleeding, fever, paralysis, inability to walk, and various unnamed ailments and infirmities.[11] He also resurrected people from the dead, an event-type that is described in the Old Testament and in the Book of Acts as well.[12] If God would thus miraculously intervene in the workings of nature, then it could not be true that the removal of any natural evil whatever would make the world worse for mankind, since a deity that is omnibenevolent toward mankind would not make the world worse for the object of his love. We applaud God for his miraculous healings, but AE throws in a twist: if such a being really did exist, then he would have done still more for humanity (the object of his love), and in particular, situation L would have been produced. The very fact that situation L does not obtain counts against the existence of such a deity. The Education Defense is clearly a failure in its attempt to protect FDE's premise (P2) against the Natural-evils Objection.

4.42. The Devil Defense

Another way to try to defend premise (P2) against the Natural-evils Objection is to declare that the alleged evils cited are not natural after all. They are, instead, moral evils which are perpetrated upon the world by Satan (or

Satan together with his cohorts, hereafter understood). For example, if an earthquake occurs, killing and injuring many people, then that was the work of the devil. Or if a child succumbs to leukemia, that, too, was Satan's doing. There is some slight biblical support for this outlook, for, as noted in section 1.7, St. Paul views Satan as having blinded the minds of nonbelievers (2 Cor. 4:4), which is presumably evil, and, according to John, the whole world is under Satan's power (1 John 5:19). So for God to have prevented such evils, he would have needed either to get rid of Satan or preferably to make him into a nice guy, that is, to have created (or caused) the devil to be altruistic. But that would have been intolerable since it would have interfered with Satan's free will and prevented him from making real choices. Let us refer to this as the "Devil Defense."

The possibility of the Devil Defense, used in support of the Free-will Defense against the Natural-evils Objection, is suggested by Alvin Plantinga, who says, "The Free Will Defender . . . points to the possibility that natural evil is due to the actions of significantly free but nonhuman persons."[13] He goes on to include such evil in the category of "broadly moral evil," the idea being that no evil is purely natural: all of it is the outcome of deliberate free actions, whether by humans or by nonhuman persons, though our world still contains more good in it than evil. Plantinga maintains that there is no evidence whatever *against* the claim that all the evil in our world is broadly moral evil and that God, while retaining all of the moral freedom there is, could not have created a better world than ours with respect to the balance of broadly moral good over broadly moral evil.[14] I am willing to grant the *logical* possibility that the given claim is true, and I think that is all that Plantinga intended with regard to it. However, the move in question has no relevance to the version of AE put forward in this book. The issue before us is not whether the Devil Defense expresses a logical possibility but whether it is *reasonable*, and it seems quite clear that it is not.

There are many objections to the Devil Defense and we need not pursue all of them. Michael Martin does a good job attacking it.[15] Probably the main objection is that it leaves far too many things unexplained, and perhaps unexplainable. For example, if Satan is behind all the apparent natural evil in the world, then why didn't he make the world still worse? Why did he leave in all the beauty and harmony that exists in nature, the delightful sights, sounds, textures, tastes, and fragrances? Why did he permit us to have as good an immune system as we have? Why doesn't he cause still more storms, earthquakes, volcanic eruptions, etc.? It is clearly not the best of all possible worlds, but also it is far from being the worst. Why didn't Satan do still more to make it closer to the worst? One might reply that God restricts Satan (just as he restricted him with regard to how much suffering Satan could impose on poor Job). But then the question simply becomes that of why God doesn't restrict Satan more than he does.

Another problem concerns the origin of evil. If Satan is the source of all apparently natural evil, how could that happen? God was supposed to have created a perfect world. Within the six days, he created everything that exists (Exod. 20:11) and the creation was finished (Gen. 2:1), and "God saw everything that he had created and declared that it was good" (Gen. 1:31). What, then, is the source of evil? How could it have come about by itself within a perfect world? Furthermore, God is supposed to be omniscient and have foreknowledge. When he first created the world, he could have seen that Satan would cause much suffering on earth and so all that God needed to do to prevent such occurrences would have been to refrain from creating Satan (or Lucifer). Obviously it would not have interfered with Satan's free will for God to refrain from creating him, since there would have been no Satan to have any free will in the first place. The only way to get around this point, it appears, is to deny God's foreknowledge, but that is highly objectionable, as will be shown later (in section B.2).

Another objection to the Devil Defense is that it creates an enormous conflict between the interests of humanity and Satan's interests, for if Satan is taken to be the cause of all apparently natural evil, then he seems bent on greatly harming humanity and to have been successful in inflicting tremendous damage. The question naturally arises why God should set up the world in such a way. Since Satan is such a powerful adversary to humanity, why have him around at all? And why should God favor Satan's side of the conflict? If the enormous suffering of billions of people could be prevented by eliminating or restricting Satan, then why not do it? What is so important about letting Satan exercise his free will? Unless these questions are answered, the Devil Defense would be not merely incomplete but actually incoherent. An all-loving deity could not sic the devil on us or allow him free reign to perform evil, for that would be incompatible with his being maximally loving toward humanity, which is supposed to be one of his essential properties, especially within the context of evangelical Christianity.

It might be said that the Devil Defense merely shifts the problem of evil over to the problem of why God created the devil. Eleonore Stump says the following:

> If earthquakes in densely populated areas, for example, are the result of free choices by fallen angels, the problem of why God allows such earthquakes is not solved. It is simply shifted to the problem of why God allows fallen angels to be successful in bringing about the evil they have willed.[16]

Plantinga could reply that he was not working on the problem of why God allows earthquakes in the first place, only on how to defend FDE against the Natural-evils Objection. But it seems that his defense is a failure within the context of Christianity unless he can somehow reconcile it with the

Christian emphasis on God's love for humanity. And that is something that he has not done.

FDEers could plead ignorance regarding God's relation to Satan. They could say that God's ways are mysterious, for example. But that is no longer a defense of FDE but a shift to a different defense. There would be no reason to retain any reference to Satan. There is practically no scriptural support for the idea that Satan is the cause of apparent natural evil. Apart from the special case of Job, the devil is depicted as a *deceiver*, not a harmer (2 Tim. 2:25–26, 1 John 5:19, Rev. 12:9). There is certainly no support whatever for the idea that God permits Satan to harm humanity out of respect for Satan's free will. Instead of the Devil Defense, one could as well say: "We do not know why God permits natural evil." That is close to what I call the "Unknown Purpose Defense," which is to be dealt with in chapter 10. So far as FDE is concerned, the failure of the Devil Defense to adequately explain the introduction of Satan into the system of things, and to show how it might be compatible with an all-loving deity, renders it counterintuitive. Therefore, the Devil Defense is a failure in dealing with the Natural-evils Objection, which is thereby shown to be a most formidable attack on FDE as it is presently formulated.

4.43. The Moral-evils Defense

One might try to deal with the Natural-evils Objection by altering FDE in such a way that it applies only to moral evils. Perhaps AE could be dealt with piecemeal, with FDE applying to moral evils and some other defense or theodicy applying to natural evils. Let situation L* be the situation of there being significantly less *moral* evil in the world than there actually happens to be at present. Then perhaps FDEers could try to make a case for their premise (P2) as applied to situation L* (instead of to situation L). The revised premise would read as follows:

(P2): The only possible way for God to bring about situation L* (a reduction in moral evil) would be to have made people altruistic.

We are assuming here that corresponding adjustments (changing L to L*) would also be made to the other steps of FDE.

That still won't save FDE, for at least four reasons. First, FDE's background assumptions (that contracausal free will is what free will is, and that it is indeed possessed by people) might be attacked, as in appendices A and B, below. Second, FDE's premise (P1) could still be strongly attacked by the Altruism Objection, as shown above in section 4.3. Third, its premise (P3) could also still be attacked, as will be shown in section 4.5, below.

And finally, even FDE's premise (P2) could be attacked, despite the change. God need not make people altruistic in order to reduce moral evil; there are other ways he could do it. One way would be for him to improve the defenses (but not the offenses) of all potential victims. For example, the world could be like the "Superman" world described in section 4.1. Such a world contains free will but not moral freedom. There would be no moral freedom because it would be impossible to harm anyone (or anything). And the reason for that would not be people's altruism but rather the great defenses mounted by all potential victims of harm. They would have those great defenses not only against natural evils but also against moral evils. This could be called the "Superman Objection," for it appeals to a world the inhabitants of which would have Superman-like defenses against any sort of harm whatever.

It should be noted that the Superman Objection could be used as a counterexample in its own right to FDE's premise (P2). God could have brought about situation L not only by eliminating or reducing natural evils or by making people altruistic but also by maximizing the defenses of potential victims against both natural and moral evil. That would be another way to refute FDE's premise (P2). Although the Superman Objection has close affinities with the Natural-evils Objection, it is distinct from it. It functions as an alternate attack on (P2) and also as an attack on the Moral-evils Defense. It is double-barreled in that it not only refutes FDE's premise (P2) as presently worded, but would also refute it when the premise is applied, as above, to situation L* instead of situation L.

We have seen three different ways of blocking the inference to FDE's step (C2), which reads, "For people to have moral freedom necessarily conflicts with God bringing about situation L." The three ways are the Altruism Objection, the Natural-evils Objection, and the Superman Objection. All of these arguments could be called versions of the "Lack-of-conflict Objection," which is simply the objection that there really is *no conflict* between people having moral freedom and God significantly reducing the amount of suffering and premature death that occurs in our world. As I see it, the claim that there is no such conflict not only appears prima facie to be a reasonable claim but also has several good reasons to back it up. The first half of FDE is therefore a great failure. Let us now take a look at the second half.

4.5. Premise (P3): The Relative-value Objection

It is a basic assumption of all versions of the Free-will Defense that God places great value on human free will. But that assumption could receive opposition from the Bible. In appendix B, it will be shown how the very existence of free will might be challenged by appeal to the Foreknowledge

Objection and the Predestination Objection, both of which receive ample scriptural support. If free will does not even exist, then it would be hard to maintain that God has it as a very high priority. A further scriptural objection might be mounted by appeal to the vast amount of divine homicide described in the Bible. When God kills people, particularly children, that deprives those people of the exercise of their free will. And God is supposed to have killed millions of people, including children. He killed millions in the Great Flood (Gen. 7:23). He killed thousands in the destruction of Sodom and Gomorrah (Gen. 19:24–25) and thousands more in the deaths of the firstborn, which seems particularly aimed at children (Exod. 12:29–30). Later, God killed Korah, Korah's men, Dathan, Abiram, and their families by having the earth swallow them up, then another 250 council members by lightning, plus another 14,700 people by plague (Num. 16:25–49). For still more examples, see section D.7 below. With all that killing, especially of children, it seems that God was not very much concerned about preserving free will on the part of humans.

One reply that might be made here is that although the divine homicide shows that God does not have human free will as his very highest priority, it does not show that situation L is a high priority either. When God kills people, that not only undermines human free will, but situation L as well, for the killing produces still more suffering and premature death. The issue is that of the relative value that God places on human free will and situation L. The divine homicide is irrelevant to that issue. All it shows is that God has higher priorities than both of them. This reply is well taken, but we still wonder why there was not some other method for God to accomplish his goals without killing so many people. For God to avoid the homicide would have been conducive to both bringing about situation L and increasing the amount of free will in the world, both of which are supposed to be desirable from God's point of view. So some explanation is needed as to why God did not avail himself of such an alternate method.

According to FDE's premise (P3), as it is usually interpreted, it is always more important to God that some people have free will than that other people not suffer. The question could be raised as to whether free will is really *that* valuable. But to raise such a question runs a certain risk. It might be objected that values are relative and that theists and atheists simply appeal to different sets of values. On that topic, David Basinger says the following:

> Both parties may well agree that in a comparison of two possible worlds the one containing the greatest net balance of good over evil is superior. But how are we to assess the quantity of good and evil in each? Let us suppose, for example, that in the mind of a given atheologian the undeserved suffering of a single individual outweighs any amount of good

which might be generated in such a world, while in the mind of a given theist the intrinsic value of "human freedom" outweighs any amount of evil such freedom might entail. How would we determine who is correct? I, for one, have no idea how an objective, nonquestion-begging determination of this sort could be made.[17]

I am quite sympathetic with Basinger's relativism regarding values, but it does not seem directly relevant in the present context. Rather, the issue has to do with the concept of an all-loving deity. The claim is made that God favors free will over the prevention of suffering. Although such a system of preferences might in some situations reflect the attitude of an omniscient, all-loving deity, there are other situations in which it clearly cannot. And, in particular, if the group of people who suffer is very large and there is only a single person whose free will is at issue, then it seems that such a deity, just to be all-loving, would have to favor the interests of the group over the interests of the individual. This is not to say that God must be a utilitarian, only that he needs to be an agapist, one who advocates performing the *most loving* act available.

The usual example brought in here is that of Adolf Hitler and the Holocaust. Suppose that the Holocaust could have been prevented if God had interfered with Hitler's free will back in, say, the year 1936. (For example, Hitler could have been made to suffer a fatal heart attack shortly following the presentation of gold medals to Jesse Owens at the Berlin Olympics.) The argument is that an omniscient, all-loving deity would necessarily have deemed the avoidance of the Holocaust to have greater relative value than the preservation of Hitler's free will, and he would have had to act accordingly. To favor Hitler over the millions who died is incompatible with agapism and with having an all-loving nature. Another example is that of Satan and the Devil Defense. For God to permit Satan to inflict on humanity all (so-called) natural evils just out of consideration for Satan's free will would be incompatible with the claim that God loves humanity.

Many other examples of the same sort could be formulated, that is, examples where the avoidance of enormous suffering for a large group of people clearly outweighs the preservation of free will for another person or small group. To say that X "outweighs" Y here implies that it is part of our very concept of an all-loving deity that such a being (given complete knowledge of the situation) would place a greater relative value on X than on Y. Consider one last example. Suppose a mother is observing her children play. But one of the children, the oldest, starts to bully all the others and to seriously hurt them. If the mother is to perform the most loving act possible, then she must intervene. For her to let the bully do whatever he wants in the interest of preserving his free will, where she sees it will lead to him seriously harming or even killing other children, would be inconsistent with her loving all of them.

Since we are applying AE and FDE to the God of evangelical Christianity, and since that God is indeed conceived to be an omniscient, all-loving deity, it follows that the Holocaust example and others that are similar could be used to refute FDE's premise (P3) as it is usually interpreted. Evangelical Christians owe us an explanation of why God places such high value on free will that he would permit people to commit such atrocities. John Hick might say that free will is important for the development of moral virtues (a defense to be considered in chapter 6), but that sounds hollow when the enormity of the Holocaust is considered. Some other explanations for the high value placed on free will by God will be considered in later chapters: that its purpose is to permit people to be tested (chap. 7), that it is to locate culpable people and have them punished (chap. 8), and that its purpose is something at present unknown to humanity (chap. 10). But all of the explanations will be shown to be deficient. They all strike me as departures from the basic idea of the Free-will Defense. To stick to that idea, I think evangelical Christians need to say simply that God regards free will as intrinsically good (i.e., good for its own sake and not just as a means to something else). But then we are back to trying to understand how God could be considered to be perfectly loving when he is willing to sacrifice millions of people for the free will of just one individual (or a small handful of people). It runs counter to our intuitions about what it is to be "loving."

The Relative-value Objection adds one more nail to the coffin that has sealed FDE shut. Within the context of evangelical Christianity, all three of its premises have been refuted, as shown in sections 4.3–4.5 of the present chapter, so FDE can be regarded as a total failure in its attempt to defend the God of evangelical Christianity against AE.

(The reader whose main interest is AE might here consider skipping chapter 5 and going on to chapter 6, where AE is again discussed.)

Notes

1. Evan Fales, "Should God Not Have Created Adam?" *Faith and Philosophy* 9 (1992): 194–95.

2. William P. Alston, *Divine Nature and Human Language* (Ithaca, N.Y.: Cornell University Press, 1989), pp. 229–30.

3. Alvin Plantinga, *God, Freedom, and Evil* (New York: Harper & Row, 1974), pp. 55–57.

4. Peter van Inwagen, "The Problem of Evil, the Problem of Air, and the Problem of Silence," in James E. Tomberlin, ed., *Philosophical Perspectives, 5, Philosophy of Religion* (Atascadero, Calif.: Ridgeview Publishing Co., 1991), reprinted in Howard-Snyder, ed., *The Evidential Argument from Evil.* See esp. pp. 158–59 of the latter work.

5. Reichenbach, *Evil and a Good God*, p. 113.

6. Martin, *Atheism*, pp. 404–12.

7. Richard Swinburne, *The Existence of God*, rev. ed. (Oxford: Oxford University Press, 1991), pp. 202–203.

8. Martin, *Atheism*, pp. 400–404.

9. Eleonore Stump, "Knowledge, Freedom, and the Problem of Evil," in *The Problem of Evil: Selected Readings*, edited by Michael L. Peterson, p. 326.

10. Ibid., p. 327.

11. Matt. 8:2,5, 9:2,20,27–31, 12:10,22, 15:28, 20:30; Mark 1:40, 2:3, 3:1, 5:25, 7:24,31–37, 8:22–26, 10:46; Luke 5:12,18, 6:6, 7:1,11–17, 8:43, 11:14, 13:11–17, 14:1–6, 17:11–19, 18:35; John 4:46–54, 5:1–9, 9:1–7.

12. Matt. 9:18–25, 27:52–53; Mark 5:23; Luke 7:11–15, 8:41; John 11:38–44; 1 Sam. 28:7–15; 1 Kings 17:17–23; 2 Kings 4:32–37, 13:21; Acts 9:40, 20:9–12.

13. Plantinga, *God, Freedom, and Evil*, p. 58.

14. Ibid., p. 61.

15. Martin, *Atheism*, pp. 393–400.

16. Stump, "Knowledge, Freedom, and the Problem of Evil," p. 328.

17. David Basinger, "Evil as Evidence against God's Existence," *The Modern Schoolman* 58 (March 1981): 175–84; reprinted in *The Problem of Evil: Selected Readings*, edited by Michael L. Peterson. The quotation is from p. 150 of the latter work.

5

The Free-Will Defense
Applied to ANB (FDN)

Whereas situation L calls for a reduction in the amount of suffering on our planet, situation S, in effect, calls for the conversion of non-Christians to Christianity. AE makes reference to L and ANB makes reference to S. I shall use the label "FDN" for the Free-will Defense as applied to ANB. FDN tries to show that ANB's premise (A3) is false because there is something that God wants even more strongly than to bring about the acquisition of belief in the gospel message *per se* by non-Christians (i.e., situation S) and that is the *free* acquisition of such belief. God wants people to come to believe in his son *freely* and not as the result of any sort of coercion. He knows that non-Christians would indeed come to believe the gospel message (that God exists and sent his son to save the world) if he were to directly implant that belief in their minds or else perform spectacular miracles before them. But for God to do that would overwhelm them and thereby interfere with their free will, which he definitely does not want to happen. Since God's desire that humans retain their free will outweighs his (conflicting) desire to bring about situation S, it follows that ANB's premise (A3) is false, which makes ANB an unsound argument.

5.1. FDN Formulated

A more precise formulation of FDN is the following, with premises labeled as "P" and conclusions labeled as "C." As before, it is understood that the term "God" here refers to the God of evangelical Christianity.

(P1): For God to have caused people to believe the gospel message would necessarily have interfered with their free will.

(P2): The only possible way for God to bring about situation S (as mentioned in ANB) would be for him to have caused people to believe the gospel message.

(C1): Thus, the only possible way for God to bring about situation S would require him to have interfered with people's free will.

[from (P1) & (P2)]

(C2): Hence, for God to avoid interfering with people's free will necessarily conflicts with him bringing about situation S.   [from (C1)]

(P3): Although God wants to bring about situation S, he wants even more strongly to avoid interfering with people's free will.

(C3): Therefore, there is something (namely, for God to avoid interfering with people's free will) which necessarily conflicts with God bringing about situation S and which he wants even more strongly than he wants to bring about situation S.   [from (C2) & (P3)]

(C4): Thus, ANB's premise (A3) is false and ANB is thereby unsound.

[from (C3)]

Note that premise (P1) is concerned with the free will of people, which is here understood to exclude Satan. There is a possible Devil Defense in relation to ANB and it would be the idea that God lets Satan deceive people into being nonbelievers out of respect for Satan's free will. That would have been an alternate defense against ANB, but it is not FDN as here understood. I shall not pursue the Devil Defense in this context, because, first of all, I do not know of anyone who seriously advocates it, and secondly, I think the basic idea behind it has already been adequately disposed of in chapter 4.

FDN is clearly a valid argument. As indicated in connection with FDE in section 4.2, for the final conclusion of FDN to follow validly, it is not necessary that the truth of the antecedent of ANB's premise (A3) be established.

Also, I think that FDN's premise (P2) is true, though it might be challenged. In particular, it might be objected that God could have brought about situation S by some other process than causing people to believe things. Suppose God were to examine a large number of possible worlds, find one in which situation S has already come about by itself, and then make that one the permanent actual world. (In appendix B, a process similar to that will be called "quasi-predestination.") Against such a suggestion it might be objected that situation S is not something that might come about by itself, without any input from God. First of all, unlike the case of choosing to do good or evil (which will be the context for the discussion of quasi-predestination in appendix B), people do not normally choose their beliefs by a direct act of will. Belief is for the most part involuntary and not directly subject to the will, a point that will be discussed in appendix C.

Secondly, there isn't anything in the natural world that might cause people to believe all the propositions of the gospel message. Possibly nature might be thought by some to provide evidence of God's existence (the first proposition of the gospel message), but it clearly contains nothing that would support the idea of salvation of the world by God's son (the third proposition). Therefore, it would be unreasonable to think that people might arrive at a belief in *all* of the gospel message without any action whatever on the part of God. It follows that the idea that God might have actualized a possible world in which situation S had come about by itself (and might thereby have brought about situation S by quasi-predestination) must be rejected. FDN's premise (P2) strikes me as clearly true, and so I shall not challenge it.

The only places at which FDN might be attacked, then, are its premises (P1) and (P3). Let us consider how some of those attacks might go.

5.2. The Lack-of-conflict Objection

The first question to be addressed regarding premise (P1) is whether it takes free will to be something applicable to belief formation. Does it presuppose (doxastic) voluntarism, the view that belief is directly subject to the will? If so, then that would be a point at which the premise might be attacked. In this chapter I assume that FDN is taking "free will" in an ordinary incompatibilist way, as applied to *actions* (which, I shall argue later, would normally exclude belief formation), that is, in the same way that it is taken in chapter 4. Although most advocates of FDN (FDNers) do presuppose a strong form of voluntarism, according to which people often form their beliefs by a direct act of will, it seems to me that they need not presuppose that. If they do, then appendix C, below, provides a challenge to their outlook. And if FDN's premise (P1) assumes a strong form of voluntarism and that view is refuted below, then that would thereby refute (P1) as well. However, there are other objections to (P1).

I shall argue that God's desire to avoid interfering with people's free will *does not conflict with* his desire to bring about situation S, as claimed in FDN's step (C2). The issue goes back to the truth of premise (P1). Why should causing true beliefs in people, say, by showing them things, interfere with their free will? On the contrary, people want to know the truth. It would seem, then, that to show them things and thereby cause them to have knowledge, would not interfere with their will, but would conform to it. Most people realize that knowledge makes a person *more*, not less free. (Jesus himself, according to John 8:32 RSV, said, "the truth will make you free.") Even the performance of spectacular miracles, leading to knowledge or awareness, need not interfere with free will. Since people want to know the truth and how the world is ultimately set up (especially insofar as it affects them), for God to perform miracles before them would only conform to that desire and would thereby not interfere with their free will. Thus, assuming that the propositions of the gospel message are true (and relevant to people's interests), people want to be made aware of them and would in retrospect be grateful for any evidence, even of a supernatural sort, that would show them that truth. There is no conflict, then, between God causing true beliefs in people, even by way of spectacular miracles, and those people retaining their free will, which makes FDN's premise (P1) false. This may be called the "Lack-of-conflict Objection." It is similar to the Lack-of-conflict Objection mentioned above in connection with FDE at the end of section 4.43.

Two different replies to the given objection might be made here. The first is to point out that not everyone wants to know the truth. Consider, for example, people with terminal illnesses. Many of them might not want to know that they will soon die. They might instead feel that their future, however short it may be, would be made happier if they had some hope of living long. In some countries (e.g., Japan, Italy, and Russia, among others), many doctors refrain from informing terminal patients that they will soon die because they think, first of all, that the patients would not want to know the truth, and secondly, that such knowledge would cause them to go into a state of depression, which would be undesirable.

There may be some point to such an example, though I myself and most people I have asked would certainly want to know the truth even if it were bad news. Furthermore, there is a great disanalogy between the two cases. The gospel message consists of good news, not bad news. (In fact, "gospel" means "good news.") Instead of depressing people, God would only encourage people and make them happy by causing them to believe all the propositions of that message. The original point could be changed to the claim that practically everyone wants to know the truth about the ultimate nature of reality, at least if it is good news, and especially if it has relevance to their lives. Since the gospel message qualifies in both respects, we can infer that practically everyone would want to know the truth of that message if indeed it were true. Even if there were a few people who are not like that, that still would not explain why God (who is omniscient) does not simply ignore them and cause *others* (the vast majority of people in the world) to believe all the propositions of the gospel message. Practically everyone who does not already believe those propositions would want to be made aware of their truth and for that reason would not have their free will interfered with if God were to reveal it to them. It follows that the first reply to the Lack-of-conflict Objection is a failure.

The second reply is to claim that the issue of whether or not people want to know the truth is irrelevant. Even if they want to know something, for God to *force* them to know it would in a way overwhelm their consciousness, thereby interfering with their free will, which God wants to avoid. One writer who has expressed this line of thought is John Hick, who says:

> In order to be fully personal and therefore morally free beings, [humans]
> have . . . been created at a distance from God—not a spatial but an epis-
> temic distance, a distance in the dimension of knowledge. They are
> formed within and as part of an autonomous universe within which God is
> not overwhelmingly evident but in which God may become known by the
> free interpretative response of faith.[1]

Although Hick is not a champion of evangelical Christianity, his concept of
"epistemic distance" might be borrowed by evangelicals to defend FDN
against the Lack-of-conflict Objection. They could say that if God were to
make the gospel message "overwhelmingly evident" (as Hick puts it), then
there really would be a conflict with human free will, and that is something
the avoidance of which is a higher priority with God than his bringing about
of situation S itself. Thus, God has deliberately created an "epistemic distance" between himself and his creatures in order to help preserve their
free will. This could be called Hick's "Epistemic-distance Reply." Like
FDN itself, it maintains that there is a conflict between God "forcing"
people to believe things and those people retaining their free will. It differs
from FDN only in that it emphasizes the "overwhelmingness" of God
directly causing beliefs in people and the irrelevance to this issue of
people's wants and preferences about knowing the truth.

Another writer who supports FDN is Richard Swinburne.[2] He maintains that a too clear indication of God's existence would render obedience
to God too prudent and rational, which would remove moral freedom.
People would have "little temptation" to do wrong and so would lose their
opportunity for a "choice of destiny." Swinburne's arguments are very similar to those of Hick, and are dealt with quite adequately by J. L. Schellenberg.[3] For the sake of simplicity, I shall simply concentrate on Hick's version of FDN, namely, the Epistemic-distance Reply. Much of what I say will
also be applicable to Swinburne's version.

Many objections might be raised against the Epistemic-distance Reply.
First of all, it is misleading to call the process of enlightening people
"forcing," for that connotes "against the person's will," which is not the
case here. The most ordinary way for God to cause beliefs is simply by
showing things to people, or having things shown to them (say, by angels),
which is not any kind of "forcing." Certainly it would be counterintuitive to
claim that people are *forced* to believe or that their free will is interfered
with whenever they are shown anything.

Second, the assumption behind the Epistemic-distance Reply that
spectacular miracles necessarily "overwhelm" people is incompatible with
Scripture, especially the Old Testament theme that God went far out of his
way to show things to the Israelites to get them to be aware of him as their
Lord. He performed miracle after miracle in getting them out of Egypt,

helping them to survive in the wilderness,[4] and later helping them to defeat others in battle. (This point is developed further in section 5.4.) And yet, despite all of God's spectacular efforts, far from being "overwhelmed," the Israelites deserted him and began to worship other gods. Others not "overwhelmed" by miracles were those inhabitants of the cities of Korazin, Bethsaida, and Capernaum who were shown miracles by Jesus (Matt. 11:20–23). In this regard, see also John 12:37. Another relevant verse is Luke 16:31, where it is said that a man could return from the dead to tell people about the afterlife and they might still not come to believe in it. The Bible's message to Hick is that he completely underestimates people's "thick-headedness." For God to show things to people, even by spectacular miracles, would certainly *not* "overwhelm" them, at least not so far as the Bible is concerned. That in itself is reason for evangelical Christians to reject the underlying assumption behind the Epistemic-distance Reply.

Third, it might be argued that advocates of the Epistemic-distance Reply presuppose a strong form of voluntarism, a form that says belief is often directly formed by the will and that people *often choose* their beliefs. But that view is incorrect, which makes the Epistemic-distance Reply itself incorrect. I shall not pursue this objection here, but do so in appendix C, below. It is a debatable matter whether John Hick is a voluntarist at all. Many of his writings are certainly voluntaristic in their phrasing and orientation, though Schellenberg maintains that that is misleading and Hick is not really a voluntarist.[5] In any case, it is not necessary that the Epistemic-distance Reply presuppose any form of voluntarism. It might be argued that even if belief is not directly subject to the will, it has close connections with the will. People's choices and actions can certainly be affected by someone causing changes in their beliefs. Therefore, since God has concern about people's free will, he wants to keep an "epistemic distance" from humanity because of such concern. So this third objection will not be pursued here, though certainly the discussion in appendix C would become relevant should a strong form of voluntarism be claimed or assumed to be true.

Fourth, even if the Epistemic-distance Reply were to presuppose a strong form of voluntarism and even if such a view were true, the defense might still be attacked for reasons suggested by Schellenberg and others.[6] The problem taken up by those writers is a bit different, for it does not relate to the gospel message but just has to do with the question why God has not clearly revealed his existence to everyone. In response to *that* question, they consider the reply that God wants to maintain "epistemic distance" in order not to interfere with people's free will. Although the issue they discuss is slightly different from the one being pursued here, some of the arguments brought up are relevant. Let us here look at two of them.

One argument is that even if God were to reveal himself to nontheists, they could still refuse to believe in him through some sort of self-deception or "denial." In a similar way, even if the God of evangelical Christianity were to reveal the truth of the gospel message to non-Christians, they could still refuse to believe the message through a kind of irrational rejection of it. There would be nothing automatic about their acceptance. I have even heard this line of thought pushed to an extreme, where it is claimed that for God to perform miracles in front of certain people would be *futile*, as shown in the scriptural references given above regarding the Israelites and others. When people are so close-minded and "hard-hearted," it is said, not even spectacular miracles would get them to change. This has even been put forward as a defense against ANB: God doesn't bother trying to enlighten non-Christians because it would be futile for him to do so. Certainly that is going too far. First, it seems doubtful that there are any actions that would be "futile" for an omnipotent being. And second, the Bible indicates that signs ought to produce belief and that some people would have believed if signs had been shown to them (Matt. 11:4–5,21,23). The Bible also maintains that those who get to witness signs are fortunate (Luke 10:23–24). So, the futility idea is no good from a biblical standpoint, but the earlier point is correct: miraculous signs could be given and subsequent belief would in no way be automatic.

Another argument put forward by Schellenberg and others is that nontheists could become theists without thereby strongly committing themselves to God or obeying his laws. Satan himself is a theist, but not committed to obeying God (James 2:19). In an analogous way, it might be argued that non-Christians could be converted (i.e., made aware of the truth of the gospel message) without thereby strongly committing themselves to the Christian God. They could become "nominal Christians," who believe the gospel message as a kind of background assumption, but who do not have a religious attitude and do not practice the religion very faithfully. They may not pray much or even think much about God and religion. They may not read the Bible or go to church or contribute to charity. Although they believe that God's son saved humanity through his substitutionary atonement for its sins, they do not dwell much upon that proposition or strive to live the way Jesus recommended in his Sermon on the Mount. James Keller has expressed the given point as follows:

> God's goal for humans is not just that humans believe that God exists . . . and certain other things about God; rather, God's goal is, roughly, that humans will . . . *[have] faith in God.* . . . [E]ven if it were obvious to everyone that God exists and even if certain things about God's nature and will were obvious, that would not by itself coerce a person to have faith in God. It would not do so because believing all these things is not equivalent to having faith in God, nor does it psychologically guarantee that humans will have faith in God (i.e., that they will love trust, and desire to follow God). The possibility of not having faith in God while holding true

beliefs about God has been noted in Christian Scripture and has been the source of considerable pastoral concern. (Original italics)[7]

Thus, even though non-Christians may become Christians, they may still have many free choices to be made regarding their lifestyles. It follows that, even if a strong form of voluntarism were true and belief is voluntary in all people, God could still bring about situation S without interfering with people's free will in any important way. Although they would be caused to believe the gospel message, they would not thereby be caused to "accept Christ" and become religious Christians, so that would still be a matter of their free will and would still be up to them. And that sort of free choice (whether or not to adopt the lifestyle of religious Christians) is really all that God is concerned about with regard to free will, according to evangelical Christianity.

Let us express the second argument, above, as the fifth objection to the Epistemic-distance Reply. The claim is usually made by evangelical Christians that in order for Christians to be *saved* mere belief is not enough: they must also (as indicated above) "make a decision for Christ." That is, they must, by an act of free will, commit themselves to the sort of life that Jesus proclaimed to be the way to heaven.[8] As is said in the Bible, "faith without deeds is dead" (James 2:17,26). People can claim to know God and yet deny him by their actions (Titus 1:16). It follows that God could bring about situation S without thereby getting everyone saved. Even after becoming Christians, people still need to commit themselves to a certain lifestyle. If they don't, then God may say to them what he is supposed to have said to the lukewarm Christians in Laodicea, "I am about to spit you out of my mouth" (Rev. 3:16). So, more is needed for salvation than mere belief. In fact, it could plausibly be argued that it is *only* those who are aware of the truth of the gospel message who could be in a position to choose whether or not to commit themselves to a Christian lifestyle. Such a choice would certainly not be open to anyone else. So, instead of interfering with people's free "decisions for Christ," for God to reveal to them the truth of the gospel message would actually be the only way to make such a free decision possible.

As the sixth objection, assuming now that strong voluntarism is false, I would argue that even direct implantation of true beliefs into people's minds need not interfere with their free will. People want true beliefs, especially if those beliefs represent "good news" and have to do with fundamental matters. People would not then care how such beliefs are obtained, and so for God to directly implant them into people's minds would comply with their free will rather than interfere with it. An analogy would be God making a large, unexpected direct deposit into your bank account. It would make you quite pleased and would not at all interfere with your free will. So, in a similar way, direct implantation of beliefs need not interfere with free will either, provided that the beliefs are true, pleasing, and pertain to important matters. Furthermore, it could be argued that Adam and Eve must have had beliefs implanted in their minds at the time of creation, since they apparently had a language and managed to survive without any adult guidance. Yet, such implantation is not thought to have in any way interfered with their free will. In fact, they must have had free will in order for them to be culpable for their actions in the Garden. So, evangelical Christians who take the biblical creation myth literally should concede my point here. By appeal to such analogies, I conclude that even direct implantation of true beliefs need not interfere with anyone's free will.

Closely related to the idea of direct implantation of belief is the Christian idea that God sometimes sends the Holy Spirit to dwell within certain people, such as the Apostles at Pentecost (Acts 2:1–4) and those who write prophecy (2 Pet. 1:21). And it is said that in the future the Holy Spirit will enter all people (Acts 2:17). This activity of the Holy Spirit seems quite incompatible with the Epistemic-distance Reply. That is good reason for Christians, especially evangelicals, to steer clear of that reply.

Finally, as was explained previously in section 2.4, there are many different ways by which God might bring about situation S. It is not necessary for him to use either direct implantation or even spectacular miracles. He could accomplish it through relatively ordinary means, thereby preserving to a large extent some sort of "epistemic distance" from humanity. One way, for example, would be for him to have gotten some very clear and specific prophecies into the Bible which are later clearly historically fulfilled, and he could further see to it that the Bible and its translations are kept totally free of contradictions and factual errors. Considering the likelihood that ancient manmade writings would normally contain some factual errors, for the Bible to be completely free of them would make the Bible itself good evidence for its own divine inspiration and hence truth. Such evidence could have become part of history and general knowledge right from the outset, back in the first century C.E. Thus when missionaries go forth to spread the word, armed only with the Bible, they could point out those fulfillments of prophecy and other amazing features of the Bible, and so would not be totally lacking in rational support for their claims.

God could further aid missionaries in their evangelistic enterprises, as he did in the first century according to the Book of Acts, by giving them the power to perform healings and resurrections that cannot be explained naturalistically. Since it would be humans performing the miracles, sufficient "epistemic distance" between God and humanity would be preserved. Such aided missionary activity could have been ongoing through the centuries. Further, God could have influenced the preservation and dissemination of knowledge about the Bible in the schools, which would have made the truth of Scripture a part of history and general knowledge, as mentioned above. Today's Internet would be an especially effective way of disseminating information to the world about the divine inspiration (and hence truth) of the Bible, assuming that it had features that would make its divine inspiration evident. The claim that for God to perform such actions would interfere with people's free will is obviously misguided.

As a matter of fact, most evangelical Christians claim that God has already caused the Bible to have the very features described here, and they would certainly deny that such action on God's part interferes with anyone's free will. They would also deny that missionaries and teachers interfere with free will when they allegedly show non-Christians that the Bible contains the given features, thereby getting them to believe the gospel message. Of course, according to my own view, the Bible is *not* like that. It does *not* contain the features in question. (I argue for this in appendix D.) But the point here is that God *could* have given the Bible those features and that would obviously have been a way of causing beliefs in people and bringing about situation S (worldwide awareness of the truth of the gospel message) without in any way interfering with anyone's free will.

The very fact that there are people who very firmly believe the gospel message and yet retain their free will shows that non-Christians could be made to be like those people without having their free will compromised. How do most people become Christians? Probably it is simply through social conditioning or indoctrination from childhood. It would be counter-intuitive to suggest that *that* way of acquiring beliefs (the force of authority) preserves free will whereas belief acquisition through the presentation of good evidence interferes with it.

It would be ludicrous to claim that free will has to be interfered with whenever anyone is shown anything. People have their beliefs affected by others every day through what they read and hear and see, and their free will remains intact. Every time there is any sort of communication or inter-action between people, whether direct or indirect, there is the strong like-lihood that someone will do or say something that will affect someone else's beliefs. This occurrence is so common that it is easy to lose sight of it. But in none of these instances would it be said that people had their free will interfered with. Even where one person deliberately sets out to change the beliefs of another, say, through persuasive reasoning, and succeeds in doing so, we would still not say that the other person's free will was interfered with. The idea that there has to be such interference seems clearly wrong.

Hick would probably say that our free will is not interfered with when other people show us things, but it would be if God himself were to directly show us something in a spectacular way. His claim is that we would be "overwhelmed" by the experience and come to "lose our autonomy." As argued above, that claim could be disputed and it is also incompatible with Scripture, but the main point here is that God could have brought about situation S without the use of spectacular miracles. He could have done it through the use of human agents, i.e., missionaries and teachers, who accomplish their goals simply because they are armed with impressive evidence regarding the Bible itself. It is clear that for a missionary to win converts would not in any way interfere with their free will, for it would involve human-to-human interaction, not the direct God-to-human type of event about which Hick is concerned. This refutes the Epistemic-distance Reply.

Hence, premise (P1) of FDN is false, and the argument collapses. In the end, as shown by the Lack-of-conflict Objection, FDN fails to refute premise (A3) of ANB because it fails to describe a desire on God's part that actually conflicts with his desire to bring about situation S. From that perspective, since such conflict is the starting point for the whole issue, it could be said that not only does FDN fail to refute ANB's premise (A3) but the whole appeal to free will is irrelevant to it.

5.3. The Relative-value Objection

Another part of FDN that can be attacked is its premise (P3). Consider an argument similar to the Relative-value Objection of chapter 4. Even if there were people whose free will would be interfered with by God showing them things, it would seem that such people would be *benefitted* by coming to know how things really are. So, FDN would not even work well for such people, for it has not made clear why God should refrain from showing them things of which they *ought* to be aware. Such interference with free will seems to be just what such people would need to get "straightened out," so it would be in their interest for God to do it.

This point becomes greatly enhanced within the context of Christian exclusivism, the view that in the afterlife only those who have "accepted Christ" will be saved. Most evangelical Christians hold that view. The question they need to confront is this. Suppose it were granted that for God to show things to non-Christians (and thereby get them to come to "accept Christ" and thus gain the opportunity to be saved) would, at least to some extent, interfere with their free will. How could it ever be more beneficial for such people to end up damned than for them to be saved by means of such divine actions? Even if their free will is to some extent interfered with, once they are saved they would in retrospect be exceedingly thankful for such interference. How could an all-loving God permit billions of people to be damned through no fault of their own, simply as a consequence of their geographically or culturally induced ignorance about his son? Even if it means interfering with their free will, it would be far better for God to enlighten such people about his son and thereby allow them to be saved than to permit them to remain unenlightened and thereby proceed to damnation in the afterlife.

Because of the great force attached to this objection, it would be useful to look into the issue between Christian exclusivism and inclusivism. Is the exclusivist doctrine really essential to evangelical Christian belief? If it is, then not only could FDN be refuted by the Relative-value Objection, but ANB itself could be supported by the argument "God wants everyone to be saved but that requires being a Christian, so God must want everyone to be a Christian." That was argument (6) in section 2.4, above.

Argument (6) would support ANB in two ways. First, it would support ANB's premise (A2), which ascribes to God the property of wanting to bring about situation S. God must want to bring about situation S because he wants everyone to be saved and, given the truth of exclusivism, it is only through situation S that that could happen. Thus, ANB's premise (A2) must be true.

Second, the argument would also support ANB's premise (A3), which ascribes to God the property of not wanting anything that overrides his desire to bring about situation S. That support could be expressed by the following argument, which was referred to in section 2.4 as argument (8). I shall restate it here:

(a) There is nothing more important regarding humanity than humanity's salvation and whatever is required for such salvation.

(b) Salvation requires belief in the gospel message prior to physical death.

(c) Hence, there is nothing more important regarding humanity than humanity's belief in the gospel message prior to physical death.
[from (a) & (b)]

(d) But for humanity to believe in the gospel message prior to physical death is equivalent to situation S.

(e) It follows that God has no purpose which overrides his desire to bring about situation S. [from (c) & (d)]

One might still attack the inference from (c) and (d) to (e), but that means claiming that (c) and (d) might be true while (e) is false. That could not be done in the context of FDN, since FDN rejects step (c), claiming that, so far as God is concerned, humanity's free will is more important than its belief in the gospel message prior to physical death. Nor could it be done on the basis of the Testing Defense, which will be discussed in chapter 7, for that, too, rejects step (c). And certainly there is no biblical basis for the notion that (c) and (d) might be true while (e) is false. It seems that attacking the given inference would be akin to the Unknown-purpose Defense, which will be discussed later, in chapter 11. If that defense also fails (as I hope to show), then there would be good reason to claim that argument (8), above, is valid. But the critical premise in it is its premise (b), which is based on (Christian) exclusivism. It could be said, then, that in an indirect way exclusivism provides some support for ANB's premise (A3), as well as its premise (A2). ANB would then turn out to be a most formidable objection to exclusivistic evangelical Christianity.

However, it does not seem that exclusivism is essential to evangelical Christianity, seeing that some evangelical Christians have supported an inclusivist or even a universalist position. Although most of them are exclusivists, some have maintained that belief in God's son is not absolutely necessary for salvation. One example of an evangelical Christian who is not an exclusivist is Thomas Talbott.[9] Another is Clark H. Pinnock,[10] who also lists still others,[11] though conceding that they are in a minority. It is easy to understand why Christians would find exclusivism objectionable: it maintains that God is all-loving and yet permits most humans to end up eternally damned. That feature of exclusivism, one not touched upon by Alvin Plantinga in his defense of it,[12] not only lends great support to ANB, but is perversely irrational in its own right. It is hard to imagine a less loving act than that of permitting people to end up damned, especially if it is merely a consequence of ignorance on their part that could have been remedied in their life. Also, those who end up damned represent a kind of *failure* for God, assuming that he wants everyone to be saved. And it is unclear what sense it could make to allow that an omnipotent and omniscient being might fail at something. To reject exclusivism seems eminently rational.

But, irrational or not, most evangelical Christians proclaim exclusivism. They all do so for just one reason: it is the outlook regarding salvation which is best supported by the Bible. The verses which they find most compelling are the following (NIV translation throughout):

> Then he will say to those on his left, Depart from me, you who are cursed, into the eternal fire prepared for the devil and his angels. . . . Then they will go away to eternal punishment, but the righteous to eternal life. (Matt. 25:41,46)
>
> Whoever believes in [God's son] is not condemned, but whoever does not believe stands condemned already because he has not believed in the name of God's one and only son. . . . Whoever believes in the Son has eternal life, but whoever rejects the Son will not see life, for God's wrath remains on him. (John 3:18,36)
>
> If you do not believe that I [Jesus] am the one I claim to be, you will indeed die in your sins. (John 8:24b)
>
> I [Jesus] am the way and the truth and the life. No one comes to the Father except through me. (John 14:6)
>
> Salvation is found in no one else [than Jesus], for there is no other name under heaven given to men by which we must be saved. (Acts 4:12)
>
> No one who denies the Son has the Father. (1 John 2:23)
>
> He who has the Son has life; he who does not have the Son of God does not have life. (1 John 5:12)

The (minority) evangelical Christians who deny exclusivism make a brave attempt to interpret these verses in some way that does not carry the exclusivist implication. But the consensus among evangelical scholars and theologians is that all such attempts fail. I myself have no view on this internal squabble. I just note that the majority position seems to be the more irrational one, in itself, and also to be the one which more readily opens itself up to ANB.

Suppose we assume that (contrary to the mainstream evangelical view) exclusivism is false and that (contrary to the result obtained in section 5.2) for God to bring about situation S, no matter how he does it, would necessarily interfere with people's free will, at least to some extent. Must it then be good for God to withhold from the main part of humanity evidence that the gospel message is true? I think not. From the standpoint of evangelical Christianity, there would still be great benefit in people becoming aware of God's truth even if that is not necessary for salvation. They would thereby get into a proper epistemic relation with God, which would be of great benefit. Also, they would come to see meaning in life and they would lose their depression and sense of alienation. Their lives would get to be "on course." They would be more likely to come to love and worship God, which according to Scripture he desires greatly. And, according to Christians, it would probably even help them to be more moral and loving toward their fellow human beings. Even atheists can grant that there are many people in the world whose conduct would be greatly improved if God were to exist and were to cause them to believe the gospel message.

Thus, weighing the two sides, it might plausibly be argued from an evangelical Christian viewpoint that there is greater value in people becoming aware of God's great truth than in completely retaining their free will, assuming that it is not possible for both to obtain. (Of course, as shown in section 5.2, it *is* possible for both to obtain, and that may be regarded as the main objection to FDN, but we are here assuming for the sake of argument that it is not possible.) Since God is supposed to be all-loving, he must want humans to have that which is of greater value to them. Therefore, he must want to bring about situation S even if that were to interfere with their free will, which refutes FDN's premise (P3). This use of the Relative-value Objection is similar to that of section 4.5, above, and is just as potent. I would say, then, that FDN can still be attacked at its premise (P3) even if exclusivism is assumed to be false.

5.4. The Scriptural Objection

In section 4.5, dealing with FDE, the issue was raised whether God as described in the Bible really places greater value on human free will than on the elimination of human suffering. A similar issue can be raised in connection with FDN. Do the actions of God as described in the Bible support

FDN's two assumptions: that for God to enlighten people by showing them signs would interfere with their free will and that God places greater value on people's free will than on their enlightenment? If both assumptions were correct, then we would not expect God to do any enlightening of people. And yet there are several biblical passages in which he does that very thing. Let us look at some examples.

In the Book of Exodus, God performed spectacular miracles before the Israelites and the Egyptians in order to demonstrate to them that he is the true God. According to Exodus 7:5, "the Egyptians will know that I am the Lord when I stretch out my hand against Egypt and bring the Israelites out of it." And Exodus 10:1-2 reads as follows:

> Then the Lord said to Moses, "Go to Pharaoh, for I have hardened his heart and the hearts of his officials so that I may perform these miraculous signs of mine among them, that you may tell your children and grandchildren how I dealt harshly with the Egyptians and how I performed my signs among them, and that you may know that I am the Lord."

Many other verses expressing that theme could be cited.[13]

God also proved things to Gideon by means of spectacular miracles. He made fire come out of a rock (Judg. 6:21). After that, conforming to tests that Gideon himself devised, God proceeded first to put dew overnight only on some fleece and nothing else and then the next night he put dew on everything else but the fleece (Judg. 6:37–40). There was no hint that Gideon's free will might be interfered with by such demonstrations. God also revealed himself to Samson's parents by showing them a miracle (Judg. 13:19–23). And he proved himself to the hundreds of people gathered on Mount Carmel by means of another spectacular miracle (1 Kings 18:1–39). In the New Testament, Jesus used miracles to cause beliefs in people.[14] He also proved something to doubting Thomas by his miraculous appearance (John 20:24–28), and the Apostles were enabled to perform many miracles (even resurrections!) in order to convert people to the new religion. Acts 14:3, for example, says the following: "Paul and Barnabas spent considerable time there, speaking boldly for the Lord, who confirmed the message of his grace by enabling them to do miraculous signs and wonders."[15] Paul himself came to have new beliefs as the consequence of a miraculous occurrence on the road to Damascus. Considering the willingness on the part of the God of the Bible to perform miracles before people in order to get them to have certain specific beliefs, it seems that either there is no real conflict between God causing beliefs in that way and the observers' free will or else God is no more concerned about the interference with free will than he is with people's nonbelief. Hence, FDN's premises (P1) and (P3) cannot both be true. FDN does not square with Scripture. Instead, Christians confronted by others' nonbelief might be inclined to pray by reciting Psalm 90:16 (as rendered by the Living Bible): "Let us see your miracles again, . . . the kind you used to do."

5.5. The Irrationality Objection

There is a further objection concerning God's motivation. FDN's premise (P3) seems to imply that since God is unwilling to provide everyone with good evidence for the truth of the gospel message, he wants at least some people to come to believe the message without good evidence. But does he really want *that*? If so, why? It would seem to be irrational for people to believe anything without good evidence. Why would a rational deity create people in his own image and then hope that they become irrational? Furthermore, it is not clear just *how* people are supposed to arrive at the gospel message in the absence of good evidence. People normally stick with the religion of the culture that they are born into. But how did the religious beliefs of a particular culture come about in the first place and how is a person to be converted to a new religion? Is picking the right religion just a matter of lucky guesswork? Is salvation then a kind of cosmic lottery? If so, then why would God want to be involved in such a questionable operation? John Hick, as we saw above, suggests that God wants people to believe through "the free interpretive response of faith." But what exactly is that supposed to be and how does it apply to the attempt by missionaries to win converts to Christianity? Anyone who advocates FDN needs to answer these questions. The Irrationality Objection is the argument that such questions cannot be answered in any coherent way, and so FDN needs to be abandoned.

In regard to the first question, whether God wants people to believe things without good evidence, an affirmative reply is sometimes supported by citing the words of the resurrected Christ to no-longer-doubting Thomas: "because you have seen me, you have believed; blessed are those who have not seen and yet have believed" (John 20:29). Also, Peter praises those who believe in Jesus without seeing him (1 Pet. 1:8). Some have taken such verses to imply that we are to believe things on authority without questioning them.[16] But the message here may not be that God wants people to believe things without good evidence. It may be, rather, that there are other forms of good evidence than seeing, for example, the testimony of friends. Perhaps God is simply indicating that he approves of belief based on the testimony of others. Note that, earlier, the resurrected Christ had upbraided some of his disciples for not trusting the testimony of other disciples (Mark 16:14). His words to Thomas may have been just a continuation of that theme. Thus, it is not at all clear from the Bible that God desires irrational belief on the part of humans. And, as mentioned, it is very unclear just *how* people might acquire an irrational belief in the gospel message or *why* God would want them to. The very fact that there is no good answer to either of these latter questions is reason to reject the whole idea that God wants people to believe things irrationally.

This suggests a reply that might be made to the Irrationality Objection which I shall call "the Great-Commission Reply." It is that the key to understanding God's preferred mode of belief-acquisition by non-Christians lies in the Great Commission. God wants them to learn of the gospel message, not from himself directly, but from other people, presumably Christians. There are two reasons for this. First, it would in no way be an irrational mode of belief acquisition. The testimony of others is good reason to believe something, as Jesus indicated in the passages mentioned above. And second, whereas direct presentation of evidence by God (or by angels) would "overwhelm" the recipients and interfere with their free will, that is not the case when the presenters are fellow humans, in which case God's "epistemic distance" would be preserved. When non-Christians are presented with the gospel message, say, by a Christian missionary, they may choose to believe the message or choose to reject it. As Jesus said (according to Mark 16:16, NIV): "Whoever believes and is baptized will be saved, but whoever does not believe will be condemned." Since this is a free-will decision to be made by non-Christians, they are morally responsible for their choice and deserve whatever outcome it leads to. God hopes that they will freely choose to believe the gospel message, but he does not want to force them to do so, as would be the case if he himself were to do the presenting. As it says in Rom. 10:17, "faith comes from hearing the message, and the message is heard through the word of Christ." And the word of Christ is the gospel as presented by Christian missionaries.

There are at least four objections to this Great-Commission Reply. The first is that the testimony of others is *not* good reason to believe something if the others do not possess any special means to acquire the information. The testimony of friends regarding their own experiences may constitute good reason because they have special access to their own experiences. So Jesus was right about that type of testimony as it applied specifically to the disciples and their report of their encounter with him. But when the testimony consists solely of religious doctrines, the situation is different. In that case, no one has any special means to acquire the information. And, in particular, Christians do not have any rational support for the gospel message when they present it to non-Christians.

As we saw above, it is sometimes claimed that the Bible itself presents evidence of the truth of Christianity, mainly through the historical fulfillment of prophecies contained in it. So when missionaries go forth to spread the gospel message, armed only with the Bible, they could point out those fulfillments and so would not be totally lacking in rational support for their claims. This is a large issue, involving hundreds of alleged biblical prophecies and their fulfillments, and I do not plan to go into it deeply in the present book. The issue is touched upon briefly in appendix D, below. But the prevailing view among philosophers and educated people generally is that such an "argument from the Bible" for the truth of Christianity is unsound and ineffectual. Thus, the Great-Commission Reply is an inadequate response to the Irrationality Objection. It has not shown, apart from God himself demonstrating the truth of the gospel message, that there is any rational support for the message to which human missionaries might appeal and which would render it rational for non-Christians to come to believe.

Of course, in actual practice, missionaries do not rely solely on the Bible to get their message across. They rely largely upon their medical and technological know-how to impress the natives. The natives reason that since this person knows a lot about medicine and technology, he or she probably knows a lot about religion and metaphysics as well. No doubt many are won to Christianity in such fashion, though it is hardly a model of rationality. But the point would be that many more could be won if the Bible were so created and constituted that it itself could be appealed to as evidence of its own truth. That would have been a way for God to bring about situation S through the use of missionaries in a way that would not compromise people's rationality, while preserving to a large extent God's "epistemic distance." The fact that that was not done counts heavily against the Great-Commission Reply.

The second objection is that the reply appeals to some false assumptions. One of them is that for God (or angels) to present evidence which causes someone to believe something would necessarily interfere with that person's free will. That claim was refuted in section 5.2. People are not made less free by being shown the truth. Education opens up options for people. As Jesus said, "the truth will set you free." And as pointed out above, there are many biblical passages which describe God as showing things to people in order to make them aware of something. In none of those passages is there any hint whatever that the people in question had their free will interfered with. Another false assumption within the Great-Commission Reply may be that of strong (doxastic) voluntarism: that belief is directly subject to the will in most people, and so when non-Christians are presented with a proposition, it is always a matter of free choice whether or not they believe it. That assumption will be critically examined in appendix C.

The third objection is that even if belief were always directly subject to the will and even if non-Christians could always "choose freely" whether or not to believe the gospel message, it would still be *unfair* to punish them for making the "wrong choice." In this case, if there is no good evidence for the message, then the "wrong choice" (nonbelief) would be the rational choice and certainly not deserving of punishment. And if there *were* good evidence for the message, the failure to accept it, producing a kind of ignorance of the truth, would then be an intellectual failure, not a moral one. Again it would be unfair to punish the nonbeliever. Such unfairness would be incompatible with properties ascribed to the God of the Bible, such as being just and impartial. According to St. Paul:

> The man without the Spirit does not accept the things that come from the spirit of God, for they are foolishness to him, and he cannot understand them, because they are spiritually discerned. (1 Cor. 2:14)

It seems that those who do not believe the gospel message are people who are "without the Spirit." The question then becomes: how are *they culpable* for being without the Spirit? How is that *their* fault? I see no good answer to this forthcoming from the Great-Commission Reply, which is for that reason an inadequate response to the Irrationality Objection.

One writer who bravely argues that it is fair for God not to provide special revelation to the vast majority of people on earth and to just let them be eternally damned is William Lane Craig. He says the following:

> [S]uch persons would not have responded to special revelation had they received it. For God in His providence has so arranged the world that anyone who would receive Christ has the opportunity to do so. Since God loves all persons and desires the salvation of all, He supplies sufficient grace for salvation to every individual, and nobody who would receive Christ if he were to hear the gospel will be denied that opportunity. As [Luis] Molina puts it, our salvation is in our own hands.[17]

This could be called "the middle-knowledge defense of Christian exclusivism." It appeals to divine knowledge of certain counterfactuals regarding people, in particular, propositions about how they would respond if they were to be presented with the gospel message. There are many objections to this theory, but I shall here state just two. First, it fails to explain why it is that America and Europe have such a high proportion of people who would receive Christ, given the opportunity, whereas Asia and Africa have such a low proportion. I can't imagine what sort of explanation might be given for that. If Craig were to suggest that God somehow distributes souls around the world on the basis of their innate openness to the gospel message, he would still owe us an explanation for why God stuck so many of the "bad" ones in Asia and Africa. What possible divine purpose might that serve? Such incompleteness in Craig's theory is a serious defect. A second objection is that most evangelical Christians would be inclined to reject the theory on the grounds that it contradicts their idea that missionary work is efficacious, that is, that there are many people who are converted to Christianity (who would otherwise have ended up damned) because they were preached to by missionaries. More will be said about Craig's (apparently unattractive) outlook and the fairness issue in section 7.23, below. We are left with the result that the Great-Commission Reply must be false, for it implies that God does things which are grossly unfair, which is an intolerable result for evangelical Christians.

The fourth and final objection is that the Great Commission itself has been a great failure: Christianity has *not* been spread to all nations. About two-thirds of the earth's population (as reported in the 1996 *World Almanac*) is non-Christian. The apostles may have gotten off to a rousing start back in the first century C.E., some of them even being empowered to perform miracles as an aid to convincing their audiences. But the enterprise largely fizzled after that. Although it enjoyed huge success in Europe and later in the Western Hemisphere, it never made any significant inroads in Asia, where the greatest population came to be. And Islam came along a few centuries later and eventually overtook Christianity in regard to the rate at which converts are won, even in the region surrounding the Holy Land in which God was supposed to have some special interest. How could the God of Christianity have permitted *that*? Equally damaging, to my mind, is the fact that the Christians never even succeeded in converting the Jews of first-century Palestine. Those Jews were the people most knowledgeable about the alleged resurrection of Jesus and other events appealed to in support of the gospel message. If *they* wouldn't accept it, then the whole idea of selling it to all nations on earth by means of human missionaries is clearly hopeless and destined for failure. That could not be God's preferred mode of belief acquisition for the simple reason that it is so obviously ineffectual. If God cares about humanity's belief in his son, then he must want a way of bringing it about that really works. He must realize "if you want a job done then you must do it yourself." Humans on their own, without divine assistance, are simply not up to the task.

So much, then, for the Great-Commission Reply. It has failed to demonstrate that there is any way for humans to spread the gospel message worldwide apart from God himself stepping in and showing the truth of it, for it has no rational support to which human missionaries might appeal and which would render the message rational for non-Christians to come to believe. The Great-Commission Reply also fails to explain why God has not (recently) helped Christian missionaries in the ways suggested above (or done anything else for that matter) to bring about worldwide awareness of the truth of the gospel message. It stands refuted by (one or more of) the four objections given above and so fails to adequately defend FDN against the Irrationality Objection. And that brings us back to ANB and the problem of nonbelief. It is clear that FDN, two premises of which can be refuted, has not dealt with the problem adequately. Thus, ANB remains a most formidable challenge to belief in the God of evangelical Christianity.

5.6. The Inappropriate-response Defense

Another defense which is very similar to FDN is proposed by Daniel Howard-Snyder in an exchange with J. L. Schellenberg.[18] Because of its similarity to FDN, I include a discussion of it in this chapter. It should be noted, however, that the issue between Howard-Snyder and Schellenberg has to do with God in general. In adapting the argument to the God of evangelical Christianity, I am here altering it. Also, there is no reason to think that Howard-Snyder would see any merit in the argument as I have here reconstructed it.

The argument, which I shall call "the Inappropriate-response Defense," proceeds from the same assumption as that used by Craig, mentioned above, in his middle-knowledge defense of exclusivism: that God knows (via so-called "middle knowledge") how non-Christians would respond if they were to be presented with good evidence for the truth of the gospel message (or were in some other way caused to believe it). And, in particular, God knows that some of them would *respond inappropriately* in that they would either refuse to comply with the message (by refusing to repent their sins and accept Christ as Savior and Lord) or would comply with it but in an unsatisfactory way (e.g., by being or feeling coerced into doing so or by somehow lacking the proper motivation for such compliance). With this material as background, the argument might be formulated as follows:

(P1)   Necessarily, if God had caused people to believe the gospel message, then many of them would have responded inappropriately to it.

(P2)   The only possible way for God to bring about situation S (as mentioned in ANB) would be for him to have caused people to believe the gospel message.

(C1)   Thus, the only possible way for God to bring about situation S would require him to cause people to respond inappropriately to belief in the gospel message.   [from (P1) & (P2)]

(C2)   Hence, for God to avoid causing such inappropriate responses necessarily conflicts with him bringing about situation S.   [from (C1)]

(P3)   Although God wants to bring about situation S, he wants even more strongly to avoid causing such inappropriate responses.

(C3)   Therefore, there is something (namely, for God to avoid causing people to respond inappropriately to belief in the gospel message) which necessarily conflicts with God bringing about situation S and which he wants even more strongly than he wants to bring about situation S.   [from (C2) & (P3)]

(C4)   Thus, ANB's premise (A3) is false and ANB is thereby unsound.
                                                                   [from (C3)]

I think that at least some of the same objections that applied against FDN would also apply against the Inappropriate-response Defense. There is some unclarity here as to just what an "inappropriate response" is supposed to be. There is also unclarity as to how God is supposed to deal with the possibility of inappropriate responses, whatever they are. Does he supply *some* people with good evidence for the truth of the gospel message (or at least evidence of his existence) when he foresees that *their* response would be appropriate but withhold good evidence from others? If so, then the same objection could be raised as with Craig's theory, above: some explanation is needed for why it is that there are so many Christians (or theists, for that matter) in North America and so few in, say, Asia. Why should such a high proportion of Asians be disposed to respond inappropriately, thereby causing God to withhold evidence from them? Is it something to do with the Asian mentality? Many points of clarification are needed here.

In whatever way the above issues might be resolved, premise (P1) of the argument might also be attacked on the grounds that God, who is all-powerful, could cause people to believe the gospel message in such a way as to forestall any inappropriate response to it (whatever that might be), and, I might add, without in any way interfering with their free will. Just *how* God might perform such a feat is a complicated matter which I shall not pursue here. But it seems reasonable to think that he could do it. It would follow that if God has a desire to avoid inappropriate responses to belief in the gospel message, then that desire *need not conflict* with his desire for situation S. In this way, the Lack-of-conflict Objection could be brought to bear against premise (P1) of the argument. But I shall bypass this issue, for it seems to me that premise (P3) is a still easier target.

Consider the Relative-value Objection applied against premise (P3) of the Inappropriate-response Defense. First let us distinguish between two groups of non-Christians. In the first group are those who would come to believe the gospel message if provided with sufficient evidence for it but whose response to such belief would be so unacceptable to God that he would damn them for it. In the second group are those whose response to such belief, though in some way "inappropriate," would *not* be so bad as to get them damned. Then let us again distinguish the two different outlooks: exclusivism and inclusivism. It seems hopeless for an exclusivist to defend (P3), for that would imply that God cares more about the appropriateness of one's response to belief in the gospel message than he does about the individual's salvation. In other words, God would permit people in the second group mentioned to end up damned for eternity simply because their response to belief in the gospel message, though it would have sufficed for purposes of salvation, would have been in some way "inappropriate." That would be totally incompatible with God's omnibenevolence and thus not an available position for evangelical Christians, to whom salvation is all-important.

It may be, however, that the Inappropriate-response Defense would fare better within an inclusivist framework. In such a framework, we are to assume that many non-Christians do get saved even though they never come to believe the gospel message within their lifetime. Might God care more about the appropriateness of one's response to belief in the gospel message than about one's acquisition of such belief itself? One reason for saying no is that no such differentiation of attitude on God's part is revealed within the Bible. So far as the Bible is concerned, it is the acquisition of the belief itself that is of utmost importance to God. That is why he, in effect, commanded such belief and why he sent his son into the world to witness to it and why he issued the Great Commission, etc. In none of all that was there any evidence of reluctance on God's part due to divine fastidiousness regarding the appropriateness of people's response to belief in the gospel message. For that reason, premise (P3) of the Inappropriate-response Defense seems incompatible with Scripture, even within an inclusivist framework. And that would make the argument unusable within evangelical Christianity.

There is another reason for maintaining that God would always care more about the acquisition of belief in the gospel message than about one's response to such belief. It is that one's immediate response may not remain fixed. A person could come to believe the gospel message and at first respond inappropriately. But after some time has elapsed, the person may come to modify his/her response. Schellenberg makes this point. He suggests that God, being all-loving, would "seek in various ways to facilitate a better disposition."[19] It seems to me that, quite apart from God doing more with the new believer, just the nature of the gospel message itself would incline one to be favorably disposed toward a belief in it. Surely it would be "good news" for people who have recently come to believe in heaven that they will eventually go there. It seems reasonable to think that such belief would inspire in them a feeling of gratitude, which presumably is the sort of response that God desires. It is hard to see how God could get any better behavior or better disposition from non-Christians by having them remain ignorant of the gospel message than by causing them to believe it. That would be still another reason to reject premise (P3) of the Inappropriate-response Defense. This treatment is perhaps rather cursory, but it does seem that the given defense can be refuted in somewhat like the way in which FDN was refuted earlier in this chapter. It seems clear that, at least from the standpoint of evangelical Christianity and the gospel message, the Inappropriate-response Defense is itself an "inappropriate response" to ANB. Whether some version of it might fare better against ANB as applied to God in general (which is the context in which Howard-Snyder and Schellenberg actually debated the issue) will be considered later in chapter 14.

(The reader who is mainly interested in ANB rather than AE is here encouraged to skip ahead to section 7.2, where ANB is again taken up.)

Notes

1. John H. Hick, *Philosophy of Religion*, 4th ed. (Englewood Cliffs, N.J.: Prentice Hall, 1990), p. 44.

2. Swinburne, *The Existence of God*, pp. 211–12.

3. Schellenberg, *Divine Hiddenness*, pp.115–30.

4. For example, providing manna from the sky (Exod. 16:11–18,31–35; Num. 11:9; Deut. 8:16), quail by the millions (Num. 11:31–32), water out of a rock (Exod. 17:6; Num. 20:8–11; Deut. 8:15), and leading the people as a pillar of cloud by day and as a pillar of fire by night (Exod. 13:21–22; Num. 14:14).

5. Schellenberg, *Divine Hiddenness*, pp. 98–102.

6. See, esp., Schellenberg, *Divine Hiddenness*, pp. 109–30; Dilley, "Fool-Proof Proofs of God?" pp. 20–23; McKim, "The Hiddenness of God," pp. 150–54; and Terence Penelhum, *God and Skepticism*, pp. 111, 113.

7. Keller, "The Hiddenness of God and the Problem of Evil," p. 18.

8. Matt. 25:41–46; John 5:28–29; Rom. 2:5–10; James 2:14–26.

9. Talbott, "Three Pictures of God in Western Theology."

10. Clark H. Pinnock, "Acts 4: 12—No Other Name under Heaven," in William V. Crockett and James G. Sigountos, eds., *Through No Fault of Their Own? The Fate of Those Who Have Never Heard* (Grand Rapids, Mich.: Baker Book House, 1991), pp. 107–15.

11. Charles Kraft, C. S. Lewis, James N. D. Anderson, John Sanders, Bruce Reichenbach, Stuart Hackett, Dale Moody, Neal Punt, John Stott, and Don Richardson. Ibid., p. 108, n2.

12. Alvin Plantinga, "A Defense of Religious Exclusivism," in Louis J. Pojman, ed., *Philosophy of Religion: An Anthology*, 2nd ed. (Belmont, Calif.: Wadsworth Publishing Co., 1994), pp. 529–44.

13. Exod. 6:6–7, 7:17, 8:10,22, 9:14,29, 11:7, 14:4,17–18, 16:6,8,12. See also Ps. 77:14, 106:8.

14. John 9:3–32, 10:37–38, 14:11.

15. See also Acts 3:6–18, 5:12–16, 9:33–42, 13:7–12, 14:1–11, 28:3–6.

16. For example, L. Beverly Halstead says of the verse from John: "That is by far the most subversive statement in this book," "Evolution—the Fossils Say Yes," in Robert Paul Wolff, ed., *About Philosophy*, 3d ed. (Englewood Cliffs: Prentice-Hall, 1986).

17. Craig, " 'No Other Name,' " p. 186.

18. Daniel Howard-Snyder, "The Argument from Divine Hiddenness," *Canadian Journal of Philosophy* 26 (1996): 433–53, followed by J. L. Schellenberg, "Response to Howard Snyder," pp. 455–62.

19. Ibid., p. 460.

6

Two More Theodicies

This chapter pertains only to the Argument from Evil. Many theodicies, or theistic explanations for evil, have been proposed in the literature. When viewed in relation to AE, every theodicy contains (as a part or as an aspect) a defense of God's existence against the argument, and specifically against AE's premise (A3). A theodicy attempts to state God's purpose for permitting so much evil (i.e., suffering) in the world. If it succeeds, it would show that God has some purpose which overrides his desire to prevent or reduce evil, and that would refute AE's premise (A3). The Free-will Defense (FDE) is part of a theodicy which identifies the purpose in question as that of providing humans with the opportunity for moral freedom. Having seen the failure of FDE (in chapter 4), we should consider some alternatives. I lack the space to discuss all the theodicy defenses that have been proposed, but will consider two in this chapter. I here refer to them as the "Contrast Defense" and the "Moral-virtues Defense," focusing on their defense aspect against AE's premise (A3).

6.1. The Contrast Defense

According to the Contrast Defense, suffering is needed in order for people to experience a certain amount of *contrast* between good and evil and thereby come to appreciate all the good that there is in their lives. Let us call the situation of people experiencing such contrast to the optimal degree "situation OC." According to the Contrast Defense, our actual world contains situation OC. That is, people experience just the right amount of contrast between good and evil. Furthermore, there is a logical conflict between

144

situation L and situation OC. To reduce the amount of suffering that occurs would necessarily disrupt the ideal balance that exists between people's experience of good and their experience of evil. Thus, it would be logically impossible for both situations to obtain at the same time. But even an omnipotent being cannot perform logically impossible acts, so not even God could bring about both situation L and situation OC simultaneously. Although God wants situation L, he wants situation OC (which is our actual situation) even more. Therefore, there is something that God wants that necessarily conflicts with his desire to bring about situation L (namely, OC) and he wants it even more than he wants L. Hence, premise (A3) of AE is false, which makes AE an unsound argument.

One merit of this defense, I think, is that it shows that some suffering is needed in an ideal world. Without any suffering whatever, the world would be bland and people could not experience the sorts of joys that they presently possess. It might be objected that the world need not be bland since people could still have preferences. For example, although they like the taste of both chocolate ice cream and vanilla ice cream, they may prefer chocolate to vanilla. But this objection fails. If people preferred chocolate and no other suffering were to occur, then to have to eat vanilla ice cream instead of chocolate would be experienced by such people as suffering. Thus, for suffering to be totally eliminated, all preferences would also need to be abolished. Clearly that would be an undesirable world. I find this to be the simplest and best way to bring out the necessity of at least a little suffering.

As pointed out in sections 1.4 and 4.3, there is a certain unclarity in the idea of an ideal world in which there occurs just the right amount of suffering. Such a world cannot be described in great detail because of all the complexities involved. And yet we can know that our actual world is *not* the ideal world. Those who deny that are simply mistaken about the matter, as pointed out previously. Having to concede that the ideal world would need to contain some minimal amount of suffering does seem to present a certain problem for AE, but I do not see it as a fatal defect.

Michael Martin denies the need for the given concession, suggesting instead that God could have given people the sense of contrast between good and evil without actually having them suffer. He says the following:

> If a contrast with evil is necessary, it is not necessary to have knowledge by acquaintance of evil, such as the suffering of a person being tortured. Vicarious and empathic acquaintance is enough. . . . God could have created *all* humans with a high degree of empathic ability. . . . By viewing art and reading literature about evil, people created with a highly sensitive empathic ability could empathically experience what is depicted and thus learn to appreciate good without experiencing evil.[1]

This strikes me as highly dubious. Just to have the concept of evil or suffering, it is necessary that there be some experience of it. For God simply to implant such a concept in people's minds without the corresponding experience seems very unclear, perhaps even incoherent. Furthermore, even if people were to have the concept of suffering implanted, it would seem to be an unpleasant concept to contemplate. The sort of viewing and reading that Martin mentions would cause some discomfort and hence slight suffering, in which case actual suffering would not be totally eliminated. I shall therefore stick with my praise for the Contrast Defense as showing in an economical way the necessity of some minimal amount of suffering.

The necessity of suffering creates a kind of paradox. We think of all reduction of suffering as good. We hail all those doctors, inventors, scientists, engineers, and others who work toward the reduction of human suffering as heroes of humanity. And yet the ideal toward which they strive cannot be a world totally devoid of suffering, for such a world would be too bland to be of value. So it is in principle possible for some reduction to be bad, and that seems paradoxical, especially if evil is equated with suffering, as in the present book. But the paradox is eliminated by the recognition that there is some ideal balance between suffering and the contrast-benefit produced by it such that any deviation from that balance in the amount of suffering that occurs, whether up or down, would be detrimental. That is, in such an ideal world, if suffering were increased, that would be bad, but if it were reduced, then that, too, would be bad (because of the detrimental effect on the contrast-benefit). What the Contrast Defense is claiming is that our world already has the ideal balance. But that idea is too far-fetched to be taken seriously. I cannot specify an exact test by which people might determine whether or not they are in the ideal state described, but I think it is nevertheless clear that our actual world is *not* such a state.

Just about every writer who has mentioned the Contrast Defense (or the idea behind it) has simply rejected the claim that situation L (the mere reduction of suffering in our world) necessarily conflicts with people's experience of contrast between good and evil. Whether or not they grant that *some* suffering is needed for the sake of contrast, they all maintain that not as much of it is needed for that purpose as there actually is. Immediately after making the point contained in the quotation above, Martin goes on to say:

> Even if God could not have accomplished this and had to have humans experience evil to appreciate good, it was not necessary that there be as much evil as we find in the world. For contrast purposes, evil could be on a much smaller scale.

As Madden and Hare put it: "We need little pain by way of contrast to get the point: One might be allowed to bite his lip occasionally rather than have cancer of the mouth."[2] Certainly that is right, and it does refute the Contrast Defense.

6.2. The Moral-virtues Defense

The Moral-virtues Defense follows a pattern similar to the Contrast Defense. It maintains that suffering is needed in order for people to develop moral virtues such as courage, compassion, forgiveness, patience, self-sacrifice, charity, tolerance (of others' irritable behavior), and so on, these being good characteristics for people to have. Let us use the label "situation OM" to stand for the situation of people having to the optimal degree the opportunity to develop moral virtues of the sort in question. According to the Moral-virtues Defense, our actual world contains situation OM. That is, people have the opportunity for the development of such virtues as courage, compassion, forgiveness, etc., to just the right degree. It couldn't be better. Furthermore, there is a logical conflict between situation L and situation OM. To reduce the amount of suffering that occurs would necessarily reduce people's opportunity for the development of such moral virtues. Not even God could bring about both situations simultaneously. Although God wants situation L, he wants situation OM even more. Therefore, there is something that God wants that necessarily conflicts with his desire to bring about situation L (namely situation OM) and he wants it even more strongly than he wants situation L. Hence, premise (A3) of AE is false, which makes AE an unsound argument.

Like the Contrast Defense, the Moral-virtues Defense brings out a certain value in suffering: One cannot "develop character" without suffering to at least some extent. Again Michael Martin attacks this connection.[3] But, again, as with the Contrast Defense, I think that there is a kind of obscurity or incoherence in the idea of acquiring the benefit without the actual experience, though I shall say no more about that matter here.

It should be noted that the contrast experience is absolutely necessary for any sort of meaningful existence, whereas the development of moral virtues is not. A world without courage, compassion, forgiveness, etc., would be undesirable, but not totally devoid of value, as would a world without the experience of contrast between good and evil. So, although the Moral-virtues Defense demonstrates that there is a certain benefit that accrues from suffering, the Contrast Defense goes further and demonstrates that some minimal amount of suffering is necessary for a meaningful life.

The basic idea behind the Moral-virtues Defense is most often associated with John Hick, who says the following:

A child brought up on the principle that the only or the supreme value is pleasure would not be likely to become an ethically mature adult or an attractive or happy personality. And to most parents it seems more important to try to foster quality and strength of character in their children than to fill their lives at all times with the utmost possible degree of pleasure. If, then, there is any true analogy between God's purpose for his human creatures, and the purpose of loving and wise parents for their children, we have to recognize that the presence of pleasure and the absence of pain cannot be the supreme and overriding end for which the world exists. Rather, this world must be a place of soul-making. And its value is to be judged, not primarily by the quantity of pleasure and pain occurring in it at any given moment, but by its fitness for its primary purpose, the purpose of soul-making.[4]

This is the concept that is sometimes called "tough-love": A loves B but lets B suffer for educational and developmental purposes. Hick's idea is that God's love for people is a form of "tough-love": God permits them to suffer so that they may learn things and develop character.

Hick's theodicy is attacked by Roland Puccetti, who points out that it is guilty of "all or nothing" thinking. He says that Hick is forcing his readers "to choose between a completely painless world and the actual world."[5] Certainly there are intermediate states between those two extremes which would be preferable to both. Puccetti mentions a world in which all animals are herbivorous. My own favorite example is of a world that contains little or no premature death, an idea which will be discussed below. There are many other attacks on Hick's theodicy in the literature. Michael Martin devotes a chapter of his book to it.[6] I do not plan to pursue the many issues raised in those works.

Hick's "soul-making" theodicy differs from the Moral-virtues Defense in that it does not appeal to the idea of situation OM in which the opportunity for the development of moral virtues is optimized, and does not explicitly claim that our actual world contains situation OM. Also, according to Hick, the "soul-making" continues into the afterlife, which is not an idea contained within the Moral-virtues Defense. For that reason, I am more inclined to identify Hick as an advocate of the Afterlife Defense (which will be discussed in chapter 9) than an advocate of the Moral-virtues Defense. Although the ideas behind the Contrast Defense and the Moral-virtues Defense are mentioned in the literature, I have not found any writer who advocates either of those defenses exclusively, at least not in anything like the form in which they are formulated above.

6.3. The Scriptural Objection

It is not my aim in this chapter to beat a pair of dead horses, but to bring out a few points regarding the Contrast Defense and the Moral-virtues Defense which I find interesting and which have not, so far as I know, appeared in the literature on the problem of evil. In order for situation L to logically conflict with situation OC as described in section 6.1, it is necessary that the afflictions that people suffer in life *optimize* the amount of contrast they experience between good and evil. But if people's afflictions were to optimize such contrast, then for God to cure people of their afflictions would interfere with situation OC. Hence, it might be argued that if God were to want situation OC more strongly than he wants situation L, then he would *not* have cured people of their afflictions in the past. However, according to the Bible, God did indeed cure many people of their afflictions. It follows that either situation L does not logically conflict with situation OC or else God does not want situation OC more strongly than he wants situation L. Since both of these alternatives are in conflict with the Contrast Defense, we may conclude that the Contrast Defense is an unsound argument. An analogous appeal to God's motivations in curing people of their afflictions could also be raised against the Moral-virtues Defense. It could be argued that either situation L does not logically conflict with situation OM or else God does not want situation OM more strongly than he wants situation L. And in either case, the Moral-virtues Defense stands refuted.

Another way of questioning God's motivations with regard to situations OC and OM has to do with the fact that, according to the Bible, God killed, or ordered killed, millions of people.[7] When people are killed, there obviously occurs an interference with those people's experience of contrast and their opportunity to develop moral virtues. Therefore, if God were to want the maximization of such qualities (i.e., situations OC and OM) even more strongly than he wants situation L, then he would not kill a great many people or order many of them to be killed. But, according to the Bible, God did just that. Hence, if God exists, then it might be argued that he does *not* want situation OC or situation OM more strongly than he wants situation L, which makes the Contrast Defense and the Moral-virtues Defense both unsound arguments.

As a sidenote, it might be pointed out that this same sort of scriptural objection could also be used against FDE. FDE could be formulated in a way which implies that God's bringing about of situation L logically conflicts with the optimization of people's free will, which we can call "situation OFW." That further implies that free will is optimized by the sorts of evils that exist in our world, including people's afflictions. But then for God to eliminate those afflictions would interfere with situation OFW. Therefore, if God wants situation OFW more strongly than he wants situation L, then he would not have cured people of their afflictions in the past. Presumably he would have let the afflicted alone so that others could exercise greater free will in their dealings with them. But according to the Bible, God did indeed cure people of their afflictions. It follows that either situation L does not logically conflict with situation OFW or else God does not want situation OFW more strongly than he wants situation L. In either case, some assumption made by FDE is false, which makes FDE an unsound argument.

Similarly, it might be argued that there occurs an interference with people's exercise of free will whenever they are killed (perhaps even more so in the case of those who do not wish to die). Thus, if God were to want situation OFW even more strongly than he wants situation L, then he would not kill many people or order many of them to be killed. But, according to the Bible, God killed or ordered killed millions of people (and we can assume that those people did not wish to die). Hence, if God exists, then he does *not* want situation OFW more strongly than he wants situation L, which makes FDE an unsound argument. This point was already addressed and attacked in section 4.5, above. For all the divine homicide that occurred, God may still prefer situation OC or OM or OFW to situation L. Since the homicide detracts from *all* the situations, including L, it does not show anything about God's relative preferences among them. However, it is still a challenge for any advocate of the Contrast Defense or the Moral-virtues Defense (or FDE) to explain why God killed so many people, or ordered them killed, especially within a Christian framework which views God as being perfectly loving.

As for the miraculous healings, there again there may be some divine motivations involved that have nothing to do with situations OC, OM, OFW, or L. It would be tempting simply to declare that God's purposes in this area are unknown to humanity. We will come to consider such a maneuver later on in chapter 10. (It is the only defense considered in this book that is totally unconnected with any theodicy.) One drawback to it in the present context is that it seems to be a radical departure from the Contrast Defense and the Moral-virtues Defense. If we do not know God's motivations in curing people, then there seems little reason to insist that certain other divine motivations have something to do with people experiencing contrast or developing moral virtues. On the other hand, perhaps it would be premature to switch from the Contrast Defense and the Moral-virtues Defense to a different type of defense. An alternate suggestion is that the miraculous healings have to do with God's desire to show things to onlookers. That was the explanation given when Jesus healed a man who had been born blind. Jesus rejected his disciples' assumption that the blindness was a divine punishment, but said instead: "this happened so that the work of God might be displayed in his life" (John 9:3). From this perspective, nothing is shown by the miraculous healings about the relative value that God places in general on situations OC, OM, OFW, or L. He may generally prefer OM, for example, to L, even though there are special circumstances in which he will do things that inadvertently promote L rather than OM. Because of the possibility of such an appeal, I regard the Scriptural Objection to be a failure.

It should be noted, however, that the idea that divine healings are performed for the purpose of showing things to people tends to support the Argument from Nonbelief. It implies that there are certain propositions that God wants people to know or believe. But then there comes to be a problem in explaining why the world contains so many people who do not believe those propositions, which conforms to the atheological theme underlying ANB.

6.4. The Impediment Objection

Another objection to the theodicies under consideration is one mentioned above in section 4.4 in connection with FDE. It is that there occur evils which are actually *impediments* to both the sort of contrast mentioned in the Contrast Defense and the sort of moral virtues mentioned in the Moral-virtues Defense. Situations such as mental retardation, grave diseases, and genetic disorders in children, as well as the early death of children in great natural catastrophes, actually *reduce* the degree to which people experience contrast between good and evil and their opportunity to develop moral virtues. Obviously, they can't experience contrast between good and evil or develop moral virtues if they are dead, gravely ill, or to a high degree mentally impaired. Therefore, if *those* evils had been eliminated, or at least significantly reduced, then that in itself would have increased both the experience of contrast and the opportunity to develop the sort of moral virtues in question. Consequently, the actual amount of suffering experienced by humans in the world at the present time, which includes such evils as mentioned above, is clearly *not* needed in order for the experience of contrast and the opportunity for developing the moral virtues mentioned in the Contrast Defense and the Moral-virtues Defense to be optimally realized. They could be optimally realized even if the amount of suffering presently experienced by humans were to be significantly reduced. As a consequence, it is logically possible for situation L and situation OC both to obtain at the same time and it is also logically possible for situation L and situation OM both to obtain at the same time. Since the Contrast Defense and the Moral-virtues Defense deny those possibilities, it is clear that they are unsound arguments.

An alternate way to pose the objection (which particularly appeals to me) is by separating premature death from other suffering. It seems that premature death is an especially great impediment to any sort of experiencing or developing. If God really were to place great value on OC or OM, then he would be strongly motivated to do away with premature death, at least among humans. He could do that by making the planet calmer and more stable and by greatly increasing people's immunity to fatal disease, or in general their defenses against whatever natural risks might confront them. Even if other suffering were retained, if premature death were eliminated (or at least greatly reduced), then that would be a much better world than ours, one which a loving God would want us to have. And the Contrast Defense and the Moral-virtues Defense would be totally undermined by this suggestion, for the described world would in a desirable way *increase* the amount of contrast experienced by humans as well as their opportunity to develop moral virtues. Some might object that a world with no (or very little) premature death would be very quickly overpopulated, but that is no problem for an omnipotent and omniscient deity. He would be able to devise humane forms of fertility reduction or birth control that would prevent overpopulation while also preventing premature death. It might also be objected that people impervious to fatal disease would need to commit suicide in order to die. But I see that as a benefit rather than a drawback. In an ideal world, people should have control over their own death. When they feel that they have had enough of life and want no more, then they should be able to push a button to bring about a painless death. It should be as simple as deleting a file on a computer. Since premature death is an impediment to both the contrast experience and the development of moral virtues, it follows that there is one way to bring about situation L (i.e., by eliminating premature death) that definitely does not conflict with either situation OC or situation OM. Hence, both the Contrast Defense's claim that L necessarily conflicts with OC, and the Moral-virtues Defense's claim that L necessarily conflicts with OM, are proven false. The Impediment Objection neatly refutes both defenses in one fell swoop.

One way for an advocate of the Contrast Defense or the Moral-virtues Defense to try to get around the objection is to appeal to what might be called the "Favorites Reply," which is the claim that God has divided people into two groups, the "favorites" who are to enjoy the sort of contrast experience or moral-virtue development mentioned in the Contrast Defense and the Moral-virtues Defense, and the "scapegoats" who are to be sacrificed for the benefit of the "favorites." There are at least two defects in this maneuver. One of them is that it conflicts with the Bible. God does not "play favorites" or show favoritism. According to the Bible, he is not partial (or as the KJV puts it, a "respecter of persons").[8] Although the Israelites were in a sense God's "chosen people," that was another matter entirely. They were chosen for responsibility and even sacrifice, not for privilege. They certainly did not enjoy the sort of contrast experience mentioned in the Contrast Defense or the sort of moral-virtues development mentioned in the Moral-virtues Defense any more than anyone else. Therefore, the Favorites Reply can be rejected. Another defect in it is that a world divided in the given way into "favorites" and "scapegoats" is a clearly inferior world from the standpoint of love: it is not the sort of world that an all-loving God would create or permit. It is only if Christian theology could explain why there should be people who do not get much, if any, opportunity in this earthly life to experience the contrast between good and evil or to develop moral virtues such as courage, compassion, and forgiveness that the Favorites Reply might have any merit at all. But Christian theology cannot do that, and so the given claim has no merit.

6.5. The Negligent-father Objection

Another objection that can be raised against both the Contrast Defense and the Moral-virtues Defense makes use of an analogy suggested above by Hick. Suppose a father were to permit his son to drown in a lake in order to maximize certain people's opportunity for an experience of contrast between good and evil. The people (perhaps those who had led very sheltered lives and needed some experience of evil in order to provide more balance) may be onlookers on the shore of the lake. Or, alternatively, suppose the father let his son drown in order to help the onlookers develop such moral virtues as courage, compassion, and forgiveness. That is, he could have saved the boy, but instead he let him die for the sake of the onlookers. He saw that they (being nonswimmers) would need courage to try and save the boy, that they would certainly feel compassion as they watched the boy drown, and that they would then have an opportunity to forgive him (the father) for his (lack of) action. Certainly no one would regard the father's behavior justifiable. It would reflect, not "tough-love," but an absence of love. In the given circumstances, the ends, even if all of them were to be achieved, would not justify the means. In a similar way, so it might be argued, the evils of our world *outweigh* the alleged benefits appealed to in the Contrast Defense and the Moral-virtues Defense. Even if those evils were to bring about situations OC and OM (i.e., optimize both the sort of contrast experience and the opportunity to develop the sort of moral virtues mentioned), that would still fail to justify them. Just as in the case of the "father" example above, the alleged benefit is not greater than the horrible means used to bring it about, but is considerably *lesser*. This shows that the Contrast Defense and the Moral-virtues Defense are both failures so far as providing a theodicy or justification of evil is concerned.

As with the Impediment Objection, the Negligent-father Objection could also be applied to FDE. Suppose, for example, that some other boy, named Butch, had deliberately drowned the son within the father's presence, but the father had permitted that to happen. Suppose that, in his defense, the father were to say, "I wanted Butch to have an opportunity to exercise his free will and that is why I did not intervene." Such a defense would still be woefully inadequate, and the same is true of the Devil Defense mentioned above in section 4.42. Even if Satan were given full rein to exercise maximally his free will, that certainly would not justify permitting him to cause as much harm as actually happens with natural evil. Similar considerations apply to the Holocaust and other examples of particularly horrendous moral evils. The opportunity for people to exercise free will is not a great enough value to justify permitting them to commit horrendous atrocities. This shows that FDE can also be refuted by the Negligent-father Objection.

The analogy of the father might be criticized on the grounds that a human father who lets his son drown is not like God. For one thing, he is not the boy's *creator* and therefore does not have any moral right to let him suffer and die. God, on the other hand, *is* the creator of every human and therefore does have the moral right to let humans suffer and die if he should so choose. This criticism of the analogy is objectionable, among other reasons, because it depends on the principle that if X is the creator of Y, then, just by virtue of that alone, X has the moral right to permit Y to suffer or die. Such a principle strikes many as morally repugnant. Most people's intuitions, I think, would inform them that some good reason is needed to justify permitting a person to suffer or die, and that merely being the person's creator would not suffice. It would be immoral, for example, for Dr. Frankenstein to torture the monster whom he had created.

Another disanalogy that might be appealed to is the claim that God, being omniscient, knows all about future consequences, whereas the human father does not. But what is the relevance of that? Are there any future consequences that would morally justify letting children suffer and die, and that would show how such apparent negligence is compatible with maximal love for humanity? If so, then what are they? Neither the Contrast Defense nor the Moral-virtues Defense have come up with any that are adequate. If the appeal is then made to future consequences that are presently unknown to humanity, then my response is that that is a departure from the Contrast Defense and the Moral-virtues Defense. A similar point was made in chapter 4 in connection with the Devil Defense. Those who bring in the "unknown purpose" idea are leaving behind the defense with which they began. Such a move shifts the discussion to the "Unknown-purpose Defense," which is a different approach to the issue. So far as the Negligent-father Objection is concerned, it appears to do a good job in showing the bankruptcy of the Contrast Defense and the Moral-virtues Defense, as well as FDE.

All three defenses of God against AE thus far considered (namely, FDE, the Contrast Defense, and the Moral-virtues Defense) appeal to some greater good that is supposed to be achieved through the use of humanity's earthly suffering. And all three can be refuted by the Impediment Objection, the Negligent-father Objection, and the related objection (commonly cited in the literature) that our actual world contains far more suffering than is required for the greater goods in question. Thus, all three defenses are complete failures. For all that they can provide, AE's case against God's existence remains as formidable as ever.

Notes

1. Martin, *Atheism*, p. 450.

2. Madden and Hare, *Evil and the Concept of God*, p. 54.

3. Martin, *Atheism*, pp. 416–17, 426.

4. Hick, *Evil and the God of Love*, p. 295; the relevant passage is reprinted in Michael L. Peterson, ed., *The Problem of Evil: Selected Readings*, p. 227. Hick mentions in a footnote that the phrase "the vale of Soul-making" was coined by the poet John Keats in 1819.

5. Roland Puccetti, "The Loving God: Some Observations on Hick's Theodicy," *Religious Studies* 2 (1967): 255–68; reprinted in Michael L. Peterson, ed., *The Problem of Evil: Selected Readings*. See esp. p. 237 of the latter work.

6. Martin, *Atheism*, chapter 17.

7. Gen. 7:23, 19:24–25; Exod. 12:29, 14:28; Num. 16:31–35; Deut. 7:1–2. For further examples of divine homicide, see section 7 of appendix D, below.

8. Gen. 18:25, Deut. 10:17, 2 Chron. 19:7, Acts 10:34, Rom. 2:11, Col. 3:25, 1 Pet. 1:17.

7

The Testing Defense

The Testing Defense appeals to the idea that people are being tested in their earthly life by God or by agents of God. In most cases, the people are not aware of the tests being conducted on them. This idea seems not to be very popular with philosophers or theologians, though it has some biblical basis and (I have found) occurs fairly often among students.

7.1. The Testing Defense Applied to AE (TDE)

When applied to AE, the basic idea behind the Testing Defense (here abbreviated TDE) is that God is testing people to separate those (like Job in the Bible) who continue to worship him, despite all the suffering they endure in life, from those who don't. If the amount of suffering in the world were to be significantly reduced, then that would necessarily upset the tests by making them too easy. But God does not want that to happen. His desire that the tests continue at the same level of difficulty is greater than his desire that the suffering in the world be significantly reduced. Therefore, there is something that God wants which necessarily conflicts with his desire for situation L (namely, that his tests not be upset) and he wants it even more strongly than he wants situation L. Hence, premise (A3) of AE is *false*, which makes the argument unsound.

7.11. The Omniscience Objection

One obvious objection to TDE is that if God exists, then, at least when it comes to understanding human beings, he is all-knowing.[1] And the same can be said of God's son.[2] Therefore, if any tests are performed on humans, God must know their outcome beforehand. But such tests as mentioned in TDE would serve no purpose if God were to already know their outcome beforehand. For that reason, God has no use for such tests, and so would not perform them, which makes TDE an unsound argument. Let us call this the "Omniscience Objection." It can also be used to attack the Testing Defense when it is applied against ANB.

But the Omniscience Objection won't stand. First of all, we can think of possible reasons why God might have tests performed on people even though he already knows beforehand the outcome of the tests. In the case of Job, God wanted to prove to Satan that Job would pass the sort of test that Satan thought he would fail (see Job 1:8–22, 2:3–10). It could be like that with people generally. Maybe angels or saints are watching and God wants them to become enlightened about human nature, just as Satan became enlightened about Job. Or maybe God wants the humans who are being tested to become enlightened about themselves. For example, perhaps they are tested so that they may come to know about their own sinful nature. On the basis of such possibilities, the given objection can be dismissed. God's tests might serve some purpose other than his own enlightenment.

Another reply is that divine tests are described in the Bible, which suggests that God does indeed perform them and has some purpose for them. For example, God is supposed to have tested Abraham (Gen. 22:1,12) and the Israelites (Deut. 8:2, 13:3). Divine testing is a common Old Testament theme (Ps. 7:9; Jer. 11:20, 17:10, 20:12). And in 1 Peter 1:7, it says that Christians will need to suffer so that their faith may be proved genuine, which is a Job-like test. They are even urged to accept their suffering so as to empathize with Christ's suffering (1 Pet. 4:12–13). So the basic idea of TDE does receive some scriptural support. But there is a certain problem regarding the Bible. When God tested Abraham and the Israelites, the tests seem to have been for his own benefit. For example, it says in Deut. 13:3 (13:4 of the *Tanakh*, the Hebrew Scriptures) that God tested the Israelites to find out which of them loved him maximally. And that suggests that God is *not* all-knowing about humans after all. Another verse which points in that direction is Jer. 3:7, in which God admits having been mistaken about what (the people of) Israel would do. The problem is that if the Bible is inconsistent on the matter of God's foreknowledge, then its support for TDE is compromised. Let us postpone further discussion of the Bible's position regarding God's foreknowledge to section B.2, below.

A closely related issue is that of whether or not God has middle knowledge, which is not foreknowledge (i.e., knowledge of what people will actually do) but knowledge of what people would do under conditions which do not actually obtain. Some philosophers deny that there is any fact of the matter with regard to such conditions, so that the very idea of middle knowledge is in a way incoherent. It would be knowledge of something that is not there to be known. Philosophers of religion have been debating whether or not God has middle knowledge, and I do not want here to support either side of the issue. However, it seems to me that if a deity needs to do any testing at all to acquire any sort of knowledge, then it is because he lacks middle knowledge, not because he lacks foreknowledge. A lack of foreknowledge would simply call for waiting to see what happens. A lack of middle knowledge calls for testing. Therefore, all those philosophers who deny that God has middle knowledge should have no objection to the idea that God does a lot of testing of people. They may still claim that God is omniscient in the sense of knowing all that there is to know, for they would deny that the counterfactual conditionals which express middle knowledge are anything that can coherently be said to be known. This would be a further defense against the Omniscience Objection.

We need not get involved in the biblical issues or philosophical issues mentioned above. Even if God is taken to be omniscient and to possess middle knowledge as well as foreknowledge, there could still be reasons for him to have humans tested, as shown by the first reply above. Thus, the Omniscience Objection is shown to be a failure in refuting TDE. And this is also the case when the Testing Defense is applied against ANB.

7.12. The Unfairness Objection

A much stronger objection to TDE has to do with the unfairness of the test to which it appeals. Presumably the test has to do with remaining steadfast in one's religious faith while enduring suffering. However, such a test seems to favor those people who have been given more religious training in childhood over those who have been given less. And it also seems to favor those people who experience less suffering in life over those who experience more. In both cases, it would be easier for the favored group to maintain their faith while enduring their suffering. It follows that the test would be *unfair*. However, according to the Bible, God is *just*[3] and, as mentioned previously, he does not show favoritism. Hence, he would not administer such an unfair test as mentioned in TDE. It follows that the basic premise of TDE, that God is testing people in the given way, must be false, which makes TDE an unsound argument.

One move sometimes made to get around this Unfairness Objection, as it may be called, is to relativize the test to the individual. Those who received more religious training in childhood need to meet a higher standard in order to pass the test than those who received less. And similarly, those who suffer less in life also need to meet a higher standard than those who suffer more. One writer who has expressed this outlook is George Schlesinger:

[W]hen we wish to assess the nobility of an individual's character and the merit he has accumulated through his works, what is of essential significance is not the absolute spiritual height to which he has climbed, but the magnitude of the impediments that were placed in his path. . . . The degree of spiritual refinement a person achieves is proportional to the amount of free-willed exertion that was required from him to raise himself to the level he has reached. . . . [H]uman judges [should] . . . introduce some of the elements of a higher kind of justice, as when the court takes into account the extenuating circumstances of the accused.[4]

Schlesinger is not here defending TDE, but what he says can be applied against the Unfairness Objection to TDE. The idea is that when God tests people and judges them, he takes into account how much religious training they had in the past and how much suffering they endure and makes his assessment of them dependent upon such extenuating circumstances.

There are still many problems with this. First, what is to be said of people who had no religious training or religious faith at all at any time in their lives? How might the test even be applied to such people? If they are taken automatically to flunk the test, then that seems grossly unfair. And at the other extreme are people who have had extensive religious training and who suffer very little in life. If the little suffering they endure has no detrimental effect on their faith, then do they automatically pass? If so, then that, too, seems unfair. We would be inclined to say that anyone at all would have passed such an easy test under those conditions.

Another problem is that such a test as mentioned in TDE would impose a line of demarcation between two groups of people (those who pass vs. those who fail) such that those just above the cutoff would be practically indistinguishable from those just below. Since all degrees of love of God or faith in the Lord and all degrees of suffering are represented among humans, wherever the line is drawn through any of the spectrums, there would be no significant gap between those on one side of it and those on the other. Even when extenuating circumstances are taken into account, wherever the line is drawn, the indistinguishability problem at the cutoff would apply. It seems, then, that any such dividing line would have to be arbitrary, which would make such a test unfair. And since God would not administer an unfair test, the basic premise of TDE is thereby false, which makes TDE unsound.

A third problem is that those who fail the test (especially ones very near the cutoff mentioned above) could always in retrospect plead that they would have passed if they had been given better religious training in childhood or if they had been given less suffering to endure. How could it possibly be established that they still would not have passed even if they had been given better religious training or less suffering? Or, alternatively, if people failed because of the higher standards imposed in their particular cases, they may plead that they would have passed if they had been given *less* religious training or *more* suffering to endure because the standards they would have had to meet would then have been suitably reduced. How could it be proven to them that they still would have failed even by the lower standards? All of this seems to call for middle knowledge. Does God even have such knowledge in the first place? And even if he has it (which is debatable), how could he prove it to the people pleading their case (and perhaps others), thereby establishing the fairness of the test and his judgment in their particular case? There is much here that is very obscure.

Still another problem is that the test does not apply at all to people who suffer premature death (except that they would all flunk it since all dead people lack faith). A similar consideration applies to people who are so ill as to be barely conscious and to those who are very severely retarded. Such people are unable to manifest religious faith. Apparently, the only way to deal with this is to shift the test from the victims of the suffering, who die or are otherwise incapacitated, to whatever onlookers there may be; that is, have the test check the onlookers' faith, given their degree of religious training and degree of suffering. But what about the victims? If they all flunk the test, then that seems to favor the onlookers over the victims. And if the victims all automatically pass the test, then that would seem to favor the victims over the onlookers. Either way, the test would be unfair. The appeal to extenuating circumstances seems not to apply to this problem.

Of course, it would not be so bad if everyone were eventually to get to heaven and the only effect of failing the earthly test is that one does not receive a gold star in heaven and a pat on the back. But most evangelical Christians believe that not everyone will get to heaven, and that if people were to fail God's test then they would end up being eternally tormented in hell. Such a view not only reintroduces the Unfairness Objection, but is morally repugnant in itself. Even if everyone on earth were tested equitably and even if there were a significant gap between all those who pass and all those who fail, it would still seem immoral for God to let people endure eternal torment. We are inclined to ask, "What could they possibly have done to deserve *that*?"

It seems that the issue of whether or not the Unfairness Objection is a serious one depends on the sort of soteriology into which TDE is to be embedded. But given the traditional soteriology of evangelical Christianity, which has to do with heaven and hell, it is indeed a serious objection. Actually, Christians do not usually build their soteriology around the Job-like test involved in TDE, since that test does not look for belief in God's son (or faith in Christ). It is more often the sort of test involved with the Testing Defense as applied to ANB, which we will get to below. So, from that perspective, it becomes unclear what the purpose of TDE's Job-like test might be, assuming that God employs it generally. If it is not to determine who gets saved, then why would he conduct the test at all? And why is the test so important that it overrides the reduction of suffering on earth? TDE seems not to have any good answer here. It is understandable, then, why no professional philosophers who work on the problem of evil advocate TDE.

7.13. The Unsuitability Objection

Millions of humans die too young or are too ill or retarded to be tested in the way described in TDE, for their faith or lack of it cannot be meaningfully ascertained. That shows the world to be far from being ideally suited for purposes of testing humans. But if God exists and wants to test humans, then, being omnipotent and omniscient, he would have made the world ideally suited (or at least close to ideally suited) for such a purpose. It follows that if God exists, then he is clearly not motivated to test humans in the way described in TDE, which makes TDE an unsound argument. We can call this the Unsuitability Objection.

A similar point, one which is related to the Impediment Objection of chapters 4 and 6, is that many of the evils that occur in our world are actually impediments to the sort of tests mentioned in TDE. Consider, for example, the many diseases, natural calamities, and other causes of premature death in children. For God to eliminate or at least reduce such evils, perhaps by having made the planet calmer or by having made children hardier, would actually aid or enhance the tests. It is obvious, then, that a reduction in the amount of suffering and premature death associated with such evils, contrary to what is claimed in TDE, would not necessarily upset the tests, which makes TDE an unsound argument. This objection does not relate to one's soteriology. Whether there is a hell or not, the earth is unsuitable for testing humans in an adequate way. There are many ways to make it more suitable and some of them even produce situation L. Clearly, then, if God exists, he cannot be testing humans in the way described, which refutes TDE. I see no way to get around this objection. It seems to me that TDE has been utterly demolished. Let us leave it and move on. (Readers interested only in AE should skip the next section and go on to chapter 8.)

7.2. The Testing Defense Applied to ANB (TDN)

The idea behind the Testing Defense as it is applied to ANB (abbreviated TDN) is that God permits people not to believe the gospel message in order to *test* them. If it is objected that God (being omniscient) has no need to test people, then it could be pointed out (as above, in connection with AE) that tests might be performed for the enlightenment of others. God's omniscience need not be a barrier to testing in general, since people may be tested for the benefit of angels or saints or other onlookers, or even for their own enlightenment. TDN is the argument that ANB's premise (A3) is false because there *is* something that logically conflicts with situation S which God wants even more than situation S, and that is to test people, or have them tested, whoever the ultimate beneficiaries of the process may be.

One question to be raised is how, exactly, the performing of a belief-test might be connected with situation S. There are at least two versions of TDN. According to one, the evidence for the propositions of the gospel message is *inadequate*, that is, it does not supply sufficient warrant to make it reasonable to believe those propositions. Thus, what is being tested is people's inclination to believe those propositions despite the inadequate evidence. If God were to do things that would make the evidence for the gospel message adequate, then that would necessarily upset such a test. Perhaps the test is to see how people respond to a persuasive speaker who has no data to back up his claims. I am reminded here of Jonah, who (according to Jon. 3:3–5, 4:11) preached a doomsday message to more than 120 thousand people in the city of Nineveh and got them all to believe him, even though he apparently had little or no evidence to present in support of his claims. Maybe God likes people to be gullible like that. This first version of TDN is related to the Free-will Defense, and encounters some of the same objections. Why, for example, should God, who is rational, as maintained in premise (A4) of ANB, create people in his own image, but then hope that they believe things irrationally, without adequate evidence? Since it is not a version of TDN that is advocated by anyone, so far as I know, I shall not pursue it here.

The second version is the one usually appealed to by evangelical Christians, so it is the one which I shall take up in the present chapter. It has been a mainstay in the revivals of the evangelist Billy Graham, who urges people to "make a decision for Christ." According to the second version, the evidence for the gospel message is already quite *adequate*. The historical evidence for Christ's resurrection and for the accuracy of the New Testament in general is certainly sufficient and is readily available to anyone who wants to know the truth. Hence, people who do not believe all the propositions of the gospel message must be *refusing* to believe them because of some spiritual defect, such as false pride. In chapter 9 of the Gospel of John, such people are called "blind." They saw Jesus heal a blind man and yet did not come to believe in him. The NIV note on John 9:39 says that the coming of Jesus divides people into two groups, those who come to believe in him and those who don't, and those in the second group end up "blind." According to TDE, God wants such people to be identified, perhaps so that they can be weeded out for eternal damnation (Mark 16:16), and it is for that purpose that the test is performed. But if God were to supply still further evidence for the gospel message, then, first of all, it might be *futile* (as suggested in John 12:37 and other verses). Second, even if the evidence were not futile but were actually so overwhelming as to surmount people's false pride and thereby get them to believe the gospel message, then that would make it too hard to discern and identify people with the spiritual defect in question. So the test would necessarily be upset, which God does not want to happen. It is this sort of belief-test or faith-test, rather than TDE's Job-like test, that is most commonly associated with Christian soteriology. So it plays a major role within the whole system. Since God's desire that the test not be upset both necessarily conflicts with and outweighs his desire for situation S, it follows that premise (A3) of ANB is false, which makes ANB unsound.

7.21. The Lack-of-evidence Objection

There are many objections to (the second version of) TDN. One obvious one is that there really is no good evidence for the gospel message, especially the tenet that God sent his son to be the savior of humanity. The alleged historical accuracy of the New Testament is totally unconvincing, as are other appeals to rational support for the Bible. (This issue is addressed in appendix D, below.) Therefore, the argument's claim that such evidence exists is erroneous.

Another objection is that even if there is historical evidence concerning Jesus or other rational support for the truth of the Bible, it is clear that billions of people in the world are unaware of it. Nor are they in any good position, barring divine intervention, to become aware of it. They are simply victims of their geographical and cultural circumstances. Thus, the claim made in TDN that the evidence for the gospel message is "readily available" to everyone is also clearly erroneous.

TDN is a failure even for those people who have ready access to the New Testament and any other ancient documents that may be relevant. If they do not believe the gospel message, then it certainly does *not* have to be because they are "refusing to believe" due to something like false pride. One alternate explanation is that they simply find the documents unconvincing. There is nothing about the Bible that clearly shows it to be true. A neutral observer has no good reason to accept Christianity over the many other religions. The Lack-of-evidence Objection to TDN is that there simply is no good evidence of an objective sort for the truth of the gospel message of which people generally are aware. Thus, the basic assumption behind TDN is erroneous.

7.22. The "Howler" Objection

Even if there were clear evidence which shows Christianity to be the one true religion, and even if everyone were to be aware of that evidence, it could be that many non-Christians have simply not reasoned correctly about the matter. They may never have managed to "put two and two together." Their failure to believe the gospel message could be due to an honest mistake in their thinking about God and religion. It is true that it would indeed be a terrible mistake, a kind of "howler," since it would lead to damnation. (If the mistake is called a "howler," then perhaps it should be on account of the non-Christians' howls of pain in hell rather than Christians' howls of laughter in heaven.) But the mistake would be simply an honest mistake in reasoning, and not at all due to any "refusal to believe." Therefore, the claim made in TDN, that all nonbelievers in the gospel message must suffer from some "spiritual defect," is clearly wrong.

Furthermore, even the Bible suggests that nonbelievers are fools, rather than knaves, at least with respect to theism in general, for it says: "The fool says in his heart, 'There is no God' " (Ps. 14:1, 53:1). The NIV has the following textual note: "The Hebrew words rendered *fool* in Psalms denote one who is morally deficient." If this were so, then the English word "fool" would be a poor translation of the Hebrew, and some explanation would be needed for its selection. The *Tanakh* instead uses "the benighted man" (which is ambiguous, ranging in meaning between "knave" and "fool"). But every other translation uses "fool." Since the translators should know what they are doing, it seems possible that biblical writers regarded nonbelievers as intellectually rather than morally deficient, in which case the "Howler" Objection would apply. But even if the Bible does not support the claim that people who fail to believe propositions for which they have good evidence are fools rather than knaves, it is still a reasonable claim to make.

Perhaps the advocate of TDN would concede that many people's failure to believe in Christianity is due to some mistake in reasoning on their part. He could then declare that *that* is at least part of what is being tested for. The trouble with such a concession is that it cannot provide an adequate rationale for the whole system of testing. Why would God do it, especially in light of the drastic consequences of failing the test? Suppose a schoolteacher were to refuse to clarify a point just to find out how many students in the class already understand it without further clarification. That would be acceptable only if the teacher were then to go ahead and provide the clarification for those who need it. The testing must be subservient to the teaching. Otherwise, the whole system would be defective, even immoral. The testing reveals who has reasoned badly, but that cannot be the end of the matter. So what if people have reasoned badly? What are you going to do, hang them? The aim of the system must be improvement, not annihilation.

One might say that the schools also have final exams and a system which permits "flunking out." But even those who flunk out of school, perhaps due to a learning disability, find some place in society. They are not executed, let alone tormented indefinitely. If execution or eternal torment really were a consequence of flunking out of school, then the teacher should take extraordinary measures to help students pass the final exam so as not to flunk out. A loving teacher would even break the rules and write the exam answers on the board for the test-takers to copy and thereby pass. Christians say that God is holy and cannot break his own rules. But that only shows a defect in Christian theology. To be perfectly loving, God needs to put love ahead of rules. As for the school system, it is for education, not punishment. Its purpose is to try to help those with learning disabilities, not to punish them. Similarly, if non-Christians "don't get it" in the case of the gospel message, then what they need is additional instruction, not punishment. TDN fails because testing cannot be an end in itself or merely a device to serve the aim of punishment. To be moral, testing must always lead to something which justifies it, and it is that final goal which TDN has failed to supply.

7.23. The Unfairness Objection

There is an Unfairness Objection that can be applied to TDN just as there was for TDE, and it is closely related to the "Howler" Objection, above. People who commit "howlers" are fools rather than knaves. They should be pitied, not punished. If there were any test going on of the sort described within TDN, it would be very unfair to non-Christians. Quite apart from the issue of whether or not they are fools, non-Christians have powerful inducements to stick with the religion or belief-system of the family into which they happened to be born. It would be unfair to punish those with the "wrong" religion for not rebelling against their family and culture and switching to Christianity. To suggest that God is engaged in such a practice runs contrary to his being loving and just, which are properties attributed to him by evangelical Christianity.

A further problem with the testing idea is that it fails to clarify how strongly one must hold the relevant beliefs in order to pass the test. Suppose someone believes the first and second propositions of the gospel message but has some doubt about the third one. After all, the concept of "saving humanity," which is appealed to in proposition (c), is hard to grasp. It is unclear, for example, just what humanity was saved from and why God needed to sacrifice his son to accomplish it. It is also unclear exactly what was involved or given up in the sacrifice, especially since God was supposed to have raised his son from the dead (to a position of great glory) shortly after the crucifixion. From that perspective, it does not seem to be a very great sacrifice. Someone could easily be excused for having doubts in that area. Would a person with such doubts necessarily fail the test? Must one have maximal certitude that proposition (c) is true?

Still another type of problem emerges in the case of a person who readily assents to and asserts the *sentence* "God's son saved humanity" but who does not, from a theological perspective, understand it properly. For example, suppose what the person actually believes is that God's son defused an atomic bomb by means of which Satan, the father of all terrorists, was attempting to blow up the earth. Would such a person pass the test or fail it? There is some suggestion in the Bible that Christian belief needs to be theologically correct in order to warrant God's approval (1 Cor. 11:19, 1 John 2:19). But the whole area of belief-tests seems filled with unclarity and conceptual snares. This relates closely to the "unfairness" idea, but it is also an important objection in its own right.

If God really were interested in identifying people who willfully refuse to believe the propositions of the gospel message, then he ought to have made the evidence for those propositions quite good and quite convincing. It is only then that the reason for nonbelief would have to be something other than "unconvincing evidence." So it is only by providing a lot *more* evidence for the gospel message than there already is that God could reasonably perform the sort of tests that TDN attributes to him. What this shows is that there is no real conflict between God's desire for situation S and his alleged desire that people's false pride be revealed. God could have gone ahead and provided a tremendous amount of evidence for the gospel message, enough to cause all or almost all people to accept the propositions, and then see who the "holdouts" are. The ones who still do not believe the gospel message after all that may very well be "willfully refusing to believe." In that way, God could have both of his desires fulfilled: he could have situation S and also perform the sort of test described in TDN. Since those desires do not really conflict, it is proven that TDN is actually irrelevant to premise (A3) of ANB and clearly does *not* refute it. Again, this connects with the "unfairness" idea but is also an important objection in its own right.

The moral repugnance of God sending anyone at all to hell was already expressed above, but the repugnance of him sending people to hell merely for having wrong beliefs is particularly great. In response to this, some have expressed the peculiar idea that God does not send anyone to hell; rather, people "send themselves" there. For example, William Lane Craig says the following:

> Those who make a well-informed and free decision to reject Christ are self-condemned, since they repudiate God's unique sacrifice for sin. By spurning God's prevenient grace and the solicitation of His Spirit, they

shut out God's mercy and seal their own destiny. They, therefore, and not God, are responsible for their condemnation, and God deeply mourns their loss.[5]

Although it is understandable why Craig would dislike the idea that the Christian God of love sends people to hell, even by his own account it is still God who does the sending. The idea of "self-condemnation" is that some people deliberately put themselves in a situation which results in God sending them to hell. I find the idea of self-condemnation to be peculiar, for almost all people on earth act in what they take to be their own long-term best interests. If they really were well-informed about God's inclination to send them to hell for rejecting Christ, then they would surely *not* reject him. So I doubt that there are many who would condemn themselves in the given sense. Yet, according to Craig and most exclusivists, more than half the humans on earth will end up in hell. This is not only ethically repugnant but also contrary to the facts about human nature.

The point has been well expressed by Thomas Talbott in an essay that aims to show an inconsistency between the idea of hell and the idea of an all-loving deity:

> As long as any ignorance, or deception, or bondage to desire remains, it is open to God to transform a sinner without interfering with human freedom; but once all ignorance and deception and bondage to desire is removed, so that a person is truly "free" to choose, there can no longer be any motive for choosing eternal misery for oneself.[6]

My emphasis would be on the ignorance factor. No one would *knowingly* choose eternal misery for oneself. To suggest otherwise is to betray an abysmal ignorance of human nature.

Instead of "mourning" the loss of the non-Christians, as Craig suggests, God should provide them with sufficient evidence to convert them to Christianity. Even if their "acceptance of Christ" were done only out of self-interest, it would still be preferable to having so many people end up in hell. For God to refuse to provide such evidence is morally repugnant, and runs afoul of the Unfairness Objection. To treat fools as knaves is obviously unfair.

Many evangelical Christians would draw some distinction between those heathens who have heard of Christ and those who haven't. They might say that those who have heard of Christ are in a position either to "accept him" or "reject him." And to "reject Christ" does involve a kind of wickedness, so such heathens are to some extent knaves and not merely fools. For God to punish them would therefore be fair.

There are many objections to this line of thought some of which were already presented in section 5.5. I think that the fundamental objection is that it presupposes a strong form of (doxastic) voluntarism, which is an incorrect theory about belief formation. Once it is recognized that people do not normally choose their beliefs but form them automatically from their experiences, it will be seen that nonbelievers can only be fools for their nonbelief (assuming they have made some mistake). It is totally wrong-headed and misguided to regard them as knaves.

The reply might be that heathens are knaves not merely for their non-belief but also for refusing to take the time and effort to investigate the matter further. But if they do not believe that there is any merit in the gospel message, that is, anything that would warrant further investigation, then it is hard to see how they could be culpable for refusing to devote the time and effort to conduct such an investigation. Most of the evangelical Christians who think along these lines have themselves been approached by missionaries preaching a doctrine different from theirs, for example, missionaries representing the Mormons or Jehovah's Witnesses, and have refused to devote time and effort to further investigation of those alternate belief systems. (And the Mormons themselves refuse to investigate further the Jehovah's Witnesses' beliefs, and vice versa.) My aim here is not to call them "hypocrites," but only to point out the naturalness of refusing to put time and effort into the further investigation of belief systems that strike one as prima facie erroneous.

Richard Swinburne and J. L. Schellenberg are two philosophers who have worked on the question of when it is that people are culpable for not adequately investigating the truth of a proposition. Their result, with which I agree, is that such people are culpable only when they themselves realize and acknowledge the impropriety of their neglect.[7] In other words, it is only *voluntary* neglect that is culpable. But I should think that voluntary neglect would be exceedingly rare, since people want true beliefs about important matters (such as salvation) and would not voluntarily neglect whatever it takes to obtain such beliefs. If people fail to investigate propositions about important matters, then it will almost always be because they regard those propositions to be highly improbable. In other words, their prior beliefs have blocked the further investigation. And if their prior beliefs are not voluntary, then their neglect to investigate further is not voluntary. To deny this is to revert to strong voluntarism, which is an incorrect view.

Even if strong voluntarism were true and people were often to choose their beliefs by direct acts of will, there would still be a fundamental objection to the idea that heathens who reject the gospel message deserve to be punished for it. It is an idea which fails to recognize a principle which Christians themselves have expressed down through the centuries: that humans are basically selfish and will aim to perform only those actions which they take to be in their own long-range best interest. People continually want to know "What's in it for me?" If heathens are presented with the gospel message and refuse to believe it, then it must be that they do not think it is in their own long-range best interest to believe it. But why do they not think that? It must be because they do not regard it to be at all probable, for if it were true, then (given the nature of the message itself) it would have to be in one's interest to believe it. So we are back to inquiring why the heathens do not find the gospel message to be probable. In particular, why do they find it so implausible as to not even be worth investigating further? The obvious answer is twofold: (1) they already have a belief system in relation to which the gospel message is just flat-out false and incredible, and (2) the person who is presenting the gospel message to them, whoever that person may be, has not put forward any good reason to think that it is true or even possibly true. In light of this, I must say that the heathens' rejection of the gospel message is reasonable, and their refusal to investigate the matter further is entirely warranted, given their circumstances. And all this would be so even under the assumption that people often willfully choose their beliefs. Even then, nonbelievers would not deserve punishment for what they do, and for God to punish them would be unfair. TDN is thus refuted by the Unfairness Objection.

The idea that people knowingly "condemn themselves," to use Craig's expression, is simply false. It is contrary not only to the facts of human nature, but to Christianity's own conception of human nature. If humans are motivated out of selfishness and greed, as Christianity claims, then one thing they would *never* do would be to knowingly "condemn themselves." One might say that the heathens "condemn themselves" but not knowingly. But the reply to that is obvious: what the heathens should receive from God in that case is not punishment, but further education. As Talbott points out, that would in no way interfere with human freedom. God should take over from the incompetent missionaries and see that the job is done right. In other words, he ought to do the thing that the Bible indicates he wants to do: bring about situation S. To abandon that for the sake of testing would be pointless and unfair. TDN, then, is clearly refuted.

7.24. The Unsuitability Objection

As we saw in connection with TDE, above, the whole idea of a worldwide test is fraught with difficulty. As was pointed out, millions of people die too young or are too ill or retarded to be properly tested. The lives of many revolve solely around the struggle for survival. The issue of the religious beliefs of such people cannot sensibly be raised. Thus, the world is far from being ideally suited for the purpose of testing humans with regard to their beliefs. That in itself is good reason to deny that any deity is involved in such a testing process or has it as a high priority.

In the particular case of TDN's belief-test, there are additional reasons for finding the world unsuitable. First of all, there are billions of people who lived before the time of Jesus. The test described in TDN is not applicable to them. Second, there have been billions of people who have lived since the time of Jesus who simply never heard of the gospel message. Those people cannot be tested in the given way either. And finally, there have been billions of people who have heard of the gospel message, but only in some disparaging way. They, too, constitute another group who are not suited for TDN's test. If God really had been interested in testing people in the way suggested in TDN, then the world would have been very much different from the way it has been down through the centuries.

The "testing" idea is encountered every now and then, and it has a slight connection with the popular Pascal's Wager. But the notion that billions of people are somehow aware of the propositions of the gospel message but are "refusing to believe" them is just too far-fetched to take seriously. And, even if there were such people, the idea that God, who is perfectly loving, is more interested in "catching" them than in correcting their ignorance is also too unreasonable to accept. It is clear that some other sort of defense is needed against the Argument from Nonbelief.

(Readers mainly interested in ANB rather than AE should skip ahead in the book to section 9.2, where ANB is again discussed.)

Notes

1. Ps. 139:1–4, Acts 15:18, Heb. 4:12–13, 1 John 3:20.

2. John 2:24–25, 6:64, 21:17; Acts 1:24.

3. Deut. 32:4; Ps. 9:8, 11:7, 33:5; Isa. 5:16, 28:17, 30:18, 61:8; Jer. 9:24; Zeph. 3:5; Rev. 15:3.

4. George Schlesinger, *New Perspectives on Old-time Religion* (Oxford: Oxford University Press, 1988), pp. 166, 190.

5. Craig, " 'No Other Name,' " p. 176.

6. Thomas Talbott, "The Doctrine of Everlasting Punishment," *Faith and Philosophy* 7 (1990): 37

7. Richard Swinburne, *Faith and Reason* (Oxford: Oxford University Press, 1981), pp. 45–71. Schellenberg, *Divine Hiddenness*, pp. 58–69.

8

The Punishment Defense

Like chapter 6, this chapter will be devoted exclusively to the Argument from Evil. It will take up the Punishment Defense, which seeks to explain human suffering on earth by appeal to the idea that it is part of God's punishment for sin. (That idea is not relevant to ANB, since nonbelief in itself is not a form of suffering and so cannot be a punishment for anything.)

8.1. Two Versions

There are two different versions of the Punishment Defense. According to the first, God wants to punish people for their sins because he is holy and just, and such punishment is what people deserve. In other words, it is right for people to suffer to the exact degree that they actually do suffer in this earthly life, and God desires to do what is right. However, God has a conflict of desires. He wants to punish, but he also wants to prevent or reduce suffering. He loves humanity and desires situation L, which makes premise (A2) of AE true, but his desire for justice both necessarily conflicts with and outweighs his desire for situation L. Therefore, there is something that God wants that necessarily conflicts with his desire for situation L (namely, that people be punished for their sins to the exact degree that they deserve), and he wants it even more strongly than he wants situation L. Hence, premise (A3) of AE is false, which makes the argument unsound. In attacking AE's premise (A3), the first version is like the previous defenses (FDE, the Contrast Defense, the Moral-virtues Defense, and TDE) in that it views God as having a conflict of desires and as having to forego his lesser desire in order to act upon his greater one.

A point mentioned in section 2.2 should again be noted, for it has application to all the various defenses against AE. In order for premise (A2) and/or (A3) to be false, it is necessary that the partial definition of "the God of evangelical Christianity" assumed in AE's (collective) premise (A) be construed as reportive rather than as stipulative. What both versions of the Punishment Defense are attempting to show is that the definition is inaccurate. People do not mean *that* by the term "God" as it is used in the Bible or by evangelical Christians. Either biblical writers and others did not actually intend to describe God as having the given property or else they were simply mistaken about God's properties. The difference between the two versions of the Punishment Defense is that the first version rejects the divine attribute ascribed in AE's premise (A3), whereas the second rejects the divine attribute ascribed in AE's premise (A2).

According to the second version, God, following the Fall of humanity, imposed an earthly punishment upon it for its sinfulness, as stated in Gen. 3:16–19. Also, God's inclination to punish people for their sins was shown by the Great Flood (Gen. 7:21–23), the destruction of Sodom and Gomorrah (Gen. 19:24–25), and many other biblical events. Several Old Testament prophets express the theme of natural disasters as divine punishment for sin, either on the "Day of the Lord" or prior to it.[1] In addition, the idea is expressed in the Apocrypha: "Fire and hail and famine and pestilence, all these have been created for vengeance" (Sirach 39:29). The very idea of divine *commandments* implies the idea of divine punishment for failure to obey them. So the idea that earthly suffering is a form of divine punishment is a very natural one among theists. Some people today think that it is also shown by such calamities as the current AIDS epidemic, though we need not get into that issue. According to the second version, the overall amount of suffering experienced in life by humans serves well God's inclination to punish them for their sins. For all of these reasons, he does *not* want the amount of suffering presently experienced by humans to be significantly less than what it is. In other words, situation L is *not at all* among God's desires, so he does not have any conflict of desires there. It is premise (A2) of AE which is false and which makes the argument unsound, rather than premise (A3).

Another way to express the second version is by claiming that God loves us only to the extent that he was willing to sacrifice his son to give us an opportunity to have eternal life (John 3:16; 1 John 4:9.) He does not love us to the extent that he is willing to set aside the earthly punishment for sin that he imposed on humanity following the Fall. In other words, there are two punishments for sin, one in the afterlife and one in humanity's earthly life, and God sent his son to save the world because he wanted the afterlife punishment for sin dispensed with, though not the earthly punishment. As pointed out above, God's inclination to impose an earthly punishment on people for their sins was shown by various biblical events. The suffering that we experience in life serves well God's inclination to punish us for our sins. Furthermore, the Bible is God's primary way of revealing himself to humankind. Therefore, if he had ever felt any pity or compassion for human beings generally for their earthly suffering, then that would have been indicated in the Bible. But nowhere in the Bible is that indicated. Thus, God does not really want to prevent or reduce the suffering that occurs in the world. In other words, he does *not* want situation L. It is not even among his desires. Hence, premise (A2) of AE is false, which makes AE unsound.

Another way to bring out the difference between the first and second versions of the Punishment Defense is to focus on the idea of desert. One possible objection to the first version is that no one ever deserves to suffer, which is a kind of paradox. The argument for it is that people's behavior, whether sinful or not, falls into one of two possible categories. Either (1) the behavior is totally determined by events and conditions of the remote past, out of their control, and possibly even by God himself (as suggested in the biblical doctrine of predestination, which will be discussed in appendix B), or else (2) the behavior is the outcome of one or more uncaused events, occurring possibly in people's brains. In either case, people are not culpable for their behavior, for they can't be blamed for the events and conditions of the remote past nor can they be responsible for uncaused events (if any) or the outcomes of such events. This is a paradox in that it seems to prove by a kind of constructive dilemma that people are never culpable for anything that they do. We may call it "the Paradox of Culpability." If people are never culpable, then it follows that they would never deserve punishment for any of their sinful behavior, which would make the first version an unsound argument. This objection applies to the first version but not to the second because only the first version insists that people *deserve* their earthly punishment. The second version leaves it open why exactly God is inclined to punish people on earth, which may be a point in its favor. I shall not here pursue issues surrounding the Paradox of Culpability but will comment on it in appendix A.

Nevertheless, I do think that the second version of the Punishment Defense is a better argument than the first. One reason is that it does not depend upon the implausible idea that everyone who suffers on earth to whatever extent *deserves* that particular amount of suffering. I call this idea implausible mainly because of the suffering of small children and animals. It seems clear that they do not deserve the suffering. Some have suggested that children deserve punishment because they are afflicted by original sin. But that idea, aside from its irrelevance to animal suffering, is totally counterintuitive anyway, and so may be dismissed. I shall not go into all the reasons. It is certainly not a doctrine of evangelical Christianity that small children who suffer are being punished by God for original sin. There is still a problem about the inequity of human suffering in connection with the second version, which will be considered below. I shall not further pursue the first version of the Punishment Defense but only the second one, which I find to be the more plausible of the two.

I was not able to find any advocacy of the defense within the literature of the philosophy of religion except a partial one by Bruce R. Reichenbach, who says the following:

> [The Punishment Defense might] explain some instances of natural evils. As we noted above, it is in character with God's justice that he mete out punishment for our sins . . . [and] it is both reasonable and consistent with divine revelation to believe that God uses natural evils as a means of punishment in his administration of justice.[2]

This is a very limited support for the Punishment Defense (whether for the first version or the second version is unclear). Most philosophers eschew it. Let us look at some reasons why.

8.2. The Historical Objection

Both versions of the Punishment Defense appeal to the Fall of humankind as a historical event. In the case of the second one, which is the version we will henceforth be considering, it is mainly because of the Fall that God "has it in for us" and is motivated to punish us by means of suffering and premature death. This is where the Historical Objection comes in: the Fall is *not* an historical event. It is obviously just a myth. John Hick expresses this point as follows:

> The time has long been with us when Christians can not only see, but must frankly say, that the Genesis story is not history but myth. For the past century evidence has been available concerning the earlier states of mankind, before the brief span of recorded history, and none of this evidence lends any support to the theory that the human race is descended from a single original pair, or that mortality and liability to disease and disaster are other than natural to the human animal in his place within the larger system of nature.[3]

That is Hick's main objection to the Punishment Defense, and certainly I agree with it completely.

It is not necessary to belabor the point about the mythical character of the story of the Fall of humankind. Some further discussion of the matter occurs in appendix D. This is a potent objection for two reasons. First, the Punishment Defense needs to appeal to the Fall as an actual event in order to explain in a clear and vivid way God's motivation to punish humanity. Without that, such motivation would be unclear and largely inexplicable. Why, for example, would God be inclined to punish primitive humans? Where and how in the process of evolution did *Homo sapiens* come to deserve divine punishment? The whole idea is exceedingly murky. Secondly, the defense also needs to appeal to the idea of "original sin" (as stemming from the Fall) in order to morally justify the punishment of small children by means of natural evils. Thus, since the Punishment Defense depends so heavily on the idea of the Fall as an historical event, and since the Fall is so clearly *not* a historical event but merely a myth, this objection can be seen to be a very potent one indeed.

Some evangelical Christians reject the idea of original sin and concede that the story of the Fall is mythical. The question might be raised whether they could consistently appeal to anything like the Punishment Defense to try to justify human suffering. It seems to me that the answer is no, and a good part of the reason for that lies in the objections to the Punishment Defense presented below.

8.3. The Loving-God Objection

According to the Bible, God is merciful[4] and there are no restrictions on his love for humanity.[5] Furthermore, he and his son feel pity and compassion for human beings for their earthly suffering.[6] But the Punishment Defense depicts God as lacking mercy, as having restrictions on his love, and as feeling no pity or compassion for human beings for their earthly suffering. Because of those three defects, the Punishment Defense is an unsound argument. We can call this the "Loving-God Objection."

Several things might be said in defense of the Punishment Defense against this objection. First of all, the three defects with which it charges the argument may not be completely relevant. The defense only talks of God's inclination to punish humans for their sins via their earthly suffering. It might seem possible for him to have such an inclination even though he does *not* lack mercy, and does feel love and compassion for humanity. If the punishment of humans is less severe than what they deserve, then it could be regarded to be a form of mercy. As for love and compassion, certainly X could love Y and feel compassion for Y while still feeling the need to punish Y. It is a common occurrence among parents.

This defense is problematic in that it would be hard to show that humans generally deserve punishment and that the punishment they deserve is more severe than their actual suffering in their earthly life. Also, the appeal to the punishment of children by parents is an appeal to rehabilitative punishment rather than retributive punishment, whereas the concept of punishment in the Punishment Defense is strictly retributive. Whether X could feel love and compassion for Y while at the same time feeling that Y deserves (retributive) punishment is hard to say. I'm inclined to think not, though the issue is open to dispute. The given defense appears not particularly strong, so let us move on to others.

A second point has to do with the claim made in the Loving-God Objection that God is merciful. Although that claim does indeed receive some biblical support, it might be argued that there is even greater support for its denial. There are a great many verses that depict God as being unmerciful.[7] And since there are so many of those contrary verses, the part of the objection that appeals to God's mercy could be regarded as weak.

Third, the claim that there are no restrictions on God's love for humanity might be challenged. The claim is sometimes supported by appeal to John 15:13, according to which for X to sacrifice his life for Y shows maximal love on X's part for Y. But that is not generally true: if X, in addition, were to release Y from Y's earthly punishment (assuming that were in X's power), then that would show even greater love for Y, since doing two good things for someone shows more love than doing just one of those things. Furthermore, the verse does not even apply to God, since it wasn't God's life that was sacrificed for humanity, but his son's. And, according to the Bible, God sacrificed only his son's earthly life and only temporarily, since he raised his son from the dead to a position of glory shortly thereafter. So the alleged sacrifice wasn't so great, after all. I realize that most Christians would make the claims that God and God's son were/are the same being and that it was a great sacrifice after all despite its temporary character. But let us not pursue those claims here.

Another passage that might be appealed to in support of God's love for humanity is Eph. 3:17–19. However, it says in effect that Christ, not God, has great love for some one group of people, and it does not clearly specify which group of people that may be. The group seems not to be humanity in general. And the love in question is not claimed to be maximal. So the passage does not imply the idea that God's love for humanity in general has no bounds.

Sometimes an appeal is made to the metaphorical saying "God is love" (1 John 4:8,16). But it is unclear what that metaphor means or how it might support the idea that God's love for humanity is maximal. It seems not to relate directly to the main point of the Punishment Defense: that if God inflicted earthly punishment on humankind following the Fall, then it appears that he has not as yet set aside, or released people from, that punishment.

It should also be pointed out that the very idea that God loves humanity maximally is hard to grasp. Does the Bible really depict God in that way? In the case of a human father, if two sons are equally loved, but one of them becomes very disobedient and disrespectful, it seems only natural that the father would come to love that son less than the other. In the biblical story of the prodigal son (Luke 15:11-32), the wayward son was given a second chance. But what if he were continually to abuse his father's love whereas the other son didn't? The story does not address that. It seems there must come a point where the bad son comes to be loved less than the good son. The idea that God's love for people remains forever the same (maximal), no matter how morally different they may become, is exceedingly hard to grasp and to accept. For that reason, some doubt may be cast on the claim that the Bible does indeed depict God in that way.

Another point is that some biblical passages say of God that he *hated* certain people. For example, it is said that he hated Esau (Mal. 1:3; Rom. 9:13) and that he hates all workers of iniquity (Ps. 5:5), which would presumably include such people as those who died in the Great Flood or at Sodom and Gomorrah. It does not seem that God can be maximally loving if there is anyone at all whom he hates or ever hated.

Finally, the verses appealed to in support of the idea that God and his son feel pity and compassion for people for their earthly suffering only show compassion on the part of Jesus, not God, and only for certain groups of people whom Jesus directly encountered, not humanity generally. Nor do any other biblical verses show any pity or compassion on God's part for people in general with respect to their earthly suffering. The alleged support is simply not there. So the part of the Punishment Defense that makes that negative scriptural claim can be adequately defended.

For all of these reasons, the Loving-God Objection to the Punishment Defense appears to be a failure in its attempt to demonstrate an incompatibility between the way God is depicted in the Bible and the way God is depicted in the Punishment Defense. However, the matter is far from settled. The issue is whether God as depicted in the Bible is a deity who is merciful, all-loving, and compassionate toward humanity in general with regard to its earthly suffering. Some verses seem to depict him that way but others point in an opposite direction. The Bible is not consistent on the matter, which leaves the Punishment Defense in a kind of limbo.

However, we are here approaching the matter from the special perspective of evangelical Christianity. So we need to ask how evangelical Christianity views God as described in the Bible. I would say that it emphasizes those verses that depict God as merciful, loving, and compassionate, and it disregards or downplays the contrary verses. Or, alternatively, it makes a valiant attempt to harmonize Scripture by casting the contrary verses in a favorable light. They are called "hard sayings" and are in one way or another reinterpreted so as to be consistent with the evangelicals' overall conception of God. I do not want to assess here whether evangelical Christianity's interpretation of the Bible is correct in the sense of capturing the original biblical authors' intention. It is enough to point out that that form of Christianity has a certain conception of God, one which it tries to support by appeal to the Bible, and that conception of God is incompatible with the Punishment Defense.

A working definition of "evangelical Christianity" was supplied in section 1.6 and supplemented in section 2.4. I shall now put forward one last version of it as follows:

> Evangelical Christianity is that form of Christianity which has the following features: (1) It regards the Bible, and only the Bible (especially the New Testament), to be the inerrant "word of God." (2) It attributes to God the property of wanting all humans to be saved. (3) It attributes to God the property of being merciful, all-loving (or maximally loving), and compassionate towards humanity in general. And (4) it emphasizes what it takes to be God's Great Commission: spreading the gospel message to all non-Christians.

What the Loving-God Objection is trying to show is that so long as God is viewed in the way indicated in item (3), above, he cannot be using earthly suffering to punish humans as claimed in the Punishment Defense.

Therefore, although the Punishment Defense might possibly be a forceful defense of *some* conception of the God of the Bible against AE, it cannot be reconciled with evangelical Christianity's conception of that God. Hence, it won't work against AE as a defense specifically of God as conceived by evangelical Christians. Within this narrow framework, I think that the Loving-God Objection can be considered successful in refuting the Punishment Defense. In chapter 12 I shall take another look at the Punishment Defense within a quite different framework.

8.4. The Inequity Objection

A third objection to the Punishment Defense is the one that is most common in the literature. It is that when people experience suffering in life, the innocent suffer as well as the guilty. Often they suffer even more than the guilty do and often they suffer greatly. Among the "innocent" would be small children and animals. Just considering the humans, it is clear that the amount of suffering experienced by people in this earthly life is *not* exactly proportional to their degree of guilt. But if God were inclined to punish people for their sins, then he would want to punish only the guilty, not the innocent. There is biblical support for that.[8] And God would want the severity of the punishment to be exactly proportional to the degree of guilt of the offender. Hence, the suffering that people actually experience in life *cannot* serve well God's inclination, if any, to punish people for their sins. Thus, the premise of the Punishment Defense which claims that such suffering does serve God's purposes well is false, which makes the argument unsound.

To defend the Punishment Defense against this objection, it might be suggested that, according to the Bible, God has in the past inflicted death and destruction on people in an indiscriminate way. In the stories of the Great Flood and of Sodom and Gomorrah, thousands of little children are killed, along with their (sinful) parents. And when the tenth plague (the death of the firstborn) was sent out in Egypt, many innocent children died. By all rights, the children should have been spared. The fact that God did not spare them shows that he had little concern about individual distributive justice in people's earthly lives back in biblical times, and so may not have such concern even today. As Jesus said in the Sermon on the Mount, God "causes his sun to rise on the evil and the good, and sends rain on the righteous and the unrighteous" (Matt. 5:45). This would show that God is unfair after all, and not concerned about distributive justice, which would refute the Inequity Objection. This response may be called the "Collectivism Reply" because it maintains that God is inclined to deal with humanity collectively and not individually. In other words, his rule is simply "If some group (or humankind generally) sins, then that group (or humankind) generally must suffer for it," and individual guilt is not taken into consideration.

The Collectivism Reply does not seem compatible with the conception of God expressed in item (3) of the above definition of "evangelical Christianity." If God is merciful, all-loving, and compassionate toward humanity in general, then he must have concern about individual cases. That is built into the very ideas of mercy, love, and compassion. To let an individual child suffer or die to punish the group would be unmerciful, unloving, and uncompassionate toward the child, which would conflict with the given conception of God. I would say, then, that although the Collectivism Reply may be available to other viewpoints, it is incompatible with evangelical Christianity.

In place of the Collectivism Reply, it might be said that God had some unknown purpose for all the death and destruction that he inflicted on people in the Bible stories cited above which would show that it was not indiscriminate (and collective in focus) after all, but actually, in the end, quite merciful, loving, and compassionate. And it might be argued that God would surely have such a purpose if he were totally rational, as maintained in premise (A4) of AE. On these grounds, God's fairness and concern for distributive justice might be defended, and the defense would be compatible with the verses cited previously in support of the Inequity Objection.

But there is no need to cling to the Punishment Defense at all if one is going to appeal to this "unknown purpose" idea. Given such a presupposition, one might as well say that God has a purpose for whatever suffering occurs, but, in many cases at least, we do not know what that purpose might be. And we do not know whether or not the purpose involves human free will or Satan's free will or an experience of contrast or the development of moral virtues or testing people or punishing people for sin or any of the other ideas brought up in discussion of the problem of evil. Perhaps it involves one or more of these factors and perhaps not. In other words, once theists appeal to the "unknown purpose" idea within any of the specific-purpose (or known-purpose) defenses that have been discussed so far, they may as well abandon the given defense and appeal to that idea directly in what I call "the Unknown-purpose Defense." They would have no reason not to. That defense, however, has problems of its own, which will be taken up in chapter 10.

My overall assessment of the Punishment Defense as presented here is that it is a failure. From the standpoint of science, the Punishment Defense succumbs to the Historical Objection. And within the framework of evangelical Christianity, it is clearly refuted by both the Loving-God Objection and the Inequity Objection. Of course, there may be other conceptions of God, ones in which he is more "mean" than the evangelicals would allow, with respect to which the Punishment Defense would be a more potent defense against AE. This issue will be addressed again in chapter 12, below.

Notes

1. Num. 16:25–49; Hos. 8:1–14; Joel 2: 1–11,25; Amos 1:3–2: 16, 5:16–19. See also relevant verses in section 7 of appendix D, below.

2. Reichenbach, *Evil and a Good God*, p. 96.

3. Hick, *Evil and the God of Love*, p. 181.

4. Ps. 86:5, 100:5, 103:8, 136:2, 145:8–9; Joel 2:13; Mic. 7:18; James 5:11.

5. John 3:16, 15:13; Eph. 3:17–19; 1 John 4:8,11,16.

6. Matt. 9:36, 14:14, 15:32; Mark 6:34, 8:2.

7. See, e.g., the verses listed in note 6 of chapter 3, above.

8. Gen. 18:25, 2 Chron. 6:23, Ps. 62:12, Prov. 17:26, Jer. 17:10.

9

The Afterlife Defense

In this book I take the word "afterlife" to refer only to a personal afterlife, i.e., the survival of death by some specific individual, so that he or she is the *same* person after death as before death. Surveys have shown that most people in the United States say they believe in the existence or occurrence of an afterlife thus defined. Attempts might be (and have been) made to defend God's existence against AE and ANB by appeal to the concept of an afterlife and that is the subject of the present chapter. Let us label all such attempts versions of "the Afterlife Defense."

One objection to the Afterlife Defense is that the very concept of an afterlife is incoherent. Although I am not definitely committed to that point of view, I am sympathetic to it and do say something in support of it in appendix E, below. But in the present chapter I shall assume that talk of an afterlife is intelligible and that the concept is perfectly coherent. My aim is to argue that, even with those assumptions, potent objections to the Afterlife Defense can be raised.

9.1. The Afterlife Defense Applied to AE (ADE)

The basic idea of the Afterlife Defense as applied to AE, which is abbreviated "ADE," is that all humans will have life after death and God has so set up the world that when they get to the afterlife, all the suffering they had endured on earth will be somehow rectified. There are two different models for how that might be brought about. One model has the suffering rendered *negligible* by its contrast with the eternal bliss that people will enjoy in heaven. This idea is suggested by St. Paul, who wrote, "I consider that our

181

present sufferings are not worth comparing with the glory that will be revealed in us" (Rom. 8:18). The other model has the suffering fully *compensated* by means of either heavenly rewards or a reduction in the amount of punishment that would otherwise be received. Maybe those who committed sins but suffered very little in their earthly lives will be punished more severely in the afterlife. This idea is not expressed in the Bible, though it may be in conformity with the verse "From everyone who has been given much, much will be demanded" (Luke 12:48).

One main advocate of ADE is John Hick, who supports the first of the two models described above. In rejecting the second model, he says the following:

> This suggests a divine arrangement equitably proportioning compensation to injury, so that the more an individual has suffered beyond his desert, the more intense or the more prolonged will be the heavenly bliss that he experiences. . . . As distinct from such a bookkeeping view, what is being suggested here . . . is that these sufferings—which for some people are immense and for others relatively slight—will in the end lead to the enjoyment of a common good which will be unending and therefore unlimited, and which will be seen by its participants as justifying all that has been endured on the way to it. The 'good eschaton' will not be a reward or a compensation proportioned to each individual's trials, but an infinite good that would render worth while *any* finite suffering endured in the course of attaining to it.[1]

Although it is clear that Hick advocates the first model of ADE rather than the second, it is not clear whether he conceives of God as having a conflict of desires. The question arises whether God desires situation L but also desires the present amount of evil in the world, that being conducive to "soul-making" in the afterlife. Hick says the following:

> God has ordained a world which contains evil—real evil—as a means to the creation of the infinite good of a Kingdom of Heaven within which His creatures will have come as perfected persons to love and serve Him, through a process in which their own free insight and response have been an essential element.[2]

The question that Hick does not answer is whether God feels bad about people's earthly suffering or whether he just shrugs it off as "an essential element" for the overall long-range good. In other words, does God nod approvingly, as people suffer, perhaps saying, "Yes, good, they're coming along," or does he suffer along with humanity, wishing he could help them but refraining from doing so because of higher priorities? Since Hick does not mention such a conflict of desires on God's part, I shall assume that it is not his view. Also, it is hard to understand why any significant reduction in earthly suffering that might occur would necessarily affect in an adverse way the eternal process of soul-making that Hick describes. The outlook wherein God has a conflict of desires will be explored further below, but for the time being, let us assume that that outlook is not part of ADE.

It seems, then, that whichever model is employed, ADE views God as having the "eternal view," not the short-range view. Thus, God is seen as being unconcerned about all the suffering that occurs in the world: he does not really want it to be significantly less than it is at present. So, God does *not* want situation L. It is not even among his desires. Hence, premise (A2) of AE is false, which makes AE unsound.

Another apparent supporter of the first model of ADE is Marilyn McCord Adams, who seems to agree with the verse from St. Paul (Rom. 8:18) which expresses that outlook.[3] It is not completely clear that when Adams refers to "the problem of evil" she means the same thing that I do, for she suggests that evil is sin,[4] whereas I take evil to be suffering and premature death. Nevertheless, I shall quote a passage from Adams which adds a peculiar twist to ADE. She says the following:

> [P]erhaps our experiences of deepest pain as much as those of boundless joy are themselves direct (if still imperfect) views into the inner life of God. . . . Any vision into the inner life of God has a good aspect, this goodness at least partly a function of the clarity of the vision. . . . [A Christian] might be led to reason that the good aspect of an experience of deep suffering is great enough that, from the standpoint of the beatific vision, the victim would not wish the experience away from his life history, but would, on the contrary, count it as an extremely valuable part of his life.[5]

There is much here that I don't understand, such as the talk of the "inner life of God" and the "beatific vision." But what struck me as most peculiar is the suggestion that someone, perhaps in heaven, might be given the option to "wish away from his life history" some bit of past suffering. Presumably that does not mean changing the past, which is a self-contradictory idea. Perhaps what the heavenly person would take the option to mean is some sort of obliteration of memory. And I agree, in that context, the person would not "wish it away" (meaning "wish the memory of it to be obliterated"). The person's sense of self-identity would be so fragile, assuming that it would be possible in an afterlife to have any sense of self-identity at all, that any memories of the past, in helping to preserve that sense, would be desirable to retain, even memories of extreme suffering. However, I do not agree that the person would "count it as an extremely valuable part of his life," as Adams suggests. On the contrary, I think he would say that his life would have been better if the given event had not occurred. Survivors of the Nazi Holocaust of World War II, for example, would probably feel that way. I would say, then, that the peculiar twist that Adams adds to ADE does not in any way bolster it but has huge difficulties of its own.

9.11. The Unsaved Objection

Even if there were such a state as an afterlife which all people enter upon physical death, God, according to the Bible, does not reward them all with bliss when they get there. In particular, those who end up unsaved do not receive any rewards.[6] Hence, it is incorrect to say, as ADE does, that all the suffering and unfairness that people experience on earth will be somehow rectified in the afterlife. The earthly suffering experienced by the unsaved never gets rectified, which makes ADE an unsound argument.

This objection is sidestepped by Hick because of his universalism. He denies that in the long run anyone will end up unsaved and makes an effort to interpret the Bible so as to be in conformity with that outlook.[7] However, it is clear that evangelical Christianity's interpretation of the Bible is quite different from Hick's. Most evangelical Christians are exclusivists, and even among those who are not, almost all would maintain that *some* people at least will end up unsaved. As with previous parts of this book, I shall in this chapter assume evangelical Christianity's interpretation of the Bible and proceed accordingly.

The only move that evangelical Christians might make in response to the "Unsaved Objection" (as I shall call it) is to modify ADE so as to apply only to those who are saved. The situation of the unsaved could be covered by some other theodicy, such as, for example, some version of the Punishment Defense. It might be suggested that the unsaved get what is coming to them and so it is morally justifiable for their earthly suffering to go unrectified. In other words, the unsaved deserve extreme punishment. Their earthly suffering merely serves part of that purpose and the rest is fulfilled by their harsh treatment in the afterlife. This approach would involve combining two different defenses, ADE as applied (only) to the saved, and some version of the Punishment Defense as applied (only) to the unsaved.

The drawback to this, of course, is that there are strong objections to the Punishment Defense. Two of them presented in chapter 8 were the Loving-God Objection and the Inequity Objection. Evangelical Christians, at least, have no good response to either of those two. That may explain, in part, why the idea of earthly punishment (as opposed to afterlife punishment) is not popular with them. In any case, they need to defend ADE against the Unsaved Objection, which requires that they develop a soteriology compatible with their concept of an all-loving God. As we saw in section 5.3, that is a rather daunting undertaking, especially for exclusivists.

9.12. The Unrectifiability Objection

Another objection to ADE is that there sometimes occur forms of suffering that are so extreme that it is impossible that they should ever be rectified, i.e., rendered negligible or fully compensated by rewards. In other words, it would have been simply better, no matter what, that they had never occurred. An example often appealed to is the Holocaust of World War II. Suppose it were suggested that the victims of the Holocaust have gone (or will go) to heaven and will enjoy eternal bliss there (contrary to exclusivism, which would send the Jewish victims, at least, to hell). Maybe the memory of their earthly suffering will be erased, though that would give rise to the problem of retaining a sense of self-identity mentioned above, and which I shall not pursue here. Even with all that, a good case could be made for the view that their extreme suffering could not be rectified. No matter how much bliss they come to enjoy, it would have been better, overall, if the Holocaust had never happened. Hence, the claim made in ADE that *all* forms of suffering (at least among the saved) will be rectified in the afterlife is an incorrect claim, which makes ADE an unsound argument. Hick considers this objection and replies to it as follows:

> It may be that the personal scars and memories of evil remain for ever, but are transfigured in the light of the universal mutual forgiveness and reconciliation on which the life of heaven is based. Or it may be that the journey to the heavenly Kingdom is so long, and traverses such varied spheres of existence, involving so many new and transforming experiences, that in the end the memory of our earthly life is dimmed to the point of extinction.[8]

The objection to be raised here is that personal identity could no longer be preserved if one's most significant earthly memories were to become "dimmed to the point of extinction." To be coherent, ADE needs to allow that people's memories are retained in the afterlife, but then it is confronted by the problem of memories that are exceedingly painful.

On the one hand, it is hard to press the Unrectifiability Objection in an objective way. Advocates of ADE could say that no one can know ahead of time that heavenly bliss cannot possibly rectify certain forms of earthly suffering. One has to actually experience the afterlife before any such judgment could be warranted. On the other hand, those who have suffered so greatly in this life as to be "crushed" by the experience might come to identify themselves with the suffering, making it part of their essence. Such people might justifiably say, "It would have been better, no matter what, if those events had never occurred, and if some future person in heaven should declare otherwise, then that person could not possibly be *me.*" Which side of the dispute is right? I think that this issue can never be resolved. There is a certain ineradicable subjectivity to the Unrectifiability Objection that prevents it from being used as an objective refutation of ADE.

9.13. The Jesus Objection

If a person's future experience in the afterlife leads God to be totally unconcerned about that person's earthly suffering, as claimed in ADE, then God would have been totally unconcerned about the suffering of his son Jesus on the cross. But that is contrary to Christian doctrine. According to Christianity, God was supposed to have been greatly distressed over Jesus' suffering. That distress was part of the great sacrifice involved in the Atonement. It follows that ADE must be an unsound argument.

This "Jesus Objection," as it may be called, is a most formidable one when it is applied against ADE as formulated above. But perhaps the part of ADE which describes God as "totally unconcerned" about human suffering on earth could be dispensed with. Certainly it is incompatible with the outlook of evangelical Christianity. As was pointed out in section 8.2, some parts of Scripture indicate that God is loving and compassionate toward humanity, and evangelical Christianity emphasizes those parts and ignores or tries to explain away whatever contrary verses there may be in the Bible. But then ADE would need to be restructured. Instead of being an attack on AE's premise (A2), it would need to be formulated as an attack on premise (A3), which would require conceiving of God as having conflicting desires. As mentioned previously, none of the advocates of ADE, so far as I know, makes explicit the idea of God's conflicting desires with regard to humanity's earthly suffering. So none of them has any adequate response to the Jesus Objection.

Whatever John Hick's view on the matter may be, the idea that God is totally unconcerned about human suffering is incompatible with the evangelical Christian concept of God as loving and compassionate toward humanity. I should think, then, that evangelical Christians need to somehow develop ADE in a way in which it attacks AE's premise (A3) instead of its premise (A2). But that calls for a theory regarding some divine conflict of desires, that is, a conflict between a desire for situation L on the one hand and an overriding desire for something else on the other hand that somehow involves the afterlife. But what might that overriding desire be? And why exactly is it in conflict with situation L, so that God could not possibly have both desires satisfied? I have never seen all that worked out, nor do I have any idea how it might be done. If God feels bad about our earthly suffering, there seems to be no possible reason within ADE for him to permit it. In the end, I suspect that all advocates of ADE within an evangelical Christian framework must eventually fall back on the Unknown-purpose Defense, which will be taken up in the next chapter.

9.2. The Afterlife Defense Applied to ANB (ADN)

The application of the Afterlife Defense to ANB, which I shall label "ADN," is a little more complicated than ADE. First of all, there is a time reference built into ANB because situation S refers explicitly to the period from the time of Jesus of Nazareth to the present. Since the present keeps changing, the argument's time reference keeps changing. Every time the argument is expressed, it refers to a slightly longer span of time. And new humans keep getting born, thereby continually enlarging the set of humans referred to in situation S. What we have, then, is a temporal series of situations, $S_1, S_2, S_3, \ldots S_n$, where the "situation S" referred to each time the argument is expressed is a new one further along in the series. ANBers concede this point, but insist that it does not affect the truth of any of the premises. It may not be exactly the same situation S from one moment to the next, but the difference is quite minor, and God still wants the new situation S anyway, so premise (A2) remains true.

What ADN claims is that ANB's premise (A2) is false, after all, because God is really not interested in any of the situation S's, but rather, a future situation somewhat like S. It is a situation in which everyone will believe the propositions of the gospel message, but most of the people will have come to believe them in an *afterlife* rather than prior to their physical death, as specified in situation S. Since it is this other situation that God wants, and not situation S, ANB's premise (A2) is false. ADN appeals to the idea of a future society in which God, or his son, reigns as king and in which everyone believes all three propositions of the gospel message (or *knows* them, as an advocate would put it). People who died without having been sufficiently enlightened about the gospel will be resurrected at the time of the future kingdom and given another opportunity "to come to the knowledge of the truth." Or, alternatively, non-Christians who believed in God in their earthly lives, perhaps in response to the "general revelation" of God's handiwork in nature, and who properly sought further information about God (and no other non-Christians), would be given the opportunity for salvation in the afterlife. There are various versions of the doctrine. Because of all this (whichever soteriology is pursued), God does not really want situation S, which relates only to belief prior to physical death, and that makes premise (A2) of ANB false.

Most evangelical Christians do not accept the idea that people who never attained a saving faith in Christ during their earthly life will gain another opportunity for such faith in the afterlife. However, some of them do accept that idea. For example, it is a mainstay of the Jehovah's Witnesses.

9.21. The Scriptural Objection

One objection to ADN's scenario is that it is not supported by Scripture and may even conflict with it regarding the doctrine of salvation. The argument claims that some people will not attain salvation by what they do or believe in *this* life, but rather, by what they do and believe in the *next* life. It is only in the afterlife that they will come to believe in God's son and thereby meet that important requirement for salvation. But the Bible does not say anything about such a possibility, and, in fact, some verses seem to conflict with it. The Bible says, "Now is the day of salvation" (2 Cor. 6:2) and "It is appointed for men to die once, and after that comes judgment" (Heb. 9:27). This seems to require that the criteria for salvation be satisfied in this life and leaves no room for anyone coming to satisfy them *after* having been resurrected into the next life.

It might be claimed that the Bible does leave some room for afterlife conversions in Peter's account of Jesus preaching in the afterlife "to the spirits in prison" (1 Pet. 3:19). However, it seems that no clear interpretation has been given to that passage.[9] In the discussion of it in the *NIV Study Bible*, three different interpretations are suggested, but each of them is shown to contain grave problems. Also in connection with 1 Peter 4:6, the comment is made: "it is necessary to make it clear that the preaching was done not after these people had died, but while they were still alive. [There will be no opportunity for people to be saved after death; see Heb 9:27.]" I take this to be the official doctrine of evangelical Christianity, since the NIV translators were specifically commissioned from the ranks of those who espouse that point of view.[10] Therefore, the idea that the conditions for salvation might be satisfied in the afterlife appears to be excluded from evangelical Christian soteriology.

Also, apart from the Bible, the doctrine that commitment to Christ must occur during one's earthly lifetime has been dominant in the Western church. This is brought out by John Sanders, who says the following:

> The idea is also present in 2 Esdras 9:10 and in other early Christian writings such as 2 Clement 8:3: "for after we have gone out of the world, no further power of confessing or repenting will there belong to us." In Roman Catholic theology and in most Protestant thought, it is assumed that death ends our period of probation and seals our destinies.[11]

Sanders also supplies references to the doctrine in Thomas Aquinas, Jonathan Edwards, several Reformed confessions, and other Christian sources.

There is another incompatibility with Scripture that might be noted. If ADN were correct, then presumably just about everyone would eventually attain salvation. People, aware of having become resurrected, who are at that time enlightened by angels about the truth of the gospel message, would there be given an opportunity to accept Christ and be saved. Such people are not likely to let such an opportunity slip by, which implies that just about all of them would come to attain salvation. Yet, according to the Bible, Jesus said that *very few* people will be saved (Matt. 7:13–14, Luke 13:23–24). So here is still another place where the argument seems to conflict with Scripture. ADN leads to the view that just about everyone will eventually be saved, whereas the Bible explicitly rejects that view.

Still another point of conflict has to do with the Great Commission, as described at the end of both Matthew and Mark. Why should it be important to God to have missionaries go forth to spread the gospel to all nations, beginning at the time of Jesus of Nazareth, if people will receive another chance at such education in the afterlife? Presumably people would learn the truth of the gospel message much more readily than under past or present conditions, for they would presumably be aware that they are in an afterlife, which in itself would make an enormous difference. Why should missionaries struggle to convince them of the gospel message in this life when the same job could be accomplished effortlessly (say, by angels) in the next life? Why should God command missionaries to do something that in the end serves no important purpose?

It might be suggested that God issued the Great Commission because awareness of the truth of the gospel message is beneficial to people even in this earthly life, quite apart from any consideration of salvation in the next. But there are problems with this suggestion. First, not only is it a departure from the theme of ADN, which has to do only with the afterlife, but it is incompatible with it. According to ADN, God has little concern with whether or not situation S is brought about, but the given suggestion provides him with a reason to be concerned about it. Second, it is not clear exactly what the benefit of the awareness is supposed to be. There are billions of non-Christians in the world, many of them not only quite happy, but apparently quite fulfilled, even from a spiritual perspective. What is it, exactly, that they are missing out on? Furthermore, according to one main doctrine, Christians are called upon to suffer and to make sacrifices in this earthly life (some of the sacrifices being quite extreme). What is the benefit of *that*? Why should it attract non-Christians to Christianity? Finally, even if there were some earthly benefit in awareness of the truth of the gospel message, that would just be a good reason for God to step in and help the missionaries. We need to know why he has not done that. They could certainly use some assistance, especially now that Christianity is losing ground worldwide. ADN has no good answer to any of this, and so the argument appears incompatible with the Great Commission as described in the Bible. This objection is particularly severe against evangelical Christianity, which takes the Great Commission to be not only its main guide to understanding God's motivations, but also its *raison d'être*.

Before leaving this section, we should note that there is excellent biblical support for premise (A2) of ANB, as shown in arguments (1)–(7) of section 2.4. ADN has done nothing to undermine that support. For that reason alone, it ought to be rejected, but the above objections to the argument also render it untenable. All of these considerations combine to form what might be called the Scriptural Objection to ADN. It seems that, because of its incompatibility with the Bible, ADN is not an option open to evangelical Christianity as a defense against ANB.

9.22. The Inexplicability Objection

Continuing with the theme suggested above regarding the Great Commission, we can see that there is a mystery of a general sort surrounding ADN. Why should God set up the world in such a way that there is a prior period when people are pretty much left on their own, followed by a kingdom-period in which God or his son reigns? What is the purpose of it all, especially if people can become resurrected from the one period to the other and have the more important portion of their existence, including satisfaction of the criteria for salvation, during the second period? Why even bother with the earlier one? If the earlier period has some significance, then it would seem that people who are in it ought to be able to attain whatever self-fulfillment is possible for them. But that would require coming to be aware of the truth of the gospel message. Those who live their entire earthly lives ignorant of that truth will have missed out on something beneficial. The question is why God would permit that benefit (of knowing the truth) to be withheld from so many people in this earthly life. ADN leaves all that not only unexplained, but inexplicable, and that is still another reason to regard it as unsatisfactory.

According to J. L. Schellenberg, as we have seen previously, since God is supposed to be perfectly loving, he *must* prevent people from missing out on whatever great benefit he might provide for them. The great benefit on which Schellenberg focuses is mere awareness of God's existence. But the proposition that God exists is only part of the gospel message. It seems to me that it is the rest of it, and in particular the proposition that God's son has made salvation in the afterlife possible for all humans, that evangelical Christians would say is the most beneficial to be aware of. Such awareness would provide people with some understanding of the afterlife and the system of salvation that God has devised for the world, and thereby provide them with great joy and a great hope regarding the future. Such understanding, joy, and hope would be of greater benefit to them than would be mere awareness of God's existence. Thus, I think that Schellenberg is on the right track: to be perfectly loving, God must provide people with some awareness of the way things are, since such awareness would be of benefit to them in their earthly life, even if it were not a requirement for salvation. But Schellenberg did not fully develop the knowledge that people should acquire. It contains more than just the proposition that God exists. For maximal earthly benefit, people need to be made aware of the truth of the full gospel message. At least that is how evangelical Christians would view the matter.

But then we come back to our original problem: why has God not done more to bring about situation S (universal awareness of the truth of the gospel message)? ADN provides no answer here, and so it is hopelessly incomplete. We need to leave it and move on in our quest. It seems we are ready to look at the idea (popular among professional philosophers) that God has some purpose for permitting the world to be the way it is, but it is a purpose presently unknown to humanity.

Notes

1. Hick, *Evil and the God of Love*, p. 377.

2. Ibid., p. 399.

3. Marilyn McCord Adams, "Redemptive Suffering: A Christian Solution to the Problem of Evil," in Robert Audi and William J. Wainwright, eds., *Rationality, Religious Belief, and Moral Commitment* (Ithaca, N.Y.: Cornell University Press, 1986), p. 262; reprinted in Peterson, ed., *The Problem of Evil*, p. 183.

4. Ibid., Audi and Wainwright, p. 253; Peterson, p. 173.

5. Ibid., Audi and Wainwright, pp. 264–65; Peterson, pp. 184–85.

6. Isa. 33:14; Matt. 13:40–42, 25:41,46; Mark 9:43–48; Jude 6–7; Rev. 14:10–11.

7. Hick, *Evil and the God of Love*, pp. 377–81.

8. Ibid., pp. 386–87.

9. For an excellent discussion of the given passage and related biblical texts, see John Sanders, *No Other Name: An Investigation into the Destiny of the Unevangelized* (Grand Rapids, Mich.: Eerdmans, 1992), pp. 181–88.

10. *The NIV St Bible: New International Version* (Grand Rapids, Mich.: Zondervan, 1985). Regarding the translators' point of view, see the preface, pp. xi–xiii, and page xv of the introduction.

11. Sanders, *No Other Name*, p. 46.

10

The Unknown-Purpose Defense
Applied to AE (UDE)

We have formulated AE by appeal to the world's vast amount of suffering (understood to include premature death). Defining "God" (or "the God of evangelical Christianity") as, among other things, the omnipotent ruler of the universe who loves humanity maximally, AE declares that if such a deity were to exist, then he would not permit there to be so much suffering. Hence, because there *is* so much of it, God, thus defined, does not exist.

As we have seen, many defenses against this argument have been formulated. One maintains that the possibility of suffering by human beings permits them to have and exercise moral freedom. Another maintains that it permits them to experience a contrast between good and evil and thereby come to appreciate whatever good there may be in their lives. Another identifies the purpose as permitting people to develop such moral virtues as courage and compassion. Another says that suffering permits them to be tested. And still another says the purpose is for people to be properly punished. Let us refer to all such responses to AE as "Known-purpose Defenses." They are all stem from theodicies, for they all attempt to identify some specific higher purpose on the part of God that would not only explain why there is so much suffering but would also fully justify it. (ADE, according to which God does not care about people's earthly suffering because he knows that it will all be taken care of in one way or another in the afterlife, is not included here for the reason that it does not put forward any purpose for the suffering but merely belittles it. It is unclear whether ADE should be taken to be part of a "theodicy.")

We have put forward objections against the various Known-purpose Defenses. The main one is that there occur forms of suffering which they cannot adequately explain and justify. An example would be the suffering of children, as from cancer. It is hard to locate any benefit that might justify such events. Sometimes parents and others associated with the children do come to exercise free will and exhibit courage, compassion, and so on, but not always. And even if they do, such results are totally insufficient as an end to justify the large amount of suffering. Another example is the Holocaust. To try to explain why God did not prevent it by pointing out specific benefits that came about because of it seems to be an exercise in futility. Whatever benefits there may have been were insufficient to justify the enormous suffering that took place. The Known-purpose Defenses stand refuted by their inability to deal with certain actual instances of suffering that might be brought up.

10.1. UDE Formulated

This brings us to a defense that can't be refuted in such a way, the Unknown-purpose Defense as applied to the Argument from Evil, or UDE for short. It is suggested by the biblical passage in which God says, "For as the heavens are higher than the earth, so are my ways higher than your ways, and my thoughts than your thoughts" (Isa. 55:9) and by St. Paul's "How unsearchable his judgments, and his paths beyond tracing out" (Rom. 11:33). Other passages also reflect that theme.[1] Since God is so much "higher" than humans, it seems possible that he should have a purpose for earthly suffering which humans have not as yet been able to figure out, despite all their efforts to do so. It may be that the purpose does not make use of the suffering directly, but rather is directed at some other situation of which the suffering is a necessary byproduct. Let us use the expression "purpose for the suffering" in a broad enough sense to include this case. UDE maintains that for every instance of suffering that occurs on earth, God has some purpose for it (in the broad sense), but in many cases (perhaps most) we do not know what that purpose is or even what it might be. Nevertheless, it is a purpose that not only adequately explains why God permits the suffering but which also morally justifies him permitting it. If at some future time (perhaps in the afterlife) we come to know what the purpose is, then we will come to understand why God did what he did and will see that the purpose is indeed an end that morally justifies the means (i.e., either the suffering or something else that required the suffering) without which the end could not have been attained.

The question might again be raised, seeing that God is omnipotent, why he could not have attained his (unknown) purpose and also prevent the given instance of suffering. That is, why should an omnipotent being need to resort to any means at all to accomplish his ends? The answer (as has been stated previously in this book) is that omnipotence must at least be restricted by considerations of logic. The (unknown) purpose is so related to the amount of the suffering which is used as a means to attain it (or required by the means) that it would have been logically impossible for God, given his essential properties, to attain the purpose in any way that involved less suffering. To put the matter in terms of AE's premise (A3), God has some (unknown) overriding purpose which not only conflicts with his desire to bring about situation L (the reduction of suffering), but which conflicts with it in a logical way, so that it would actually be inconsistent or self-contradictory for him, given his essential nature, both to fulfill the purpose and bring about situation L. God could no more do that than he could "have his cake and eat it too," which is impossible even for an omnipotent being.

The basic idea behind the Unknown-purpose Defense as applied to AE is appealed to by many writers on the topic. We have already seen (in chapter 9) how John Hick appeals to it (along with FDE, the Moral-virtues Defense, and ADE). Most of these who appeal to it do so without any explicit reference or label. For example, Alvin Plantinga says the following:

> Why does God permit all this evil, and evil of these horrifying kinds, in his world? . . . The Christian must concede that he doesn't know. That is, he doesn't know in any detail. On a quite general level, he may know that God permits evil because he can achieve a world he sees as better by permitting evil than by preventing it; and what God sees as better is, of course, better. But we cannot see *why* our world, with all its ills, would be better than others we think we can imagine, or *what* in any detail, is God's reason for permitting a given and specific and appalling evil.[2]

As pointed out in section 4.42, above, Plantinga denies that there is any evidence against the Devil Defense. Nevertheless, he apparently sees some deficiency in that defense, for it does not square with the idea that God aims to permit all humans to live worthwhile lives. The Devil Defense implies that God often sides with Satan in Satan's battle with humanity by letting him have his way, even to the extent of causing people to die (unlike the case with Job, whom Satan was not permitted to kill). As previously mentioned, there is no scriptural support for the Devil Defense, and so one might as well replace it, together with the whole Free-will Defense, by the more general Unknown-purpose Defense (UDE). Instead of saying, "No one knows why God places so much store on the free will of Satan that he permits Satan to cause as much evil as he does" or simply, "No one knows why God permits Satan to cause so much evil," one could as well say, "No one knows why God permits so much evil," which is, in effect, what Plantinga says in the quotation above. So, why bring in any appeal to free will or Satan at all? There is no scriptural support for any of that. One could as well simply advocate UDE from the outset.

Another writer who goes along with Plantinga on the given point is Marilyn McCord Adams:

> As Plantinga points out, where horrendous evils are concerned, not only do we not know God's *actual* reason for permitting them; we cannot even *conceive* of any plausible candidate sort of reason consistent with worthwhile lives for human participants in them. . . . Finally, there are reasons that we are cognitively, emotionally, and/or spiritually too immature to fathom (the way a two-year-old child is incapable of understanding its mother's reasons for permitting the surgery). I agree with Plantinga that our ignorance of divine reasons for permitting horrendous evils is . . . of [that] type. (Original italics)[3]

I gather that both Plantinga and Adams advocate UDE, though not by that (or any similar) name. We may call them "UDEers." Another writer whom I would put in that category is Bruce R. Reichenbach. He says the following:

> What the atheologian must do . . . is show *both* that the theodicies and defenses . . . are not sound *and* that . . . God would not have other good reasons for not eliminating more evil than he does. . . . If the atheologian is to conceive of a better world, what he must do, first, is develop other possible world systems . . . [which] would result in less evil than the present world-system. This project . . . seems quite impossible. . . . To do this would necessitate knowing all the implications of both natural systems, a task suited only for an omniscient mind. (Original italics)[4]

Reichenbach here alludes to God's good reasons for permitting evil. If he were actually to state what the various reasons might be, then we could place his treatment of the problem of evil into the category of "Known-purpose Defenses." He himself apparently regards it as being in that category, since in his preface he says, "We will present a theodicy for evil, attempting to show that a morally sufficient reason can be given for the evil present in our world."[5] But he never does state what "God's good reasons" might be. It seems natural, then, to construe those allusions as appeals to *unknown* divine purposes, which makes Reichenbach just another "UDEer," like Plantinga and Adams.

I think that anyone who avoids advocating any particular theodicy but instead simply leaves the issue with the pronouncement that the atheologian has not proven his case (and cannot do so since it would require being omniscient) is making an implicit reference to UDE. That would apply to Reichenbach, above, and also to David Basinger, who says the following:

> The atheologian has yet to demonstrate that God could create a significantly modified natural system which, when considered in terms of the entire world system of which it would be a part, would produce signifi-

cantly less natural evil and yet preserve the integrity of human freedom
and retain as much good as we have in our present world.[6]

The problem comes in with Basinger's requirements for the atheologian's
"demonstration." Consider the following "world-system":

> a world just like ours except that all humans are born with a genetic
> immunity to all forms of cancer, which they gradually begin to lose after
> the age of seventy.

This description seems to meet Basinger's requirements. It is a "significantly
modified" system which produces "significantly less natural evil," since
millions of young and middle-aged people would not suffer horribly and die
prematurely from the ravages of cancer. It would not only "preserve the
integrity" of human freedom but, as mentioned previously, would even
increase it, since millions of people would make free-will decisions that they
would not otherwise have made (having died prematurely or become
extremely incapacitated from cancer). It would seem to me to retain at least
as much good as we have in our present world. Perhaps it is there that
Basinger would say: "You have not demonstrated that. Maybe there are
things going on with regard to cancer that we don't know about, things which
make cancer a kind of 'blessing in disguise.' In that case God could have
good reason for permitting cancer to strike people of all ages." It seems evident that what this would boil down to is an appeal to unknown divine purposes. So, on that basis, I would put Basinger into the category of "UDEer."
Anyone should be classified that way who leaves the problem of evil, not
with actually stating what God's good purpose for evil might be, but with the
atheologian's alleged "failure to demonstrate" that God lacks any such purpose. Three other philosophers who attack some version of AE by an appeal
to some version of UDE, and who therefore could also be classified as
"UDEers," are William Alston, Peter van Inwagen, and Daniel Howard-
Snyder.[7] I find that it has become exceedingly difficult to find philosophers
who attack AE in the recent literature on any basis other than UDE.

    If a theodicy is an explanation of why God permits suffering, then UDE
does not purport to be a theodicy or part of a theodicy. It only informs us that
there is or may be some explanation for the suffering without in any way sup-
plying that explanation. However, although not (part of) a theodicy, UDE is
nevertheless an attempted *defense* of God's existence against AE, for it is
actually nothing more than a bare denial of AE's premise (A3). It is in effect
stating that AE is unsound because its premise (A3) is just flat-out false. So
what it amounts to is, in effect, the statement that there is (in the abstract)
an adequate theodicy but we just haven't found it yet. Let us consider
whether or not UDE should be regarded as a successful defense against AE.

10.2. The Burden-of-proof Objection

One objection to UDE that might be raised is that it has a burden of proof which it fails to fulfill. There is a methodological principle to the effect that anyone who claims the existence of something has a burden of proof to show that it exists. If I claim that there exist leprechauns, then my claim is worthless if I cannot at all support it. I could, of course, point out that no one has ever proven the nonexistence of leprechauns, but that would be merely an appeal to ignorance. Apart from special cases (such as square circles), it is not possible to prove nonexistence. No one has ever demonstrated the nonexistence of leprechauns, satyrs, dragons, unicorns, or mermaids, yet that is simply due to the logical structure of the proposition in question and is no reason whatever to think that such things exist. Except in special cases, unrestricted negative existential statements are not provable. One cannot be everywhere in the universe simultaneously to perceive that nowhere are there any members of the given class. For that reason, wherever one group of people claims an unrestricted existential statement to be true and another group claims it is false, it is the group that claims it is true which has the burden of proof. If they fail to support their claim, then it is the opposing group that has the more reasonable position. That is why we regard it as more reasonable to *deny* the existence of unicorns and leprechauns, etc., than to affirm their existence.

In the case of UDE, an existence claim is being made: that there exists an explanation for why God permits in the world as much suffering as there actually is, an explanation that morally justifies such a great quantity. In opposition, AEers (i.e., advocates of AE) are making a negative existential statement: that no such explanation exists. According to the above methodological principle regarding existence claims, it is the UDEers who have the burden of proof. However, they have not fulfilled that burden, for they have not produced any reason to think that the sort of explanation they claim to exist actually does exist. UDE is therefore seen to be an unreasonable response to AE. This may be called the "Burden-of-proof Objection" to UDE.

Against this objection, three different replies might be made, which I shall refer to as the "Argument from the Bible," the "Possibilist Reply," and the "Standoff Reply." Let us look at each of them. The Argument from the Bible is that the Bible contains features which show beyond a reasonable doubt that it is the "word of God" and that therefore the God of evangelical Christianity really does exist. Hence, since he is a perfectly loving deity, he *must* have some purpose for permitting so much suffering in the world. This would satisfy the burden of proof called for and thereby refute the Burden-of-proof Objection in a strong way. Let us postpone (to appendix D) a scrutiny and critique of the Argument from the Bible. It will be shown to be a complete failure. Note that in this context a mere proof of the existence of God in general would not be relevant. Only an argument for the existence of the God of evangelical Christianity would suffice, because AE, UDE, and the Burden-of-proof Objection are here being considered only in relation to that particular deity.

Let us turn, then, to the second reply to the given objection, the "Possiblist Reply." We need to distinguish two different versions of UDE, which may be called the actualist version and the possibilist version. Both affirm God's existence. But it is only the actualist version which declares that *there actually exists* a purpose on God's part which explains and justifies all the suffering in the world. The possibilist version claims not that God definitely has such a purpose, but only that it is *possible* that he does, in which case AE's premise (A3) is merely *possibly* false. It thereby aims to show only that AE fails as a conclusive proof of God's nonexistence because it does not establish a necessary connection between God's existence and the prevention of suffering. That is, AE fails to show that if God exists then he could not possibly be satisfied with the world as it presently is but must instead have been inclined to do things to prevent or reduce the suffering. AE needs to establish that there cannot possibly be any purpose on God's part that would fully explain and justify all the suffering in the world (in effect, that there cannot be any adequate theodicy), but it has failed to do that. Thus, whereas the actualist version of UDE is, in effect, claiming that there actually exists an adequate theodicy but we just haven't found it yet, the possibilist version is merely claiming that possibly there is such a theodicy. The Possibilist Reply to the Burden-of-proof Objection, then, is that the objection does not apply to the possibilist version of UDE, which does not make any existential claim, only a possibility claim. Thus, if it is the possibilist version that is being advocated, then the given objection is irrelevant.

The possibilist version of UDE has some merit and I agree that the Burden-of-proof Objection is irrelevant to it. Among other things, it shows that AE is not a conclusive proof of God's nonexistence. In order for AE to be conclusive, all of its premises would need to be indubitable. But its premise (A3) is obviously *not* indubitable, and so AE is not a conclusive proof. Those atheologians, such as J. L. Mackie, who maintained a contradiction between God and evil, were in effect claiming that AE is conclusive. But when their proof is fully formulated so as to be deductively valid, somewhere within it there would need to be something like premise (A3), and at *that* point the conclusiveness crumbles. (It is not necessary to go into an extended "Free-will Defense," as Alvin Plantinga does, to establish this result. A mere scrutiny of premise (A3), or its analogue, reveals its nonindubitability, and the nonconclusiveness of the proof or argument along with it.)

Despite the merits of the possibilist version of UDE, I do not think that it is useful within the present context of discussion. It may indeed show that

AE is not a conclusive proof of God's nonexistence, but AE was not intended to be that in the first place. Whether framed in a deductive or in an inductive way, AE purports merely to show that there is good reason to deny God's existence. It claims its premises to be true, but not indubitable. Premise (A3) in particular is put forward in AE as a proposition which may be true and which therefore challenges the evangelical Christian to come up with a counterexample. Merely to state that (A3) is possibly false, as the possibilist version of UDE does, is not to attack AE, for AEers concede the point. The issue between UDE and AE is that of which outlook, evangelical Christianity or its denial, is the more reasonable one to accept, given the evidence available. So for UDE merely to claim that AE is *possibly* unsound is too weak a claim and does not win the battle as we have here characterized it. An argument can be possibly unsound and yet be a strong inductive or evidential argument. The possibilist version of UDE is a point that might be raised by someone neutral on the issue of whether or not the God of evangelical Christianity exists, but it is not an adequate defense of that God against AE by an evangelical Christian.

Another way to view the matter is in terms of the *problem* of evil. If the problem is that of explaining why God permits so much suffering in the world, then the actualist version of UDE claims, in effect, that there definitely is some solution but we do not at present know what it is. On the other hand, the possibilist version is merely claiming that there *may* be a solution, not that there actually is one. That is obviously too weak a claim. The problem of evil must be confronted by all those for whom it is a serious problem. People cannot reasonably continue to believe a proposition in the face of a putative refutation of it if all they can say in response is that *possibly* the refutation fails. For them to continue to believe the proposition requires that they actually deny the refutation. The refutation plays the same role here as the negation of the proposition. If you affirm P, then you cannot merely say of not-P that it is possibly false. Rather, in order to reasonably continue to affirm P, you must say of not-P that it is definitely false. And in the same way, you must definitely reject any putative refutation of P. Although the attack on AE by the possibilist version of UDE is an argument that could be put forward by someone who is neutral on the issue whether there is any solution at all to the problem of evil or whether the God of evangelical Christianity can be cogently argued not to exist, it is not sufficient on the part of evangelical Christians as a defense of their God's existence. For that reason, the Possibilist Reply is inadequate as a response to the Burden-of-proof Objection. In what follows, I shall disregard the possibilist version of UDE and take the actualist version of it to be the only viable one within the present context.

It might be claimed that the actualist version of UDE is also too weak. It is a mere defense and not a theodicy. It fails to explain why there is so much evil and is therefore not a "genuine answer" to the problem. Madden and Hare say of the theist: "if he does not have a genuine answer to the problem of evil he has no right to say that he *knows* that God exists."[8] I think that this is going too far. If there were excellent evidence that God exists, proving it to be a fact, then theists could reasonably claim to know the fact even though the existence of evil would present a kind of anomaly for them. For example, God could announce from the sky, "I have a purpose for all the suffering, but it is beyond your comprehension." The theists would still have no "genuine answer" to the problem of evil, yet they could justifiably claim to know that God exists.

Another opponent of (what I take to be the actualist version of) UDE is Roland Puccetti, who says the following:

> Suppose someone who knew Adolf Eichmann well and wants to defend him says this: "I agree that Eichmann did all the things you cite. . . . But I am confident he has—indeed he must have had—a morally sufficient reason for acting the way he did." . . . It is not part of our decision-making process in such cases to ask if it is *logically* possible someone had a morally sufficient reason for what he did, or failed to do. We ask only if it is *practically* possible, that is, whether any reason has been put forward plausible enough to warrant an acquittal or suspension of judgment. When that is not forthcoming we regard the matter as closed. (Original italics)[9]

Since the actualist version of UDE does not supply any morally sufficient reason for God to permit so much evil, according to Puccetti, UDE fails to show that it is "practically possible" that he should have one, even though it may be logically possible. So God should no more be "acquitted" on the basis of UDE than should Adolf Eichmann. I think that Puccetti is in effect putting forward the Burden-of-proof Objection and rejecting UDE on the grounds that by failing to produce a divine purpose for permitting so much evil UDE fails to meet its burden of proof. His conclusion, I gather, is that nontheism is the reasonable position to take on the matter.

Again this is too extreme. If there were excellent evidence for God's existence, then it would be quite reasonable for theists to proclaim that fact, despite the anomaly of evil. The actualist version of UDE would be a quite adequate response to the problem of evil. Of course, Puccetti would deny that there is any good evidence for God's existence, especially in the case of the God of evangelical Christianity. I agree with him on that point. Suppose we are right. Would there *then* be any way to defend UDE against the Burden-of-proof Objection? I think there is and will try to show that.

There is a third response to the Burden-of-proof Objection that I call the "Standoff Reply." It appeals to a kind of "Mexican standoff" between the two sides. UDEers may grant the sort of methodological principle mentioned: anyone who affirms the existence of something has a burden of proof. They may even grant that their appeal to the existence of an unknown purpose is subject to that principle and that by failing to come up with any actual candidate for the purpose they have failed to satisfy the principle. However, they could in a way try to sidestep the issue by pointing out that there is another methodological principle relevant here, namely, that anyone who claims to show or establish anything at all has a burden of proof. AEers are indeed claiming to establish God's nonexistence even if they deny that their argument is intended to be conclusive. Hence, if there is a controversial step in their argument, then they have the burden of showing that it is indeed true. If they do not fulfill the given burden, the argument can be reasonably rejected.

The particularly doubtful step in AE is of course premise (A3), which claims, in effect, that there is no adequate theodicy, that is, no purpose or end on God's part that would explain and morally justify his permitting all the suffering that occurs in our world. So long as there is any doubt about the truth of that step, AEers have the burden of establishing it. And if they fail to do so, then they cannot claim that the argument is successful as a proof or that it has successfully established its conclusion. Thus, AEers also fail a burden-of-proof test and so cannot claim that their position is any more reasonable than that of UDEers. There is a kind of "Mexican standoff" between the two sides regarding the burden of proof. Neither side has *refuted* the other, for neither side has shown any premise or inference in the other's argument to be false or incorrect. All that has been shown is that neither side has actually proven or established anything, for neither side has satisfactorily discharged the burden of proof that has been imposed upon it by one methodological principle or the other.

My own view is that, given the status of the discussion up to the present point, the Standoff Reply is successful and that, therefore, the Burden-of-proof Objection has thus far failed to refute UDE. We saw in section 2.2 that some scriptural support could be given for AE's premise (A2). However, there was none given for premise (A3), even of an indirect sort. So, in that respect, AE's (A3) is in the same category as the existence claim within UDE. Both call for some sort of support, and yet none is forthcoming for either of them. Both arguments, UDE and AE, have thus far failed the "burden-of-proof" requirement placed upon it by proper methodology. For that reason, it cannot be said that UDE is at present in an unfavorable situation vis-à-vis the burden of proof, which makes the Burden-of-proof Objection thus far a failure. However, it may be that additional considerations introduced into the discussion will tip the battle towards AE and thereby end the Mexican standoff. Let us see about that.

10.3. A Further Property of God

In the context of AE as applied to the God of evangelical Christianity, God has been defined as the omnipotent ruler of the universe who loves humanity maximally and who feels compassion for human beings with respect to their earthly suffering. (Scriptural support for those divine attributes was discussed previously, in sections 2.2 and 8.2.) But I think some further property can justifiably be introduced into the definition. God can be said to have, by definition, the further property of strongly desiring a personal relationship with humans, and, in particular, desiring that they reciprocate his great love for them. Some such property is assigned to God by various religions, with Christianity, and especially evangelical Christianity, being the most prominent. It should be noted that humanity is commanded to love God maximally in both the Old Testament (Deut. 6:5) and the New Testament and that the commandment in question is called the "greatest" one (Matt. 22:37-38; Mark 12:29-30 NIV). The idea here is that God most desires worship from humans and it is worship which proceeds from maximal love, or at least great love, that would be the best kind. We may find resources for such great love because it could be based upon God's love for us (1 John 4:19).

In any case, to redefine "God" as possessing the further property of desiring great love from humans would certainly be relevant to UDE, for, presumably, if God has that property, then he would not want to keep his purposes secret from humanity, at least not those that have a significant effect on humanity's relationship to him. If God wants people to love him greatly and he has some purpose for permitting all the suffering that occurs in the world, then it would behoove him to reveal that purpose to humankind. Too much secrecy is clearly an obstacle between God and humanity. It undercuts the relationship between them that is the main theme of evangelical Christianity. Some find Christianity preferable to both Judaism and Islam because it depicts God as less remote from humanity and more concerned with its problems. But UDE makes God remote again, which counts against it from a religious perspective. For this reason Christians should appeal to the "unknown-purpose" idea only as a last resort.

It is very hard for people to love greatly a ruler who permits them (and others) to suffer, especially when so-called "horrendous evils" are taken into consideration. But if God were to somehow transmit to people an explanation of how so much earthly suffering is logically required for some higher end, an end which fully explains and justifies it, even for "horrendous evils," then that obstacle to people's love would be removed. In contrast, it makes God into an irrational being when UDEers declare that although God wants people to love him greatly, he nevertheless places an obstacle between people and himself that thwarts such love, namely, all the secrecy surrounding his purpose for permitting so much suffering. It might be suggested that it is not so much a matter of secrecy but rather our inability to comprehend the purposes of an omniscient mind. But even if that were so, God should have at least placed into Scripture a clear statement to the effect that he has *some* purpose for permitting humanity's earthly suffering which would fully justify it although it is one that humans are unable to comprehend. Such a statement by itself would have gone far toward removing the obstacle to people's love mentioned above. But there is no such statement in Scripture, and so it *is* proper to refer to God's "secrecy" on this matter. If the definition of "God" used in AE were to include the given further property (desiring humanity's great love) as a divine attribute, then that would greatly strengthen it as an argument for the nonexistence of God, defined in that new way.

One UDEer who claims to see nothing in the Bible to support AE is Terry Christlieb.[10] He instead finds the Bible to imply UDE. But Christlieb has not looked in the right places. He should look at those biblical passages which show the "further property" mentioned above: that God desires a certain response from people, in particular that they love him greatly. Given that further divine attribute, it seems highly unlikely that God would both permit people to suffer as much as they do and keep secret from them his purpose for doing that (even the very fact that he has such a purpose). Thus, the basic premise of UDE is rendered highly unlikely by the Bible, which then indirectly supports AE.

Another reason for God to reveal to humanity his purpose for permitting so much suffering (or at least that he definitely has some such purpose) would be to refute AE itself, and thereby eradicate whatever nonbelief may be based on it. There are many nonbelievers in the world who would believe in God were it not for AE. Bruce Reichenbach expresses the point as follows:

> The apparent randomness and unjustified calamity of natural evils, their prevalence and intensity, can turn people away from God. "How can a good God allow a child to suffer from spina bifida or leukemia, or thousands to suffer homelessness and starvation from floods and earthquakes?" they query, with diminishing faith.[11]

Of course, God could readily cure such people of their nonbelief by appearing to them in a suitable manner. But even apart from that, if God were merely to reveal to *some* people his purpose for so much suffering (or at least the fact of its existence, together with the information that it is beyond human comprehension), allowing *them* to spread the news to others, especially nonbelievers (perhaps via the Internet), then that in itself would help refute AE and eliminate the nonbelief that is based on it. A god who desires humanity's great love should certainly do such a thing, for it would be the rational thing to do, given his desire.

UDEers need to explain why God has not revealed to us his purpose for permitting so much suffering (or the fact of such a purpose's existence), especially if he desires our great love. In order to do that, they must appeal to a *second* purpose on God's part, namely, his purpose for all the secrecy. But that second purpose is also an *unknown* one. That is, God keeps secret from us, not only his purpose for all the suffering, but also his purpose for all the secrecy itself, which also seems irrational. If God is rational, then even if he has some reason for keeping secret from us his purpose for all the suffering, he should at least inform us of that reason. To do so would allow us some minimal basis for understanding his motivations and thereby allow us to begin to develop the sort of relationship with him that he, by definition, desires.

It should be noted that God's second unknown purpose, his purpose for all the secrecy, would need to be a self-referential one. It would need to include not only secrecy surrounding his first unknown purpose, but also secrecy surrounding the second unknown purpose itself. That would be the only way to avoid an infinite regress of unknown purposes on God's part: (1) his purpose for permitting so much suffering, (2) his purpose for secrecy about the first purpose, (3) his purpose for secrecy about the second purpose, and so on. By speaking of "his purpose for *all* the secrecy," advocates of UDE could include that self-referential aspect, which would avoid such an infinite regress of unknown purposes.

UDEers might say that God has some reason not only for permitting all the suffering in the world and for all the secrecy surrounding his purpose for the suffering, but also for all the secrecy surrounding the secrecy. That is, for some reason beyond human comprehension, God does not reveal to people why he keeps all this secret from them. Well, even if that were so, God should at least inform people that there is such a reason. The fact that they have not been so informed imposes still another obstacle to their love of God.

The objection to UDE that is being developed here is that it makes God appear utterly irrational. If he has the additional property in question which at least evangelical Christianity ascribes to him, then he wants people to love him greatly (and has even commanded them to do so, calling this his "greatest" commandment). And yet he thwarts such love by withholding something quite essential to it: an understanding of his motivations toward people, both his motivation for permitting so much suffering in the world and his motivation about all the secrecy itself. He even withholds the information that he has the relevant motivations. UDEers could of course make their position more reasonable by *not* including the given further property (God's desire for people's great love) among the divine attributes. But if they are evangelical Christians, then they are inclined to include it, despite the fact that it weakens their argument.

In effect, UDE is not an outlook well suited to evangelical Christianity. UDEers need to be people who regard God as hidden, mysterious, and remote. But evangelical Christians are not like that. They hold up the Bible and proclaim: Look, God is not hidden, but has revealed himself here in this book. God is not mysterious, for the book allows us to understand him. And God is not remote, but is here among us, interacting with us, desiring a close personal relationship with us and desiring from us our love and worship. When Christian philosophers appeal to UDE, they need to realize that such a maneuver undermines whatever "evangelicalness" they may have had within them.

10.4. The Ignorance Objection

There is an old version of AE which attempts to sidestep UDE. It has been called "the Noseeum Argument."[12] I prefer the title "Nondiscovery Argument." Here is a formulation of it:

(1)   If God were to exist, then he would have some purpose for permitting so much suffering in the world.
(2)   For centuries the brightest people have sought such a purpose.
(3)   So, probably, if there were any such purpose, it would have been discovered by now.   [from (2)]
(4)   But the purpose in question has not been discovered.
(5)   Thus, probably there is no such purpose.   [from (3) & (4)]
(6)   Hence, probably God does not exist.   [from (1) & (5)]

This version of AE is one of those described by Bruce Russell and mentioned above in section 1.4. It is the kind which proceeds (by inductive reasoning or a sampling methodology) from a statement of our inability to justify the amount of suffering in the world to the proposition that much of it is *pointless* (i.e., cannot be justified). Daniel Howard-Snyder calls it an inference from "inscrutable evil" to "pointless evil."[13]

The place where UDEers would attack the above argument would be the inference from (2) to (3). They would claim that God's purposes are beyond human comprehension. Even the brightest people are all like infants compared to God, so we could not expect them to discover God's purposes. This is in effect a defense of UDE against the Nondiscovery Argument. It is expressed by Stephen J. Wykstra as follows:

> The observed sufferings in the world do require us to say that there are outweighing goods connected to them that are entirely outside our ken.

... [I]f we think carefully about the sort of being theism proposes for our belief, it is entirely expectable—given what we know of our cognitive limits—that the goods by virtue of which this Being allows known suffering should very often be beyond our ken.[14]

I think that Wykstra is right about humanity's cognitive limits. If God exists, then no doubt his purposes would very often be beyond our ken. Such an argument would refute Madden and Hare's tennis analogy, which they formulated as follows:

Consider the case of a determined and ingenious tennis player who consistently loses key matches. He tries strategy after strategy and notices that with some strategies he loses less badly than with others. He is convinced that there is a strategy he has not yet tried which will lead to victory. . . . While it is always logically possible that he may devise a new winning approach, in view of the available evidence such an outcome does not seem likely.[15]

Madden and Hare use this example to try to refute UDE, construed as the claim that there must be some adequate theodicy even if we have not as yet discovered it. Wykstra would no doubt reject the analogy on the grounds that tennis strategies are not beyond human comprehension, whereas an adequate theodicy probably is (since it would need to refer to divine purposes which are probably beyond human comprehension). I would agree with Wykstra that the tennis analogy is weak.

On the other hand, two points should be made here. First, even if some divine purpose may presently be beyond human comprehension, it should be possible for an omnipotent deity to give people enough of a "brain boost" or else use his infinite power of explanation (or both) to get them to comprehend the given purpose. UDEers need to postulate still another unknown divine purpose to explain why God does not do that, which further weakens their theory. The second point is that we need to "call 'em as we see 'em." If humanity has tried as hard as it can to discover something, but without success, then it *does* seem reasonable to hypothesize (for the time being at least, until new evidence comes in) that the thing probably does not exist.

Consider an analogy. Suppose Mr. X were to believe that there is a worldwide conspiracy against him. He thinks that people all over the world are plotting against him, as their main occupation in life. Mr. X's psychiatrist points out to him that they are not in fact exhibiting such "plotting" behavior. They do not gesture or glance at Mr. X when he is in their vicinity or try to follow him. Suppose Mr. X concedes that point, but counters with the claim that people are sly and crafty. Although they are plotting against him, they are smart enough to conceal that fact. Then the absence of "plotting" behavior would not be evidence against the plotting. The claim that people are sly and crafty makes Mr. X's conspiracy hypothesis unfalsifiable, for Mr. X could always say, "They effectively conceal their plotting." In a similar way, Wykstra's hypothesis that God's purposes are beyond our ken makes his theism unfalsifiable. No matter how much suffering we point out, Wykstra could always say, "God still loves humanity but has his reasons (which are beyond our ken) for behaving in an apparently nonloving way." In the absence of positive evidence for God's existence, it is hard to find any basis for regarding Wykstra's theism as more reasonable than Mr. X's conspiracy hypothesis.

The "Mysterious God" idea is very much like the malicious demon to which epistemological skeptics appeal. That there is some unknown outweighing good to justify all the horrendous suffering in the world is like the idea that reality is not at all the way it appears to us (e.g., maybe we are all just brains in a vat and have been duped by a powerful demon into believing otherwise), and our cognitive faculties are just too limited to reveal that great truth to us. Bruce Russell argues that UDE is like the skeptical hypothesis that God created the universe just one hundred years ago and, for reasons beyond our ken, has deceived us into thinking that it is much older.[16] But he goes on to refute the given hypothesis by pointing out that the alternate naturalistic hypothesis that the universe is much older is a *simpler* one and is therefore more reasonable to accept. Such a refutation would also apply to Mr. X's conspiracy hypothesis mentioned above. And it should also be relevant to the Mysterious God idea, which is very much like a skeptical hypothesis. For that reason alone, I am not totally convinced by Wykstra's defense of UDE.

Still another objection to Wykstra's argument is raised by Evan Fales, who points out that it seems to prove too much, for it leads to a kind of moral skepticism. If the ethical situation that we are contemplating may be "beyond our ken" when we are working on the problem of evil, then that could be the case no matter what problem we are working on, which entails that we could never trust any of our moral judgments. Fales says the following:

> In matters of morals, we seek to know what the *total good and evil* associated with contemplated states of affairs are. . . . But if our knowledge of the moral value of these states of affairs is as radically defective as the theist has to claim—states of affairs which are not only common but often within our power to produce or prevent—then we have indeed lost our grip upon the possibility of using moral judgments as a guide to action and evaluation. (Original italics)[17]

I think this objection is well taken, but I shall not pursue it in the present book, since my framework for AE and UDE is one in which I seek to avoid the language of morals (as explained in section 1.3). There are other frameworks for the problem of evil, and Fales's attack on Wykstra's version of UDE, viewed in one of them, would be indeed severe.

For the reasons given, I have strong misgivings about Wykstra's line of thought. However, even if we were to grant that Wykstra has refuted the version of the Nondiscovery Argument formulated above, the considerations raised in section 10.3 permit a revised version of the argument to which his reasoning would be less applicable. To keep matters straight, let us give the revised version a new name: call it the "Ignorance Argument" (not to be confused, of course, with *Argumentum ad Ignorantiam*, which is something else entirely). It may be formulated as follows:

(1) If God (that is, the God of evangelical Christianity) were to exist, then he would want people to love him maximally.

(2) Humanity's failure to understand God's purpose for the great amount of suffering in the world is an obstacle to such love.

(3) The absence of a clear statement within Scripture that God definitely has such a purpose (though the purpose may be beyond human comprehension) is still another obstacle.

(4) Humanity's failure to understand the reason behind all the secrecy about the purpose in question is still another obstacle.

(5) The absence of a clear statement within Scripture that God definitely has the reason mentioned in (4), above (even though the reason may be beyond human comprehension), is still another obstacle.

(6) God could have removed the obstacles mentioned in (2) & (4) [say, by means of a "brain boost" or through the art of perfect explanation] and he could have removed the obstacles mentioned in (3) & (5) [simply through Scripture].

(7) Hence, probably, if God were to exist, then he would have removed at least one of the four obstacles mentioned in (2)–(5), above. [from (1) & (6)]

(8) But none of the obstacles has been removed. That is, humanity is still ignorant regarding all the divine purposes and reasons mentioned.

(9) Therefore, probably God does not exist.   [from (7) & (8)]

As formulated here, the Ignorance Argument is a version of the Nondiscovery Argument, for in its premise (8) it in effect appeals to the fact of humanity's failure to discover the relevant purposes (a fact conceded by UDEers). But the use made of that fact is different from that of the old version of the argument. The appeal is not to humanity's cognitive abilities but to God's desires (as may be gathered from Scripture), in particular, his inferred desire that humanity *not* be ignorant regarding those purposes of his that directly relate to his relationship with humanity. So Wykstra's belittling of humanity's cognitive abilities is no longer relevant.

As formulated above, the Ignorance Argument (like the Nondiscovery Argument) is another argument for God's nonexistence, on a par with AE. But in what follows I shall want to take it simply as an objection to UDE, i.e., framed as an attack on the idea that God has some (unknown) purpose for permitting all the suffering that occurs in our world. Here is a possible formulation of such an argument:

(1) If God were to exist, then he would want people to love him greatly and would probably remove whatever obstacles there might be to such love that are not of human origin.

(2) If God were to exist and were to have a purpose for permitting all the suffering that occurs in our world, then for him to have revealed it, or at least revealed that there is such a purpose, or at least revealed something about a need for secrecy regarding these matters, would have helped to remove an obstacle to the love mentioned in (1) that was not of human origin.

(3) Therefore, if God were to exist and have such a purpose, then he probably would have revealed one of the matters mentioned in (2).
[from (1) & (2)]

(4) But none of those matters has been revealed.

(5) Hence, if God were to exist, then he probably would not have a purpose for permitting all the suffering that occurs in our world.
[from (3) & (4)]

(6) It follows that (the actualist version of) UDE is probably unsound.

In order to distinguish this version of the argument from the one which aims at establishing God's nonexistence, let us call it the "Ignorance Objection." It is simply an objection to UDE and nothing more. I find it to be very forceful. Of course, the "unknown purpose" idea could still be raised against its premise (1), but with little plausibility.

A reply to Wykstra was made by William L. Rowe,[18] though its thrust is totally opposite that of my reply (the Ignorance Objection). My reply is that even if Wykstra's defense of UDE were to work for God in general, it would not work for a more specific concept of deity such as the God of evangelical Christianity. In contrast, Rowe conceded that Wykstra's defense may work for a more specific concept of deity, but not for God in general. He describes one such specific concept of deity as a god whose purpose for the suffering in the world will be realized only at the end of the world. Such a purpose would be too remote for humanity's limited cognitive abilities, and that would adequately explain humanity's failure to discover it, thereby refuting the inference from step (2) to step (3) in the old version of the Nondiscovery Argument, above. But according to Rowe, such reasoning does not apply to God in general, only to the more specific concept of deity in question.

Wykstra could agree with Rowe that a deity whose purpose for suffering will be realized only at the end of the world would indeed be a specific concept of deity and not God in general. But he would no doubt say that the concept of God that he appealed to was not that one but rather simply God in general, who is defined (in part) as omniscient, and that it can be inferred from omniscience alone that most of God's purposes are beyond our ken. I would agree with Wykstra that it is part of the standard concept of God (as an omniscient being) that most of his purposes are beyond human comprehension. However, the issue has to do with God's purposes that relate specifically to the realm of human happiness and suffering. It is not clear to me that *those* purposes are probably beyond human comprehension. William Alston characterizes the realm in question as "a territory about the extent, contents, and parameters of which we know little."[19] Whether or not we know so little of the realm in question that we cannot forcefully combat UDE with regard to it, is a matter about which I am still undecided. Both the Rowe side and the Wykstra-Alston side contain persuasive considerations.[20] As a consequence, although I would say that the inference from step (2) to step (3) in the old Nondiscovery Argument could be strongly attacked, whether or not it can be definitely proven invalid is still unclear to me.

In any case, I do think that Wykstra's argument can be attacked on other grounds, even when it is applied to God in general, as suggested above by the analogies of Mr. X's conspiracy hypothesis and the skeptical hypotheses (also by Fales's line of attack). Furthermore, and perhaps even more importantly, Wykstra's argument does not apply to the revised version of the Nondiscovery Argument (referred to as the Ignorance Argument) or to the Ignorance Objection, above. Those two can be used to attack any appeal to UDE that is applied to the God of evangelical Christianity. As UDEers grant, we are ignorant about God's purposes for permitting both all the suffering in the world and all of our ignorance concerning the matter. But if the God of evangelical Christianity were to exist, then (for reasons that can be gathered from Scripture) he would not want us to be ignorant about those purposes. Ergo, God (conceived in the given way) does not exist. This mode of reasoning is a supplement to AE. It can be used in either of two ways: (1) as merely the Ignorance Objection, which is an objection to UDE taken as a defense of the God of evangelical Christianity against AE, or (2) as the Ignorance Argument, which is a separate argument for the nonexistence of that God. When it is used in the latter way, as a separate atheological argument, it is similar to ANB, for it appeals to the idea that there are certain things of which people are not aware even though God, if he exists, would want them to be aware of those things. This theme will be developed further in the next chapter. At any rate, since UDE is refuted by the Ignorance Objection, it is not important for me to explore here the intricacies of the debate between Rowe on one side and Wykstra and Alston on the other regarding the force of the Nondiscovery Argument. I am sympathetic to Rowe's side of that debate, but my own intended contribution lies elsewhere. Whether the argument is formulated as AE and backed up by the Ignorance Objection to UDE or whether it is formulated as the Ignorance Argument, it strongly supports an atheistic position with respect to the God of evangelical Christianity.

The question might be raised whether the further divine property mentioned in section 10.3 and the Ignorance Objection, which makes appeal to that property, can be used to provide indirect support for AE's premise (A3). I think it can. According to (A3), if God were to exist then he would not have any purpose which overrides his desire to bring about situation L (a reduction in humanity's earthly suffering). I think that such considerations as God's desire that people love him maximally (and the fact that, according to the Bible, God *commanded* people to love him maximally, calling that the "greatest" commandment) do support the given premise. If God were to have a purpose which overrides his desire to bring about situation L, then, even if it should be a purpose beyond human comprehension, it would behoove him to reveal to humanity either the fact that there is such a purpose or something that shows a need for secrecy regarding it. To do so would remove at least a little of the ignorance surrounding these matters that acts as an obstacle to humanity's maximal love for God. So the fact that nothing has been done to remove such ignorance constitutes good evidence that there isn't any divine purpose which overrides God's desire to bring about situation L. This provides some strong support for AE's premise (A3), even though it is of an indirect sort.

Since good support for AE's (A3) can be mustered, the Mexican standoff between that proposition and UDE's existence claim (that there exists an unknown divine purpose of a certain sort) is eliminated. That permits a resuscitation of the Burden-of-proof Objection to UDE. It is now legitimate for us to declare UDE refuted by its failure to meet its burden of proof. And if UDEers ask for support for AE's premise (A3) that would satisfy *that* proposition's burden of proof, then such support could be given by an appeal to the Ignorance Objection in the way shown above.

10.5. The Probability Objection

If AE were taken as a *conclusive proof* of God's nonexistence, then it could be attacked on the basis of the possibilist version of UDE. Although AE would not be shown to be unsound, it would be shown not to be conclusive, even when the further property mentioned in section 10.3 is included among the divine attributes, for it would still fail the second burden-of-proof requirement mentioned in section 10.2. What atheologians need to do, then, is to take AE as an inductive or evidential argument. One way to formulate it would be to say that the vast amount of suffering in the world, together with the absence of any adequate theistic explanation or justification for it (and together with the absence of any adequate theistic explanation for all the secrecy surrounding the matter), constitutes *good evidence* for God's nonexistence, especially when the further property mentioned above is included in the definition of "God." Since evangelical Christianity does indeed include the further property, it becomes that much more difficult for anyone adequately to explain and justify the suffering (and the secrecy) within the framework of evangelical Christianity.

Viewing the matter inductively, what we are confronted by is a choice between two hypotheses or worldviews. Let us call them the "Anti-evangelical hypothesis" and the "Unknown-purpose hypothesis, applied to AE," or AEH and UEH for short. They may be formulated as follows:

AEH: At least one of the following disjuncts is true: (1) there is no divine power of any sort that rules the universe, or (2) there is such a power but it is not in the form of a single personal being, or (3) there is such a being but he or she is not both all-powerful and all-knowing, or (4) the being is not completely rational, or (5) the being does not love humanity greatly and feels no great compassion for humanity's earthly suffering, or (6) the being does not desire that humanity love him or her greatly.

UEH: All of the following are true: (1) there is some sort of divine power that rules the universe; and (2) that power is in the form of a single personal being; and (3) he (i.e., said being) is all-powerful and all-knowing; and (4) he is completely rational; and (5) he loves humanity maximally and feels great compassion for humanity's earthly suffering; and (6) he desires that all humans love him greatly in return (even commanding them to do so and calling that his "greatest" commandment); and (7) he has some purpose for permitting the great amount of earthly suffering endured by humanity which would fully explain and justify it all, a purpose unknown to humanity; and (8) he has some purpose for permitting all the ignorance surrounding the purpose (mentioned in (7), above), also unknown to humanity, which if known would fully explain and justify not only his permission of that ignorance but also his permission of all the ignorance surrounding itself (i.e., this very purpose mentioned here).

Note that UEH gives rise to an anomaly or mystery surrounding the great amount of suffering that occurs in the world and humanity's ignorance surrounding the purposes mentioned in its conjuncts (7) and (8), because it seems impossible, or at least highly unlikely, given the deity's properties mentioned in conjuncts (3)-(6), that he might have such purposes and that he might permit humanity to be ignorant of them. In contrast, AEH does not give rise to any such anomaly or mystery. More will be said about this point in the next section.

UDE might be attacked on the grounds that AEH is a more reasonable hypothesis than UEH. There are two versions of this attack. Let us call the first one the "Probability Objection." It claims that, of the two hypotheses, AEH has the higher a priori probability. This is due to their logical structure. AEH is in the form of a disjunction that leaves open many possibilities. UEH, in contrast, is in the form of a conjunction that makes a very exact specification of the way things are. Such a hypothesis has a considerably lower a priori probability simply because of its much greater specificity.

An analogy would be the example of ten boxes. One hypothesis simply states that at least one of the boxes is empty, whereas another hypothesis states that none of the boxes is empty. Without any further information about the matter, it is obvious that the first hypothesis is more likely to be true than the second, for we could assign a probability of one-half to the proposition that any given box is empty. Then the probability that at least one of the ten boxes is empty would be over 99 percent. It is for a similar reason that AEH is much more likely to be true than UEH and is therefore the more reasonable hypothesis of the two.

It might be objected that the analogy fails because we do not know any probabilities regarding God's existence or God's properties, and so we cannot know any of the initial probabilities of the individual disjuncts of AEH or the individual conjuncts of UEH. Thus the "God" case is different from that of the boxes, in which the initial probability that each box is empty is assumed to be one-half. However, in the "God" case, even given that the initial probabilities for the various possible situations are not equal, we still do not know what they are. We do not have any data that would alter the a priori probability assessment which makes AEH more likely than UEH, i.e., the probability assessment which just looks at the respective logical forms of the hypotheses. Thus, simply by looking at the hypotheses' logical forms, we may conclude that AEH is more likely true than UEH.

Consider the matter in another way. Suppose we are presented with a huge conjunction of propositions all of which are individually controversial. That is, there is no clear evidence that any of them is true. Each is a matter of ongoing debate among "experts" in the field. The question is then raised which is more likely true: the huge conjunction or its negation. It seems that there would be point to saying that the negation is more likely true, simply from its logical structure together with the information that none of the individual conjuncts in the conjunction has been well confirmed. All that the negation needs to be true would be for one of the individual conjuncts to be false, and that is more likely the case than that all the conjuncts should happen to be true. The argument could be posed in the following form:

(1) Conjunction C consists of ten conjuncts.
(2) None of the conjuncts is clearly supported by the available evidence: each of them is a matter of ongoing debate among specialists in the field.
(3) Therefore, the negation of C is more likely true than C.

If this argument is strong (as I think it is), then the Probability Objection is also strong. Although AEH is not exactly the negation of UEH, it comes close. UEH is a huge conjunction of propositions, and AEH comes close to being simply a negation of that conjunction. So, by the sort of reasoning provided here, I think a case could be made for saying that AEH is more likely true than UEH, which shows that AEH is a *more reasonable* hypothesis to hold than UEH. And that in turn shows UDE to be a weak defense against AE.

What is needed in order to maintain that the huge conjunction UEH has a probability at least as high as the huge disjunction AEH is evidence that each of the conjuncts in it has a very high probability. By analogy, in the ten-boxes example, if each conjunct in the conjunction "None of the boxes is empty" were to have a probability of 94 percent, then the conjunction itself would have an overall probability slightly greater than its negation, but if each conjunct were to have a probability of 93 percent, then the negation would have the higher overall probability. This shows approximately how high the probabilities of the individual conjuncts of UEH would need to be in order to bring the overall probability of UEH up to that of AEH. Is there any evidence to support the individual conjuncts of UEH? My own view is that there is no evidence whatever for any of them. Since the propositions in question relate to the God of evangelical Christianity, presumably what would be needed would be evidence that shows the Bible to be totally true. In appendix D, I argue that no such evidence exists. My conclusion is that the sort of case needed to regard UEH as having as high a probability as AEH is completely absent, and therefore there is good reason to regard AEH as being more likely true than UEH. This Probability Objection, then, is a strong attack on UDE as a defense against AE.

10.6. The Explanation Objection

Another reason for maintaining that AEH is a more reasonable hypothesis to hold than UEH is that it can explain the suffering in the world without recourse to the idea of *mystery*. The AEH explanation for the suffering is simply that it comes about naturally or it is caused or permitted by some sort of deity, but not one having all the properties specified in UEH. For example, it might be caused or permitted by a deity who does not greatly love humanity. There is no anomaly or mystery in that. But for a deity as described in UEH to permit so much suffering in the world and then not reveal to humanity his purpose for the suffering or even his purpose for all the secrecy surrounding the matter, all of that *does* present an anomaly or mystery. For an explanatory hypothesis to appeal to mystery is self-defeating, inasmuch as the purpose of explanation is to enlighten and thereby remove any mystery that surrounds a phenomenon. UEH conceives of God as a doubly mysterious being, failing to explain not only why he permits all the suffering that occurs, but also why he keeps his motivations on this matter secret from us, including his motivation for the secrecy itself. Since we appeal to hypotheses for illumination, to solve mysteries and to eliminate anomalies, we naturally prefer those that do not leave us in the end with new anomalies and even greater mysteries. So that is another reason, beyond the Probability Objection, above, to prefer AEH over UEH and for saying that AEH is the more reasonable hypothesis of the two. Just the fact that there is a phenomenon which AEH can adequately explain but which UEH cannot adequately explain makes AEH the preferable hypothesis. We can call this the "Explanation Objection."

It might be objected that hypotheses which explain things are not always superior to ones which don't. For example, to say "There is no single, definitive cause for all the crime in the world" is preferable to saying "All crime is caused by the influence of Satan," even though the former statement does not put forward any explanation, whereas the latter does. But the former statement does suggest a framework for explanation: a set of several naturalistic hypotheses regarding crime in the world. It certainly makes no appeal to mystery, and so in that respect it is not analogous to UEH. I think that once the various supplementary hypotheses regarding Satan are unpacked, the latter statement will look more like UEH and the former more like AEH.

Another example might be that of quantum theory. The prevailing (accepted) hypothesis in that area does not explain the various phenomena, many of which are regarded as anomalous. A competing hypothesis is one which appeals to hidden variables which would enable quantum mechanics to be reduced to classical mechanics. It may seem that it is the competing hypothesis, which most physicists reject, that attempts to explain phenomena, whereas the prevailing hypothesis doesn't. This is supposed to show that hypotheses which explain are not always preferable to ones which don't. It is hard to know what to make of this example. I suspect that no current hypothesis within quantum theory accomplishes much by way of explanation, and that the so-called prevailing hypothesis is not one with which physicists are perfectly content. So I do not think that this example is successful. But I need to leave it to investigators who are more knowledgeable about quantum theory than I am.

Even if there should be a case in which a nonexplanatory hypothesis is preferred to an explanatory one, that may not be relevant to the issue between AEH and UEH. The basic purpose underlying evangelical Christianity is that of proclaiming the gospel message to the world and trying to show how it explains things better than any of its rival worldviews. If it were to be shown that Christianity really has no adequate explanation for the earth's condition, the evangelistic enterprise would be undermined. And it has been shown that UEH, in virtue of its appeal to mystery, is antithetical to explanation. For that reason, evangelical Christianity needs to try to steer clear of UEH.

It is sometimes said that the evaluation of inductive reasoning, as AE is here claimed to be, needs to take into account the total evidence available and not just some portion of it. Thus, in the issue between atheism and theism, if an atheological argument is put forward as merely inductive or probabilistic in character, then the evidence for theism must also be considered. For example, Michael Peterson says the following:

> One point emerging from discussions of the probabilistic version of the evidential argument is that the final probability assigned to theism on the basis of the facts of evil depends in large part on the initial probabilities of various propositions, and that these initial probabilities will almost assuredly be different for the theist and the nontheist.[21]

That is a point well taken. However, in our present context of discussion, the deity at issue is not God in general but the God of evangelical Christianity. And the competing hypotheses are not atheism and theism, but AEH and UEH. In order for there to be evidence to support UEH, all of its conjuncts need to be supported. It is debatable whether there is any evidence for any of them, but there is certainly no evidence for all of them. The only support that would be relevant would be an argument from the Bible, but, as will be shown, such an argument would be very weak. As for the application of UDE to God in general, that will be considered in section 14.1, below.

Philosophers like Alvin Plantinga say that theists can be regarded as reasonable in their basic beliefs even if they cannot support those beliefs by appeal to evidence.[22] Whether or not that is true is a debatable matter, but even if it were, it would be true only in a totally neutral context, where there is neither evidence for the beliefs in question nor evidence against them. The context of this book is one in which theistic beliefs are under attack and the issue is whether or not they can be adequately defended. It is true that an inductive attack can be defended against by the presentation of counterevidence. But in the case of UEH, which is based heavily on the Bible, there seems to be no counterevidence that is of any weight or significance. In any case, the present context is not a neutral one, and so the appeal to unsupported basic beliefs is irrelevant.

In summary, we have seen in this chapter that although UDE can initially escape the Burden-of-proof Objection, it eventually succumbs to it when a further property of God is brought in. And there are still other attacks that it cannot escape, in particular, the Ignorance Objection, the Probability Objection, and the Explanation Objection. They show severe weaknesses in UDE. The hypothesis or worldview on which it is based is a most unreasonable one. We have seen that AE cannot be taken as a conclusive proof of God's nonexistence, but needs to be taken as an inductive or evidential argument. However, taken *that* way, AE is a *strong* argument. The hypothesis on which it is based, namely AEH, can be shown to be superior, as an explanation, to its rival, UEH. It follows that UDE is itself a failure as a defense of God's existence against AE, taken inductively. UDE needs to show that the evidential version of AE is a *weak* argument, i.e., that UEH is at least as good a hypothesis as AEH, but that is something that UDE has failed to do.

Notes

1. 1 Cor. 1:19,25, 2:7, 13:12; Eph. 3:2–6; 1 John 3:2.

2. Alvin Plantinga, "Self-Profile," in James E. Tomberlin and Peter van Inwagen, eds., *Profiles: Alvin Plantinga* (Dordrecht, Boston, and Lancaster, Pa.: Reidel, 1985), p. 35.

3. Marilyn McCord Adams, "Horrendous Evils and the Goodness of God," *Proceedings of the Aristotelian Society,* Supplementary Vol. 63 (1989); slightly revised and reprinted in Marilyn McCord Adams and Robert Merrihew Adams, eds., *The Problem of Evil* (Oxford: Oxford University Press, 1990). The quotations are taken from the latter work, pp. 215–17.

4. Reichenbach, *Evil and a Good God,* pp. 40 and 116.

5. Ibid., p. x.

6. David Basinger, "Evil as Evidence against God's Existence," p. 148.

7. See their essays in Howard-Snyder, ed., *The Evidential Argument from Evil.*

8. Madden and Hare, *Evil and the Concept of God,* p. 67.

9. Roland Puccetti, "The Loving God: Some Observations on Hick's Theodicy," *Religious Studies* 2 (1967); reprinted in Peterson, ed., *The Problem of Evil,* with the quotation taken from the latter work, pp. 244–45.

10. Terry Christlieb, "Which Theisms Face an Evidential Problem of Evil?" *Faith and Philosophy* 9 (1992): 60.

11. Reichenbach, *Evil and a Good God,* p. 99.

12. Stephen J. Wykstra uses the expression in his essay "Rowe's Noseeum Arguments from Evil," chapter 7 of Howard-Snyder, ed., *The Evidential Argument from Evil*.

13. Daniel Howard-Snyder, "The Argument from Inscrutable Evil," in his anthology *The Evidential Argument from Evil*.

14. Stephen J. Wykstra, "The Humean Obstacle to Evidential Arguments from Suffering: On Avoiding the Evils of 'Appearance,'" *International Journal for Philosophy of Religion* 16 (1984); reprinted in Adams and Adams, eds., *The Problem of Evil*. The quotation is from pp. 160 and 159 of the latter work.

15. Madden and Hare, *Evil and the Concept of God*, pp. 14–15.

16. Russell, "Defenseless," pp. 196–97.

17. Fales, "Should God Not Have Created Adam?" p. 203.

18. William L. Rowe, "Evil and the Theistic Hypothesis: A Response to Wykstra," *International Journal for Philosophy of Religion* 16 (1984): 95–100; reprinted in Adams and Adams, eds. *The Problem of Evil*, pp. 161–67.

19. William P. Alston, "The Inductive Argument from Evil and the Human Cognitive Condition," in James E. Tomberlin, ed., *Philosophical Perspectives, 5, Philosophy of Religion*, reprinted in Howard-Snyder, ed., *The Evidential Argument from Evil*, p. 121 of the latter work.

20. See, especially, Rowe's and Alston's more recent contributions to the discussion in Howard-Snyder, ed., *The Evidential Argument from Evil*.

21. Michael L. Peterson, "Introduction," *The Problem of Evil: Selected Readings*, p. 8.

22. See, for example, Alvin Plantinga, "Reason and Belief in God," in Alvin Plantinga and Nicholas Wolterstorff, eds., *Faith and Rationality* (Notre Dame, Ind.: University of Notre Dame Press, 1983), pp. 16–93.

11

The Unknown-Purpose Defense Applied to ANB (UDN)

Attempts have been made to explain why God permits (and has permitted for a long time) billions of people to go through life on earth without any awareness of the truth of Christianity's gospel message. It is a natural question why he hasn't done something to prevent it. According to FDN, he is afraid that such divine intervention in human affairs would interfere with people's free will, which he wants to avoid. And according to TDN, he is testing people as regards their beliefs and wants to avoid upsetting the tests. Both of these are "Known-purpose Defenses" of the God of evangelical Christianity against ANB. (I here exclude ADN, according to which God does not care about people's nonbelief on earth because he knows that all such nonbelief will be eradicated in the afterlife, since it does not put forward any purpose for nonbelief but merely belittles it.) Both FDN and TDN were refuted in earlier chapters. It is simply not true that for God to enlighten the billions about the truth of the gospel message would necessarily interfere with their free will, and the idea of testing people has been shown to be bogus from the start. So both Known-purpose Defenses against ANB have turned out to be failures.

11.1. UDN Formulated

This brings us to a defense that cannot be so easily refuted, the Unknown-purpose Defense as applied to ANB; call it "UDN." According to UDN, God does have some purpose for permitting all the nonbelief in the gospel message, but it is an unknown purpose so far as humanity is concerned. Contrary to the suggestion made in ADN, God *does* want to prevent or eliminate the nonbelief, i.e., to bring about situation S. But there is something else that necessarily conflicts with that desire, something which he wants even more than to bring about situation S. If we were to learn what that "something else" is, then we would fully understand why God has permitted so many people to live their earthly lives without any awareness of the truth of the gospel message.

UDN is a direct attack on ANB's premise (A3). In fact, it is nothing more than a flat-out denial of it. The logical relationship of UDN to ANB is exactly the same as that of UDE to AE, as presented and discussed in chapter 10. And most of the same results arrived at there can be applied here in this chapter.

Like UDE, UDN has both an actualist and a possibilist version. According to the latter, ANB is *possibly* unsound and therefore fails as a conclusive proof of God's nonexistence. Such a proof would need to establish that God cannot possibly have any purpose which would falsify premise (A3), but this is something that ANB has failed to do. As with the possibilist version of UDE, it is a point that ANBers are willing to grant. However, it does not say much. ANB can be a sound argument even if it is possibly unsound and not a conclusive proof. The possibilist version of UDN is too weak to function as a defense of God's existence by evangelical Christians. Since they want to affirm the existence of the particular deity against which ANB is raised, they need to show that ANB is definitely, not just possibly, unsound. For that reason, it is only the actualist version that is relevant in the present context of discussion. In what follows, then, I shall take "UDN" to refer only to its actualist version.

11.2. The Burden-of-proof Objection

As with UDE, a Burden-of-proof Objection can be raised against UDN. Advocates of UDN (UDNers) are making a specific existence claim: there actually exists a divine purpose for permitting all the nonbelief in the gospel message that there is in the world. So they have the burden of showing that such a purpose really does exist, a burden which they have not at all fulfilled (assuming that the Argument from the Bible is a failure). But they may try to sidestep this objection by applying it against their opponents. Since ANBers are trying to prove or establish something (even though their proof is not intended to be conclusive), they also have a certain burden of proof: to show that each of their premises is indeed true. In the case of AE, I maintained that, initially at least, its premise (A3) is not adequately supported, and so there is a kind of Mexican standoff between the two sides: they each have a burden of proof which they have failed to fulfill. However, it was later argued that the Ignorance Objection could be used to support AE's premise (A3) and thereby upset the standoff. So, in the end, UDE does succumb to the Burden-of-proof Objection after all.

What is the situation in the case of ANB? The issue comes down to whether there is any controversial step in ANB which ANBers have failed adequately to support, thereby failing to fulfill the burden of proof that is upon them. If so, then UDNers can seize that point in an attempt to sidestep the Burden-of-proof Objection raised against their own existence claim. The main candidate for such a step is again premise (A3), according to which God does not have any purpose which necessarily conflicts with and outweighs his desire to bring about situation S. But our treatment of ANB's (A3) in chapter 2 was somewhat different from our treatment of AE's (A3) in that we actually came up with some scriptural support for it. This took the form of arguments (8) and (9) back in section 2.4. Argument (8) presupposes argument (6), which appeals to the exclusivist idea that people who do not believe the gospel message by the time they die will end up damned. According to argument (8), since situation S pertains to people's eternal destiny and since there cannot be anything more important than that, God cannot have any purpose which overrides his desire to bring about situation S, which makes ANB's premise (A3) true. Of course, the exclusivist presupposition behind that mode of reasoning might be challenged, though it is important to note that most evangelical Christians accept it.

The other argument used to support ANB's premise (A3) was argument (9), which appeals to the forcefulness of arguments (1)–(4). In the case of arguments (1) & (2), the idea is that since God *commanded* all people to love him maximally and to believe in his son, he cannot have purposes which override his desire for situation S (which is needed for such love and such belief). Also, the maximal love commandment is said to be the *greatest* of all the commandments, which indicates that this is not a matter to be overridden by other considerations. And in the case of argument (3), the idea is that since Jesus declared that his purpose in coming into the world was to testify to the *truth* (presumably) of the gospel message, it is not likely that God would have some other purpose which overrides the spreading of the gospel message. Finally, in the case of argument (4), the idea is that God actually empowered some of the apostles to perform *miracles* in order for them to spread the gospel message, it is unlikely that he has purposes which override his desire that the message be spread. All of this, then, is good scriptural support (albeit of an indirect nature) for ANB's premise (A3).

Thus, the fact of the matter is that there is good support for ANB's premise (A3) whereas (assuming the failure of the Argument from the Bible) there is absolutely none for the existence claim within UDN. Because of that, we need not pursue the course followed in chapter 10 and call the issue between the two propositions an initial "Mexican standoff." On the contrary, right at the outset ANB does clearly satisfy the burden-of-proof requirement placed upon it, whereas UDN does not. Hence, the Burden-of-proof Objection *can* be plausibly raised against UDN, and unlike UDE, UDN has no good way of sidestepping that objection, not even initially.

11.3. The Further-properties Objection

In chapter 10 it was pointed out that, in addition to the usual divine attributes, evangelical Christians ascribe to God the further property of wanting people to love him maximally, or at least greatly. It was then argued that a deity who possesses the additional property must want people to know why he permits them (and others) to suffer, or at least that he has some reason for it, since absence of such knowledge would be an obstacle to the aforementioned love. The fact that it all remains unknown to humanity in itself greatly weakens UDE as applied to the God of evangelical Christianity. It was also argued that if there were some reason why God needs to keep secret his purpose for permitting humanity's earthly suffering (and even the fact that there is such a purpose), then he should reveal that reason or at least reveal that there is such a reason. For in that case, people could come to understand at least some of God's motivations relevant to the matter and thereby have some slight basis for developing the sort of attitude toward him that he wants them to have. The fact that *none* of it has been revealed (the purpose for permitting the suffering, the fact that there is such a purpose, the reason for all the secrecy, even the fact that there is such a reason) is strong support for the hypothesis that the God of evangelical Christianity does not exist. And UDE has no good way to attack that support.

The idea that God has the further property of wanting people to love him maximally can also be used in support of ANB against UDN. Such a deity must want people to believe the gospel message, since that would increase their awareness of what he has done for humanity and thereby help them to love him. Even if a person who is not aware of the gospel message were to love God already, he would come to love God still more if he were to become aware of it; so God must want people to be aware of that message. Furthermore, as shown previously, the fact that, according to Scripture, God actually *commanded* people to love him maximally and called that his *greatest* commandment can also be used to support ANB's premise (A3). What can UDNers say in opposition? If God really does have the sort of overriding purpose that they say he has, then why did he issue the "maximal love" commandment and call it his "greatest" one? It would make no sense for him to do that.

Consider an analogy. Suppose my class is about evenly divided into two groups of students, those I want to have certain information, X, and those I don't want to have X because of some overriding consideration. Then I order them *all* to perform task T and even inform them that that is my "most important" order. But performing task T requires having information X. I think that I could here quite properly be said to be irrational. It would make no sense for me to order people to do something I really want them to do where for them to do it requires having information which I do not want them to have. This is very much like the situation in which UDNers place God. They concede that he wants all of us to love him maximally and has even ordered us to do so as his "greatest" commandment. But for us to do that, we need to be aware of the gospel message. Then the UDNers claim that there is some unknown divine purpose which overrides God's desire to make us aware of the gospel message. If God has such an overriding purpose, then why should he issue the given commandment? We can't understand it. UDN makes God appear irrational.

Another reason for God to reveal to humanity his purpose for permitting so much nonbelief in the gospel message (or at least the fact that he has such a purpose) would be to provide ammunition which would refute ANB's premise (A3) and thereby ANB itself. That would help eradicate whatever nonbelief there may be that was based upon ANB, which presumably God would like to see happen if he were to exist. No doubt there is in the world more nonbelief based on AE than on ANB, but that may change in the future. In any case, it would behoove God to nip ANB-based nonbelief in the bud. His failure to do so is still a further sign of irrationality, or, rather, nonexistence, since the God of evangelical Christianity is by definition rational.

Our ignorance regarding both God's purpose for permitting in the world so much nonbelief and his reason for all the secrecy surrounding the purpose in question could be appealed to in order to construct an argument for God's nonexistence. A rational deity who has commanded us to love him maximally (as his "greatest" commandment) could not possibly permit so much ignorance. Such an argument would correspond to the Ignorance Argument which was put forward in chapter 10. But I think that ANBers can go even further than that, as I shall attempt to show.

Another property of God (beyond the usual ones and in addition to the property mentioned above) is that of his having done the following three things: (1) he sent his son to "testify to the truth" (of the gospel message); (2) he directed missionaries (by way of his son) to spread the gospel message to all nations; and (3) he even empowered some of the missionaries with the ability to perform miracles in order to help them get the message across. According to the Great-Commission Reply, which we considered in section 5.5, that only shows that God wanted situation S, not that he wanted to bring it about himself. Having human missionaries do the job was more important to God than the result itself. But that in itself is very peculiar. When Christians try to explain why God issued the Great Commission, they normally think the reason to be that God wanted the gospel message spread to all nations. That is, they regard the final result to be what is of main importance. To claim that it wasn't the result but the process itself that was most important to God would leave many questions: in particular, why? Why should having humans bring about the result be more important than the result itself? The result here is worldwide awareness of the gospel message. How could *that* be secondary in God's priorities to the activity of the missionaries? And why did God stop empowering missionaries with the ability to perform miracles? They would have been much more likely to succeed in fulfilling the Great Commission if they had retained that power and if still more of them had it. Also, why did God permit the Bible to contain defects (to be shown below in appendix D)? To put the matter in a more general way, why hasn't God done more to help humans spread the gospel message? If he really wanted them to succeed in their assigned task, then he should have done more to assist them. These are points discussed previously in section 5.5.

UDN could be brought in here. It might be said that there are answers to all these questions, but humanity is unaware of them. For some reason, God has not revealed the answers. Nor has he revealed the purpose for all the secrecy surrounding the matter or even that there exists such a purpose. There are at least two objections to this sort of move. First, there is no reason to cling to the Great-Commission Reply if one is going to appeal to UDN. One may just as well say that we do not know any of God's purposes regarding the widespread nonbelief in the gospel message and let it go at that. There is nothing in Scripture to warrant connecting such purposes with the Great Commission. To do so is pure speculation. The second objection is that here again UDN makes God appear irrational. The situation is like that with human suffering, discussed in chapter 10, except that the present framework is more constricted. It is even clearer from Scripture that God really does want "all men to come to a knowledge of the truth" than that he wants any reduction in earthly suffering. Jesus himself declared that he came to earth to "testify to the truth." And so the "unknown purpose" idea has less conceptual space in which to operate. We saw weaknesses in UDE, but it seems that there are even greater weaknesses in UDN.

The present objection to UDN, which goes even beyond the considerations raised in the Ignorance Argument, could be labeled "the Further-properties Objection." On the basis of Scripture, it ascribes to God the further divine properties of (1) wanting (even commanding) all humans to love him maximally and (2) having sent his son and missionaries to spread the gospel message worldwide. The argument is that UDN becomes utterly implausible when confronted by these further properties.

Still another argument could be brought up against those evangelical Christians who are exclusivists. According to Scripture, God wants everyone to be saved. But exclusivists say that salvation is denied those who fail to believe the gospel message. So this must provide God with powerful motivation to bring about situation S (or universal belief in that message). How could he have a purpose which overrides *that*? As the Bible implies, there is nothing more important, so far as humanity is concerned, than salvation (Matt. 16:26, Mark 8:36). The conceptual space here for an unknown divine purpose is exceedingly limited. Yet UDNers might still try to interject their appeal to mystery. We would like to ask them: how could humanity develop a soteriology (a theory about salvation) if there lurks in the conceptual background some unknown divine purpose that pretty well upsets whatever Christians think they have learned about salvation from Scripture? In the end, the appeal to UDN would cause exclusivist Christians to regard God as remote, hidden, and mysterious. Not much could be said about salvation with such unknown purpose(s) in the background. Much of the evangelical missionary effort would thereby be undermined, for exclusivist missionaries with the UDN outlook could not answer questions about salvation. They would have to say things like "That is not for us to know," which would run counter to the missionary message of "Here is the truth!"

Even some evangelical Christians find that exclusivism depicts God as irrational. A deity who wants all humans to be saved but who permits two-thirds of them to be damned for lack of information essential to salvation appears to be quite irrational or insane. This can be regarded as an extension of the Further-properties Objection. When God is viewed as having the further property of wanting all humans to be saved, exclusivism is shown to be so implausible that not even UDN can rescue it. To appeal to UDN within that context would undermine the missionary effort and thus be inimical to evangelicalism.

What I have tried to show is that it is utterly irrational for evangelical Christians to appeal to UDN, especially if they espouse an exclusivist soteriology. Even without exclusivism, I regard the Further-properties Objection to refute UDN within the context of evangelical Christianity. It is not necessary to pursue the matter further. However, to demonstrate analogies between ANB and AE, I shall discuss arguments similar to those considered in the latter part of chapter 10.

11.4. The Probability Objection

Even apart from consideration of the Further-properties Objection, UDN might be attacked. In chapter 10, the problem of evil was posed in terms of competing hypotheses or worldviews. I think that the problem of nonbelief in the gospel message can be posed in the same way. In place of AEH and UEH, I offer hypotheses ANH and UNH, as follows:

ANH: At least one of the following disjuncts is true: (1) there is no divine power of any sort that rules the universe, or (2) there is such a power but it is not in the form of a single personal being, or (3) there is such a being but he or she is not both all-powerful and all-knowing, or (4) the being is not completely rational, or (5) the being does not have a strong desire to bring about universal awareness of the truth of the gospel message among humans, or (6) the being does not desire that humans love him or her greatly.

UNH: All of the following are true: (1) there is some sort of divine power that rules the universe; and (2) that power is in the form of a single personal being; and (3) he (i.e., said being) is all-powerful and all-knowing; and (4) he is completely rational; and (5) he has a strong desire to bring about universal awareness of the truth of the gospel message among humans (and even sent his son to "testify" to it and commanded missionaries to spread the message worldwide, even empowering some of them to perform miracles in order to accomplish that); and (6) he has some overriding purpose for permitting the great lack of awareness of the truth of the gospel message that exists among humans, a purpose unknown to humanity, which if known would fully explain it; and (7) in addition, he has some purpose for all the secrecy surrounding the purpose mentioned (in [6], above), also unknown to humanity, which if known would fully explain both that secrecy and all the secrecy surrounding itself (i.e., this very purpose mentioned here); and (8) he strongly desires that all humans love him maximally (even commanding them to do so and calling that his "greatest" commandment).

The reason for formulating conjunct (5) in UNH in terms of God wanting to bring about the awareness rather than in terms of God simply wanting the awareness itself is that in the context of UDN we are assuming that the Great-Commission Reply and all other Known-purpose Defenses have been abandoned. The UDNer has backed down on all those battles and has come to concede that, as claimed in ANB's premise (A2), God must want to bring about situation S. The battle line, then, is totally at premise (A3).

The reason for mentioning God's desire for humanity's love in ANH's disjunct (6) and UNH's conjunct (8) is that it creates an anomaly when conjoined with (6) and (7) in UNH. A god who strongly desires that humanity love him maximally should not have purposes which he keeps hidden from humanity. Such secrets only create an obstacle to the desired love. It might be claimed that the purposes are not kept secret from us but are simply beyond our comprehension. But even if that were so, God could at least reveal to humanity that the purposes exist. He could have had passages inserted into Scripture which reveal that he has purposes which are beyond our comprehension, such that, if we could understand them, they would clarify for us why he permits so much nonbelief in the gospel message. That would go far toward removing the obstacle in question. But because God did not reveal to humanity (even the existence of) any of the relevant purposes, the anomaly remains.

I make the same claims regarding these hypotheses or worldviews as those made in chapter 10 about AEH and UEH. Between ANH and UNH, UNH appears to have the lower a priori probability because of the logical structure of the two hypotheses. ANH is a huge disjunction and UNH is a huge conjunction. The only way for the conjunction to be at least as likely true as the disjunction would be for the individual conjuncts to have a much higher probability than that for the individual disjuncts. But that is not the case here. There is no reason whatever to regard the conjuncts as more probable than the disjuncts, especially since each of the conjuncts is itself highly problematic and controversial. Thus, all things considered, ANH is the more reasonable hypothesis to accept.

11.5. The Explanation Objection

Furthermore, ANH is more reasonable than UNH because it does not make any appeal to mystery, whereas UNH does. As explained in chapter 10, hypotheses which appeal to mystery defeat the purpose of explanation itself. And it is important to evangelical Christianity's missionary effort to be able to put forward explanations for phenomena. The missionaries need to show their listeners that Christianity can explain things better than rival worldviews. So the appeal to divine mysteries and "unknown purposes" would be counterproductive and out of place there. Furthermore, not only does UNH appeal to mystery, it creates a much greater mystery than the initial fact to be explained (which was the widespread nonbelief in the gospel message). The greater mystery is the anomaly created by the secrecy surrounding the purposes mentioned in UNH's conjuncts (6) and (7). Not only is humanity ignorant of those purposes, but it seems impossible, or at least highly unlikely, given the deity's properties mentioned in UNH's conjuncts (3)–(5) & (8), that he might have such purposes and permit humanity to be ignorant of them. In contrast, no such anomaly or mystery pertains to ANH. Since ANH is clearly the preferable hypothesis of the two, it is reasonable to accept it as the better supported position. It would be reasonable, then, not only to reject UDN, but to deny the existence of the God of evangelical Christianity as well.

As mentioned above, these further objections to UDN, the Probability

Objection and the Explanation Objection, are "overkill," seeing that UDN is utterly demolished by the Further-properties Objection. However, they are forceful and important. And it is illuminating to draw the parallels between AE and ANB. Furthermore, it will be illuminating to compare the treatment of UDN within the context of evangelical Christianity with its treatment within the context of other belief systems. Three such other belief systems will be the subject matter of the next three chapters.

Part III

Other Concepts of God and an Assessment

12

The God of Orthodox Judaism

We have dwelt upon evangelical Christianity for eight chapters and it is time to consider other applications for our two atheological arguments. This may cause the reader a bit of a jolt. Of course, once the meaning of the term "God" in AE or ANB is changed, then in a strict sense that produces a new argument. To still call it "AE" or "ANB" requires that those labels be used, not for particular arguments, but for general argument structures. This is particularly true in the case of ANB. It could be thought of as the following general argument form:

(1) If God were to exist, then he would cause everyone to be aware of the truth of a certain set of propositions.
(2) But not everyone is aware of the truth of those propositions.
(3) Therefore, God does not exist.

Within the context of evangelical Christianity, the set of propositions in question is the gospel message, but within a different context it would be a different set. For ANB to be applied within the context of different belief systems, some quite drastic changes need to take place in the formulation of the argument given in section 2.3. Some may say that it is incorrect to still call the argument "ANB" when it is so radically changed. This is simply a terminological point, and I have no particular view on the matter. For expediency I shall stick with the labels "AE" and "ANB," though I concede that it would be more accurate to make up different labels for the different arguments. In chapters 12-14, I shall consider applications of AE and ANB to the following deities: the God of Orthodox Judaism, the God of liberal Christianity, and finally God in general. In each case, the main issue will be how strong the argument is in the given context.

I take Orthodox Judaism to be for the most part fundamentalist Judaism. Although there are different forms or branches of it, they have some tenets in common, such as the total inerrancy and divine inspiration (without human input) of the *Tanakh*, which is the set of Hebrew Scriptures as interpreted according to the Rabbinic tradition. When interpreted that way, the Hebrew Scriptures are for the most part similar to a literal reading of what Christians call the Old Testament. Although there are some important differences, we need not get into them here. (However, all biblical references in this chapter will be to the English translation of the *Tanakh*.) Because there is much greater uniformity among Orthodox Jews than among liberal Christians, there is less of a problem in referring to "*the* God of Orthodox Judaism" than there will be in the case of liberal Christianity. There is still a slight problem, but for simplicity's sake I shall ignore it. Our task, then, comes down to an evaluation of AE and ANB when applied to the God of Orthodox Judaism.

12.1. The Argument from Evil (AE)

There are two different versions of the problem of evil which might be considered here, one in which "evil" refers only to suffering among Jews, and another in which it refers (as before) to suffering among people generally. I shall here leave it as an open question whether (and to what extent) Orthodox Judaism treats those two problems differently. For the purpose of the cursory sketch to be given in this chapter, I shall deal only with the latter version of the problem, which is the same as the version we have been considering throughout the book.

Thus, in the case of AE, situation L remains the same: the situation of the amount of suffering experienced by humans in the world at the present time being significantly less than what it actually is at present. And AE remains the same except that it is being applied to the God of Orthodox Judaism rather than to any Christian God.

Does AE present a serious problem for Orthodox Jews? Since they regard the Hebrew Scriptures as totally inerrant, the issue comes down to whether those writings support the various parts of AE's premise (A). Certainly there is no issue regarding the power or rationality of the God of Orthodox Judaism. It is clear that he is able to have prevented or reduced the suffering in the world and that he is a rational being. Thus, AE's premises (A1) and (A4) are clearly true within the given framework. But premises (A2) and (A3) are more problematic. Does the God of Orthodox Judaism have great love and compassion for humanity in general? That is very hard to say. Almost all Orthodox Jews believe in the literal interpretation of the Adam and Eve story, according to which God placed a curse upon the earth following the Fall. With the stories of the Great Flood and of Sodom and Gomorrah highlighted, appeal to the concept of divine punishment on earth seems to be more prevalent within Judaism than within Christianity, the latter emphasizing more the idea of punishment in the afterlife. So the greatness of God's love and compassion for humanity regarding its earthly suffering might very well be called into question. Most of the biblical verses that Christians would cite to support the claim that God feels great love and compassion for humanity come from the New Testament, which is not available in the case of Judaism. The question to be raised is just what there is in the *Tanakh* to support that claim.

Psalm 136 contains twenty-six verses each of which ends with "His steadfast love is eternal." But the story being told in that chapter is the story of how God helped the Israelites escape bondage in Egypt and win battles against their neighbors. So the love that is repeatedly alluded to is presumably not love for humanity in general but only love for the Israelites. It seems irrelevant, then, to the problem of evil as posed with respect to humanity in general. Another verse that might be appealed to is Psalm 145:9, which says, "The Lord is good to all, and His mercy is upon all His works." That one does appear to apply to all of humanity, and so it is one to which Orthodox Jews need to respond. We can pose the problem of evil just with regard to it, as follows: "According to Psalm 145:9, God is good and merciful to all, so why, then, does he permit so much suffering in the world?" The weakness here is that it centers about a single verse. The problem would be more forceful if there were more support within the Hebrew Scriptures for the claim that God feels great love and compassion for humanity in general. How much more there may be is unclear to me.

The various defenses against AE considered (and rejected) earlier can all be attacked in pretty much the same way within the context of Judaism, except that all appeals to the New Testament are ruled out. I shall not here go through the various defenses and the objections to them to see in detail what effect is produced by that restriction. For the most part, the effect is not very great. For each of the defenses, even if some objections become eliminated or reduced in force, there are others that can be appealed to as an attack on the defense, which leads me to the conclusion that AE still poses a serious problem for Orthodox Judaism.

I think that almost all Orthodox Jews fall into one of three categories with regard to the problem. There are those who appeal to the Punishment Defense, those who appeal to the Afterlife Defense (ADE), and those who appeal to the Unknown-purpose Defense (UDE). We saw in chapter 8 that the Punishment Defense faces three formidable objections, namely, the Historical Objection, the Loving-God Objection, and the Inequity Objection. It does not seem to me that Jews have any better way to deal with the first and third of these than do Christians. However, the Loving-God Objection seems to me to be not be so forceful for them. Some people may be "theologically thick-skinned" enough to be able to say that God does not have any great love for humanity in general. If there are proportionately more people like that within the community of Orthodox Jews than among Christians, then certainly it could be said that the Punishment Defense becomes slightly more available to Orthodox Jews (and AE thereby presents less of a problem for them) than in the case of Christians. The Punishment Defense is repudiated within the New Testament (Luke 13:1–5; John 9:1–5), but not within the *Tanakh*. Some may think that the Book of Job repudiates it, but that is not really so because of Job's special circumstances. In any case, even if the Loving-God Objection is not pursued, the Historical Objection and Inequity Objection remain as serious problems for the Punishment Defense, even within the Jewish community. So if AE is less of a problem for Jewish advocates of the Punishment Defense, it is only just slightly less. I suspect that Orthodox Jews who wrestle with the problem of evil do not settle for the Punishment Defense but move on to either ADE or UDE.

ADE provides a way to deal with the Inequity Objection: in the afterlife people get exactly what is coming to them, so any inequities that occurred on earth will all be rectified in the afterlife. John Hick referred to that idea (perhaps disparagingly) as the "book-keeping" model (as mentioned in section 9.1). However, it may have more of an appeal to Jews, who have a very strong sense of justice. (See, for example, Jer. 17:10, 21:14, 32:19.) Certainly it is an approach that evades what was called in chapter 9 the "Unsaved Objection." Jews do not believe in heaven and hell the way Christians do, and so may be more open to the idea that everyone in the afterlife comes under the very same system of dispensing justice. Another objection to ADE evaded by Judaism is what was called the "Jesus Objection." There does not appear to be any strong support from the Hebrew Scriptures for the idea that God has great concern regarding humanity's earthly suffering. So Orthodox Jews who believe that everything will be rectified in an afterlife could very well reject AE's premise (A2).

But there remain two objections to ADE which may be obstacles to believing that everything will be rectified in an afterlife. The first of them is what was called in chapter 9 the "Unrectifiability Objection." It is the idea that some evils are so horrendous that they could never be rectified, even in an eternity of heavenly bliss. The Holocaust of World War II is a prime example that is often appealed to. Different Orthodox Jews have different views about the Holocaust, some regarding it as a special case of divine punishment. However, I think that very few of them, if any, would be inclined to belittle it by saying, "Oh, that will all be made right in the afterlife." I think that the Unrectifiability Objection is more forceful within Judaism than within Christianity, largely because of the example of the

Holocaust. And that makes ADE somewhat problematic for Orthodox Jews as a defense against AE.

The other objection to ADE is that the very concept of an afterlife is incoherent. This is a topic addressed in appendix E, below. I think that it is an objection which prevents many Orthodox Jews from appealing to ADE at all or at least from employing it without strong misgivings. Those who refrain from appealing to the Punishment Defense or ADE usually concede that they do not have any good solution to the problem of evil and are inclined simply to fall back on UDE, which is the idea that God has some purpose which would adequately explain why he permits so much evil in the world but has not as yet revealed to humanity what that purpose might be.

Part of the issue surrounding UDE is whether or not God wants humanity to love him maximally, or at least greatly. If he does, then presumably he would be less inclined to be the way UDE describes him: as keeping his purposes hidden from humanity. In the case of Orthodox Judaism, the question could be whether God wants his people (the Jews) to love him maximally. They were certainly commanded to do so (Deut. 6:5), and such love is said to be tested (Deut. 13:3). But if God exists, then he would be keeping his purposes hidden from Jews just as much as from Gentiles. And that creates an obstacle to their love, which is counterproductive from God's point of view. Thus, Orthodox Jews are confronted by the question: if God wants Jews to love him maximally, then why should he keep his purposes secret from them? It is a little unclear how they would answer that. If they cannot do so, then any appeal to UDE becomes more problematic for them than it would otherwise be.

Another way to express this point would be in terms of the so-called Ignorance Objection, which was expounded in section 10.4. All people, Jews included, are ignorant not only of God's purpose for permitting so much suffering in the world, but also of his reasons for all the secrecy surrounding the given purpose. Yet it seems counterproductive for a deity who desires people's great love to permit such ignorance. So that becomes, then, a good reason to deny the existence of such a deity. It should be noted, though, that the idea that God strongly desires everyone's great love is even more prominent within Christianity than within Judaism, and it receives powerful support from the New Testament, as shown in chapter 10. So the Ignorance Objection, though certainly applicable to Orthodox Judaism, is even more forceful within the context of Christianity.

In chapter 10, UDE was also attacked by means of the Probability Objection and the Explanation Objection. Although Judaic versions of those objections could be constructed, they would be less forceful than the original versions. The Probability Objection, for example, makes use of both the idea that God, as conceived, strongly desires all people's maximal love and that he loves humanity maximally. Those ideas are not particularly prominent within Judaism and they are harder to support by appeal to the Hebrew Scriptures alone. So the argument would have a diminished strength there, though it would still have some force to it.

As for the Explanation Objection, that one was applied mainly against evangelical Christianity and its missionary effort. Appeals to divine mystery tend to weaken missionary efforts. Such a consideration does not apply to Orthodox Judaism, which has no missionary effort, at least among Gentiles. Also, there seems to be more inclination within Judaism to regard God as a mysterious being. (The very fact that devout Jews never write the word "God," but use "G-d" instead, may be indicative of such an inclination.) For these reasons, the Explanation Objection has less force when applied within the context of Orthodox Judaism than within that of evangelical Christianity. However, both objections do have some force, and need to be taken into account by those Orthodox Jews who are inclined to defend their God against AE by appeal to UDE.

Overall, I would say that there are important objections to the three defenses in question (the Punishment Defense, ADE, and UDE) within the context of Orthodox Judaism, enough to warrant saying that Orthodox Jews do not have any very good defense against AE. However, those objections are not as powerful as the corresponding objections (plus additional ones) that might be raised against the three defenses within the context of evangelical Christianity. So, although the problem of evil is a great problem for Orthodox Jews, it is a significantly greater problem for evangelical Christians. If the strength of inductive (or evidential) arguments were to be rated on a scale from zero to 100, with fifty being in the middle between "weak" and "strong," then I would assign to AE as applied to the God of Orthodox Judaism a score of sixty-five, but I would assign to AE as applied to the God of evangelical Christianity a score of eighty-five. I shall say more about this sort of rating scale later on.

12.2. The Argument from Nonbelief (ANB)

When we apply ANB to the God of Orthodox Judaism, some radical changes need to be made, mainly in the definition of "situation S." First, in place of the gospel message, let us put what may be called "set P," consisting of propositions that pertain to the ancient Israelites. Then situation S could be defined in terms of set P. There are various possible formulations for such a set and for situation S. Here is one of them:

Set P = the following three propositions:
  (a) There exists a being who rules the entire universe.
  (b) That being has a "chosen people," namely, the Israelites referred to in the Hebrew Scriptures.

(c) He gave them a set of laws, the Torah, which he wanted them to follow and which he wants their descendants to follow.

Situation S = the situation of all, or almost all, descendants of the Israelites since the time of Moses believing all the propositions of set P.

Because of these changes, I shall write out the revised ANB completely. Making use of the above definitions of set P and situation S, ANB can be formulated in terms of Orthodox Judaism as follows:

(A) If the God of Orthodox Judaism were to exist, then he would possess all of the following four properties (among others):
   (1) *being able* to bring about situation S, all things considered;
   (2) *wanting* to bring about situation S, i.e., having it among his desires;
   (3) *not wanting* anything else that necessarily conflicts with his desire to bring about situation S as strongly as he wants to bring about situation S;
   (4) *being rational* (which implies always acting in accord with his own highest purposes).
(B) If a being who has all four properties listed above were to exist, then situation S would have to obtain.
(C) But situation S does *not* obtain. It is not the case that all, or almost all, descendants of the Israelites since the time of Moses have believed all the propositions of set P.
(D) Therefore [from (B) & (C)], there does not exist a being who possesses all four properties listed in premise (A).
(E) Hence [from (A) & (D)], the God of Orthodox Judaism does not exist.

How serious a problem is ANB for Orthodox Jews? I think that all of them would readily accept its premises (A1) and (A4). But what about premise (A2)? Probably almost all Orthodox (and Conservative) Jews believe all of set P. (Even evangelical Christians would accept set P, but only if the present tenses in propositions [b] and [c] were changed to past tenses.) The problem of nonbelief would pertain mainly to the descendants of the ancient Israelites, who are (at least from the standpoint of Judaism) today's Jews. What is God's attitude toward those people, according to Orthodox Judaism? On the basis of the Hebrew Scriptures, I would say that God wants his people, among other things, to continue to worship and glorify him and to follow the Torah. But that calls for (the new) situation S, which involves belief in all of set P. Jews who deny any part of set P would have little or no motivation to follow the Torah. Hence, we may infer that the God of Orthodox Judaism, as he is described in the Hebrew Scriptures, wants all, or almost all, Jews (i.e., the descendants of the ancient Israelites) to believe all of set P. But that is situation S. So a good scriptural case could be made here for ANB's premise (A2), just as in the case of ANB applied to evangelical Christianity.

However, when we observe the Jewish community in the world today, we find that a very large proportion of them do not believe all of set P. Reform Jews, especially, do not regard the Hebrew Scriptures in the way that the Orthodox do, as divinely inspired, mostly literal, and totally inerrant, and so they do not accept the idea that God is looking down on them, very unhappy over their nonobservance of his laws. A few of them would even reject proposition (a), but among those who accept (a), a fairly sizable proportion would reject proposition (c), and perhaps (b) as well. The existence of such a sizable group of nonbelievers among Jews makes ANB's premise (C) true.

How could the God of Orthodox Judaism have allowed such a thing to happen? How could he have permitted the Reform movement even to get underway (in the early nineteenth century)? He could have shown his people mighty signs, as he did in ancient times, to keep them on track. The problem of nonbelief here is the question why the God of Orthodox Judaism, assuming he exists, did not do things that would (directly or indirectly) cause his people to keep believing all of set P. It seems to me that this is indeed a serious problem for Orthodox Judaism.

In earlier chapters, we considered the problem within the context of evangelical Christianity and looked at four solutions to it in the form of four defenses of God's existence against ANB. The four defenses were FDN, TDN, ADN, and UDN (taken up in chapters 5, 7, 9, and 11, respectively). Objections were raised against all four. In some cases, similar objections could be raised against the corresponding defenses within the context of the above formulation of ANB and Orthodox Judaism. I think that FDN and TDN, in particular, can be disposed of by objections analogous to those raised in chapters 5 and 7. So I shall not discuss them further here.

ADN is a quite separate matter. It really has no clear counterpart in connection with the revised form of ANB or within Judaism. The new situation S is that of Jews believing set P (which, essentially, reduces to the proposition that God wants them to follow his laws). It really would make no sense to suggest that God might be satisfied if situation S were to become fulfilled in the afterlife. The whole point of situation S is to have Jews do certain things in this earthly life, so the very idea of fulfillment in the afterlife is off the track. Although appeal to the afterlife could have some bearing on the problem of evil, it has no bearing on the problem of nonbelief in the context of Orthodox Judaism. In effect, there is no ADN here.

I am fairly certain that in response to the problem of nonbelief Orthodox Jews would ultimately appeal to mystery and the Unknown-purpose Defense (UDN). They would say that God works in mysterious ways, and it is a sin even to question his motivations. However, for reasons similar to those given above in chapter 11, I find such a response to be weak. It is more reasonable to deny the existence of the given deity than to try to defend his existence by an appeal to mystery.

However, the issues surrounding UDN are somewhat different within the context of Orthodox Judaism than within that of evangelical Christianity. The main issue still revolves around the truth of ANB's premise (A3), which claims that God has no purpose which conflicts with and over-rides his desire to bring about situation S. UDN is simply a flat-out denial of that premise. In the case of evangelical Christianity, actual scriptural support was provided for the premise. Could that be done in the present context? I think it can and will try to show that by appeal to the *Tanakh*.

The most fundamental concept within Orthodox Judaism is that God selected the Jews to be his chosen people. He made a covenant with Abraham that is to be everlasting (Gen. 17:7). It was confirmed with Isaac (Gen. 26:2–4) and Jacob (Gen. 28:13–15) and then reestablished with the Israelites at Mount Sinai. David says of God:

> He is ever mindful of His covenant, the promise He gave for a thousand generations, that He made with Abraham, swore to Isaac, and confirmed in a decree for Jacob, for Israel, as an eternal covenant. (Ps. 105:8–10)

It is absolutely essential to the covenant that the Israelites' descendants be aware of it, for they are to constitute a prophet nation. That idea is expressed as follows:

> And this shall be My covenant with them, said the Lord: My spirit which is upon you, and the words which I have placed in your mouth, shall not be absent from your mouth, nor from the mouth of your children, nor from the mouth of your children's children—said the Lord—from now on, for all time. (Isa. 59:21)

The Israelites' descendants are to be a model nation, known worldwide as God's chosen people (Isa. 61:9). God will put his teaching "into their inmost being and inscribe it upon their hearts." All of them will heed God (Jer. 31:33–34). According to the *Tanakh*, God said the following:

> They shall be My people and I will be their God. I will give them a single heart and a single nature to revere Me for all time, . . . I will put into their hearts reverence for Me, so that they do not turn away from Me. (Jer. 32:38–40)

It might be objected that this covenant between God and the Israelites was abrogated when they did not fulfill their side of it (even though they had promised to do so at Exod. 24:3–8). They were to receive God's blessings if they obeyed the Torah (Deut. 28:1–14) but were to be cursed if they disobeyed (Deut. 28:15–68). However, Scripture also says the following:

> I will deal with you as you have dealt, for you have spurned the pact and violated the covenant. Nevertheless, I will remember the covenant I made with you in the days of your youth, and I will establish it with you as an everlasting covenant. (Ezek.16:59–60)

It seems that the Israelites are to be punished for their disobedience, but the covenant still remains as an everlasting one.

My interpretation of all this is that the most fundamental doctrine underlying Orthodox Judaism is that God's covenant with the Jews still holds. They are still God's chosen people and are expected to obey the Torah, thereby eventually serving as a model to all nations. As God stated:

> I will also make you a light of nations,
> That My salvation may reach the ends of the earth. (Isa. 49:6)

(See also Isa. 42:6 and 60:3.) But there is no way for that to come about unless Jews themselves are aware of it all. At the very least, they must believe all the propositions of set P. In fact, it specifically says in Scripture (quoted above) that God will inscribe the message upon their hearts. How, then, could God have some other purpose which overrides this one? He said in effect that belief in set P will be implanted in the minds of the Israelites' descendants. Thus, he must want to bring about situation S. For God to have a purpose which overrides that desire would undermine the most basic concept of Orthodox Judaism. It would in effect be an annihilation of that which in Scripture is said to be everlasting. It seems, then, that there is excellent scriptural support for ANB's premise (A3) within the context of Orthodox Judaism. This refutes UDN, which was Orthodox Judaism's last defense against ANB.

Further objections to UDN, patterned after the ones expounded in chapter 11, could be put forward. Since God demands that Jews love him maximally (Deut. 6:5, 13:4), he must want them to be aware of his covenant with them and related matters, which requires situation S. And that precludes God having purposes which override his desire for situation S. Even if he were to have such a purpose, his demand that his people love him would require that he reveal the purpose to them, or at least reveal that there is such a purpose. Secrecy surrounding this matter would be counterproductive from God's point of view, for it would put up an obstacle to his people's maximal love.

The Probability Objection and Explanation Objection could also be raised against UDN within the context of Orthodox Judaism, but they do not carry quite the force that they have in the context of evangelical Christianity. The situation is similar to that of UDE, as discussed in section 12.1, and so the same sorts of considerations apply here as applied there.

Overall, I find ANB to be a much more powerful argument for the nonexistence of the God of Orthodox Judaism than is AE. On the scale of zero to 100 mentioned above, I would rate ANB's strength as eighty-five, whereas AE would only get a sixty-five. Orthodox Judaism has ways to try to deal with the problem of evil, but has much less maneuvering room with the problem of nonbelief. Basically, the main reason for the discrepancy lies in premise (A3), and the fact that Orthodox Judaism (like evangelical Christianity) is a "religion of The Book." In the case of ANB, premise (A3) receives excellent scriptural support, but in the case of AE, it does not. More will be said about the relative strengths of AE and ANB in chapter 15, below.

Comparing ANB within the contexts of Orthodox Judaism and evangelical Christianity, respectively, I would say that both arguments are very powerful, but the latter is even more so. I would give ANB within the context of evangelical Christianity a rating of ninety-five, compared with Judaism's eighty-five. The main factor which inclines me in that direction is the fact that every one of evangelical Christianity's defenses against ANB can be utterly demolished, whereas that is not quite so evident in the case of Orthodox Judaism. In some ways Judaism is less open than evangelical Christianity and there is less clarity surrounding it and its doctrines. Nevertheless, from what I can fathom of it, it does seem not to have any good way to deal with the Argument from Nonbelief.

13

The God of Liberal Christianity

I take what I call "liberal Christianity" to be Christianity that does not accept (as inerrant) a thoroughgoing literal interpretation of the Bible and that does not maintain an exclusivist doctrine of salvation by faith in Jesus Christ. Since it is unclear to me how liberal Christians interpret Scripture, in this chapter (and the next) I shall not be making reference to specific biblical verses. Perhaps some readers will breathe a sigh of relief, while others may wish to skip ahead to chapter 15.

It is easier to say what liberal Christians reject than what they accept. As I understand their view, I take them to believe that there was something special about Jesus of Nazareth and that his ethical system (e.g., as preached in his Sermon on the Mount) is unsurpassed. They at least believe that if God had a last and greatest prophet on earth, then it was Jesus, rather than Muhammad. Almost all of them believe that Jesus was the Messiah or the Christ, prophesied in the Old Testament. Most believe that Jesus is a divine or supernatural being who was resurrected from death and is presently alive somewhere, presumably in heaven. And most believe the gospel message that Jesus is God's son, sent to save humanity (by means of his substitutionary atonement). But the main issue before us here is that of the attributes ascribed to God. In particular, do liberal Christians view God as an omnipotent ruler who loves humanity maximally, or at least greatly, and who strongly desires that that love be reciprocated? I think we simply have to say that there is no uniform position here. Probably most liberal Christians view God that way, but not all of them do.

In the United States, there is a great spectrum of Christian views about God, Jesus, and the afterlife, with evangelical (or conservative) Christianity occupying about one-half of the spectrum and liberal Christianity occupying approximately the other half, and with each half itself admitting a wide spectrum of views within it. In light of the great diversity among liberal Christians themselves, it is really pointless to speak of "*the* God of liberal Christianity." Since there are many different concepts of God there, not just one, the expression "the gods" would be more correct sociologically (though misleading, since it would connote polytheism, which we do not want at all). On the other hand, speakers of English do normally use the word "God" itself in an unqualified way, even though there is an even greater variety of concepts of God among theists in general than among liberal Christians. So to stick with the expression "the God of liberal Christianity" need not be regarded as totally incoherent.

One way to try to deal with the problem is by speaking of the deity in question as "the God of the average liberal Christian." However, that is unsatisfactory because there is no way to compute an average. Heights and weights can be averaged, but not beliefs. What I shall do, instead, is try to pick out from the great variety a more definite conception of God with regard to which the problems of evil and of nonbelief arise. These chapters 12–14 are not intended to be rigorous or complete, but only to present an outline of some further issues. A more complete treatment, which would need to be itself book-length, would attempt to disentangle the many different concepts of God within liberal Christianity and apply AE and ANB to each of them separately. Barring such a treatment, let us simply take the issue before us in this chapter as whether either of our two atheological arguments is sound (or strong) when applied to a certain more-definite concept of God (to be specified) within the overall framework of liberal Christianity.

Many liberal Christians believe in what was referred to earlier as "the God of the philosophers." They ascribe to God some of the predicates which in chapter 3 I called meaningless or at least unclear. Among those predicates are "transcendent," "nonphysical," "omnipresent," and "triune." It is still my aim to try to steer clear of such language. If I should encounter liberal Christians who insist that "God" be defined in terms of such predicates, and who refuse to discuss God's existence or nonexistence apart from them, then I suppose I would need to forsake my atheological enterprise in relation to such people. There is no point in trying to construct arguments the conclusion of which contains a meaningless word. With regard to the God-talk of such people, I would "move to the left" and take the position of noncognitivism (described in chapter 3). However, it seems to me that the questionable predicates could be bracketed off and disregarded for the purposes of our topic. I see no reason why that could not be done, and so I proceed here and in the next chapter on the assumption that there is (or at least could be) some concept picked out by the word "God" as used by liberal Christians or theists in general that is intelligible to both sides of the issue.

13.1. The Argument from Evil (AE)

When AE is applied to liberal Christianity, the definition of "situation L" remains the same: the situation of the amount of suffering experienced by humans in the world at the present time being significantly *less* than what it actually is at present. And the formulation of AE is the same as in chapters 2 and 12, except that "God" is understood to refer to the God of liberal Christianity rather than the God of evangelical Christianity or the God of Orthodox Judaism.

I have maintained that AE presents a serious problem for both evangelical Christians and Orthodox Jews, especially the former. However, I do not make any such unqualified claim in the case of liberal Christians. Since they do not ascribe to God any definite set of attributes, the most we can say is that AE may or may not present a serious problem for them. By a "serious problem" I mean one to which the given belief system gives rise but is not able to solve satisfactorily. I think it would be a mistake to say in an unqualified way that AE presents a serious problem for Christianity in general or for liberal Christianity. People could be Christians and yet deny that God is omnipotent. Many "process theologians," for example, are Christians in that category. People could also be Christians and deny that God loves humanity greatly. They may have an outlook in which God is very angry at humanity and has been punishing it severely. Or, alternatively, they may have such a nonanthropomorphic concept of God that the property of "loving humanity" would be quite inappropriate. (Possibly Paul Tillich's concept of God as the ultimate ground of being is like that.) Such people need not be bothered by any problem of evil. However, it would surely be premature simply to abandon our atheological enterprise at that point. The vast majority of liberal Christians *do* affirm God's omnipotence and great love for humanity (as do all evangelical Christians). To try to locate those for whom AE presents a serious problem, let us think in terms of going around to liberal Christians and asking them the following two questions (call them Q1 and Q2):

Q1:   Could God have prevented or reduced the suffering and premature death that exists or occurs in our world?

Q2:   Does God have great love and compassion for humanity?

I think that most liberal Christians would say yes to both questions. The problem of evil, formulated as "Why does God permit so much evil (i.e., suffering and premature death) in the world?" does indeed appear to be a serious problem for such people, just as it is for evangelical Christians. I do not see any way for them to definitely refute AE once they answer Q1 and Q2 affirmatively. We have explored the various attempts to do so in earlier chapters, especially attacks on AE's premise (A3), and have found all of them to be weak or defective or lacking in one way or another.

However, unlike evangelical Christians, not all liberal Christians would say yes to both questions Q1 and Q2. And, indeed, the problem of evil would not arise for those who say no to at least one of them. So far as AE is concerned, premise (A1) or (A2), or both, could simply be rejected, despite anything written in the Bible. Liberal Christians do not have the same commitment to Scripture that evangelical Christians do. Indeed, those willing to reject sections of the Bible are immune to all the sorts of atheological argument mentioned in this book. Nevertheless, such people may have other problems in their belief systems. For example, what is the role of Scripture supposed to be in human life? And if it is not much of a role, then what basis could there be at all for Christianity? In other words, "If you reject the Bible, then why call yourself a Christian?" Usually, liberal Christians say that they don't "reject the Bible" but just interpret it nonliterally. But then the problem becomes that of *how* to interpret Scripture. If the words are not taken literally, then there seems to be no "fact of the matter" as to what they mean. Anything goes. Under such conditions, it becomes exceedingly unclear what role the Bible might play in one's system of beliefs.

There is a third question (call it Q3) which we might pose to all who fall within the category of liberal Christians. It is the following:

Q3:   Does God want humans to love him maximally, or at least greatly?

This question corresponds to the "further property of God" that was discussed above in section 10.3 and which figured prominently in the attack on UDE. The idea there was that if God wants humans to love him greatly, then it would be counterproductive for him to keep his purposes secret from them. (The purposes include not only that for permitting so much suffering in the world but also that for all the secrecy surrounding the matter.) Even if the relevant divine purposes are beyond human comprehension, as most UDEers claim, humanity could have at least been informed *that they exist*. That bit of information is something that could have been clearly revealed in Scripture, and such revelation would have gone far toward removing the obstacle to humanity's love for God that has been brought about by all the secrecy surrounding the matter. Furthermore, even if there were some divine reason for the secrecy and even if that divine reason were beyond human comprehension, it could have been revealed in the Bible *that such a reason exists*. God could have told people that, for some reason which is beyond their limited minds, it is necessary for him to keep secret from them his purposes regarding evil as well as his purposes for all the secrecy surrounding the matter. Even such a statement within Scripture would have helped remove some of the obstacle to humanity's love for God that is created by the fact of evil and all the divine secrecy surrounding it. To let the obstacle remain would be, from

God's point of view, counterproductive, assuming that he wants people to love him greatly. So the question is what proportion of liberal Christians would say yes to Q3. I suspect that it is not as high as in the case of Q1 and Q2, but is still well over 50 percent. For those who say yes to all three questions, the problem of evil would be even more difficult to deal with than for those who say yes only to the first two. Such Christians could not as easily try to evade the problem by an appeal to UDE, for the reasons given above.

If liberal Christians were asked questions Q1-Q3, I suspect that most of them would say yes to all three. Hence, the problem of evil is indeed a serious problem for most liberal Christians. Nor do they have any better way of dealing with it than do evangelical Christians. If the relevant parts of the Bible are accepted, then all the evangelical Christian defenses that were considered and refuted in chapters 4 and 6-10 could as easily be refuted within the rubric of liberal Christianity. Of course, liberal Christians may not accept certain parts of the Bible. But even if a defense is not to be attacked by appeal to Scripture, there are other objections which might be raised against it.

Consider, for example, the Free-will Defense (FDE). Presumably liberal Christians would formulate it in the same way as given in section 4.2. And then the very same objections could be raised against it: the Altruism Objection, the Natural-evils Objection, and the Relative-value Objection. Since none of those objections make any special use of the Bible or presuppose exclusivism, they all apply to liberal Christianity just as well as to evangelical Christianity. Thus, since FDE was thoroughly refuted in chapter 4 (with a couple more licks to be thrown in, below, in appendices A and B), there is no need to critique it again here.

In the case of the Contrast Defense and the Moral-virtues Defense, we did consider in chapter 6 the Scriptural Objection. That one could be omitted within the context of liberal Christianity. However, the Impediment Objection and the Negligent-father Objection, which were also expounded there, do still apply and do suffice to refute the defenses in question. Similarly with the Testing Defense, discussed in chapter 7, the Unfairness Objection and the Unsuitability Objection should dispose of that one, even within the context of liberal Christianity.

The Punishment Defense is different, since it involved quite a lot of discussion of Scripture. But I think that when liberal Christians answer our question Q2 (whether God has great love and compassion for humanity) affirmatively, then the Punishment Defense is not so readily available to them. There is also the Inequity Objection, which does not rely on Scripture for its force. That one is usually regarded as decisive against the Punishment Defense. From my own observation, liberal Christians do *not* appeal to the Punishment Defense to try to deal with the problem of evil, and so we need not spend more time on it.

The Afterlife Defense (ADE), though, *is* one that liberal Christians sometimes appeal to. Nevertheless, we are narrowing our focus to those who answer our question Q2 affirmatively. It would be inconsistent for such people to allow that God is totally unconcerned about humanity's earthly suffering, which is part of ADE, and also affirm that God has great compassion for humanity for its earthly suffering. So, from that perspective, ADE is not available to those liberal Christians who are within our target group. Furthermore, some of the other objections to ADE, which are raised above in chapter 9 and below in appendix E, may also apply. For these reasons, I think that ADE can be refuted within the present context.

Probably almost all liberal Christians confronted by AE would fall back on the Unknown-purpose Defense (UDE) as their defense against it. It is what I have found in the philosophical literature as well as in discussion with Christians. But then the considerations raised in chapter 10 become relevant. UDE cannot adequately deal with the Ignorance Objection, which was discussed in section 10.4. Furthermore, I think that the Probability Objection and the Explanation Objection can also be raised against it, especially in relation to those who answer Q3 affirmatively. It is true that evangelical Christianity is particularly challenged by the Explanation Objection because of its missionary effort and its corresponding need to explain phenomena, but the objection seems to me to carry some force against liberal Christianity as well. Hypotheses that give rise to greater mysteries and anomalies are just generally inferior, other things being equal, even if they are not used to explain things to others. People who desire comprehensiveness and clarity within their belief systems need to avoid trying to brush off the evil of our world by appeal to "God's unknown purposes."

For the purpose of assessing AE, it would be useful for us to divide liberal Christians into three groups, G1-G3, as follows:

G1: those who answer Q1 or Q2 negatively.
G2: those who answer Q1 and Q2 affirmatively, but Q3 negatively.
G3: those who answer all three questions affirmatively.

I do not think that the problem of evil is a serious problem for (the minority of) liberal Christians in group G1, so they can be disregarded for our purposes. The ones for whom AE presents the most serious problem are those in group G3 (which I think is the group into which most liberal Christians would fall). Appealing to the scale of zero to 100 mentioned in chapter 12, I would rate AE as having a strength of seventy-five in relation to that group. For the few in group G2, I would give AE a lesser score, perhaps around sixty-five, since UDE (as a defense against AE) would be more available to such people than to those in group G3. Of course, UDE would still have objections to it, but they would not be as forceful as in the case of the G3 people. There comes to be a cloud of unclarity surrounding God's motivations pertaining to humanity if one were to say that God has great love and compassion for humanity but does not want that love to be reciprocated. (As pointed out previously, one could not support such an outlook by appeal to the Bible, since there is at least as much scriptural support for an affirmative answer to Q3 as for an affirmative answer to Q2.) I suspect that if Christians were to reflect on the oddity of the outlook represented by G2, then very few of them, if any, would put themselves in that group. But if there are any who would do so, I would say that AE still presents a problem for them, though not as serious a problem as for those in group G3. Since most liberal Christians are in G3, I would say that AE presents a quite powerful argument for the nonexistence of the deity in which most liberal Christians say they believe.

One last question remains here. Suppose we were to dispense with the survey questions and inquire about the strength of AE merely in relation to liberal Christianity *per se*. That is, how strong is AE as an argument for the nonexistence of the deity believed in by liberal Christians as a group not restricted or narrowed down in any way? I think that the argument would have some force, but not much. I would give it a score of twenty, which indicates a quite weak inductive argument. One reason for assigning any force at all to it is that almost all Christians would answer question Q2 affirmatively. In other words, Q2 is practically redundant as a question put to people identified as "Christians." One can say that the property of loving humanity is almost an essential divine attribute within the Christian concept of God. On that basis alone, AE has a certain force which it lacks when applied merely to God in general. Furthermore, even those few Christians who refrain from saying that God loves humanity greatly would apply some property or other to God that makes connection with the problem of evil. Another way of putting the matter would be to say that the term "Christian" must have some content to it that is relevant to the suffering in the world. If we were to consider the two (overlapping) groups of people, Christians and theists in general, and were to raise the question "Which group is more greatly bothered by the great suffering that occurs in our world?" then the proper answer would be the Christians. That would be a reason for assigning a score of twenty (or so) to AE within the context of liberal Christianity, whereas it should not receive more than zero within the context of theism in general. More will be said about this matter in the next chapter.

13.2. The Argument from Nonbelief (ANB)

When it comes to ANB, the first question we need to raise is that of the outlook of liberal Christians regarding non-Christians. They certainly are not exclusivists, pitying all non-Christians as destined for perdition. But they need not be universalists either. That is, if they believe in salvation in the afterlife at all (which I think just about all of them do), then they need not regard it as the eventual automatic destiny of everyone. Many of them believe that one's salvation is largely a matter of one's good works rather than one's beliefs (perhaps on the model of the Good Samaritan, described in Luke 10:30-37). They might say that non-Christians can attain salvation, provided that they believe in God and meet some minimal standard of morality, perhaps aided by an appreciation of the ethical doctrines of Jesus. However, even on that theory, it would be desirable for non-Christians to receive some information from God regarding salvation. He should want all of them at least to know that it is available (or occurs). So the fact that God has not made them aware of it is a problem for anyone who believes in salvation, even if the salvation does not require awareness of the truth of the gospel message.

In order to accommodate the broader outlook of liberal Christians regarding salvation, in the formulation of ANB I shall replace the gospel message of chapter 2 (and set P of chapter 12) by the following slightly looser set (call it again "set P"):

Set P = the following three propositions:
   (a)   There exists a being who rules the entire universe.
   (b)   There is an afterlife for humans.
   (c)   In the afterlife, there is some sort of salvation for humans which in some way involves Jesus of Nazareth.

The wording of situation S remains essentially the same as in chapter 2, i.e., "the situation of all, or almost all, humans since the time of Jesus of Nazareth coming to believe *all three* propositions of set P by the time of their physical death," though it must be kept in mind that since "set P" has a different referent from "the gospel message," "situation S" also has a different referent. I shall not write out ANB. The formulation of it remains the same as in section 2.3 except that "God" is understood to refer to the God of liberal Christianity rather than the God of evangelical Christianity, and "set P" and "situation S" have different referents, as indicated above.

The wording of ANB's premise (C) remains essentially the same, i.e., as follows: "Situation S does *not* obtain. It is not the case that all, or almost all, humans since the time of Jesus of Nazareth have come to believe all three propositions of set P by the time of their physical death." I would say that the premise is still true, even though "set P" and "situation S" have different referents here. Very nearly all the two-thirds of the earth's population who do not believe all three propositions of the gospel message also do not believe all of set P, with proposition (c) again being the most polemical one. I think that ANB remains a sound argument, even when it is changed in the ways indicated above. Thus, ANB can be taken to establish the nonexistence of the God of those liberal Christians for whom the problem of non-belief arises at all. However, unlike the case with evangelical Christianity, that is certainly not all of them, though I think it does include most of them.

As with the problem of evil, since there is no definite set of doctrines or beliefs that apply to all liberal Christians, again the most we can say is that ANB *may* present a serious problem for them. It would be a mistake to claim in an unqualified way that the problem is a serious one for Christians in general or for liberal Christians. However, it certainly is such a problem for a very large proportion of them. To try to locate those for whom ANB does present a serious problem, we could ask liberal Christians the following two questions (call them Q4 and Q5):

Q4:   Could God have done things that would have caused everyone, or almost everyone, to believe all three propositions of set P?

Q5:   Does God strongly desire that everyone, or almost everyone, have such belief?

Although I have not conducted any poll on this matter, I think that most liberal Christians would say yes to both questions. The problem of nonbelief, as reformulated, is indeed a serious problem for such people, just as for evangelical Christians. There seems to be no way for them to definitely refute ANB once they answer Q4 and Q5 affirmatively. All the various attempts considered in this book were found to be unsuccessful.

I grant that some liberal Christians would say no to at least one of the questions. The problem of nonbelief, as reformulated, does not arise for those people. They are immune to the given version of ANB. Presumably they do not have the same sort of commitment to the Bible that evangelical Christians do. However, there may be challenges of a different sort for them, for example, what to make of biblical passages that definitely support an affirmative answer to both Q4 and Q5. They at least have a kind of "problem of Scripture," just as do those Christians who would say no to question Q1 or Q2. They need to explain why they call themselves "Christians," seeing that they reject at least some important parts of the Bible, which is the main pillar (if not the sole basis) of Christianity.

For those who do answer Q4 and Q5 affirmatively, it seems that ANB would present a strong argument for the nonexistence of the deity in which they say they believe. They may try to defend against it, using one or more of the defenses which were considered in part II of this book, but those defenses would again succumb to most of the same sorts of objections that were brought up there.

Consider, for example, the Free-will Defense (FDN), which claims that even though God wants people to believe certain propositions, he permits them to go through life not believing them in order to avoid interfering with their free will. The set of propositions relevant to liberal Christianity (set P, above) is different from those in the context of evangelical Christianity (the gospel message), but the objections to FDN presented in chapter 5 are still applicable to FDN within the new context. We can drop the Scriptural Objection, which has little relevance to liberal Christianity. But the other objections to FDN that were raised still apply, especially the Lack-of-conflict Objection and the Irrationality Objection. (The Relative-value Objection also still applies, but with lesser force in the case of liberal Christians, almost all of whom are universalists or inclusivists with regard to salvation.) The objections still refute FDN, even within the new context. See chapter 5 for details.

It is unclear how the Testing Defense (TDN) might be applied to the new set P. Perhaps God would be testing people to see whether they come to believe in the afterlife and salvation just on the basis of the (limited) evidence available and refrains from providing additional evidence to avoid upsetting the test. The whole idea is rather far-fetched. It seems to me that pretty much the same objections that were raised against TDN in section 7.2 could also be raised against it here in regard to the new set P and that those objections do indeed refute TDN. Not much more need be said.

When it comes to the Afterlife Defense (ADN), the situation is quite different from that of section 9.2. It does not make much sense to suggest that God might postpone getting people to believe in the afterlife until after they die, since the whole point of claiming that God wants them to believe in the afterlife at all is that such belief is beneficial during people's earthly life, providing them with a sense of hope. The only objection from chapter 9 that would apply to ADN in the context of liberal Christianity would be the Inexplicability Objection, but it does seem to refute the defense. Assuming that belief in set P would benefit people here on earth, it would be inexplicable why God, who is all-loving, would put off bringing about such belief. Thus ADN would present a basically incomplete theory. Liberal Christians who start out trying to defend against ANB by making some sort of appeal to the afterlife usually end up shifting over to the Unknown-purpose Defense (UDN).

Since UDN is based on just a flat-out denial of ANB's premise (A3), we need to inquire whether any support can be given for that premise. But here in the context of liberal Christianity the support must not be from Scripture (as it was in the context of both evangelical Christianity and Orthodox Judaism). It seems to me that there is no support for (A3) beyond whatever nonscriptural support might be cited for premise (A2). It would need to consist of reasons to say of God that he wants to bring about (the new) situation S, which here involves people believing in an afterlife and salvation. I can think of three sorts of reason why God would want them to have such beliefs, as follows:

(1)   Belief in an afterlife and salvation is beneficial, for it gives people a sense of hope regarding the future. Thus, since God loves people and wants them to have that which is beneficial, he must want them to have such belief.

(2)   God wants people to love him maximally, or at least greatly, and it would help them do that if they were to be aware that he has provided them with an afterlife and an opportunity for salvation.

(3)   The propositions of set P are fundamental truths about reality. Awareness of such truths is intrinsically good. Thus, since God loves people and wants them to have whatever is intrinsically good, he must want them to be aware of the truth of set P.

These are reasons for maintaining that God wants to bring about (the new) situation S. They could be used as nonscriptural support for ANB's premise (A2). Of course, we do not here need to establish the truth of that premise, since in the present context we are envisioning that ANB is simply being presented to those liberal Christians who answer question Q5 affirmatively, and such people have already conceded the truth of ANB's premise (A2). However, premise (A3) goes further and claims that God does not have any purpose which necessarily conflicts with and outweighs his desire to bring about situation S. There is not much that one can do to support such a claim beyond looking at the support for premise (A2) and saying of it that it is so forceful that it seems highly unlikely that God might have a purpose which overrides the desire on his part to which (A2) appeals. In other words, ANBers simply invite people to reflect upon the three reasons, (1)–(3), stated above, which are reasons for God to bring about situation S. They then ask those people how God might have a purpose which overrides his desire for situation S. It becomes more of a challenge than an argument, but it seems to me to be an extremely difficult challenge for the liberal Christian to try to deal with.

It is clear that questions Q2 and Q3 are also relevant to the application of ANB to liberal Christians. Those who answer Q2 and Q3 affirmatively are saying of God that he has great love and compassion for humanity and that he wants people to love him greatly in return. Such Christians would be in a lesser position to appeal to UDN to try to evade the problem of nonbelief, for they would be more inclined to accept at least one or two of the three reasons given above in support of ANB's premise (A2). It is true that they may still reject premise (A3) on the grounds that God has some unknown purpose which overrides his desire for situation S. But, as pointed out above in connection with AE, even if the relevant divine purpose is beyond human comprehension, as most UDNers claim, humanity could have at least been informed *that it exists*. Such revelation would have gone far toward removing the obstacle to humanity's love for God that has been brought about by all the secrecy surrounding God's purpose for permitting so much nonbelief in set P. If God really wants people to love him, then it would be counterproductive for him to be so secretive about the relevant purposes. UDNers would probably say that God has some reason for all the secrecy. But if that is so, then why has he not revealed to humanity that he has such a reason? For God to reveal that would help humanity get into the sort of relationship with him that he presumably desires. It is clear, I think, that those liberal Christians who answer questions Q2 and Q3 affirmatively are in a weak position to try to appeal to UDN as a defense against ANB.

If there are any liberal Christians who say no to Q2 or Q3 but yes to Q4 and Q5, then UDN would be more available to them than to those who answer all four questions affirmatively. However, the problem of nonbelief would still be a serious problem for such Christians. Simply answering Q4 and Q5 affirmatively places one in a position that gives rise to the problem, for it is natural to ask why God does not bring about a situation if indeed he wants it. Furthermore, there are other objections to UDN that would need to be considered, such as the Probability Objection and the Explanation Objection. But I shall not pursue these issues further, for the given class (liberal Christians who say no to Q2 or Q3 but yes to Q4 and Q5) strikes me as being an extreme minority. Although I have not conducted a poll on the matter, from my discussions with liberal Christians, I would say that the vast majority of them would answer all five questions, Q1–Q5, affirmatively.

The question might be raised how strong ANB is with respect to liberal Christians as an unrestricted group, i.e., quite apart from the use of any survey questions. In such a framework, I assigned (above) AE a score of twenty. I would also assign ANB a score of twenty. Like AE, ANB would have some force, but it would be very slight. Christians in general have some inclination to view God as a being who wants people to believe certain things, but without further qualification that does not carry much weight. More will be said about these matters in the next chapter.

The question with which we began was "How strong are AE and ANB as arguments for the nonexistence of the God of liberal Christianity?" There are at least two separate considerations there. One of them is the proportion of liberal Christians who would answer all five of our survey questions affirmatively. And the second is how strong each argument is with respect to those who would do so.

Taking the first consideration first, as I said previously, I think most liberal Christians would answer the five questions affirmatively, but I do not have much sense of what the exact proportion would be. As a very rough guess, I would say probably around three-fourths. Among the one-fourth who are negatives, I wonder if question Q5 (which is related to the problem of nonbelief) would draw more "no's" than would question Q2 (which is related to the problem of evil). If so, then perhaps AE would have a (slightly) greater applicability among liberal Christians than does ANB. Should we say in that case that the problem of evil is a more serious one for liberal Christians, overall, than is the problem of nonbelief, for more of them are affected by it? Or do other considerations (apart from our survey questions) have a bearing on this matter? I am not sure what to say here, so (for the time being) I shall assign scores of twenty to both AE and ANB when they are applied to liberal Christianity as an unrestricted group.

I shall now turn to the second consideration. Although some case might be made within the context of liberal Christianity for ANB's premise (A3), it is clear, I think, that it is a weaker case than in the context of either evangelical Christianity or Orthodox Judaism. Without an appeal to Scripture, (A3) appears rather conjectural, and there comes to be more room for UDN. It is true that objections could still be raised against UDN, but they are not as forceful as those raised within the context of evangelical Christianity or Orthodox Judaism. For this reason, my assessment of ANB within the context of liberal Christianity, even narrowed down to the target group of those who answer all five survey questions affirmatively, is that it is not as strong as it is in those other contexts. Assigning numerical values on our scale of zero to 100, I would say that, relative to the target group, ANB has a strength of eighty. That is more than the seventy-five assigned above to AE, but less than the ninety-five and eighty-five assigned to ANB within the contexts of evangelical Christianity and Orthodox Judaism, respectively.

Comparing AE and ANB within the context of liberal Christianity, I would say that possibly AE has the greater applicability but ANB definitely has the greater strength. That is, possibly more liberal Christians have a conception of God (as all-loving) which gives rise to the problem of evil than a conception of God (as desiring a certain set of beliefs among people) which gives rise to the problem of nonbelief. If that is so, then perhaps the problem of evil is the more serious one for liberal Christians. On the other hand, with regard to those liberal Christians for whom both problems do arise (the ones who would answer all five survey questions affirmatively), which I believe is a great majority of them, ANB definitely presents a stronger argument for God's nonexistence than does AE. I tried to capture this point by assigning scores of eighty and seventy-five to ANB and AE, respectively. The main reason for that lies in the fact that the "conceptual space" surrounding the problem of nonbelief is more restricted than for the problem of evil. There is less room for the Christian to maneuver and try to find defenses. Thus, although possibly fewer liberal Christians are challenged by the problem of nonbelief than by the problem of evil, the ones who are thus challenged are (by a narrow margin, admittedly) more clearly shown by ANB to be irrational for clinging to their belief in God than by AE. There will be further discussion of the relative strengths of ANB and AE in chapter 15, below.

14

God in General

By the expression "God in general" I simply mean God as generally conceived, i.e., apart from any specific religion or set of theological doctrines. The traditional problem of evil was usually applied to the so-called God of classical theism. For various reasons, some of which were discussed earlier, I find that concept to be unclear. The property of being wholly good is problematic, as well as such properties as transcendence, nonphysicality, and omnipresence. I have tried to steer clear of them in the present book. On the other hand, if we simply aim to find some common meaning for uses of the word "God" in ordinary language, that, too, gives rise to problems. It is hard to find any such common meaning, seeing that the word is used by such diverse groups as theists, deists, and pantheists. The problem of multiple concepts of God that we encountered with liberal Christianity comes in here to an even greater extent.

Perhaps the dictionary can assist us. The first definition of "God" given in *The Random House Dictionary*, second edition, is "the one Supreme Being, the creator and ruler of the universe." Expert lexicographers have presumably ascertained that *that* is the common meaning of "God" in English. I am willing to accept that result, despite the fact that the definition does seem to exclude the pantheistic concept and perhaps deism as well. (Deists might say, "creator, yes, but ruler, no.")

The dictionary definition does not ascribe to God either the property of loving people or the property of wanting something back from them (and thus caring about their beliefs). Nor does it ascribe to God anything that would imply possession of either of those properties. For that reason, I would say that neither AE nor ANB presents any problem for belief in God as defined in the given way. If that is all that God in general is, then the problems of evil and nonbelief are not serious ones for belief in God in general. On a scale of zero to 100, I would assess the strength of both AE and ANB as applied to God in general (with no further qualification) to be zero. That is, they could not even be considered (as they were with regard to unrestricted liberal Christianity) as weak inductive (or evidential) arguments. Rather, they would have no force whatever.

The idea that AE has no force against God in general is expressed by Terry Christlieb, who says the following:

> Generic theism is simply *too* generic to be susceptible to an evidential attack. Unless the set of propositions that constitutes generic theism is somehow supplemented, its relation to propositions about the evils of this world will remain obscure. It will certainly be too obscure to justify the claim that a significant evidential relation exists between them.[1]

Although I agree with the wording of this statement, my definition of "generic theism" is different from Christlieb's. I take it to be belief in God as defined by the dictionary, which does not include the property of omnibenevolence. However, Christlieb takes it to be belief in God defined as having that property. I would argue that when the property of omnibenevolence is included among the divine attributes, then the force of AE, though still weak, should be something greater than zero. It is reasonable to think that an omnibenevolent deity would strongly desire situation L. As pointed out in chapter 10, Christlieb goes so far as to assess AE's force as zero even against the God of the Bible, and that is a big mistake. However, so far as unrestricted theism in general is concerned, I am willing to concede that AE has no force whatever. If some atheologians disagree, then they are simply wrong about the matter.

Nevertheless, this approach to the topic may seem too quick. Many readers no doubt feel that the problem of evil *is* a serious problem for general (or standard) theism. The technique that was employed for liberal Christianity was first to acknowledge that the problems of evil and nonbelief do not arise for all members of the given group but then to formulate survey questions as a way of locating a sizable subgroup for whom the problems would indeed be serious ones. Let us see how such a methodology might work in the case of theists and "God in general."

14.1. The Argument from Evil (AE)

When AE is applied to God in general, situation L remains the same as before and AE itself also remains the same except that the term "God" refers to God in general rather than any specific god. Let us set our target population to be those who could properly be called "theists." That would exclude deists, pantheists, and certain (other) religious minorities within the United States. The question is whether or not AE presents a serious problem for theists.

We need to inquire, first of all, how many of them would say yes to both question Q1 and Q2 as formulated in chapter 13. Those were the questions whether God could have prevented or reduced the evil in the world and whether God has great love and compassion for humanity. For all those who respond to both questions affirmatively I would say, as before, that the problem of evil is a serious problem. And indeed, by my rough estimate, most theists in the United States would answer the questions affirmatively, though in slightly smaller proportion than for the class of liberal Christians. And so, yes, the problem does arise for most theists. They need to explain why God, seeing that he has great love and compassion for humanity, does not do more to prevent or reduce the enormous amount of suffering that occurs on our planet. The very fact that more is not done appears to be good evidence that such a being does not exist.

An analogy could be used to bring out the force of AE as a probabilistic argument. Suppose a man is missing and the issue is raised whether he is still alive. Certain evidence could be produced that he is no longer alive. Suppose he has a wife and children whom he loves very much and suppose he is a man of great wealth and power. Suppose also that his family has fallen on hard times. They have become destitute and gravely ill. We are here assuming that if the man were still alive, he would be aware of his family's plight and would be able to help them. Thus, the fact that he has not come to his family's rescue, despite the fact that he loves them very much, is good evidence that he is no longer alive. It does not conclusively establish the truth of the proposition, but it does render it highly probable. In a similar way, AE renders highly probable the nonexistence of a deity for whom our survey questions Q1 and Q2 would yield affirmative answers.

The complaint might be made that if the survey is only done within the United States, then the class of theists is pretty much made up of Christians. So, having discussed evangelical and liberal Christianity, it would be largely redundant for me to now discuss theism in general in our country. I acknowledge the huge overlap in the target classes, but proceed with the discussion anyway because I think it would be illuminating. It has been a longstanding problem within the philosophy of religion whether AE refutes theism. My answer is that it does not do so when "God" is defined as in the dictionary or in a way (if there were any) acceptable to all theists within the United States. However, almost all theists have a more specific concept of God in mind, and AE does present a serious problem for most adherents of those specific concepts. I see it as strongly supporting the nonexistence of the deity in which they claim to believe.

We need to inquire whether non-Christian theists who answer Q1 and Q2 affirmatively have any tools at their disposal for refuting or evading the problem of evil which are not available to Christians. I think they do. Non-Christians could answer question Q3 negatively, i.e., they could deny that God wants people to love him greatly. I think that if they were to do that, it would make the Unknown-purpose Defense (UDE) slightly more open to them. They would at least not be confronted by the additional problem of explaining how God expects people to come to love him greatly if he permits so much evil in the world and also keeps his purposes secret from them. So when they say, "I have no explanation," they would only be saying that in relation to the question "Why does a loving God permit so much evil in the world and also keep his purposes on the matter secret?" In contrast, almost all Christians would answer question Q3 affirmatively. Hence, if they adopt UDE as a defense against AE, then they would be saying, "I have no explanation" to the more complex question "Why does a loving God, who wants humanity to love him greatly in return, permit so much evil in the world and keep his purposes on the matter secret?" To say, "I have no explanation" in the latter case (instead of simply giving up on Christianity) is less reasonable than such an appeal to UDE by theists in general.

The point could be brought out by the Negligent-father Objection which was appealed to in chapter 6. Suppose a father permits his son to drown, where it is clear that he could have prevented it. Also suppose that there are many onlookers, and when they later ask the father why he permitted his son to drown, he gives no reply. Two theories are put forward about the father. Theory no. 1 says of him only that he loved his son greatly. Theory no. 2 says of him that not only did he love his son greatly but he also wanted the onlookers to think very highly of him. Advocates of both theories are asked the question "Why did the father let his son drown and then refuse to explain to the onlookers why he did that?" Both sets of advocates simply reply, "I have no explanation." I think it is clear that both theories are implausible, but theory no. 2 is still more implausible than theory no. 1. For advocates of theory no. 2 not to give up their view but instead cling to it through a use of the "unknown-purpose" idea is more unreasonable than for advocates of theory no. 1 to do so. In an analogous way, considering people who adopt UDE as a defense against AE, those who are Christians and who answer question Q3 affirmatively are more unreasonable in clinging to their position than those who are non-Christian theists and who answer Q3 negatively.

I do not have any view on what proportion of non-Christian theists who answer Q1 and Q2 affirmatively would answer Q3 negatively. It would be an interesting survey to conduct. But, in any case, I would maintain that the Probability Objection and Explanation Objection (raised in chapter 10) could be applied against UDE in the present context and would be a strong attack against it, even when the further property of desiring humanity's love is not ascribed to God. Hence, the sort of move considered regarding the problem of evil (i.e., answering Q3 negatively) would still not totally eliminate the problem. To appear unreasonable in one's worldview, given the enormous amount of suffering that occurs in the world, it is enough merely to say, "God exists and God loves humanity greatly."

As for other defenses against AE, it seems that the same sorts of objections can be raised against them within the present context (theism in general) as within the context of liberal Christianity. So the considerations raised in section 13.1, showing the failure of all the various defenses, are also relevant here. Many of the details regarding specific defenses can be found in earlier chapters. Unlike the case of ANB, the issues surrounding AE are the same as in those chapters. My overall conclusion is that the defenses all fail, though the best of them is UDE.

There is another approach that may be taken here. It could be conceded by those theists who answer Q1–Q3 affirmatively that the vast amount of evil in the world does indeed constitute evidence against the existence of their deity. But they may claim to have other evidence of a positive sort in favor of the existence of that deity, such as the traditional arguments of natural theology. In the case of the God of Christianity and the God of Orthodox Judaism, divine attributes are ascribed that cannot in any way be supported solely by appeal to such arguments. But since it is God in general that is at issue here rather than any specific deity, those traditional arguments become relevant. The claim could be made that when the total evidence is considered, both for and against the existence of God (in general), the positive evidence outweighs the negative. Hence, since the process of induction requires that the total relevant evidence be taken into account, it would be incorrect to say of AE that it inductively establishes the probable nonexistence of God.

That is certainly a large issue, and I do not plan to pursue it at any great length in this book. However, I have inserted appendix F as some partial support for my overall skepticism regarding the arguments of natural theology (most of them dealing with issues of science and the adequacy of naturalistic explanations for various phenomena). I find natural theology to be ultimately unsuccessful and most obviously so when "God" is defined as (among other things) "a being who loves humanity greatly." The given arguments seem totally irrelevant to such a deity. Yet most theists include that property as an essential property of God. My conclusion, then, is that the attempt to show (as by natural theology) that the positive support for God's existence outweighs the negative evidence (based on evil) is a failure, and most obviously so when it is applied to the concept of God as all-loving, which is the concept of deity possessed by most theists. In other words, just as AE and ANB have a strength of zero when applied to God in general, so also all the arguments for God's existence have a strength of zero (and this is most obvious when the property of being all-loving is taken to be a divine attribute). I grant, though, that to establish this conclusion would call for a careful scrutiny and refutation of natural theology and that is something that has not been attempted in the present book beyond the contribution of appendix F. Others have done a lot more with the topic,[2] and I pretty much go along with their results.

As with liberal Christianity, there are two separate issues involved in assessing the strength of AE as an atheological argument. The first issue is that of applicability: what proportion of theists (say, in the United States) would answer our three survey questions (Q1–Q3) affirmatively and thereby be confronted by the problem of evil? Among liberal Christians, I made a rough guess that about three-fourths of them would be in that situation. In the case of theists in general, my (very rough) guess is that it is about two-thirds. So, is the problem of evil a serious problem for theists in general? I would say: for most of them, yes. However, for a significant number of theists, no, AE does not present any serious problem.

The second issue has to do with the force or strength of AE in relation to those theists for whom the problem of evil *is* a serious problem, say, for those who would answer all three survey questions affirmatively. I think that AE is not quite as forceful here as in the case of liberal Christianity. On the scale of zero to 100, I would give it a score of seventy. (That applies only to theists who answer all three questions affirmatively. For those who answer Q3 negatively, the score would be still less. And for theists in general, without use of the survey, the score would be zero.) I rated AE higher (with a score of seventy-five) within the context of liberal Christianity. The main reason is that Christianity provides a kind of framework which restricts the sorts of defenses that might be brought up against AE. When that framework is removed (even when the three survey questions are answered affirmatively), there is more room for defenses, which in turn reduces the force of AE, even though, I maintain, none of the defenses is in the end successful, anyway.

So my final verdict on AE as an atheological argument is that it is more forceful against the God-concepts of evangelical Christianity and liberal Christianity (with scores of eighty-five and seventy-five, respectively) and less forceful (though still "packing a punch") against God in general and the God of Orthodox Judaism (with scores of seventy and sixty-five, respectively). In the case of the God of liberal Christianity and God in general, it is assumed here that a certain specific concept of God has been extracted through the use of survey questions and AE is applied just to that specific concept. Not to extract some such specific concept, that is, to apply AE to the total classes of liberal Christians or theists in general would not produce any forceful atheological argument. For significant numbers of people within each of those classes, AE simply does not present any serious problem, since they do not conceive of God in any way that gives rise to the problem of evil. Atheologians who have claimed otherwise are simply mistaken and misguided on the matter.

14.2. The Argument from Nonbelief (ANB)

When it comes to the problem of nonbelief, there are again different ways of posing the issue for theists in general. One way would be that of William Alston, as noted above in section 1.7: "Why does God allow such a diversity of incompatible systems of belief about Himself?" Presumably there are propositions that describe God correctly. Why hasn't God (directly or indirectly) caused everyone, or just about everyone, to believe *those* propositions? Is the very fact that there is such a diversity of religions in the world good evidence that God (in general) does not exist?

Another way to pose the issue is in terms of mere theistic belief. According to the 1996 *World Almanac*, 20 percent of the earth's population consists of people who have no religion or who are atheists. Another 25 percent have some sort of non-Western religion which does not view reality in terms of a single personal deity who rules the universe. Why hasn't God done more to enlighten such people and make believers of them?[3] And, again, is the fact that there are so many nontheists in the world good evidence that God does not exist? Let us consider the problem when it is formulated in this fashion.

There are at least two different approaches to the issue. One of them is that of J. L. Schellenberg. He formulates the Argument from Nonbelief in a way that emphasizes what he calls "reasonable nonbelief" and applies it to God in general without any qualifications. Another approach, the one that I favor, is to take ANB as previously formulated in this book, modify it in a way that would make it applicable to God in general, and then apply it only to a certain subgroup of theists. Let us consider these two different approaches in more detail.

14.21. Schellenberg's Approach

Schellenberg formulates his atheological argument as follows:
   (1) If there is a God, he is perfectly loving.
   (2) If a perfectly loving God exists, reasonable nonbelief does not occur.
   (3) [But] reasonable nonbelief occurs.
   (4) [Thus, from (2) & (3)] no perfectly loving God exists.

(5) [Hence, from (1) & (4)] there is no God.[4]

A minor semantic point here is that the term "God" usually functions as a proper name or as a word with the same logical grammar as a proper name. But in putting the indefinite article in front of it (writing "a God") Schellenberg is very clearly using it as a common noun. I would prefer either using the common noun "god" in place of the name "God" or else restructuring the argument. As noted in the preface, I myself use "God" with the definite article (as in "the God of Christianity"), which is not totally correct from a linguistic point of view. However, to use "God" with the indefinite article strikes me as still worse. Nevertheless, this is not an important issue.

Another objection pertains to the expression "reasonable nonbelief." It is unclear just what its contrast might be. That is, what might "unreasonable nonbelief" refer to? Informal logicians sometimes talk about what they call "the fallacy of slothful induction."[5] That is the fallacy that people commit when they fail to draw a warranted conclusion from strong evidence of which they are aware. An example would be a mother who discovers drugs and drug paraphernalia in her son's room. She fails to draw the conclusion that her son is a drug addict, perhaps partly because such a belief would cause her great consternation. It might be said that she is deceiving herself or is in a state of "denial" (though those characteristics are not part of the definition of "slothful induction"). One possible interpretation of "unreasonable nonbelief" is that it is nonbelief which is the outcome of slothful induction. But that seems not to be how Schellenberg understands it. He says that it is nonbelief which is "the result of culpable actions or omissions on the part of the subject,"[6] which are actions or omissions which arise through the subject's fault and for which the subject is to blame.

The idea of actions resulting in nonbelief for which the subject is to blame is unclear to me. Part of my problem lies with what is referred to in appendix A as "the Paradox of Culpability." By a constructive dilemma it can be proven that people are never culpable for any actions they may perform. But even apart from the paradox, I find the idea of culpability for actions resulting in nonbelief to be obscure. Perhaps it has some connection with the principle "Ignorance of the law is no excuse." But that principle might be applied in different ways, and has exceptions to it. In any case it is unclear how any analogous principle might work in the case of ignorance of God's existence. For one thing, I know of no good evidence for God's existence that could be analogous to civil laws. And for another thing, even if there is such evidence, it appears that billions of people are or have been simply without a clue as to its existence. What could it be that they might have overlooked, and how could it be that they were somehow obligated to not overlook it? In the example of the mother who is in a state of "denial" over her son's drug addiction, is she culpable and to blame for the self-deception which produced her nonbelief? Could she relieve herself of culpability by pleading "temporary insanity"? What actions (or omissions), exactly, did she perform for which she would be considered culpable? Is she culpable only if her nonbelief in some way causes harm to someone else (e.g., harm to her son caused by a delay in treatment)? Or can people be culpable for nonbelief that affects no one else but themselves (e.g., not believing that smoking causes cancer)? None of this is clear. Nor does Schellenberg cast any light on such issues.

Let us seek guidance on this matter from a reviewer of the Schellenberg book, namely, Daniel Howard-Snyder, who says the following:

> [I]t is useful to consider the variety of ways in which theistic nonbelief can be *culpable*. (We can thereby better appreciate how easily we may be culpable.) I might spurn God's manifest love, develop a deaf ear to His overtures and lose theistic belief. Or, I might neglect to investigate the matter properly. . . . First, I might culpably fail to gather grounds for theistic belief. The possibilities here are legion. I might fail to look for evidence, or bias the evidence I consider. I might ignore or suppress an inner prompting to believe, neglect spiritual disciplines, want theism to be false for various reasons, and so on. Second, I might culpably fail to assess my grounds properly. Perhaps I culpably fail to appraise my epistemic standards, or I culpably hold theses unfriendly to theism (e.g., meaning verificationism or radical constructivism). Might God permit such culpable nonbelief, for a time? Why not? It doesn't seem worse than any other way to permit us freedom in relating personally to Him.[7]

Instead of being enlightened by Howard-Snyder's remarks, I am baffled by them. What is it to "spurn God's manifest love"? No such love is manifest to nonbelievers, especially ones who put forward AE. What are God's "overtures"? Such a metaphor is a complete dud in this context. How could nonbelievers be culpable for failing to look for evidence of God's existence? No good evidence has been presented to them. Why should they have any duty to look further? Howard-Snyder says that nonbelievers may "bias the evidence" that they consider. How might they do *that*? Some example is needed. As for nonbelievers ignoring or suppressing inner promptings to believe, neglecting spiritual disciplines, or wanting theism to be false, what does all that come to? And why think that anything like that ever occurs? It makes nonbelievers seem utterly irrational. Why think that they are? And even if they *are* irrational, why should they be regarded as in any way *culpable* for their situation?

Howard-Snyder suggests that nonbelievers may *culpably* fail to do certain things or *culpably* hold "theses unfriendly to theism." But that is begging the question. We want some *reason* to declare nonbelievers culpable for being in their situation. To simply pronounce them "culpable" is not to provide any reason. Thus, for all of his talk of "the variety of ways" and "how easily" we may be culpable, I do not see that Howard-Snyder has provided any clarification as to what it is supposed to be about. It is not only that he has failed to prove or support the claim that nonbelievers might be culpable, but that he has not even clarified what the claim is supposed to mean. For all that he says, the whole idea of culpable nonbelief remains obscure.

It would have been enlightening if Schellenberg, in his book, had provided a numerical estimate of the proportion of nontheists in the world whose nonbelief is reasonable (in his sense of "reasonable," i.e., inculpable). Whereas many Christians would say that it is zero percent, my own view (at least to the slight extent that I can understand the concept) is that it is 100 percent. Presumably Schellenberg thinks that it is somewhere between these extremes. It would have been helpful toward comprehending his outlook to know approximately where he would place it. For example, if he thinks the correct figure to be only about 1 percent, then would he still regard his argument to be a strong one? And on the other hand, if he were to think the correct figure to be about 99 percent (which would make the expression "reasonable nonbelief" close to being redundant), then would he still want to frame his argument using that expression? Answers to such questions would have helped the reader better understand his theory.

Since I would say that all nontheism is reasonable in Schellenberg's sense (i.e., not culpable), I would readily accept his premise (3). It should be noted, though, that there are many theists, especially within the evangelical Christian community, who would reject it. Schellenberg devotes a chapter of his book to refuting their outlook. Although I agree with what he says there, I object to a certain apparent underlying assumption behind his argument. It is that if his premise (3) were false and all nontheism were somehow culpable, then it would be possible for a perfectly loving deity not to do anything about nontheists but just leave them in their state of self-deception. It seems to me that such people would be in an unfortunate situation and in need of some sort of treatment or "straightening out." Like people in a foreign country who are ignorant of its laws and like the mother who deceives herself about her son's drug abuse, nontheists would be in need of enlightenment about the true nature of reality. Even if their nonbelief were somehow their own fault, that fact seems irrelevant to me. A perfectly loving deity would set vindictiveness aside and still want to help them, despite their culpability. All it would take, for most, would be a "great sign" (like skywriting), or perhaps, as Schellenberg prefers, a religious experience. As James A. Keller has said: "[E]ven if our ignorance is in part or entirely our fault, if God loves us and wishes us to have faith in God, then there is good reason for God to do what God can to make our situation more clear to us."[8] This seems quite right. Thus, although I accept

Schellenberg's premise (3), I reject the distinction which underlies it, between culpable and inculpable nonbelief. The real force of ANB lies in the fact of nonbelief itself. The issue of whether the nonbelief is culpable or inculpable is irrelevant.

The Schellenberg book was also reviewed by Robert McKim, who put forward some interesting criticisms of it. McKim begins his critique as follows: "Presumably, according to Schellenberg, it is the *human* side of a personal relationship between God and us that is difficult (or even impossible) if nonbelief is rational." (Original italics)[9] I think that this is a misconstrual of Schellenberg's position, which is that if there are nonbelievers and their nonbelief is rational, then God (who is perfectly loving) could not possibly permit it, since he couldn't bear having people (i.e., the nonbelievers) so deprived. So it would be the divine side, not the human side, that would be impossible if nonbelief is rational.

McKim talks of the "goods of mystery" (which are the benefits of nonbelief) and the "goods of clarity" (which are the benefits of awareness of God) and views the issue as that of which set of goods outweighs the other. He takes Schellenberg to be claiming that the goods of clarity outweigh the goods of mystery, and that is why God (in order to be perfectly loving) needs to reveal himself to humanity. I think that would be an accurate representation of Schellenberg's position only if it were added that there are no goods of mystery that we know of, whereas there are indeed very definite goods of clarity. McKim grants that there are goods of clarity, citing "the good of personal relationship with God" and the (intrinsic) good of having a true belief about God. Another such good (a "biggie"), not mentioned by either McKim or Schellenberg, would be the good that would be available only to believers if exclusivism were true: that of the opportunity for salvation in the afterlife.

Schellenberg and I deny that there are any goods of mystery, but McKim suggests that free will might be one. He says: "Our being able to decide what to believe about religious matters in circumstances in which a number of options are rational may also be a good of mystery."[10] But that idea is refuted by Schellenberg in his chapter 5. I hope also to have disposed of it in my own chapter 5. There are many objections to it, one of which is its presupposition of strong voluntarism (attacked below in appendix C) and another its presupposition that it is good to be in a situation of epistemic ambiguity. I see nothing good about that. The classic example of the man in an arena forced to choose (in a state of ignorance) between two doors, behind one of which is a beautiful lady and behind the other a tiger, should count against it. If McKim had come up with some plausible candidate for a good of mystery, then he might have begun to mount a strong objection to Schellenberg. But he didn't, and so he lacked any such objection.

However, McKim does appeal to the Unknown-purpose Defense (UDN), which is certainly a move to be taken seriously. Referring to the contest between the goods of mystery and the goods of clarity, he says: "[W]e have no way to rule out the possibility that there are more unknown goods on one side than there are on the other, or that such goods are only on one side."[11] The expression "unknown goods" as applied to the "goods of mystery" side is a way of referring to unknown purposes that God might have for (reasonable) nonbelief. Some of what was said about UDN in chapter 11 would be relevant to McKim's appeal to it here. More will be said about this issue later (in section 14.23).

My main criticisms of Schellenberg's actual argument, as formulated above, pertain to premises (1) and (2). I reject (1) because there are theists who do not view God as perfectly loving. There may be many Orthodox Jews in that category and even a few Christians as well. They think of God as an angry deity who is bent on punishing people for their sins (or whatever). Certainly a god who would order the genocidal annihilation of the Amalekites, including all their children and all their animals (1 Sam. 15:3), is not a perfectly loving god. And certainly a god who would predestine some of his creatures to eternal torment in hell (as accepted by many Calvinists) is not a perfectly loving god. It is possible that many Muslims also think of Allah as a being who is something other than perfectly loving. McKim comments on this point as follows:

> Many theists put more emphasis on the need to worship and fall before a God who is mysterious and awe-inspiring, before whom we are as dust, in whose presence reverence rather than a search for friendship is appropriate for us, and with whom we are not capable of a mutual and reciprocal relationship. Muslims, with the exception of some Sufis, put little emphasis on an intimate personal relationship with God: they put more emphasis on submission on our part, and on compassion, mercy, and justice on God's part. Many Catholic Christians put more emphasis on a relationship that is mediated by the Church.[12]

On this point I am in agreement with McKim. Even if many of the theists who conceive of God in the ways described here would say, "God is perfectly loving," it is their mental picture of God that is important, and that seems to be something else, despite the words. Thus, the property of "perfectly loving" is too specific to be applied to God in general. No doubt that is why the lexicographers omit it, and they are right to do so. If included, it would make the definition of "God" too narrow.

In the discussion of his position on this matter, Schellenberg says:

> Any being who lacked [Divine love] would be a being whose greatness could be surpassed, and therefore not God. Love of the sort in question is

clearly one of the highest manifestations of personal being; so if God is conceived as embodying the perfections of personal life, he must be conceived as perfectly loving.[13]

I really do not know what to make of this claim since the concept of "unsurpassable greatness" (like that of being "wholly good") eludes me, as indicated in section 1.3. There is much in religious language that is obscure and in my view the given expressions are like that. In any case, the fact remains that there are a great many people out there who believe in a god who ordered the total annihilation of the Amalekites (and who performed many other acts which, if done by humans, would be regarded as atrocities, subject to investigation by a war-crimes tribunal). And there are a great many people who believe in a god who predestines people to hell. It is clear that they do not conceive of such a deity as perfectly loving, despite whatever lip service they might pay to the concept of divine love. Hence, to ascribe that property to God in general, without qualification, seems to me to be a mistake.

Of course, one could simply ignore the above objection and take Schellenberg's essential argument to be his steps (2)–(4). Certainly if he were successful in proving *that* argument to be sound, then that would be a great achievement in the philosophy of religion, so let us scrutinize it more closely. The main point at which Schellenberg's argument should be attacked is its premise (2). The question is: even assuming that God is perfectly loving, why should a loving deity have to want people to believe in him? We could have pets (e.g., turtles or birds) which we love dearly without any desire that they be aware of our existence. A man could even have children whom he loves and supports in circumstances in which they are not aware of his existence. He may prefer it to be that way, perhaps because for certain reasons he thinks they would be better off not knowing about him. For example, maybe he is a moody person with periods of violent behavior. Or maybe he is hiding from bomb-throwing terrorists, so anyone close to him is at risk. There is nothing in the concept of love itself that would warrant the inference drawn in premise (2). There is no contradiction (or even oddity) in the statement "X loves Y, but X does not want Y to be aware of X's existence." The idea of "loving from afar" is a familiar theme in literature.

Schellenberg would no doubt object that these considerations do not apply to God because he has additional properties which forestall them. God is all-powerful and all-knowing, but more importantly, God is all-good. And it has to be in people's best interests to be aware of the existence of such a being if indeed he exists. But what does "all-good" mean? And *why* must it be in people's best interests to be aware of such a being? There are many nontheists out there who lack such an awareness and yet who seem to be perfectly happy anyway. What is the great benefit that such people are missing? This is something that Schellenberg should have made clearer.

Another consideration is that God may be so far beyond us that we are incapable of comprehending him. Maybe theists have such a poor understanding of God that there is no significant difference between them and nontheists, so far as God is concerned. In other words, people's nonbelief does not bother God because the only sort of belief of which humans are capable is of little, if any, value to him. Yet, he might be perfectly loving, notwithstanding. I could love my pet canary even though its comprehension of *me* is exceedingly limited. I may also love the robin out in my backyard. I *could* make an effort toward revealing myself to the robin, but why bother? The most I could achieve within the robin would be a comprehension of me that is akin to that of my canary, which would not be worth the effort. What this shows, I think, is that divine love, by itself, is insufficient to motivate God to bring about universal (or near-universal) theistic belief, which refutes Schellenberg's premise (2).

It can be gathered from Howard-Snyder's treatment of Schellenberg's argument[14] that if he were to focus on the version of it stated above (which is Schellenberg's own formulation), then he would attack its premise (2). He would raise two main objections to that premise. One of them would be the Inappropriate-response Defense, which was discussed in section 5.6, above, and the other would be an appeal to UDN. According to the Inappropriate-response Defense, God may very well permit nonbelief in his existence as a way to avoid inappropriate responses among people who are caused to believe in God. I think that when the issue has to do with nonbelief in God in general, that defense becomes a little more plausible than it is in the context of the God of evangelical Christianity and nonbelief in the gospel message. Nevertheless, Schellenberg's reply to it[15] still strikes me as quite strong. This issue was covered previously and we need not go into it again here. Furthermore, it is not of great importance for me to enter into the intricacies of the given debate, for even if Howard-Snyder were to prevail in it, he would be refuting a premise which I myself reject, and, more importantly, his argument does not fare well against my own formulation of ANB, which will be discussed below. I shall also discuss below the use of UDN against ANB applied to God in general.

There is good point in claiming that the God of evangelical Christianity wants people to be aware of his existence. However, the support for such a claim cannot simply be that the deity in question is perfectly loving. It ought to include an appeal to Scripture. It is mainly because the claim can be supported by biblical passages that it can carry the weight of an atheological argument. Suppose the Bible had instead said explicitly that God loves humanity maximally but nevertheless wants to maintain some sort of "epistemic distance" from it (and did not contain any verses that convey a contrary message). Then two points would be warranted. One of them is that there would be no contradiction there. Whatever reason God might have for wanting to maintain an "epistemic distance" from humanity, it need not automatically impugn his perfect love. The other point is that ANB would have no basis. The fact of people's nonbelief would in that case be no good reason whatever to deny the existence of the deity in question. This shows the importance of Scripture for Schellenberg's line of reasoning. It is because he makes no appeal to it that I find his argument unconvincing. Premise (2), by itself, lacks sufficient force.

Thus, my conclusion regarding Schellenberg's atheological argument is that it is a failure. To make a case for premise (1), it should have been exclusively applied to some such deity as the God of Christianity rather than God in general. And to strengthen premise (2), it should have included an appeal to Scripture or to other divine attributes rather than put all its weight on the concept of divine love. The closer the argument might come to the version of ANB formulated above in section 2.3, the stronger it would be.

14.22. My Approach

We first need to recognize that there are many different concepts of God in general, even when the domain is restricted to the United States. For many of them, the problem of nonbelief is not a serious problem. One could simply assert that God does not give a hoot whether or not people believe in him and that would end the matter right there. However, there are many people in the United States, especially Christians, whose conception of deity is not so nonchalant, so let us not give up too soon. The United States is a Christian nation.

Some theists, possibly including some liberal Christians, may hold the view that God greatly loves people but does not expect anything back from them. Hence, God is not as concerned about people's beliefs as evangelical Christians make him out to be. It is true that the problem of nonbelief would not be such a serious one for such theists, but there would be a different problem: Why believe that God greatly loves people? One cannot in this position appeal to the Bible, for there is at least as much evidence from the Bible that God wants something back from people as that he greatly loves them. So it seems that the belief in God's love would in that case be without foundation.

There are many theists for whom the problem of nonbelief would be a serious one, and we could use survey questions similar to the ones mentioned in chapter 13 in an effort to locate them. In particular, questions Q4 and Q5 could be rephrased as follows:

Q4: Could God have done things that would have caused everyone, or almost everyone, to believe that he exists?

Q5: Does God strongly desire that everyone, or almost everyone, believe that he exists?

I think that more than half the general theist population of the United States would answer both questions affirmatively, but with a slightly smaller percentage than in the case of questions Q1 and Q2. For those people who say yes to both questions, there is the problem of nonbelief, which in this context is for the most part the problem of explaining why there are so many atheists and nonreligious people in the world. If God wants such people to believe in him, then why hasn't he simply appeared to them or done something else that would have effectively cured them of their nonbelief? I do not know of any cogent and reasonable explanation that might be given here.

That gives rise to ANB as an argument for the nonexistence of God in general. In formulating it, we need to eliminate specific religious content from set P, which is simply to delete its second and third propositions. That leaves us with just a single proposition, P, which is the proposition that there exists a being who rules the entire universe. Some may prefer to expand the proposition to say, further, that the ruler of the universe is a being who is omnipotent, omniscient, omnibenevolent, eternal, and the creator of the universe (that is, to express what is called "classical theism"). However, for our purposes here, it is not important exactly what form the theistic proposition takes. Situation S would be simply the situation of all, or almost all, present-day humans believing proposition P, whether P is given the narrower or the more expanded form. Having defined "situation S," we can formulate ANB with respect to God in general as follows:

(A)   If God were to exist, then he would possess all of the following four properties (among others):
   (1) *being able* to bring about situation S, all things considered;
   (2) *wanting* to bring about situation S, i.e., having it among his desires;
   (3) *not wanting* anything else that necessarily conflicts with his desire to bring about situation S as strongly as he wants to bring about situation S;
   (4) *being rational* (which implies always acting in accord with his own highest purposes).

(B)   If a being who has all four properties listed above were to exist, then situation S would have to obtain.

(C)   But situation S does *not* obtain. It is not the case that all, or almost all, present-day humans believe proposition P (even when it is given the narrower formulation).

(D)   Therefore [from (B) & (C)], there does not exist a being who possesses all four properties listed in premise (A).

(E)   Hence [from (A) & (D)], God does not exist.

Is this argument a powerful proof of the nonexistence of the deity believed in by all theists who would answer our questions Q4 and Q5 affirmatively? An affirmative answer to Q4 would certainly entail premise (A1). But what about an affirmative answer to Q5 (which affirms that God strongly desires that everyone, or almost everyone, believe that he exists)? Would that entail either premise (A2) or premise (A3)? We need to ask whether God might desire universal theistic belief without wanting to bring it about himself. Also, might God want to bring it about but still not do so because of some other conflicting desire that outweighs that one? We here get into issues analogous to the ones we discussed earlier in connection with the God of evangelical Christianity. But now we do not have the Bible to which to appeal. The difficulties confronting support for (A2) and (A3) are therefore more formidable. We need to look at what might be said in their behalf.

In addition, we need to say something about ANB's new premise (C), which was not an issue in the previous formulation. I have actually had people tell me that everyone on earth (even Madalyn Murray O'Hair) really "knows deep down" that God exists, and so ANB's (new) premise (C) is false. What can one say to such people in reply? I have said, "Look, I myself do not believe that God exists and I should know my own state of mind better than anyone else." But that fails to deter them. They say, "Deep down, in your heart of hearts, you know He exists." Such a conversation can be exasperating. It seems arrogant for them to declare that they know me better than I know myself. Their thesis, if it could be called that, would be totally unverifiable and unfalsifiable. It lacks content. I shall have to say simply that in the present book it is assumed that there are billions of nontheists out there. They claim to be nontheists (though not necessarily in those words) and that seems to me to be enough to establish that they really are nontheists. If that doesn't establish it, then what would?

Furthermore, the issue could be raised why God permits so many people simply to *claim* to be nontheists. If God exists, then presumably claims that he does not exist would tend to upset him, so the theists owe us an explanation for why he permits it. All God need do would be simply to reveal himself to everyone in a very clear way. That would cause the putative "nontheists" to stop making the claim in question and start calling themselves "theists." I conclude that even if it were conceded that everyone on earth really (deep down) believes that God exists, an argument like ANB could be constructed around the fact that billions of people *claim* to be nontheists (or claim that God does not exist or seems not to exist). Such an argument would suffice to establish God's nonexistence. Thus, in the end, ANB's premise (C) could as well be conceded. There is nothing in it conceptually problematic, as there is in Schellenberg's corresponding premise (3).

In earlier chapters we considered various defenses which might be raised against ANB in the context of evangelical Christianity. In my opinion they were all refuted in one way or another. But the concept of God in general is of special importance. So it would be worthwhile to consider in some detail whether or not any of the defenses might fare better in the context of general theism, i.e., as defenses against the particular version of ANB formulated above.

First consider FDN. Might God refrain from revealing himself to people in a clear way for fear of interfering with their free will? I think that some of the same objections that were raised against FDN in the context of evangelical Christianity (chap. 5) would apply here as well. For example, the Lack-of-conflict Objection would apply because people's free will is *not* interfered with simply by them learning or being shown the truth about something, even by God. As explained previously, there are a great variety of ways by which God might impart knowledge about himself to humanity. He need not do it by means of spectacular miracles, though even if he were to do it that way I would still argue that there is no interference with anyone's free will. Schellenberg thinks that if God were to exist then he would reveal his existence to people by providing them with some sort of religious experience.[16] Maybe that would work, but I have no clear idea what sort of experience it might be, despite Schellenberg's (and others') discussion of the topic, so I shall not pursue that line of thought. Another way for God to impart knowledge of himself would be by inspiring humans to write Scripture that possesses some special properties. But enough has already been said on that topic in chapter 5, so I shall not rehash it here. The idea that divine revelation would necessarily interfere with people's free will is a clearly counterintuitive notion.

Possibly some atheologians might want to make a case for the Relative-value Objection as an objection to FDN in the present context, though I shall not myself pursue that. Consider instead the Irrationality Objection. There are well over a billion people on the planet earth who lack a belief in a ruler of the universe (and probably over three billion if proposition P were made to express "classical theism," as described above). Assuming that God wants all those people to come to believe in him, how does he expect them to do that if he is unwilling to provide the evidence they need? Does he want them to arrive at the belief in some irrational manner? In a recent essay, Douglas Drabkin tries to answer such a question, as follows:

> Why, if God exists, doesn't God take up his responsibilities as our Ultimate Parent and Teacher, reveal himself to us, and steer us with a firmer hand onto the path of virtue? Does God's apparent hesitancy to reveal himself give us reason to suppose that he *doesn't* exist? . . . Perhaps the process of learning is itself something good, and not merely as a means to other things. If so, then there may well be a point in having us begin life ignorant of God's existence, born into a world where some people even

appear to achieve happiness through wrongdoing: it would give us the opportunity to seek God and discover him for ourselves through a life of struggle (perhaps continuing endlessly into the future). It is not clear to me that the best of all possible worlds wouldn't be one that improved continuously and endlessly through the efforts of persons struggling against ignorance to do what they ought to do. (Original italics)[17]

It seems to me that the Irrationality Objection comes back in here. What does it mean for us to "seek God and discover him for ourselves through a life of struggle"? How, exactly, are we to come to "discover God for ourselves"? Is it some sort of guessing game, where people hit upon the right religion by chance? Surely that would make the whole system irrational. Without further clarification, Drabkin's response to his initial challenge (explaining why God's hiddenness does not imply his nonexistence) comes up empty.

When confronted by the Irrationality Objection, theists may claim that although there is no evidence for the existence of the God of evangelical Christianity (the Argument from the Bible being a failure), there *is* evidence for the existence of God in general. Hence, theistic belief is in no way irrational. But how does that square with FDN? If people are aware of evidence for God's existence, then how is their belief in God "free"? FDNers need to walk a tightrope here. They may say that there is just the right amount of evidence: enough to make their theistic belief rational but not so much as to interfere with their free will. However, if God were to provide still more evidence of his existence, no matter how slight it might be, then that would cross the line and interfere with free will.

There are many problems with this. One of them is that there really is no evidence for the existence of God in general. (See appendix F.) Another is that even if there is such evidence, apparently billions of people are unaware of it and are in need of something extra. Presumably for God to provide that little bit extra would not interfere with those people's free will, for it would only bring their level of awareness up to that of the theists who (with no interference with their free will) already are aware of the given evidence. Thus, there would be no good reason for God to permit nonbelievers to remain that way. If there is a level of evidence sufficient for belief but less than the level that interferes with free will, then God should see to it that every person on earth capable of theistic belief becomes aware of evidence for theism that is at the right level. But all of this discussion is moot, anyway, for it assumes that giving people evidence for the truth of something can interfere with their free will, and (as shown above) that is a false assumption. So far as I can see, FDN is still refuted by both the Lack-of-conflict Objection and the Irrationality Objection, even when the Bible is disregarded and the context of discussion is simply God in general.

Drabkin speaks of people's "struggle against ignorance" (whatever that might be in this context) as "continuing endlessly into the future." Does he mean to imply that people will die and then wake up in an afterlife? Here again his point is unclear. If he intends to bring in the Afterlife Defense (ADN), then he would need to defend it against (among other things) the Inexplicability Objection that was raised in section 9.22. Some explanation is needed for why an all-loving deity would permit billions of people to go through their earthly lives deprived of the knowledge that he exists. If they had been armed with such knowledge, they could have somehow led fuller lives and would have been more inclined to love God and give him whatever it is that he wants from humanity. What possible benefit might be conferred on them by their ignorance? Drabkin needs to explain this in order for his theory to have any merit. But he hasn't, and so it doesn't.

As might be gathered, I think that ADN can be refuted even when it is applied to the new version of ANB. For one thing, the whole concept of an afterlife seems to me conceptually shaky and perhaps incoherent. But even if we allow the conceivability of an afterlife, it still fails to explain why God would permit billions of people to go through their entire earthly lives in a state of ignorance about him. What possible purpose might be served by humanity's earthly life if knowledge of God's existence is so unimportant within it that God would not do anything to bring it about? I think the Inexplicability Objection undermines ADN whether applied in the context of evangelical Christianity or in the context of general theism.

As for the Testing Defense (TDN), that was a failure before and it is still a failure here. It is understandable why Schellenberg doesn't even discuss it in his book. We would need to know what sort of test might be appealed to by TDN in the context of God in general. How might God be testing us by remaining hidden? Whatever the answer, the world is obviously unsuitable for purposes of testing since so many people die young or live in some sort of incapacitated condition. So that in itself would be a reason to deny that any sort of general testing is going on. Furthermore, whatever sort of test might be applied to people regarding their theistic beliefs, it would have to be an unfair test because of people's widely disparate circumstances. Most theists would deny that God would perform unfair tests, for it would be not only immoral but irrational as well. So that would be another objection to TDN. In chapter 7 there was also raised against TDN what was called the "Lack-of-evidence Objection." In the present context, that may be connected with the issue of whether there is any evidence for theism. I have already said that there is no good objective reason to believe that God exists, but a full defense of that claim will have to be undertaken elsewhere. In any case, so far as the refutation of TDN is concerned, even if the Lack-of-evidence Objection were insufficient, the Unfairness and Unsuitability Objections would do an adequate job.

The upshot of all this is that ANB still prevails against FDN, TDN, and

ADN, even in the context of general theism. In other words, there is good reason to deny that if God exists then he keeps hidden from people out of any concern regarding free will, testing, or the afterlife. Of these three factors, Schellenberg discusses only free will at length, devoting his chapter 5 to it. Apparently he would agree with my negative verdict regarding FDN.

In his chapters 6 and 7, Schellenberg brings up some other possible explanations for God's hiddenness. They are the following:

(1) God's hiddenness stimulates people to realize their wretchedness and to seek God, and it prevents them from becoming arrogant or presumptuous in relation to (their knowledge of) God. [This is attributed to Blaise Pascal.]

(2) God's hiddenness stimulates people to choose to believe in God in some irrational way, which creates in them a kind or "inwardness" or "subjectivity," which God wants them to have. [This is attributed to Sören Kierkegaard.]

(3) God's hiddenness places people in a situation of "intellectual probation," thereby providing them with certain temptations which they would not otherwise have and which God wants them to have. [This defense, which strikes me as similar to FDN, is attributed to Joseph Butler.]

(4) God's hiddenness gives rise to great religious diversity, which God likes.

(5) God's hiddenness, by a kind of indirect process, brought about the existence of those people who actually exist, and God wanted specifically *those* people to exist.

(6) God's hiddenness allows some people the opportunity to be morally responsible in helping others seek God, and God desires that there be such opportunity for moral responsibility.

(7) God's hiddenness provides people with certain cognitive benefits which he wants them to have.

(8) God's hiddenness gives rise to all, or almost all, the above-mentioned benefits, which, taken cumulatively, provide an adequate explanation for it.

None of these defenses makes much sense to me. From what little I understand of them, they strike me as exceedingly weak. (Perhaps Schellenberg would say the same of TDN and ADN, which he does not address.) In any case, Schellenberg refutes all of the above defenses, and I have no objections related to those refutations. Any reader who would like to see any of the given defenses taken on is urged to look them up in Schellenberg's book.

14.23. UDN Revisited

We are finally led to the last of the defenses raised against ANB earlier in the present book, namely, the Unknown-purpose Defense (UDN). It could be thought of as the ultimate "last-resort" defense. Many writers apparently accede to it. Daniel Howard-Snyder is one of them, as mentioned above. Another is Frank B. Dilley, who says the following:

> The failure of religious excuses for the lack of public demonstrations [of God's existence] constitutes a good reason for concluding that there is no God of the sort described as the God of Abraham, Isaac, and Jacob. . . . However I admit that there might be sufficient hidden reasons which would offer persuasive excuses for the God of the ordinary believer.[18]

To focus more precisely on this matter, it would be useful for us to reintroduce a distinction drawn earlier in the book, that between the possibilist version of UDN (according to which it is logically possible that God exists and has unknown purposes that would adequately explain why he chooses to remain hidden) and the actualist version of it (according to which God exists and actually has such purposes). Dilley may be acceding only to the possibilist version of UDN. But one who may espouse the actualist version of it is Robert McKim, who says the following:

> I just take it for granted that the nontheists are wrong, and that God does exist. . . . The correct h-explanation [i.e., explanation of God's hiddenness] may include considerations other than those I have mentioned, perhaps other than those which anyone has conceived of, or even *could* conceive of. This is a reason for thinking that the question of whether or not there are h-explanations which adequately explain why God is not even a little less hidden than God is . . . is one on which we should suspend judgment. (Original italics)[19]

Since McKim maintains that God does exist, presumably he thinks that there is some explanation for God's hiddenness but it has not as yet been revealed to humanity. Instead of saying that we should suspend judgment on the issue of whether there are any such explanations, McKim, as a theist, should express confidence that God has his reasons even though we may not at present know what they are. In any case, I gather that these writers assign enough force to UDN to warrant taking no more than a neutral position regarding the soundness or forcefulness of ANB.

In contrast, Schellenberg regards ANB to be a forceful argument for God's nonexistence. He says the following:

> Without strong independent evidence for the denial of my argument's conclusion, S [a person] has no reason to appeal to the possibility of an explanation unknown to her, perhaps beyond her grasp. Without the indirect support for an appeal to the possibility of unknown explanations afforded by strong independent evidence of God's existence, S must, if she agrees with this argument, come to believe that there is no God.[20]

It seems to me that Schellenberg is here rejecting UDN out of hand without due consideration. In one sense, he is right that anyone who "agrees with" his argument must believe that there is no God, since that is the conclusion of his argument. But in a more interesting sense, it seems to me that someone could agree with the basic points of his argument and yet "suspend judgment" (as McKim urges) on whether or not there might be some purpose which would adequately explain why God remains hidden from (at least a large part of) humanity. In fact, Schellenberg himself seems to allow that possibility, for he denies that his book is an attempt to show that God does not exist. He says:

> My description [of my argument] may seem to suggest that it is my wish to defend atheism—to show that God does not exist. But this is not an accurate representation of my intent; and I would like to emphasize that it is not. . . . I by no means wish to rule out the possibility that better [counter]arguments than the ones here discussed may one day be devised. . . . I myself have been unable to find reason to suppose that it is so much as plausible that a perfectly loving God would be hidden, and so the prospects for a future counterargument that would remove the threat to theism and revive the possibility of belief must appear dim. . . . But it may be that new evidence will turn up. Perhaps stronger counterarguments can be devised. I hope that because of my efforts, others will be inspired to show that this is indeed the case.[21]

Although in the previous passage Schellenberg seems to rule out UDN, in this passage he seems to be acceding to it.

Perhaps the reason why Schellenberg insists that he is not defending atheism in his book is that he does not attempt to refute the traditional arguments for God's existence. He simply makes it one of his initial assumptions that none of those arguments is successful.[22] Maybe he feels that no book which is structured in such a way should be taken to be a defense of atheism. But one can be taken to be supporting (even trying to prove) a proposition even if one does not discuss alleged support for the proposition's negation. As a terminological point, there would be nothing wrong with characterizing Schellenberg's book as an argument for atheism. Whether it is a sound argument and whether it succeeds in its endeavors are of course separate issues.

It may be that the best way to characterize Schellenberg's position, which would make it perfectly consistent and also in agreement with my own position on the matter, would be to say that, according to Schellenberg, the possibilist version of UDN is sound (and serves to show that ANB is not a conclusive proof of God's nonexistence) but the actualist version of UDN is unsound. If that is indeed his view, then certainly he should say more about *why* the actualist version is unsound. And instead of denying that he is trying to show the truth of atheism, Schellenberg should say that such a task is indeed at least part of his aim, though he could grant that his argument for atheism is not intended to be a conclusive proof.

What I shall now turn to is a consideration of the issue which Schellenberg neglected to consider: whether there is any good reason to reject (the actualist version of) UDN when applied to God in general. First, unlike Schellenberg, I concede right from the start that ANB is a failure when applied to God in general without qualification. There are plenty of theists out there who believe in a deity who is totally unconcerned about humankind's belief or lack of belief in him. ANB simply has no application to such a deity. Having granted that point, we could narrow our investigation. Let us confine it, initially at least, to theists who would answer our revised questions Q4 and Q5 affirmatively, and thus who believe in a deity who strongly desires that everyone, or almost everyone, be aware of his existence. Assuming that such a deity is hidden (at least from a large part of humanity) and that all the attempts to explain that hiddenness are failures, what are we to make of an appeal to (the actualist version of) UDN: the claim that God exists but has some unknown purpose which, if known, would adequately explain why he has chosen to remain hidden? It would be a purpose which necessarily conflicts with his desire for universal theistic belief among humans but which outweighs and overrides it, thereby falsifying premise (A3) of ANB. Is there any good reason to deny that there is a deity who has such an unknown purpose?

When we considered this matter in chapter 11, we did so within the framework of evangelical Christianity, and that gave us resources which we do not have here within the framework of theism in general. For example, the Burden-of-proof Objection was quite potent. Although it was conceded that in the battle between UDN and ANB's premise (A3) both sides faced a certain burden of proof, the ANB side could meet its burden because of biblical support that could be mounted in its favor, whereas the UDN side failed to meet its burden of proof. However, within the context of theism in general, it might be claimed, the situation is reversed. The UDN side can meet its burden of proof by appeal to arguments for God's existence from natural theology. (Such arguments support UDN, for if God exists then, being rational and in control of things, he *must* have some purpose for permitting in the world whatever it is he permits, even if such a purpose is at present unknown to humanity.) On the other hand, the ANB side cannot meet its burden of proof once the appeal to Scripture is abandoned. There then comes to be no reason to accept ANB's premise (A3).

I do not agree that there is evidence for the existence of God in general. The arguments from natural theology are all failures. However, I must concede that the case for ANB's premise (A3) here within the context of theism in general is considerably weaker than it was within the context of evangelical Christianity. For that reason (as well as the absence of a complete discussion of natural theology within the present work), I do not think it would be fruitful to pursue here the Burden-of-proof Objection. For the time being, let us say that the two sides are in the situation of a "Mexican standoff." Each has a burden of proof which it has failed to fulfill.

Another of the resources appealed to in chapter 11 was the Further-properties Objection. It is a basic Christian assumption that God strongly desires a personal relationship with people and that they love and worship him. And evangelical Christians also take God to have sent his son to earth to "testify to the truth" and to have directed missionaries to spread the gospel message worldwide. In the context of general theism we cannot appeal to such considerations. However, we are confining our investigation, at least initially, to theists who view God in a certain way, in particular, to those who answer the revised questions Q4 and Q5 affirmatively. They are willing to say that God strongly desires that everyone, or almost everyone, believe that he exists. Certainly a person who makes such a claim should be reluctant to go on to declare that God nevertheless has some (unknown) reason to stay hidden from (a large part of) humanity. But it would not be an incoherent position to maintain.

Furthermore, there is now a difference with regard to the hierarchy of divine purposes. When we dealt with God's purpose for permitting so much nonbelief in the gospel message, we could go on to ask why he keeps that purpose secret from us. It seems counterproductive for him to do that. But now we cannot in a perfectly analogous way go on to ask why God keeps secret from us his purpose for staying hidden, for whatever purpose he may have for staying hidden, it would also explain why he keeps it secret from us: not to keep it secret would eliminate his hiddenness. The most we could ask for here is that God reveal to some of the theists of the world why he remains hidden from the nontheists. He should at least reveal that there *is* some purpose for it, even if he does not reveal the actual purpose itself. What UDNers might say is that God refrains from revealing any of those things because of the purpose that he has for staying hidden from the nontheists, whatever it may be. That is, if he were to reveal anything at all about this matter, even to some of the theists, that would risk upsetting the given purpose, which explains why he does not do it. Since such a move could not be made within the framework of evangelical Christianity, UDN has a slight advantage here in regard to general theism that it did not possess within that other framework.

Another objection raised against UDN in chapter 11 was that the worldview to which it appeals (called UNH) has a lower probability than that of the worldview associated with ANB. But part of the force of that objection had to do with the complexity of UNH within the context of evangelical Christianity. Here in the context of general theism, even assuming affirmative answers to questions Q4 and Q5, UNH is not so complex. It simply says that, although God could bring about and strongly desires universal theistic belief, he has some overriding (unknown) purpose for staying hidden (at least from a large part of humanity). One might still try to maintain that the opposing worldview (that such a deity does not exist) is more likely true, but the force of such a claim is considerably less than in the context of evangelical Christianity.

Finally, there was the objection that UNH is no good as an explanation since it appeals to mystery, which is antithetical to explanation. That argument had a great deal of force within the context of evangelical Christianity because evangelical Christianity places explanation high on its list of priorities. When Jesus went out to "testify to the truth," his object was to get people at least to understand the gospel message, whether or not they came to accept it. And when Christian missionaries go forth, they are claiming, among other things, to explain the way things are. So when UNH, with its appeal to mystery, departs from the explanatory aim, it becomes inimical to the evangelistic enterprise. For that reason, the given objection to UDN within the context of evangelical Christianity was an extremely powerful one. But, now, within the context of general theism, even with the assumption that God strongly desires universal theistic belief, the same sort of objection is not so forceful. There is no need for theists in general to place explanation high on their list of priorities. If their worldview, according to which God has some unknown purpose for staying hidden, is no good at explaining anything, the theists can simply say, "So what?" Such theists have no program for enlightening the world. They can remain in their shells, comfortable with the idea of divine mystery, and willing to try to ward off ANB by appeal to UDN.

My initial result, then, is a negative one. Although the earlier defenses (FDN, TDN, and ADN, as well as all the additional ones Schellenberg considers) are failures, even within the context of general theism, UDN has enough force to it to warrant saying that ANB is not so strong within this context. Even when theists are willing to say yes to Q5 (and thereby grant that God strongly desires universal theistic belief), they could bring up UDN in regard to the nontheists of the world. They could say that God has some (unknown) purpose for leaving those people in their ignorance, which overrides his desire for universal theistic belief. Maybe someday we will come to know what that purpose is. Such a move would be highly objectionable within the context of evangelical Christianity, but here in the context of general theism, it seems to be a more effective rejoinder.

Let us, however, focus our investigation still further. We considered theists who would answer our revised questions Q4 and Q5 affirmatively. But let us go further and consider the slightly narrower group of theists who would also give affirmative answers to questions Q2 and Q3. Those questions asked whether God has great love and compassion for humanity and whether God wants people to love him maximally (or at least greatly). It seems to me that if theists were to give affirmative answers to all four questions, Q2–Q5, then they would be in a less favorable position to appeal to UDN. Let us see why.

One reason is that something like the Further-properties Objection of chapter 11 would become relevant. If God wanted people to love him greatly, then it would obviously be counterproductive (and perhaps even irrational) for him to stay hidden from them. Of course, this could again be a matter of conflicting desires: God wants people's love (just as he wants their belief), but he also has some (unknown) purpose which overrides that desire. Nevertheless, God's position is here more conceptually precarious than before. That is, because of the further divine attributes introduced, UDN has now become more counterintuitive or far-fetched than before.

Another reason is the sort of consideration which is the focal point of Schellenberg's argument. If God has great love for people, then he presumably wants whatever would benefit them in the long run. But surely that would include a close personal relationship with himself. How in that case could God deny a large portion of humanity such a benefit by staying hidden from them? If he loves people maximally (or at least greatly), then surely he could not permit them to be so deprived. The appeal to UDN again becomes increasingly far-fetched, though, admittedly, more is needed here to clarify the benefit that nontheists are supposed to be missing out on.

In addition to clarifying the benefit in question, Schellenberg should have further restricted the concept of God on which he was working. He should have added such divine attributes as those that are implied by affirmative answers to our survey questions Q3 and Q5, as given above. The divine attribute relevant to Q3 is that of wanting people to reciprocate God's love for them, and the one relevant to Q5 is that of wanting people to believe that God exists. The latter desire is implied by the former one, since people cannot reciprocate God's love without believing that he exists. But it is also implied by other divine attributes, including omnibenevolence (as Schellenberg points out). Some theists might also claim that belief in God is *intrinsically* valuable, quite apart from its connection with other matters. And that would be further reason to think that God wants people to have it. Here is a suggestion as to how Schellenberg ought to have formulated his "Argument from Reasonable Nonbelief":

(1)   If there were to exist a God who (a) is perfectly loving, (b) strongly desires that humanity reciprocate that love, and (c) wants people to believe that he exists, then reasonable nonbelief would not occur.

(2)   But reasonable nonbelief occurs.

(3)   Hence, there does not exist a God who (a) is perfectly loving, (b) strongly desires that humanity reciprocate that love, and (c) wants people to believe that he exists.

In addition to putting forward arguments in support of premise (1), it would be useful here to argue also that the God of the Bible is supposed to have the three attributes mentioned in that premise. And I think a good case could be made that most theists in the United States would ascribe those attributes to the deity in which they believe. At any rate, if Schellenberg had formulated his argument in the way suggested, then it would have been less susceptible to UDN than it actually is. For the fact is that UDN can be brought strongly to bear against Schellenberg's present premise (2) (as quoted above in section 14.21), a fact indirectly exploited by Howard-Snyder at the end of his critique.[23] On the other hand, UDN becomes considerably less plausible when applied against premise (1) in the suggested formulation above.

Still another reason why UDN would be less plausible when applied to the "restricted God in general" has to do with the Probability Objection. That is, the Probability Objection could be given new life by having the theist's conception of God complicated by affirmative answers to questions Q2 and Q3 (as well as Q4 and Q5). In addition to desiring universal theistic belief, God would be regarded as loving humanity greatly and desiring that that love be reciprocated. In addition to making God's permission of nonbelief still more anomalous, such additional complications would reduce the a priori probability of UNH (the worldview associated with UDN) by increasing the number of conjuncts within its formulation. (For further details about that point, see section 11.4.) It might be suggested that UNH within the context of theism in general is less complex than UNH within the context of evangelical Christianity. That may be so, but when affirmative answers to questions Q2–Q5 are incorporated into the former, the difference between the two becomes greatly reduced. Just as UDN did not fare well against ANB as applied to the God of evangelical Christianity, so also it does not fare well against ANB as applied against the "restricted God in general."

It might be suggested that there is independent evidence for God's existence which increases the probability of UNH within the context of theism in general. I have two comments about that. First, when "God" is defined as (among other things) loving humanity greatly and desiring in return both humanity's love and universal theistic belief (which are properties supplied by affirmative answers to our survey questions), then the arguments allegedly presenting evidence for God's existence become *non sequiturs*. None of them aims to support the existence of *such* a being! My second comment is that none of the theistic arguments within natural theology is any good anyway, even when aimed at a "bare-bones" deity. What I say in appendix F relates to that topic.

Finally, even the Explanation Objection might be put forward here. It is true that the general theist, unlike the evangelical Christian, may feel no need to explain things to others and so may be quite content with a worldview that appeals to mystery. However, he should not be content with that. A worldview that centers around an appeal to mystery is just generally inferior, other things being equal, even if it is not used to explain things to others. Such a worldview or hypothesis reduces the comprehensiveness and clarity of any belief system in which it plays a prominent role. For that reason, people who desire such features within their own belief systems need to avoid appeal to "God's unknown purposes."

My overall assessment of ANB as applied to God in general, then, is as follows. I readily grant that the argument has no force whatever if the concept of God is left unrestricted (using, for example, just the dictionary definition of "God"). However, most theists have a more definite concept of God, and ANB becomes much stronger when it is applied against that more definite concept. Let us consider the concept of God possessed by those theists who would answer all four of our survey questions Q2–Q5 affirmatively. There are again two issues here, the applicability of ANB and its force or strength. Taking the applicability issue first, I would guess that more than half the theists in the United States would answer all four questions affirmatively and so are confronted by the problem of nonbelief. ANB, as formulated above, presents a formidable case for the nonexistence of their deity. Thus, I would say that the problem of nonbelief is a serious one for most theists in the United States.

Regarding ANB's strength, I would say that it is quite a strong argument for the nonexistence of the given deity (the one believed in by theists who answer the four questions affirmatively). On the scale of zero to 100, I would give it a score of seventy-five. (Of course, that figure would be reduced for theists who do not answer all four questions affirmatively, and it would be zero for theists in general, apart from the survey questions.) For a comparison of the respective strengths of AE and ANB, see the next chapter.

Because of the more restricted framework involved, ANB applied to the God of liberal Christianity (to which I gave a score of eighty) is stronger than ANB applied to God in general. In the context of theism in general, even when all four survey questions are answered affirmatively, there is still more room for maneuvering in response to ANB than when the framework of Christianity is also imposed. The differences, though, are admittedly slight. In the next chapter I shall discuss my overall assessment of ANB as an atheological argument. So far as theism in general is concerned, I would say that ANB is still a strong argument when it is applied to the concept of God possessed by most theists in the United States. It may not prove beyond all reasonable doubt that their deity does not exist, but it does render that result likely. ANB has presented a serious challenge for such theists that they have yet to overcome.

Notes

1. Christlieb, "Which Theisms Face an Evidential Problem of Evil?" pp. 56–57.

2. See, for example, Martin, *Atheism*, and Mackie, *The Miracle of Theism.*

3. The issue is suggested by the title of R. C. Sproul's book *If There's a God, Why Are There Atheists?* (Wheaton, Ill.: Tyndale House Publishers, 1988).

4. Schellenberg, *Divine Hiddenness*, p. 83.

5. For example, Stephen F. Barker, *The Elements of Logic*, 4th ed. (New York: McGraw-Hill, 1985), p. 246.

6. Schellenberg, *Divine Hiddenness*, p. 59.

7. Daniel Howard-Snyder, Review of Schellenberg's *Divine Hiddenness and Human Reason* in *Mind* 104 (1995): 431.

8. Keller, "The Hiddenness of God and the Problem of Evil," p. 20.

9. Robert McKim, Review of Schellenberg's *Divine Hiddenness and Human Reason* in *Faith and Philosophy* 12 (1995): 275.

10. Ibid., p. 276.

11. Ibid., p. 276.

12. Ibid., p. 274.

13. Schellenberg, *Divine Hiddenness*, p. 11.

14. Howard-Snyder, "The Argument from Divine Hiddenness."

15. Schellenberg, "Response to Howard-Snyder."

16. Schellenberg, *Divine Hiddenness*, pp. 47–57.

17. Douglas Drabkin, "The Moralist's Fear of Knowledge of God," *Faith and Philosophy* 11 (1994): 90.

18. Dilley, "Fool-Proof Proofs of God?" p. 35.

19. McKim, "The Hiddenness of God," pp. 143, 158.

20. Schellenberg, *Divine Hiddenness*, p. 211.

21. Ibid., pp. 12, 213–14.

22. Ibid., pp. 11–12.

23. Howard-Snyder, "The Argument from Divine Hiddenness," pp. 452–53. I say "indirectly" because Howard-Snyder does not explicitly address the exact version of Schellenberg's argument which I formulate above in section 14.21. That is actually a point of contention between them in their exchange, though it does not seem to me to be of as great significance as Schellenberg makes it out to be in his "Response."

15

Assessment

The problems of evil and nonbelief have been formulated in terms of AE and ANB, which are not specific arguments but argument-types applicable to various concepts of God. For each concept of God, AE and ANB can each be expressed as a specific argument for the nonexistence of that particular deity. The problem (for theists) in each case is how to respond to the given argument, whether AE or ANB. Since different groups of people have different concepts of God, we have, in effect, relativized the arguments and thus the problems to different groups of people.

In the present book, four groups have been considered: evangelical Christians, Orthodox Jews, liberal Christians, and theists in general. The first three groups are mutually exclusive and the fourth includes them all plus others besides. Each group is called upon to explain within the context of its own theistic belief system two different phenomena. In the problem of evil it is the existence of widespread suffering and premature death in the world. In the problem of nonbelief it is the existence of widespread nonbelief of a certain sort. Both problems are serious ones for most people in each of the four groups in two different ways. First, each group is confronted by the problems in that it has a system of beliefs that gives rise to a kind of anomaly: a god who has great love and compassion for people and yet permits them to suffer and die prematurely or a god who wants people to be aware of something but who permits them to remain ignorant of it. The problem in each case is to dispel the anomaly by means of a suitable explanation. Second, the problems are not readily solvable. In fact I would say that they are not solvable at all, which implies that each of the theistic belief systems which gives rise to the anomalies is probably erroneous, postulating a deity who in fact does not exist, as shown by the argu-

285

ments. My assessment of each argument, AE and ANB, is that it is a sound deductive argument as formulated. Some of the premises call for inductive support. I would say that such support is strong in each case, and in some cases, very strong. If the support were to be made part of the argument, thereby producing an expanded AE or expanded ANB, then the argument would be a strong inductive (or evidential) argument. (I believe that the arguments could also be very effectively applied to other deities, e.g., the God of Islam, but that is a further project.)

Both problems, evil and nonbelief, are most serious for evangelical Christians because of their great reliance on the Bible, especially the New Testament. There is excellent reason to maintain, by appeal to the Bible and especially the New Testament, that if God existed, then he would have done more to prevent or reduce the enormous amount of evil and nonbelief that exist or occur on our planet. When applied to the God of evangelical Christianity, AE and ANB are both sound arguments with premises that receive excellent support from the Bible. For example, ANB claims that if the God of evangelical Christianity were to exist, then he would want all, or almost all, people to be aware of the truth of the gospel message, and indeed that premise is very strongly supported by the Bible.

15.1. AE vs. ANB

Part of my project in the present book, as suggested by its title, has been to compare AE with ANB. Although both arguments are excellent within the context of evangelical Christianity, I claim that ANB is a (slightly) stronger atheological argument than is AE. And that is so for all four groups of theists under consideration, at least when they are restricted in appropriate ways.

The reason why the problem of nonbelief is a greater problem than is the problem of evil in the case of evangelical Christianity is as follows. There is biblical support for the claim that the God of evangelical Christianity wants people to love him and to believe the gospel message. Call that evidence B. From evidence B one may infer that if the given deity were to exist, then he would have done things to prevent or reduce the amount of nonbelief in the gospel message that exists on our planet. There is also biblical support for the claim that the God of evangelical Christianity loves people maximally, or at least greatly, and has great compassion for them regarding their earthly suffering. Call that evidence L. From evidence L one may infer that if the given deity were to exist, then he would have done things to prevent or reduce the great amount of suffering on our planet. There are two reasons why the problem of nonbelief is the greater problem for evangelical Christians. One is that evidence B is superior (both in quantity and quality) to evidence L. And the second is that the inference from evidence B to the conclusion drawn from it is a more forceful or cogent inference than the corresponding one in the case of evidence L. I shall look at these two reasons more closely.

Evidence B consists of biblical verses that support the claim that God wants people to love him and to believe the gospel message. Several such verses were presented in arguments (1)–(6) in section 2.4. Evidence L consists of biblical verses that support the claim that God has great love for humanity and feels compassion for its earthly suffering. There are a few such verses, but not as many as in the case of evidence B, and the few that there are do not support the claims so clearly. The truth of the matter is that nowhere in the Bible does it say explicitly that God loves humanity greatly and nowhere does it say that God feels any compassion for humanity in general regarding its earthly suffering. Furthermore, there are contrary verses that suggest that God definitely does not love certain persons or groups of people. For example, according to the Bible, God hated Esau and apparently disliked the Amalekites intensely. Also, it seems doubtful that God loved those who drowned in the Great Flood or died in the destruction of Sodom and Gomorrah. And it seems impossible that God should love those, if any, whom he predestines for damnation. The predestination idea can be supported by appeal to Scripture, though the matter is somewhat unsettled. In any case, it is clear that for various reasons evidence L is inferior to evidence B in both quantity and quality.

The second point, the argument from evidence B to the conclusion that if God existed then he would have prevented or eliminated nonbelief in the gospel message (which is the basic idea within ANB), is more forceful or cogent than the corresponding argument from evidence L to the conclusion that if God existed then he would have significantly reduced the amount of evil in the world (the basic idea within AE). One way to bring out this point pertains to the pivotal role played by premise (A3) in AE and ANB. Premise (A3) says, in effect, that God has no overriding reason not to do the thing in question. It is an essential premise without which the argument cannot go through. We saw previously that some biblical support for (A3) can be mustered in the case of ANB, but none at all in the case of AE. AE's premise (A3) needs to rely completely on what might be called "intuitive support." This shows that the reasoning involved in ANB is more forceful or cogent than that involved in AE, at least within the context of evangelical Christianity. Both arguments are strong, but ANB is still stronger, as I have tried to express by assigning it a score of ninety-five (vs. eighty-five for AE).

Another way to bring out the greater cogency of ANB is to point out that ANB's conceptual framework is simpler and clearer than that of AE. And this applies to all the various concepts of God, not just to the God of evangelical Christianity. There are four main factors, as follows:

1. The problem of nonbelief arises within the conceptual framework of human belief, especially its rational support. The corresponding framework for the problem of evil is that of human happiness and suffering. It is arguable that the latter framework is broader than the former. And that gives rise to a greater variety of possible defenses, which in turn tends to weaken AE. This is not to say that AE is a weak argument, only that it is weaker in the given respect than ANB.

2. It would be easy for God to bring about situation S without any interference with the laws of nature or the initial conditions of the planet earth, but that may not be so easy in the case of situation L. It should be noted, of course, that for God to bring about situation S would also automatically bring about situation L, since there would be genuine benefits for humanity in situation S, including, possibly, an increase in moral behavior. So, from that standpoint, bringing about S could not be easier than bringing about L. But if we focus simply on what it would take to reduce *natural* evil, it is not so clear that *that* is easily accomplished. Although we can be fairly certain that a reduction in nonbelief at one time and place will not lead to an increase in nonbelief at another time and place, this is not so for a reduction in human or animal suffering. It seems easier for me to eliminate my neighbors' nonbelief (e.g., by showing them things) than for me to eliminate their suffering or premature death. And that sort of difference may apply to God as well as to humans. Even the limited God of process theology could easily bring about situation S, whereas it might be harder for him to bring about situation L, at least through a reduction in natural evil. And some of the complications involved with situation L may be of a conceptual sort, which would restrict even an omnipotent deity. Because of these factors, it ends up harder to explain God's failure to bring about situation S than his failure to bring about situation L.

3. From God's point of view, the ideal situation regarding the elimination of nonbelief (which would be its *total* elimination) is conceptually clearer than the ideal regarding the elimination of suffering, since, for reasons discussed in chapter 6, the world is better off if it contains some slight suffering than if it were to contain no suffering at all. What ideal situation could possibly serve as a model for situation L? That is, if God were to keep producing situation L, i.e., reducing suffering in the world in an effort to make its residents more satisfied, then at what point would they say, "Stop, we're maximally happy now"? Since the ideal state calls for the occurrence of some minimal amount of suffering, it becomes obscure and difficult to describe in any detail. (This point was discussed in section 1.4 as "the Regress Objection.") That affects the cogency of the argument that if God were to exist then he would have produced situation L (i.e., prevented or reduced the suffering that presently occurs). There is a kind of unclarity about the whole process that does not exist in the case of ANB. Our

inability to conceive of the ideal situation regarding suffering makes the idea of God bringing about situation L conceptually more obscure, which weakens AE.

4. Closely related to (3) is the fact that situation S is *more definite* than situation L. Unlike the case of situation S, there are an infinite number of disparate situations, all of them meeting the description of situation L. (It should be noted that if AE had been formulated as the Unjustifiability Version, discussed in section 1.4, then the situation to which the argument would have appealed would not have had such indefiniteness. But then there would have been still other problems with AE, such as the relativity of value, that we were spared in this book.) The extreme indefiniteness of situation L, in contrast with situation S, makes ANB more sharply focused, and hence stronger, than AE.

There may be additional factors, but each of these is a reason to assess the forcefulness or strength of ANB to be greater than that of AE. I do not mean to imply here that AE is a weak argument. On the contrary, I regard it as strong, despite the above misgivings. However, ANB is even stronger. And that applies to other concepts of God as well, not just the God of evangelical Christianity.

In the case of Orthodox Jews, there are additional reasons for regarding the problem of nonbelief (formulated in the appropriate way) to be the more serious problem of the two, even though their rabbis may not as yet have recognized that point. That is, although the problem of evil is indeed a problem for them, it is not as serious because of certain ideas which can be used as defenses, such as divine punishment on earth and the fundamental mysteriousness of God, both of which are ideas that are more prominent within Judaism than within Christianity. Hence, for both biblically based groups, the problem of evil is a lesser problem than the problem of nonbelief, appropriately (i.e., biblically) formulated, but for Orthodox Jews the discrepancy is even greater because they possess resources for dealing with the problem of evil not possessed by evangelical Christians.

When we try to apply the two problems to the other two groups, liberal Christians and theists in general, we must first recognize that for some of them the problems simply do not arise because the people in question do not make the necessary basic assumptions. Those assumptions, expressed by affirmative answers to questions Q1–Q5 as formulated in chapters 13 and 14, were mostly taken from Scripture. Since people could be theists or even Christians without assuming the authority or accuracy of Scripture, they could be members of those groups without answering any of the questions affirmatively. However, most people within each group do make the basic assumptions, and so the two problems do indeed arise for the majority.

In the case of each of those two groups, there are reasons for regarding the problem of evil to be the more serious one. First, the problem of nonbelief is more oriented toward the Bible. People who reject much or all of the Bible would not be so affected by it. Second, the idea that God loves humanity is a more common theme both within liberal Christianity and within theism in general than is the corresponding theme that God wants people to believe certain things. (Possibly that will change in the future, especially if my book or Schellenberg's is to have much effect.) It might be claimed that since God's love connects more directly with the elimination of suffering than with the elimination of nonbelief, it becomes more of a puzzle why suffering has not been eliminated.

I grant that these are relevant considerations, but it is hard for me to weigh them against the ones mentioned previously which tend to make ANB a more forceful or cogent argument than AE. Part of the problem lies in the great heterogeneity of the two groups in question when they are taken in a totally unrestricted way. In the case of theists in general, because of the enormous variety of concepts of God found within the group, I do not claim that either evil or nonbelief is a serious problem for them. In assessing the strength of AE and ANB applied to God in general, with no further qualification (which comes down to God as defined by the dictionary), I assign to each a score of zero.

I am reluctant to also assign a score of zero to AE applied to the God of liberal Christianity, because to do so would suggest that Christianity does not ascribe any divine attributes beyond those ascribed by theism in general that have any bearing on the suffering that occurs in our world, and that seems wrong. Christianity must have some concept of God that goes beyond the bare-bones dictionary definition in a relevant way. It is hard to state precisely what the additional characteristics might be, but perhaps the idea of being omnibenevolent or all-loving would capture it best. Although not every Christian would assign those characteristics to God, almost all of them would. From that point of view, the problem of evil emerges for liberal Christians, and when AE is applied to their deity, it should receive a score greater than zero. In chapter 13 I assigned the score of twenty to show that AE, though still quite weak, has more to it when applied to the God of liberal Christianity than when applied to God in general.

I also assigned a "twenty" to ANB within the context of liberal Christianity. One reason is Schellenberg's consideration: a perfectly loving deity (as the Christian God is supposed to be) would want people to believe certain things because of the benefit that it would have for them. Such beliefs, aside from the possible intrinsic value of making people aware of the truth, would make people happier and more hopeful regarding the future. Another consideration is the clarity and definiteness of ANB. If AE is to receive a score of twenty, it would be hard to justify assigning a lesser score to ANB. I gave it the same score because of my indecision about how to assess the arguments within such a nebulous framework as unrestricted liberal Christianity.

It might be suggested that at least within the context of theism in general, evil is a greater problem than nonbelief because suffering is a more *practical* concern than nonbelief. Everyone experiences it to some extent. It is more of an "in your face" type of situation. From the human point of view, there is a more evident benefit to be derived from the elimination of suffering than from the elimination of nonbelief, and that would show the problem of evil to be the more serious threat to belief in God. Relief from suffering is more valuable to humans than is mere theistic belief. It is better to be an atheist free of suffering than to be a theist in great pain. Hence, it should be more important to God to relieve humanity of its great suffering than to relieve it of its great nonbelief, and so the fact of suffering points more clearly to God's nonexistence than does the fact of nonbelief.

I can see merit in this line of thought, though it also has drawbacks. First, the point should be made that issues of relative value need to be viewed from God's, not from humanity's, point of view. In other words, the question needs to be the following: If God were to exist, then which would upset him more, great suffering among humanity or great nonbelief among humanity? I suspect that a great many theists in the United States would say that, because of God's long-range plans for humanity, it is the nonbelief that he finds to be the more upsetting. From God's point of view, human nonbelief is more of an "in your face" type of situation than is human suffering. So, from the perspective of such theists, it would be the fact of great nonbelief, rather than great suffering, that would be the greater challenge to theism.

Second, the argument assumes that God loves or has concern about humanity, and that is not part of the concept of God in general, though probably most theists would include it. If we are proceeding simply on the basis of the dictionary definition of "God," then not only is neither atheological argument stronger than the other, but neither of them should be assessed as having any force at all. Furthermore, even if there were here a point in favor of AE as opposed to ANB, I think that the considerations cited previously (showing ANB to be the superior argument) would serve to cancel out this one. But all those considerations are irrelevant in this context, anyway. In the end, I think that it is simply not fruitful to apply AE or ANB to God, as defined in the dictionary.

15.2. The Scores

In chapters 12–14, I used numbers to express my assessments of the various arguments. Those numbers are recapitulated in the chart below.

CONCEPT OF GOD	AE	ANB
The God of evangelical Christianity	85	95
The God of Orthodox Judaism	65	85
The God of liberal Christianity, unrestricted	20	20
The God of liberal Christianity, restricted	75	80
God in general, unrestricted	0	0
God in general, restricted	70	75

By "restricted" is meant: defined by the giving of affirmative answers to all five of the survey questions, Q1–Q5, specified in chapter 13 or 14 for the given deity. For those people in the relevant groups who would answer some of the questions affirmatively and others negatively, the numerical assessment would be less than the figure given here. I take "God in general, unrestricted" to represent God as defined by the dictionary.

As indicated before, the numbers range from zero to 100, with zero indicating that the given argument has no force whatever and 100 indicating a conclusive proof. The number fifty would represent the cutoff between weak arguments (below fifty) and strong arguments (above fifty). There is no definite relation intended between the above score representing the strength of the argument and the probability conferred by the argument upon its conclusion. But as a very rough measure, it could be said that if the conclusion has an initial probability of 50 percent, then the argument confers upon it an additional probability that is 1/200 (or 0.5 percent) of the given score. Thus, for example, since for the God of liberal Christianity, restricted, ANB receives a score of eighty, it might be said that that argument makes the probability that that deity does not exist 90 percent [since $0.5 + (1/200 \times 80) = 0.9$]. In other words, for liberal Christians who answer all five survey questions affirmatively, ANB shows it to be 90 percent probable that their God does not exist. However, all this is very rough. I think that the concept of probability is out of place in assessing theological propositions (an exception being the propositions considered in sections 10.5 and 11.4, above), since the relevant data are not of a numerical sort.

The main function of the scores in the above chart is not so much to provide absolute strengths as to indicate the differences in assessment that I assign to the various arguments and to provide a vehicle by which I can present *reasons* for those different assessments. In each case, it is not so much the number that is important but the reasons behind it.

15.3. My Claims

Of all the arguments, the strongest is ANB as applied to the God of evangelical Christianity. It receives a score of ninety-five. The score shows that the given version of ANB is something less than a conclusive proof (which would have a score of 100), but it comes close. In saying that that version of ANB is such a strong argument, I am saying that, by far, the preponderance of evidence is on the side of the claim that the God of evangelical Christianity does not exist. So this result does indeed strongly support an atheistic stance with respect to that particular concept of God. It is argued for on the basis of ANB in chapters 2, 5, 7, 9, and 11. The same conclusion can also be supported, though with slightly lesser force or to a slightly lesser degree of cogency, by appeal to AE as applied to the God of evangelical Christianity, as shown in chapters 2, 4, and 6–10. Of all the results in the present book, that particular atheistic conclusion is the main one.

The question might be raised whether the pair of arguments, AE and ANB, taken together, present a stronger cumulative case for the nonexistence of the God of evangelical Christianity than ANB alone. I am inclined to think that they do. Even though AE's score is only eighty-five, compared with ANB's ninety-five, when AE is taken into account, it enhances the case that ANB makes against evangelical Christianity. I would assign a score of ninety-seven to the cumulative case. (The question might be raised whether such a high score warrants a knowledge claim. That is, does anyone *know* that the God of evangelical Christianity does not exist? That is a large issue that I would prefer not to address at present. It calls for an examination of the concept of "knowing" which is beyond the scope of this book.)

The cumulative-case situation also applies to other concepts of God, including God in general. The matter could be viewed in terms of phenomena to be explained. ANB's "no-God" hypothesis is the best explanation for the world's widespread nonbelief. But it becomes an even better explanation because there is another phenomenon, the world's widespread evil, for which it is also the best explanation. The more phenomena a hypothesis explains, the better it is, overall, as an explanation. If some third phenomenon were to be discovered for which the "no-God" hypothesis is clearly the best explanation, then that would give rise to a third (evidential, God-vs.-world) atheological argument. And the cumulative case made by the three arguments combined would be still stronger than that for just AE + ANB. This point relates to each of the different concepts of God that we have discussed, though the cumulative case with regard to the God of evangelical Christianity is the most pronounced.

There is another way for the cumulative-case situation to be viewed. Sometimes philosophers grant that there is some evidence for God's existence but claim that it is canceled out or neutralized by the fact of suffering, which constitutes some evidence that God does not exist. Such philosophers speak of reality as being "ambiguous" with regard to God's existence. In this framework, ANB might play a role. It might tip the tide in favor of God's nonexistence by pointing out that a situation of ambiguity would be unacceptable to God if he exists, and so the very fact that there *is* such a situation becomes evidence for his nonexistence. When viewed this way, ANB is not like a second army joined to AE for a direct assault, but rather, it is a reinforcement that turns the tide of battle after AE has fought the enemy to a standstill. At any rate, whichever way it is viewed, the cumulative case for God's nonexistence presented by AE and ANB combined is indeed formidable.

How could evangelical Christians continue to believe in their deity when such a strong case could be made for its nonexistence? My explanation is that they have not adequately thought through the implications with their own doctrines. That is not to say that they should become atheists, but that they should reconsider ascribing certain attributes to God. Perhaps they should regard God as more remote than they take him to be, a deity less loving and less concerned about humanity's beliefs. Or perhaps they should regard God to be considerably less powerful than they supposed. That too would be a way to escape the force of AE and ANB.

The results having to do with other conceptions of God in chapters 12–14 are not intended to be as definite as those in part II of the book, for they are presented in a more sketchy fashion, with many details omitted. But they do introduce some forceful atheological arguments that apply when certain theological doctrines are assumed to be true (in particular, those expressed by affirmative answers to the various survey questions discussed). Those results also serve to present the overall framework or methodology for atheological reasoning which I think is unique to the present work and which I think is superior to other discussions in the literature. The sooner philosophers of religion cease talking about the "God of classical theism" and come to relativize their arguments to particular concepts of God, the sooner they will make genuine progress on the various issues involved.

With regard to God in general, the question might be raised whether theists have support for their belief that allows them to be regarded as *rational* in holding it. An atheist could give an affirmative answer here if rationality is viewed as an internal feature of people in relation to their own belief systems. William Rowe refers to such a position as "friendly atheism,"[1] distinguishing it from "unfriendly atheism" according to which theists are irrational even within the context of their own belief system. The friendly atheist grants that theists have support for their belief which rationally justifies them in holding it. One form of such support might be religious experience. My own position on this matter would be what Rowe calls "indifferent atheism." I grant the *possibility* that theists may have such rational support, particularly in the form of religious experience, but I would not go so far as to say they actually have it. In any case, viewing rationality in the relevant way, I would concede that theists *may* be rational with regard to their theistic belief, even though, from an objective point of view, AE and ANB do present strong evidence that the belief is false. I would agree with Rowe that the positions of "indifferent atheism" and even "friendly atheism" are internally consistent ones to hold.

However, I would not go so far as to maintain "indifferent atheism" with regard to the God of evangelical Christianity. I can understand how someone's subjective religious experience might support a belief in God in general, but I do not understand how it could support a belief in the God of evangelical Christianity. It may be that I do not know enough about religious experience, but from what I do know, it seems to me that evangelical Christians are irrational, even from the perspective of their own belief system. The arguments of part II, above, aimed at that result, among others.

Here is a summary of the main claims of this book:

1. The four versions of AE and the four versions of ANB presented and discussed in chapters 2 and 12–14 are all sound deductive arguments.

2. Although not all of the objections to the various defenses against AE and ANB are sound, almost all of them are. Furthermore, each defense is refuted by at least one objection.

3. When the support for the premises is included, we may speak of the expanded AE and ANB. Those expanded arguments are strong inductive (or evidential) atheological arguments, applied to various concepts of God, with their scores given in the chart in section 15.2, above. Disregarding the unrestricted arguments, the scores range from sixty-five to ninety-five, or from fairly strong to nearly conclusive.

4. As shown by the scores, the expanded ANB is in every context a stronger atheological argument than the expanded AE. (Reasons for that were given in section 15.1.)

5. It could be said that, whichever of the four concepts of God is considered, God's nonexistence has been established beyond a reasonable doubt, though I tend more to see the matter as one involving degree and the "preponderance of evidence." If God exists, then we have good reason to expect situations L and S also to exist, and the fact that they do not becomes good evidence for God's nonexistence. It is especially within the context of evangelical Christianity that theism is an unreasonable set of beliefs, at least when "reasonable" is understood in an objective way. If rationality is construed subjectively, with religious experience being relevant, then I grant the possibility that those who believe in God in general are "rational" in relation to their own belief system. I would not go so far with regard to theistic belief related to other, more definite concepts of God, but let further discussion of that issue be set aside as a separate project.

My hope is that these claims and the arguments supporting them will stimulate philosophers of religion to pursue topics and lines of thought that they had not yet dreamt of in their philosophy.

Note

1. William L. Rowe, "The Problem of Evil and Some Varieties of Atheism," *American Philosophical Quarterly* 16 (1979), reprinted in Daniel Howard-Snyder, ed., *The Evidential Argument from Evil.* See pp. 8–9 of the latter work.

Appendices

The main project of my book is finished and yet there are many pages of appendices. They might be thought of as extended endnotes. They are not essential and could be skipped. On the other hand, some readers may find issues and topics within them of great interest.

Appendices A and B go with chapter 4. They contain further objections to FDE. The objections are not to specific premises within FDE but to certain background assumptions that FDEers usually make. Appendix A attacks the background assumption of incompatibilism, the view that people cannot have free will if all of their choices and actions are completely determined by remote causal antecedents. I myself am not fully committed on the matter but lean toward the opposite view, namely, compatibilism. In appendix A, I give my reasons for that outlook.

Appendix B attacks FDEers' background assumption that people have the sort of free will which is incompatible with determinism, often called "contracausal free will." I raise two different types of objection to that assumption. One is determinism itself, a certain form of which I am inclined to think is true. The other is that there is an inconsistency in the FDEers' system of beliefs, actually two different inconsistencies. One is that people have contracausal free will and yet God exists and knows everything that they do before they do it. The other inconsistency is that people have contracausal free will and yet God has in one way or another predestined everything that happens, including people's choices and actions. Among other things, appendix B goes into the different notions of predestination that may be involved there.

I have three reasons for addressing the issues in question in appendices rather than in the main text. First, I don't feel I need the given arguments to refute FDE. The objections raised in chapter 4 are more than adequate to do the job. Second, it is not totally clear to me that FDEers really need the background assumptions that are attacked in appendices A and B. I suspect that they do need them, but the issue is not completely settled. In any case, they all do make those assumptions. And finally, my own views on the given issues (compatibilism, determinism, etc.) are not definite. I lean certain ways rather than other ways, but I am still quite open on these matters. In contrast, the views I express and defend in chapters 1–15 are more definite than that. I had something to say there and made an effort to say it clearly.

Appendix C is related mainly to chapter 5 and indirectly to section 7.2. It explores issues related to (doxastic) voluntarism, the view that belief is directly subject to the will. I put that material into an appendix (rather than taking it up within, say, chapter 5) for three reasons. First, it is not completely clear that all FDNers presuppose voluntarism. I think that all who are evangelical Christians must do so (in order to follow Scripture), but there may be others around who do not. Second, even if voluntarism were to be presupposed, there would be other objections to FDN that are quite compatible with a voluntaristic outlook, and it was those other objections that I wished to present in chapter 5. Finally, the issues related to voluntarism are large and complicated. They go off in their own direction, quite apart from their connections with ANB. That is still another reason for giving them "their own space."

Appendix D takes up the Argument from the Bible, which is relevant to chapters 5, 7, 10, and 11. (The connections are stated at the beginning of it.) One point that should be noted regarding appendix D is that the Argument from the Bible is an argument in natural theology, though it is one not often addressed by professional philosophers. Another point is that appendix D is very incomplete. It is only a sketch in great need of filling out, which would require an extensive treatment to be adequate. Finally, readers who lack an interest in the Bible are encouraged simply to skip appendix D.

Appendix E relates to chapter 9. It provides an alternate attack on the Afterlife Defense, but one which is highly controversial and in which I do not feel a great deal of confidence. It, too, is a sketchy part of the book and, like the previous appendices, itself in need of a lengthy treatment. I include it mainly to show that the concept of an afterlife is in no way free of conceptual problems and to express some of the misgivings that people have had with it.

Appendix F is mainly connected with chapter 14. Like appendix D, it is concerned with natural theology, which is relevant to any inductive (or evidential) God-vs.-world arguments. It represents a kind of sample. I have objections to each of the usual arguments for theism, but lack the space to present them in the present work. So, in appendix F I consider just one of those arguments and present objections to *it*. The objections are analogous to ones that I would put forward to attack other theistic arguments and thus may be regarded as a sample of such objections. The importance of attacking theistic arguments for my overall project is explained at the start of the appendix, though it should be noted that the connection is an indirect one. The connection would have been quite direct if I had tried to infer God's nonexistence by the Lack-of-evidence Argument, mentioned in section 1.5. However, I have not appealed to that argument but used other God-vs.-world arguments instead.

The final appendix, G, aims to show, among other things, what effects the present book would have if people generally were to accept it. Possibly readers will find some of those effects thought-provoking, even alarming, which will encourage them to work harder at finding opposing arguments. That would certainly be welcome. It would make for progress in the field of philosophy.

Appendix A

Compatibilism vs. Incompatibilism

A.1. The Issue

Incompatibilism is the view that if determinism were true then no one could have genuine free will or make any real choices. It is a view that seems to be held by all advocates of FDE (the Free-will Defense as applied to AE). It would be interesting to speculate how FDE would fare without it, and that question will be touched upon below. But for now I shall assume that FDE needs incompatibilism and that to attack incompatibilism would be an alternate way to attack FDE, i.e., beyond the ways presented and discussed above in chapter 4. Let us see how that might go.

An incompatibilist definition of "real choice" may be formulated as follows (call it "D1"):

D1: A real choice is a choice among actions all of which are avoidable, given the agent's complete background, where this is interpreted in a contracausal way as excluding choices that are totally determined by the remote past.

It may be objected here that there are better definitions to consider. One of them is the following (call it "D2"):

D2: A real choice is a choice among actions all of which are avoidable in the sense that, for each of them, if the agent had tried to avoid performing the given act then he would not have performed that act.

This implies that, for any act which is the consequence of a real choice, if the agent had tried to avoid performing the act then he would not have performed it. Note that D2 is not an incompatibilist definition, for it does not require that real choices be "contracausal." Even if an act were totally determined by the past, it could still be true that the agent would have avoided performing the act if he had tried to avoid it. Thus, people could still make real choices in the D2 sense even if determinism were true. Taking compatibilism to be the view that free will is compatible with determinism, D2 would be a compatibilist definition.

However, D2 is objectionable in that it is too broad. It has the unwanted consequence that just about any choice whatever would be a "real choice" or "free-will choice." In ordinary language, there are many situations where we say that a person did not do something of his "own free will" or did not have a "real choice" in the matter at hand, even though it is true that the person would not have done what he did if he had tried to avoid doing it. For example, if I hand over my wallet to a robber at gunpoint, it would probably be said that I had no "real choice" in the matter, yet it would still be the case that if I had tried to avoid handing over the wallet, I would have succeeded in not handing it over. Although being avoidable in the given sense is a necessary condition for "real choice" (or "free-will choice"), it is not a sufficient condition. Hence definition D2 is a failure.

In light of this objection, let us give up D2 and consider some other compatibilist way to define "real choice." A more promising definition is the following (call it "D3"):

> D3: A real choice is a voluntary choice, that is, a choice among actions none of which is *compelled*, i.e., chosen by the agent, A, but caused by some intrusive force that conflicts with A's own normal desires, causing A to do something contrary to A's normal course of behavior.

So long as the agent A is choosing voluntarily, i.e., in accord with A's own normal desires, it is a "real choice" and A is exercising free will. This definition is another compatibilist one. It is clear that even if determinism were true, A's choice need not be caused by any intrusive force that conflicts with A's own normal desires. So, if the expression "real choice" were defined in the way given by D3, then compatibilism would be true, i.e., free will (or the making of real choices) would be compatible with determinism. But in that case, FDE's premise (P1) (which says that for God to have made people altruistic would necessarily prevent them from having moral freedom) would be false. God could create people to be staunchly altruistic, meaning that they would always be inclined to do things for the sake of others, and they could still have moral freedom, i.e., make real choices (as defined by D3) between doing good and doing evil (causing others happiness or causing others suffering). Staunchly altruistic people, by definition, would never choose to do evil but would always choose to do good. Nevertheless, they could still be making real choices in the given sense, for their choices need not be caused by any intrusive force that conflicts with their own normal desires. Thus, God could make people altruistic (even staunchly altruistic) without preventing them from making real choices between doing good and doing evil, which would refute premise (P1). This gives rise to an attack on FDE, based on definition D3. The objection is that D3 is a better definition than D1, and when moral freedom is understood in terms of D3, FDE's premise (P1) becomes false.

A.2. Examples of Compulsion

Let us explore D3 further. When compatibilism is based on it, the key distinction is between real choices and compelled choices. One example of a compelled choice would be that mentioned previously, a robber who demands your money at gunpoint. If you surrender your money to him, your choice to do so is compelled in the sense that it is caused by an intrusive force (the threat of being shot) that conflicts with your own normal desire (in this case your desire to keep your money). In ordinary language, people say of such cases, "You had no real choice in the matter" or "You did not give him your money of your own free will." If the police capture the robber but he says that you gave him the money of your own free will, then you would certainly deny that!

(Note that this sort of example should be distinguished from that of a pickpocket who steals your money without there being any action on your part. That case is irrelevant in the present context, for there would be no action of handing over money to be classified as being "done of free will" or "not done of free will." The same would be true if a group of muggers were to totally overpower you and take your money without you in any way surrendering it to them. A compelled choice always requires that there be some *action* on the part of the person who suffers the compulsion.)

It might be objected here that whenever you *surrender* your money, even if it is done at gunpoint, you still have some choice in the matter. After all, you could have tried to put up a fight or perhaps just run away. Some people have been known to choose to resist in such circumstances and when they do so, it would probably be said of them that their action was done of their "own free will." How can it be that if you have a choice between X and Y and choose X (resistance) then it is a "real choice," whereas if you choose Y (surrender) then it is not a "real choice"? It is hard to maintain that only act X was the result of a "normal" desire, namely, your desire to retain your money, for act Y, too, was the result of a certain "normal" desire, namely, your desire to avoid being shot.

I have two kinds of reaction to this. First, it is not completely clear to me that if you choose to resist the gunman then your choice is one of "free will," for the overall situation is still being foisted upon you. It would at least not be the sort of action that anyone would use for a paradigm example of a free-will choice. My second reaction is to wonder whether the objection is really serious. After all, it seems quite clear that there is an important difference between handing over money voluntarily, say, to a charity, and handing over money at the threat of being shot. People normally say that in the latter case your action of surrendering the money was compelled, and not done freely, and that you had no "real choice" in the matter. The difference between the two cases is quite sharp. Furthermore, if we deny that handing over money at gunpoint is a compelled action, then it is rather hard to see what the distinction between "free" and "compelled" amounts to. What, then, would be a paradigm example of a compelled choice? To deny the given distinction is obviously a radical departure from ordinary usage.

The compatibilist's problem appears to be that of framing an adequate definition that would draw the sort of distinction wanted. Granting for the moment that you act freely if you resist the gunman, I think a case could be made for saying that if you resist the gunman then your choice is caused by your *own* desires, for you have not subordinated them to anyone or anything else. On the other hand, if you surrender to the gunman then your choice is not caused by your own desires, but is instead the result of someone else's (the gunman's) desires. I grant that the wording of D3 may be in need of some improvement, but the point of the gunman example and the distinction it exemplifies should be clear. In a certain sense, if you resisted then you were not compelled to do so, but if you had surrendered then you were compelled to do so, or so it would normally be said, in retrospect, in ordinary language.

Another example of a compelled choice would be that of a drug addict who is driven to steal money in order to buy drugs. We are assuming here that the person's normal desire is to not steal. Then the drug addiction is an intrusive compulsion that causes behavior contrary to the agent's own normal desire, which entails, on the given definition, that the choice to steal is a compelled rather than a real choice. This example is different from the previous one in that the immediate intrusive compelling force, namely, the drug addiction, is internal rather than external. However, if we push the case back far enough, possibly we could trace the chain of events to a past external force that introduced drugs into the addict's life. More will be said about that later. It should be noted that some cases of mental illness, e.g., kleptomania, would be similar to that of the drug addict who is driven to steal, and could also be classified as "compulsions."

A third example of a compelled choice is one that is somewhat artificial, but is sometimes appealed to and rather instructive. It is the so-called "robot-person." Suppose Joe is kidnapped by Martians who implant an electrode in his brain by means of which, after Joe is released, they are subsequently able to control his beliefs and desires, and thereby his actions. Joe was law-abiding in the past, but the Martians now cause Joe to want to steal money for them. Knowing the facts, we would say of Joe that when he now goes out to steal, he does not do so of his own free will, but is compelled to do it (by the Martians). And D3 would accommodate that intuition. Although Joe wants to steal, that is not his normal desire. Rather, it is brought about by an intrusive force (the electrode implanted in his brain) that conflicts with his normal desires, those being the ones (including the desire to obey the law) that he had in the past, prior to the kidnapping.

It has been suggested that for God to make staunch altruists of people, i.e., make them into beings who *always* aim at the morally right act, he would have to do something to them akin to the implantation of electrodes in their brains. But if that were so, then such people would necessarily lose their moral freedom, quite apart from whether determinism is true or false. Even if determinism were true, for God to make staunch altruists of people, he would need to use an intrusive force contrary to their normal desires, and by definition D3 that would eliminate their moral freedom. Thus, there would be no need for advocates of FDE to defend either indeterminism or incompatibilism. They could put forward and defend FDE's premise (P1) within a determinist and compatibilist framework, using D3 instead of D1 as their definition of real choices (or moral freedom).

I think that this suggestion is no good. First, there could very well be staunch altruists whose *normal* desire is always to do the morally right act, for they could be that way from birth. So, for God to make people like that, he need not use any intrusive force that conflicts with their normal desires. He could just see to it that they are that way as a result of genetics or nature. By D3, such people would have moral freedom, which would refute FDE's premise (P1). Furthermore, the appeal to staunch altruism is misguided anyway, for God could greatly reduce the moral evil in the world simply by making ordinary altruists of people (ones who are strongly motivated to avoid morally wrong actions though not strictly determined to do so). It seems to me that the only way for advocates of FDE to get their premise (P1) to be true would be for them to reformulate it in terms of "staunchly altruistic" people (instead of merely altruistic people) and to stick with their incompatibilism and definition D1. (However, as was pointed out in section 4.3, that requires that the advocates of FDE reformulate their premise (P2) in a way that would make it obviously false. So their enterprise is doomed anyway.) At any rate, I shall continue to assume that FDE needs incompatibilism as a background assumption and that to attack incompatibilism is to attack FDE.

Let us return to a scrutiny of D3. Suppose Joe were kidnapped by the Martians at birth and the electrode were implanted in his brain while he was still an infant. In that case, he would have no "normal" desires with which his desire to steal would conflict. Would he then be making real choices as defined by D3? I think a case could be made that his desires would not be "normal," because they would be produced by an object or situation that is quite abnormal in comparison with other humans. I think we would still be inclined to say that Joe's behavior is being compelled and that he is not making real choices as we usually think of them. Admittedly, this is exceedingly vague, but there seems to be no way of getting around that.

What if the Martians got Joe to steal for them, not by implanting an electrode in his brain, but by surgically operating on his brain while he was still an infant and making it into the sort of brain that robbers have? When he then later steals for the Martians, would he be doing so as the consequence of normal desires? Or would Joe's case still be an example of compulsion? It is very hard to answer this question. Suppose there were a brainscan machine that could distinguish "law-abiding" brains from "criminal" brains. Some people would be found to have the one type while others would be found to have the other type. Joe's brain would show up as a "criminal" brain, but in no way distinguishable from other brains of that type which are possessed by people who became criminals in quite ordinary ways. (It would have no electrode in it.) Maybe some distinction could still be drawn here. Knowing Joe's history, we could say that his particular criminal desires are not normal, for they were produced by Martian surgery, which is quite abnormal in comparison with the situation of other humans. Focusing on that aspect of Joe's case, we could then say that, by D3, when Joe makes choices, they are not real choices, for they are brought about by desires which are in conflict with Joe's normal desires. But what *are* Joe's normal desires? He has been a robber from a very young age. Would it make sense to say that Joe's normal desires are those he would have had, given his heredity, had he not been kidnapped and operated on by the Martians? To say that would require that normal desires could be merely hypothetical (rather than actual) ones. It would surely be stretching the concept too far to say that. What, then, are we to say about D3? Is it shown to be too broad by the case where the Martians simply operate on Joe when he is an infant? Is that a case where Joe does *not* make real choices and yet does so according to D3? I think it is very hard to make a judgment here.

A similar example is that of predestination. Suppose that God plans out Joe's nature and life prior to his birth and then sets up the world in just that way which would fulfill his plans for Joe. Would Joe be making real choices or not? Again, it is hard to decide such a case. Joe's behavior would not be compelled according to definition D3, for God's predestination is not an intrusive force conflicting with any normal desires. So, by D3, Joe's choices would be real ones. But whether that makes definition D3 too broad is hard to say. (The idea of predestination will be discussed further in appendix B.)

Apart from the issue of whether or not D3 is too broad, it seems that our third example of compulsion shows that there is an area of vagueness surrounding the concept and that it could be hard to say whether or not certain acts are compelled. But the same area of vagueness shows up with the two previous examples as well. Let us look into that matter further.

A.3. The Degree Objection

One feature of D3's distinction between real choices and compelled choices that should be emphasized is that it is a matter of *degree*. There is no sharp division here. Rather, it is a spectrum of cases ranging at one end from choices that are very strongly compelled by an intrusive force (that sharply conflicts with the agent's normal desires) to the opposite end consisting of choices that are not affected by any influence whatever outside of the agent's own normal desires. In the latter situation, the agent might be said to be doing his "own thing." All three of the above examples of compulsion could be used to bring out this feature of degree. Instead of a gun, the robber could threaten you with a knife or perhaps just a beating. There could be a group of robbers, which would increase the degree of compulsion. Or, alternatively, you could be part of a group of victims threatened by a lone robber, which would lessen the degree of compulsion. Many other factors would be relevant here, such how much money is at stake, whether you have an opportunity to run away or put up a fight, and in that case how fast a runner or how good a fighter you are. Some of these factors would reduce the degree of compulsion while others would increase it. Certainly in ordinary language we do say that a person might be "more free" or "less free," depending on the circumstances that the person is in. I am also inclined to view the resistance case in these terms. That is, even if you resist the gunman, you are not making a completely free choice, for you are still in a situation that conflicts sharply with your own normal desires. Few people, if any, would want to be addressed at gunpoint. I would say, then, that the victim who resists acts "more freely" than the victim who surrenders, but it is still not a case of complete free will.

The example of the drug addict-turned-thief also admits of degree. How addicted is he and how long has he gone without the drug? How much inclination did he have, prior to becoming addicted, to avoid stealing? That is, how much conflict is there between the stealing and the agent's normal desires? Still another way to ask this question is to inquire just what are or what were the drug addict's normal desires? Was there ever a period in his life that could be called "normal"? Suppose that the person had an abnormal childhood and exhibited delinquent behavior from early youth. Would that make his later choice to steal in order to support a drug habit more free or less free? It is hard to say, I think because the abnormal childhood increases the force upon the individual to steal while at the same time, in eliminating normalcy, it reduces the conflict between the stealing and the person's "normal" desires. But our difficulty in assessing the matter only shows further how there is no sharp line between free and unfree choices. There are many factors determining the forces that cause the drug addict to steal, and they prevent a sharp cutoff between cases in which the person makes a real choice to steal and those in which it is not a real choice but the result of some sort of intrusive compulsion.

Similar considerations could be raised in connection with kleptomania and other mental illnesses. And we have already seen how they can be raised in connection with the example of Joe and the Martians. The boundary between "real choices" and compelled behavior is exceedingly vague. And this is reflected in ordinary language, for people would readily grant that it is sometimes quite unclear whether a given person did or did not act of his own free will, even when all the relevant facts are known.

The fact that we are inclined to view free will as a matter of degree seems to support the compatibilist as opposed to the incompatibilist definition. The incompatibilist definition, namely D1, is in terms of "avoidability": free will is choosing among options all of which are avoidable, given the agent's complete background. So if the agent's complete background causally determines a choice of option X rather than option Y, then option X becomes unavoidable, given that background, which makes the choice something other than a "real choice," and that eliminates the agent's free will in this matter. But avoidability does not admit of degree. An option is either completely determined by the past or it isn't, and the element of degree plays no role here. So if free will does admit of degree in ordinary language, then that shows that the incompatibilist definition fails to capture our ordinary-language concept of free will. This attack on incompatibilism could be labeled the "Degree Objection."

One reply that the incompatibilist might make to the objection is that it rests on a confusion between freedom of the will and freedom of action. He might claim that only freedom of action admits of degree, and that freedom of the will does not. But what exactly is the difference between the two? How can a person have one but not the other? Suppose a man is totally paralyzed and unable even to tense his muscles. He could still *try* to move while having no ability whatever to do so, so perhaps one might say that he has freedom of the will but no freedom of action. It might also be said of him that he could exercise his will in performing mental acts, such as remembering, daydreaming, and planning. The trouble with this is that if remembering and daydreaming, etc., are to be regarded as a kind of action, then to that extent the prisoner does have a certain degree of freedom of action, for he is indeed free to perform *those* acts. And what about *trying* to move itself? If that, too, is a mental act, then even in trying to move, the man is performing some sort of action, and to that extent has *some* freedom of action. If we regard such mental events as remembering and trying to move as "actions" of a certain sort, then we have not come up with an example where a person has free will but no freedom of action. The incompatibilist might attempt to circumvent this objection by construing mental events as nonactions or by defining "freedom of action" so as to apply only to *physical* actions. Then a person could be said to have free will, defined here as the ability to try to do something, without having freedom of action (i.e., the ability actually to perform physical actions).

But another objection to the definition of "free will" as "trying" comes in with our example of drugs. While under the influence of a drug or while deprived of a drug to which he is severely addicted, a man might behave in a strange manner and it might be said of him that he is not doing things of his own free will. Also, some cases of mental illness might be regarded in that way. It is often said of such people that they lack free will. And yet it is clear that they do *try* to do things. Some try to resist the influence of their drug addiction or mental illness, but fail. It seems that we are forced to abandon the attempt to define "free will" by appeal to the concept of "trying." What other alternatives are there?

Could it be that what distinguishes cases in which free will is absent is simply that the things which the people try to do are very strange or uncharacteristic things, which we do not expect them to do? What about the case where Joe has an electrode implanted in his brain by means of which the Martians send signals to him? For example, if they want Joe to sit down, then they send the appropriate signal to Joe's electrode and that causes him immediately to sit down. When Joe performs the given action, most people who know of the circumstances would say of him that he did not do it of his own free will. Why? Is it that the action is somehow inappropriate, i.e., not in character for Joe, or one that does not fit in with his long-range goals and plans? That does not seem to work here, for most people would deny that Joe has acted of his own free will even if some of the actions he performs are indeed ones that he would do (such as sitting down) under normal conditions. Clearly, some other definition of "free will" is needed.

One suggestion is that free will has to do with the *kinds* of causes that preceded the action. That is, when it is one kind of cause we say the person had free will, but when it is a different kind (including a case involving a foreign object that is implanted in the brain) we say the person lacked free will. Well, suppose the Martians did not control Joe by means of any physical device, or even by any special surgery, but did so by a process of conditioning. Let us say that for many years they trained Joe to behave in certain ways. For example, suppose that through extensive use of reward and punishment the Martians trained Joe to steal for them. When Joe subsequently does the stealing, would he be acting of his own free will? This is a difficult case which seems to fall in the border area between free and unfree. And it certainly does seem that the element of *degree* comes into play here. It seems reasonable to say that the more extensive the process of conditioning imposed by the Martians, the less Joe possesses free will. If the conditioning is minimal, then Joe's free will is hardly interfered with, but if the conditioning is maximal, then his free will is pretty well eliminated. But then this sort of definition will not serve the incompatibilist's purpose of showing that freedom of the will does not admit of degree.

It seems that when the incompatibilist tries to distinguish freedom of the will from freedom of action, the concept of free will becomes rather unclear. It seems not to be just the ability to *try* to do something and it seems not to be just the ability or inclination to act normally or in ways that are characteristic of the person. Furthermore, to say simply that free will has something to do with the kinds of causes acting on the person seems exceedingly vague. The relevant kinds need to be specified. So the problem of defining the concept in a way which distinguishes it from freedom of action has proven very difficult.

Even if the distinction between free will and freedom of action could be clearly drawn, there is still reason to say that in ordinary language free will admits of degree. Consider cases like drug addiction and kleptomania. People may be victims of them to a greater or lesser degree. We say that such conditions are more or less severe. Yet such conditions clearly do inversely affect freedom of the will and not merely freedom of action (assuming the distinction could be drawn). It follows that freedom of the will admits of degree. The stronger the addiction or kleptomania, the less freedom of the will is possessed by its victim. Thus, it is time for the incompatibilist to concede that free will does indeed admit of degree, and so D1 can no longer be upheld as an accurate definition.

The incompatibilist might concede that the Degree Objection refutes D1 and replace that definition by the following (call it "D4"):

D4: A real choice is one that:
(1) meets definition D1 (i.e., it is made from actions all of which are avoidable, given the agent's complete background, which entails that the choice was not completely determined by the remote past), and
(2) is voluntary in the sense provided by definition D3, above.

In virtue of part (2) of definition D4, real choices do admit of degree. The stronger the intrusive force and the more it conflicts with the agent's own normal desires, the more the choice is "compelled" and the less it is a "real choice" or one made by free will. Thus, since voluntariness admits of degree and since voluntariness is a necessary condition for being a real choice, it follows that the property of being a real choice, i.e., one made by free will, also admits of degree. That brings the incompatibilist's definition into conformity with ordinary language on that score, which takes care of the Degree Objection. However, incompatibilism is retained because, in addition to voluntariness, there is also part (1) of the definition, which makes free will, or being a real choice, incompatible with determinism. If the incompatibilist revises his definition of "real choice" in this way, then he succeeds is getting around the Degree Objection while still retaining incompatibilism. I do not know of any incompatibilist who has actually gone this route, but it seems to me to be the only way to deal adequately with the Degree Objection. For that reason, I shall assume in what follows that D4 is "the incompatibilist's definition."

A.4. The Criterion Objection

Another objection that might be raised against the incompatibilist definition of free will (or "real choice") is that it fails to square with the *criterion* that is employed in everyday life to ascertain whether or not an actual choice made was a "real" one or one made by free will. Suppose that such an issue were to arise, say, in a legal context. Taking our first two examples of compulsion (the realistic ones), we can imagine a courtroom setting in which the issue is raised. When the victim, X, handed money over to the robber, was it done of X's own free will? When X stole money to buy drugs (or as a result of kleptomania), was it done of X's own free will? How do people try to answer such questions? What criterion do they appeal to?

The compatibilist, appealing to definition D3, would maintain that the only criterion is that of voluntariness. People would say that X acted of his own free will if and only if the action was voluntary, that is, caused by X's own normal desires rather than some intrusive compulsion that was in conflict with his normal desires. Granted, this is sometimes hard to judge and there are many borderline cases. That has to do with the element of degree that was pointed out above. Nevertheless, despite the vagueness, *that* is the criterion to which people would appeal. But the appeal to voluntariness is only part (2) of the incompatibilist's definition of "real choice," given above, namely, definition D4. The definition also has a part (1), the requirement that real choices not be completely determined by the remote past. Well, do people ever appeal to *that* consideration in their assessments of free will? In other words, in judging whether X gave the money to the robber of X's own free will, or whether X stole money to support a drug habit of his own free will, is the issue ever raised whether or not X's act was completely determined by antecedent causes? I would say, "Hardly ever." One possible exception was Clarence Darrow's appeal to determinism in his defense of the murderers Leopold and Loeb in 1924, but that is a rare situation. Not only do people not normally raise such an issue, they would not even comprehend how to raise it. What would one look for to ascertain whether or not X's act was completely determined by remote causal antecedents? There seems to be no way to try to ascertain that. Although it is an empirical issue, it is highly abstract and hard to address in practical terms.

This gives rise to another objection to incompatibilism, which may be called the "Criterion Objection." The incompatibilist's definition of free will, D4, contains two parts, but people normally appeal only to the second part as their criterion of free will. The first part plays practically no role in the making of assessments as to whether or not a person acted of his own free will or had a "real choice" in some matter. It follows that the definition is faulty and that, to capture the ordinary-language use of the relevant terms ("free will" and "real choice"), its first part should be omitted. (Note that the original incompatibilist definition, D1, would fare even worse by this objection, for *all* of it would be shown to be criteriologically irrelevant.) As people use the relevant terms in everyday discourse, they clearly have in mind some concept other than that of the incompatibilist. So some other definition, presumably the compatibilist's (namely, D3), is called for.

One reply that an incompatibilist might make here is that the reason people would not appeal in everyday discourse to the first part of definition D4 is that they already assume that it is satisfied. For example, if X hands over money to the robber and the question is raised whether or not it was a real choice (or whether X did it of X's own free will), then it is already assumed that the action was not completely determined by remote causal antecedents. It is true that the only practical issue is that of voluntariness, but that is so simply because the other issue (the determinism-indeterminism issue) is not even brought to mind. If it were to be raised, say, by a philosopher, then people would take an incompatibilist stance on the matter. That is, if it were suggested that when X handed the money over to the robber, X's action was completely determined by the remote past, then people would reply that in that case X had no "real choice" and lacked free will. It follows, according to the incompatibilist, that the first part of definition D4 is indeed needed, even though it does not play any role in the everyday usage of the expressions "free will" and "real choice."

The predestination example could also be appealed to here by the incompatibilist. Suppose that X's action had been predestined by God prior to X's birth. That is, God had planned that X would be the way he is and would choose to do exactly those things that X in fact does. Would X in that case be making real choices and have free will? We have already seen that an appeal to definition D3 would yield an affirmative answer, for God would in no way be intruding upon X's normal desires. But, according to the incompatibilist, most people would say no, which shows that compatibilism and its Criterion Objection are incorrect and misguided.

It is hard to judge whether this response to the Criterion Objection is successful. It seems to depend on what people would actually say if confronted by the idea of determinism or predestination. Would they say that if determinism or predestination were true then no one would ever have free will or make real choices? Or would they say, instead, that the issues of determinism and predestination are irrelevant, and that people have free will and make real choices just so long as they are acting voluntarily and are not being forced to do what they do by any sort of intrusive compulsion (a situation that could still obtain even if determinism or predestination were indeed true)? This is a linguistic matter on which I do not feel competent to make a call. I think that different people would go different ways. It may be that there are two distinct concepts in ordinary language and that one of them makes free will compatible with determinism and predestination whereas the other does not. In that case, we could not say that FDE's premise (P1) has been definitely refuted by compatibilism. Our lengthy excursion into semantics has not produced a definite result.

A.5. The Randomness Objection and Agent-causation Theory

One last stab at attacking incompatibilism can be made by inquiring as to the exact nature of a "real choice" as the incompatibilist conceives it. In virtue of part (1) of definition D4, such a choice would not be completely determined by remote causal antecedents, which implies that there is some sort of indeterminacy (in the physicists' sense) in its background. Are we to call it an "uncaused choice," one that just pops up at random in the agent's brain? That would be a most unpleasant notion. People's free-will choices would then be pure chance and a matter of luck. If a bad choice should pop up randomly, then that would be bad luck for the agent. Such a concept of free will would be absurd. Agents would be not at all responsible for their "real choices," since no one can be responsible for anything that occurs at random or by pure chance. And instead of being something desirable, free will would be something to be dreaded, a kind of unpredictable happening that could get one into trouble through no fault of one's own. This could be called the "Randomness Objection." It maintains that the incompatibilist definition of "real choice" must be rejected because it is committed to the untenable proposition that a real choice is an uncaused choice, a kind of brain event that just pops up on occasion at random. That would make the whole idea of free will absurd.

To get around the Randomness Objection, most incompatibilists draw a distinction between our usual notion of causation as a relation between events and what they call "agent causation," which is a special kind of causation relating agents to the actions they perform. Actions, they say, are not caused by events but by agents. The agents initiate the actions in something like the way the First Cause of the universe was supposed to have initiated things. Each agent, in performing an action, is the first cause in a series of causes extending into the future. But whereas the causes extending into the future are event causes, the initiating first cause of the whole series is something different, being an agent cause. Agent causationists not only deny that free will is subject to determinism, but they also deny that it is random or indeterminate, which gets around the Randomness Objection. Choices are not random events going off in people's brains, but a special kind of event caused by an agent. In what follows, I shall assume that all incompatibilists and advocates of FDE are agent causationists.

A.6. The Mysteriousness Objection and Culpability

Since agent causation is different from event causation, which is the sort that occurs out in nature, it is a kind of nonnatural causation, presumably outside the domain of the usual scientific methodology. It does not support prediction and explanation in the way done by event causation. That makes free will a rather mysterious feature of the human situation. Although the idea of agent causation usually seems acceptable to theists and others with a supernaturalistic worldview, it does not usually seem so to those who subscribe to naturalism or physicalism.

One of the questions that we would like to put to the agent causationist is what sort of connection exists between a "real choice" and the agent's *nature*, which includes his character, goals, beliefs, and desires, as formed from his past. If the choice is not completely determined by the nature, then how might the relation be described? Is it only one of influence? I should think it highly peculiar that my nature (including my desires) will only have an influence over my choices and not determine them totally. I would then have to regard it rather risky to make "real choices." How could I set out to deliberate about some course of action, expecting that my deliberation will culminate in a real choice, if indeed my deliberation will not in the end totally determine the choice but only influence it? What exactly is the additional factor that fills in what is missing from my nature to produce the choice? Is there any way that I could somehow take account of it in the course of deliberation? The whole matter is exceedingly mysterious and seems to smack of supernaturalism. Let us call this the "Mysteriousness Objection." It is an attack on any form of incompatibilism that appeals to agent-causation theory, and shows, I think, that the theory is rather unclear, if not incoherent.

One reply to the Mysteriousness Objection that the agent causationist might make is to appeal to what might be called the "Paradox of Culpability," mentioned previously in section 8.1. To develop the paradox, let us consider the following two principles, both of which seem quite reasonable:

(I)   No one is culpable for any event which was completely determined by causal antecedents that occurred prior to one's own birth.

(II)   No one is culpable for any uncaused event or any event which is an effect of an uncaused event.

It might be argued that every event falls into one of those two categories. We can record this as a third principle:

(III) Every action either is completely determined by causal antecedents that occurred prior to the agent's own birth or else is an uncaused event or an effect of an uncaused event.

From the three principles taken together, it is possible to deduce that no one is ever culpable for any action that he performs, which would be a most paradoxical conclusion. What could we mean by "culpability" if it never actually applies to anything? Well, the agent causationist has a solution. Principle (III) can be denied on the grounds that there is a third alternative to actions being completely determined by the remote past and actions being uncaused events. The third alternative is that actions are "agent caused." This is supposed to provide a way out of the given paradox. And if the theory of agent causation is rejected, then one is stuck with the Paradox of Culpability with no way out.

I am inclined to agree that there is an important problem here. How can the paradox be escaped if no appeal is made to agent causation? Many compatibilists readily deny principle (I), which is the first premise of the above argument, and that strikes me as a possible solution. However, principle (I) does seem plausible, especially when culpability is understood to entail desert. In that context I myself lean toward agreement with all three principles and do not have any solution to the paradox apart from simply accepting the conclusion that no one is ever culpable for any action and trying to live with that. I think that, with a utilitarian (or consequentialist) outlook and perhaps the right worldview, one could indeed learn to live with the conclusion without incurring conceptual or ethical problems. However, it may also be that principle (I) is wrong and can indeed be attacked. I have no settled view on the matter. In any case, it appears that, with the appeal to agent causation, incompatibilism has some resources which have not been totally discredited.

Still another objection to compatibilism might be raised once principle (I), that determinism is incompatible with culpability, is granted. It could be posed as the following argument:

(a) Determinism is incompatible with culpability.

(b) Free will is both necessary and sufficient for culpability.

(c) Therefore, determinism is incompatible with free will.

The big issue here is premise (b) and, in particular, whether free will is sufficient for culpability. I think there are ordinary-language senses of the relevant terms by which one might be said to make a real choice (of one's own free will) without being culpable (or blameworthy) for that choice. Some choices made by small children might be good examples of this. Although the choice is voluntary, it is also excusable. So free will, in that case, would not be sufficient for culpability, which would make premise (b) false and the objection unsound. I conclude, then, that the incompatibilist's appeal to culpability provides us with food for thought, but it does not in itself refute compatibilism, even when compatibilism grants principle (I), mentioned above.

As for the Paradox of Culpability, if I am right and there are ways to deal adequately with the problem without making appeal to the idea of agent causation, then the agent causationist's attempt to evade the Mysteriousness Objection is not entirely successful. He still owes us an account of what agent causation is and how it connects with those aspects of human nature that appear, when studied scientifically, to completely determine human action. So long as such an account is not forthcoming, the appeal to agent causation will always carry with it an aura of obscurity.

Another point regarding agent causationism is important. In section 4.2 it was shown how God could have made people altruists without interfering with their free will. That is because being an altruist (as opposed to being a "staunch altruist") only inclines one away from (or gives one an aversion toward) harming others. It does not make harming others impossible or contrary to natural law. So, one could have an altruistic nature and still make real choices in the incompatibilists' sense (definition D1). What I want to note here is that this point regarding altruism would be and needs to be supported by agent causationism, which denies any fixed connection between an altruist and his altruistic nature. If one's nature only influences (and does not completely determine) one's behavior, then God could have given people altruistic natures without thereby completely determining their behavior. (He would have merely influenced the behavior without completely determining it.) As pointed out in section 4.2, for God to have done that would have brought about situation L by a great reduction in crime and immoral conduct without any interference with free will, even given an incompatibilist definition of "free will." So long as the incompatibilist espouses agent causationism, he cannot consistently deny the point made regarding altruism. Thus, agent causationism actually tends to support the attack on FDE's premise (P1) that was made in chapter 4.

A.7. The Undesirability Objection

Still another objection to the agent-causation theory is that it makes free will rather undesirable, for it seems to sever the connection between a free-will action and the agent's nature, which includes his character, goals, beliefs, and desires. This could be called the "Undesirability Objection." If people were to express their preferences on the matter, I would expect them to say that they prefer performing actions that are *completely* the outcome of their natures, as determined by the past, rather than performing actions which are only influenced or partly caused by their natures, thus determined. To perform completely determined actions would provide them with confidence in what they are doing. If one's choice could go contrary to one's nature, as determined by the past, then there would always be a kind of uncertainty in all of one's deliberations. In the back of one's mind, one would always think, "Here I am deliberating about whether or not to perform act A, and no matter what result I end up with, I might (through agent causation, whatever that is) choose in a way contrary to my nature which is the source of the deliberation." There would then always seem to be an element of indeterminacy in one's free-will decisions, which I should think would be an undesirable feature of them. It would appear that people should then be fearful or apprehensive about their deliberations. Free will is normally regarded as very valuable, so for a theory to make it into something undesirable is certainly a drawback to the theory. This line of thought seems to show that, however it fares against the Mysteriousness Objection, the agent-causation theory is, in the end, untenable. But once that theory is discredited, then the incompatibilist has no adequate defense against the Randomness Objection. When pushed in this direction, compatibilism has finally seemed to gain some force as an attack on FDE's premise (P1).

Another reason why the Undesirability Objection is so forceful is that the advocate of FDE needs to emphasize the desirability of free will. In fact, he is claiming that free will is so valuable that overall human happiness can justifiably be sacrificed for it. That is the basis of FDE's premise (P3). So, if it can be shown that the agent-causation theory makes free will undesirable, then that would bring out a fundamental inconsistency in the use of that theory to try to defend FDE.

It may be that I have misunderstood the agent-causation theory and that agent causation is neither as mysterious nor as undesirable as I have depicted it here. In that case, FDE cannot be refuted by compatibilism. I really do not have a settled view on this matter, though I lean strongly towards the compatibilist side of the controversy. In any case, even if compatibilism should fail, at least FDE was very definitely refuted by the objections raised against it in chapter 4.

Appendix B

Challenges to Contracausal Free Will

In the previous appendix, objections to incompatibilism were presented and discussed, but in this one I shall simply assume that incompatibilism is true and that our ordinary concept of free will is what is usually called "contracausal free will," i.e., the ability to make choices and perform actions that are not totally determined by the remote past. So I shall use "free will" to mean "contracausal free will." Moral freedom, in turn, is defined as free will as applied to real choices between causing others to be happy and causing them to suffer unjustifiably. Do people ever have moral freedom in that sense? Is there such a thing as (contracausal) free will? In this appendix, some reasons for saying no will be scrutinized. The first one will be a reason open to everyone, while the others will be only for theists of a certain sort.

B.1. The Determinism Objection

In chapter 4 it was pointed out that the Free-will Defense (FDE) normally contains the premise that people have moral freedom (as defined above). Although that assumption is not absolutely necessary for FDE to combat the version of the Argument from Evil put forward in this book, I take it to be a background assumption because all FDEers assume it and FDE would be highly implausible without it. Now, according to determinism, all human actions and decisions are completely determined by causal antecedents that extend back indefinitely into the remote past. So if determinism were true, then there would be no such thing as free will or moral freedom, which would make FDE's background assumption false. Thus, we need to consider the truth of determinism.

There are two sorts of counterexample to determinism that are frequently cited. One is subatomic events which are supposed to be causally indeterminate. The other is the original first cause, whatever it may be. I am not convinced by either of these. It seems to me that subatomic indeterminacy may not be real, but merely an illusion brought about by the incompleteness of our physical theories. And it also seems to me that there need not ever have been a first cause. Causal chains may simply extend infinitely backward in time. Granted, that is hard to conceive, but so also is the idea of a first cause. The conceptual problems associated with the idea of a first cause strike me as just as intractable as those associated with causal chains that have no beginning, so to appeal to such problems does not favor either idea over the other.

Even if we concede that general determinism has the sorts of exceptions to it mentioned, it is still not clear that those exceptions have anything to do with human action. The level at which human actions take place is so far removed from the subatomic level that they could be thought to be in separate categories. Could human actions be totally determined even if subatomic events aren't? Why couldn't so-called "near determinism," the view that all human actions are totally determined by the remote past, still be true, even if general determinism has exceptions to it? It might be argued that some actions performed by quantum physicists who are studying subatomic events through the use of sophisticated measuring instruments are actually affected by those events. For example, suppose a subatomic particle is ascertained by scientist X to have come to be in one physical state rather than another, where that was an uncaused event. Suppose that X records that information. In that case, the (uncaused) subatomic event, by way of the complex measuring instrument, indirectly caused X to record what he did. Hence, some subatomic events would, on occasion, cause human actions. So if the subatomic event was uncaused, then the given human action would not be completely determined by the remote past, which would falsify even "near determinism."

It is unclear to me whether there actually do occur such causal sequences as described above. I do not know enough about subatomic physics to pronounce upon this matter. But even if it sometimes happens, that is still far removed from the sorts of human action involved in the free will issue and FDE, namely, choices that people make in everyday life. It might be claimed by a still more restricted form of determinism that all of *those* actions (the kinds of ordinary actions performed in everyday life) are indeed completely determined by remote causal antecedents. Whether or not this is true is of course an empirical issue and one which has not as yet been resolved in the sciences. It does seem to me, though, that many of the results of scientific investigation of human behavior, to date, do support the hypothesis of the above-described form of restricted determinism. And since FDE is intended to apply to the sorts of choices people make in everyday life, that would count against its assumption that (contracausal) free will exists. Certainly those who are sympathetic with that form of restricted determinism (as I am) must be inclined to reject that assumption.

However, because of my ignorance regarding quantum physics and its possible application to human actions, I shall take a neutral stance on the determinism-indeterminism issue. That is, I shall not here claim that the Determinism Objection refutes FDE's background assumption regarding free will. That assumption will receive enough flak from other sources, so the determinism issue is not essential. However, I realize that, having backed down somewhat in my defense of compatibilism in appendix A, I must appear rather irresolute for not staunchly standing up for determinism. Despite the disappointment of those to my left, I shall continue simply to "call 'em as I see 'em."

B.2. The Foreknowledge Objection

Another attack sometimes directed against the claim that people have free will is that God exists, and God, being omniscient, knows the future completely, which includes knowing ahead of time everything that anyone ever does or will do. This may be termed the "Foreknowledge Objection." It seems reasonable to say that if God knows beforehand that person X will do act Y, then X must do Y, which makes Y unavoidable for X. But that eliminates any real choice on X's part between doing Y and not doing Y (in the incompatibilists' sense of "real choice," as discussed in appendix A). Such a choice would be a real one only if both doing Y and not doing Y are avoidable. But even if the choice is not completely determined by the past, if God knows that X will do Y, then doing Y becomes unavoidable for X. That makes X's choice not a real one, which in turn eliminates X's free will. This attack on free will differs from the Determinism Objection in that it presupposes theism, whereas the Determinism Objection doesn't, but that need not be a serious flaw in the present context. All advocates of FDE are theists, so they all need to defend against the Foreknowledge Objection. The objection, then, is not that free will does not exist, but that it would be inconsistent for theists to believe in it.

There are at least two ways for theists to try to deal with the Foreknowledge Objection. One of them introduces the idea of backward causation, and could be labeled the "Backward-causation Reply." We normally think that if there is a causal relation at all between events A and B, then the earlier event must be the cause of the later event. But God's relation to time is so peculiar, so this reply goes, that if the earlier event is that of God knowing something, or coming to know something, then it is possible for the later event to be the cause of the earlier one. Suppose, for example, that God knows on Monday that I will choose to eat an egg on Tuesday morning. According to the Backward-causation Reply, it was my (freely) choosing to eat the egg Tuesday morning that caused God to know on Monday (and still earlier) that I would do it. Therefore, since my choice was not determined or caused in any way by God's foreknowledge, it was a real choice: I *could* have chosen, instead, not to eat the egg Tuesday morning, in which case God would have been caused to know (in the past) that I would not eat the egg. It is my (free) choice that determines what God knows, rather than the other way around, even though the choice occurs at a later time than God's knowing. Thus, my choice was a real choice (and avoidable) even though God knew about it beforehand in the temporal order.

To me, the idea of backward causation is incoherent. It is neither conceivable nor intelligible. And it does not help to say that God "transcends time" or exists "outside time" or anything similar. As was pointed out in section 3.3, certain ways of speaking about God are in a certain sense meaningless, and that includes talk both of God being "outside time" and of God-related events being subject to backward causation. If a theist were to insist that either of those ways of speaking has to be part of the definition of "God," then I would say that rational discussion with such a person would be exceedingly difficult and atheological arguments such as AE and ANB might be out of place. It is reasonable to appeal to arguments only when they have intelligible conclusions, and for an atheological argument to have an intelligible conclusion, the concept of God which it uses must be coherent and intelligible.

A second way of dealing with the Foreknowledge Objection is simply to deny that God has foreknowledge of future free choices. It might be claimed that in virtue of the indeterminacy of free choices, the future is open, not closed, with respect to them, and so propositions about future free choices have no truth value. Either they come to have a truth value at the time to which they refer or else at that time they are superseded by present-tense (or past-tense) propositions about the given events which do have a truth value. It follows that it is impossible for propositions about future free choices to be known at all by anyone, even God. Although God is omniscient, that just means he knows everything there is to know. And he may indeed know everything about the future that is totally determined, but that excludes free choices in the incompatibilist's sense. Since propositions about future free choices are not anything to know, God's failure to know them does not detract in any way from his omniscience. However, it does detract from God's complete foreknowledge and would thereby refute the Foreknowledge Objection.

I have four misgivings about the idea that God does not know what people will choose to do in the future. The first is based on determinism, which I claim implies God's foreknowledge. If restricted near-determinism is true, and all human actions and choices of an everyday sort are completely determined by the past, then an omniscient being should be able to know about such events, ahead of time, just from his knowledge of the past and his knowledge of the relevant causal laws that connect the past to the future events. This would of course eliminate free will, at least with regard to ordinary human choices, simply by virtue of the Determinism Objection, but the point here is that it also implies God's (an omniscient being's) foreknowledge. However, I do not want to press this objection, even though I tend to agree with it, for it depends on the truth of restricted near-determinism, a view which I am not in this work claiming or assuming to be true.

My second misgiving has to do with the effects of the indeterminate events about which God is supposed to lack knowledge. Assuming, as the advocate of FDE does, that such events occur with great frequency, if God cannot know about them ahead of time, it appears that there is very little he could know about the future. Even if God could reason about causally determined events, the indeterminate events would throw up barriers to such reasoning. They would have greater and greater effects as time progresses, since their effects would have effects. But for God to know about any of those effects, he would need to know about the causes. And if the chain leads back to causes that are themselves unknown to God, then he could not know about any of the effects either. Thus, if God cannot know about humans' free-will choices ahead of time, then, even if, initially, there were relatively few such events, their effects would multiply rapidly through time so that in the long run there would be very little about the future that he could know at all. It would be like the physicist who could predict where every billiard ball will end up just from his knowledge of the present state of the billiard table. All that knowledge would be useless if some unforeseen disruptive force were introduced into the system (like someone sticking out his hand to stop one of the balls). If the physicist could not figure in the effects of that disruptive force, then all his predictions about the future state of the billiard table would be worthless, and probably false. Since God would be in such a situation regarding the planet earth, with people's free-will choices being like unforeseen disruptive forces, there would be, in the end, very little that God could know about the future. It would then sound very hollow indeed to declare God to be omniscient.

My third misgiving pertains to ESP. Some people are said to be gifted with precognition, the ability to glimpse the future directly. I don't believe in it myself, but a great many others do, including a great many theists. It seems to me at least logically possible that people have such an ability, even with regard to uncaused events if there should be any. In the context of such widespread beliefs and claims, it seems incongruous to deny such an ability to God. If humans can have it, then God should have it also, and to an even greater degree. However, these first three misgivings are minor ones.

My fourth and main misgiving pertains to the Bible. There are places in Scripture that suggest definite foreknowledge on God's part with regard to future free choices. David wrote, "Before a word is on my tongue, you know it completely, O Lord" (Ps. 139:4). And fulfilled prophecy is said to be the test of divinity (Deut. 18:22). Numerous prophecies are made, some of them of a very specific sort that involve free choices on the part of individuals. Here are a few examples:

1. When Jacob dies, his son Joseph will administer the last rites (Gen. 46:4).

2. When Moses goes to the Israelites, they will pay attention to him (Exod. 3:18).

3. Pharaoh will make trips to the water on certain specific days (Exod. 7:15, 8:20).

4. Josiah, a descendant of David, will be born and will perform certain actions (1 Kings 13:2).

5. Jereboam's wife, pretending to be someone else, will ask about her son (1 Kings 14:5).

6. Jehu will kill a certain group of people and Elisha will kill another group (1 Kings 19:17).

7. Four generations of descendants of Jehu will sit upon the throne of Israel (2 Kings 10:30).

8. Regarding Jehoiakim's corpse, people will neither mourn over it nor bury it (Jer. 22:18–19).

9. Hanamel will utter certain specific words (Jer. 32:7).

10. The sanctuary will be profaned for exactly 2,300 days (Dan. 8:13–14).

11. Amaziah's wife will become a prostitute and his children will fall by the sword (Amos 7:17).

12. A certain child to be born (John the Baptist) will be a lifelong teetotaler (Luke 1:15).

13. Certain disciples will not believe Jesus and a specific one of them will betray him (John 6:64).

14. The disciples will be scattered and leave Jesus all alone (John 16:32).

15. Before the rooster crows, Peter will deny Jesus exactly three times (Luke 22:34).

Certainly evangelical Christians, who affirm the existence of moral freedom, place great store on both biblical prophecy and biblical inerrancy, so they need to accept the view of God presented by such verses as the above. Just in regard to Christ's atonement for the sins of humankind through his crucifixion, in order for God to have known about that ahead of time, he needed to know that Judas would betray Jesus, that the Jerusalem mob would choose Barabbas (for release) instead of him, that Pontius Pilate would accede to their choice, that the Roman soldiers would be brutal in scourging Jesus, and so on. Thus, the claim that God lacks foreknowledge of future free choices is not available to evangelical Christians. The Bible is not totally consistent on this point, as there are verses which suggest a lack of foreknowledge on God's part,[1] but the verses which indicate foreknowledge far outnumber those. Because of that and because of the emphasis on fulfilled prophecy among evangelical Christians, they cannot deny that God has foreknowledge.

Thus, almost all evangelical Christians appeal to the Backward-causation Reply (or the "Atemporality Reply," which I would regard to be equivalent) in trying to deal with the Foreknowledge Objection. But, as maintained above, that reply is incoherent. As I see it, then, the Foreknowledge Objection is a most formidable one when applied to the claim that people have moral freedom as made from within a biblical framework such as that of evangelical Christianity, and thereby when applied to any appeal to FDE made from within such a framework.

B.3. The Predestination Objection

Although evangelical Christians try to refute the Foreknowledge Objection by appeal to the Backward-causation Reply, there is another God-related objection (to the existence of moral freedom) to which that reply is inapplicable. It can be called the "Predestination Objection." According to the Bible, God does not merely have foreknowledge of the future, but *predestines* it in the sense that he has a great plan for the world and actually manipulates events behind the scenes so as to guarantee that his plan is completely fulfilled. As declared in Acts 17:26, he determined exactly when nations would rise and fall and "the exact places where they should live." Here are some other examples of that in Scripture:

My [God's] purpose will stand and I will do all that I please . . .; what I have planned, that will I do. (Isa. 46:10–11)

The Lord works out everything for his own ends, even the wicked for a day of disaster. (Prov. 16:4)

In his heart a man plans his course, but the Lord determines his steps. (Prov. 16:9)

. . . it is the Lord's purpose that prevails. (Prov. 19:21, see also Prov. 20:24 and Jer. 10:23)

For those God foreknew, he also predestined . . . and those he predestined, he also called. (Rom. 8:29–30)

For he chose us in him before the creation of the world . . . he predestined us . . . in accordance with his pleasure and will. . . . We were . . . predestined according to the plan of him who works out everything in conformity with the purpose of his will. (Eph. 1:4–5,11)

The suggestion here is that God somehow pulls the strings backstage so that everything works out the way he wants. The whole story of the Bible is the story of an omnipotent deity who is seeing to it that things work out the way he has wanted them to from the beginning of time. It is hard to see how people can have free will if that is the way things are. The idea of backward causation is irrelevant in this context.

Some evangelical Christians, especially those with Calvinist leanings, accept the doctrine of predestination as described above. However, most of them resist it, making a brave effort to interpret the problematic verses in some way that avoids the idea that God predestines everything. It is unclear, though, just how God should be understood, given that he has fore-knowledge but does not meddle in human affairs the way he is said to do in the doctrine of predestination. Is God pleased with the way things are going? If not, then why did he create the world in the first place? Why didn't he destroy it as soon as he came to see how badly it was going to turn out? It is hard to understand why anyone would do anything that he knows ahead of time would displease him greatly. There are an infinite number of possible worlds that God could have created. Why should he create *this* particular one when there are no doubt many others that would please him a lot more?

The question might be raised whether God has middle knowledge, which is knowledge about how nonexistent possible worlds would turn out if they were to be created, assuming that those worlds contain beings who make free choices. There is some suggestion in Scripture that God does have such knowledge (Matt. 11:21–23), but the idea has also been attacked by philosophers.[2] The main objection to it is that there would be no fact of the matter for God to possibly know about. Although I do not wish to take a stand on the issue regarding God's middle knowledge, it does seem to me that the question might be raised whether God might acquire such knowledge using foreknowledge. Suppose he were to create a world. Could he then use his foreknowledge to see how that world would turn out if it were to continue, record the given information, and then destroy the world? The question is whether it would still be foreknowledge, seeing that it would here have a counterfactual character. Let us say that it would be a kind of foreknowledge since it would be knowledge about what is at the given time the *actual* world. Being a fast worker, God could perform such an operation for a very large number of possible worlds in a very small amount of time. At the end of the process, he could recreate (for good) that world which he had ascertained (by this special kind of foreknowledge) would please him the most.

Let us call the process described above "quasi-predestination." If it succeeds, it would lead to the same outcome (God having a world that pleases him) that would be arrived at through predestination. (Possibly it is a process a little like the one that Alvin Plantinga refers to as "weak actualization."[3] However, Plantinga's concept is different at least in that it is not as temporalized.) We could call the claim that God used quasi-predestination to produce a world that is maximally pleasing to himself the "Quasi-predestination Theory." If that theory were correct, then it might be said that God is "behind" everything that happens, by way either of predestination or of quasi-predestination. Assuming that he could use his foreknowledge to obtain a world maximally pleasing to himself, it would be irrational for him not to do so. But God is definitely rational, so if he has foreknowledge, then either predestination or quasi-predestination must have occurred.

Before considering an objection to the Quasi-predestination Theory, let us look at the ideas of predestination and quasi-predestination more closely. The first idea is that of God predestining everything, which FDEers would concede really is incompatible with free will on the part of humans. The other idea (quasi-predestination) has God merely permitting the world to continue, because he had originally created it in such a way that it was destined to contain humans and their free actions, which he, using his foreknowledge, had come to know about at the outset. Is there a big difference between these two ideas? If God is our creator, then everything that we do is *partly* caused by God. Just as the presence of oxygen is part of the cause of any combustion, so also God is part of the cause of anything that happens, for without his original act of creation there would be no world at all. Therefore, so-called contracausal free will cannot be totally contracausal. God, the creator, has to be part of the cause. And another part of the cause is God's pleasure (to use a term from Ephesians). If God did not receive pleasure from a person's action, then God would not have let the world continue, but would have replaced it by a different world.

Suppose, for example, that I freely choose to eat an egg on a certain morning. Using foreknowledge, God could have known immediately after creating our world that I was going to do that. If the foreseen act did not please him, then he could have very quickly destroyed the world and created a different one, in particular, one which did please him. So part of the cause of my eating the egg was God's creation of our world and another part of the cause was God's pleasure over my eating the egg (an act which he glimpsed by way of foreknowledge). My action loses some of its alleged contracausality just from that, for, in effect, no one can do otherwise than what he actually does unless the action is pleasing to God. Let us call the act that is actually performed "X" and some alternate act "Y." Presumably X is an act pleasing to God, since he let the world go on, knowing that X would occur. If Y is an act that would have displeased God, then at the time of creation, if Y had been "in the works" instead of X, God would have quickly destroyed that world and replaced it by one that he foresees to contain X. So, from that perspective, our alleged contracausal free will is restricted, since in a certain way we can never do anything that displeases God. Whatever difference there may be between this view of God's creative activity (quasi-predestination) and predestination itself, it seems that the difference is not as great as may at first appear. Thus, even if we assume that backward causation is possible and that it is involved in divine foreknowledge, if the Quasi-predestination Theory were correct, there would appear to be some problem in maintaining that humans have moral freedom or contracausal free will. An advocate of FDE, or anyone who maintains that people have free will in the incompatibilists' sense, may need to deny that God has complete foreknowledge, which most evangelical Christians are reluctant to do.

There is an objection that might be raised against the Quasi-predestination Theory. It claimed that God could sequentially create many different possible worlds, take a look at how each one would turn out (that being possible for God, using foreknowledge, with regard to any world that is at the given time the actual world), destroy each world after he took that look, and then at the end of the process *recreate* that world which he found would please him the most. But there is a problem here. When God uses foreknowledge to take the look at how the world will turn out, he is glimpsing the choices made by beings who possess (contracausal) free will. We are assuming here that it is those choices that provide God with his foreknowledge, by some sort of process of backward causation. So when God goes to recreate the given world, there is no way that he can guarantee that all (or any) of those choices would go the same way as before. If the first time the present world had been actual I chose to eat an egg on a given morning, there is no guarantee that I would choose exactly the same way if God were to recreate the world. He can only determine the nature of the world exclusive of the free choices that occur in it. The free choices are up to the beings who make those choices, not God. It follows that the Quasi-predestination Theory is false: God cannot use quasi-predestination to produce a world that is maximally pleasing to himself. Therefore, the alleged restriction on our free will (that we cannot do anything displeasing to God) does not exist. So we *can* indeed be morally free after all.

I think that there is no way to refute this objection to the Quasi-predestination Theory so long as we follow incompatibilism (taking free will to be contracausal) and so long as we assume that God cannot have knowledge of the free-will choices of merely possible beings (as opposed to foreknowledge of the choices of actual beings). I challenged incompatibilism in appendix A. As for the second assumption, God having "middle knowledge," I have no definite view about that, so I shall not attempt to refute it. I thus concede that within an incompatibilist framework the attack on moral freedom based on the Quasi-predestination Theory is a failure.

There is one point that might be made here, though. Even if God could not guarantee for himself a world of free beings that would please him the most, it seems reasonable to think that he could have done better than our present world. We can imagine God creating worlds, taking a look (via fore-knowledge) at how they would turn out, and then eventually making permanent one that he finds minimally acceptable. For example, suppose he had started such a process with a very high standard, say, 99.9 percent of free actions being good and only 0.1 percent being bad. But after, say, a googolplex number of tries, none of the worlds created met the standard, and each one was destroyed. Perhaps God would then reduce the standard slightly to, say, 99.8 percent of free actions being good and 0.2 percent being bad. He could then proceed to create another googolplex number of worlds to see if any of them meet the new reduced standard. By such a procedure, even if God could not guarantee a world that is maximally pleasing to himself, he should have been able to come up with (and make permanent) a world that is, from a moral point of view, far superior to our present world.

Although the attack on moral freedom based on the Quasi-predestination Theory proved unsuccessful, my overall conclusion regarding that type of free will is rather negative. It conflicts with the restricted form of determinism (mentioned in section B.1), which many of us would claim is supported by science. And (as shown in section B.2), assuming that backward causation is impossible, it also conflicts with the doctrine of God's complete foreknowledge, which is a doctrine supported by Scripture and accepted by all evangelical Christians. In addition, it conflicts with the doctrine of predestination, which is also supported by Scripture (though not as well as the doctrine of foreknowledge). I conclude, then, that the proposition that people have moral freedom, even if it only functions as a kind of background assumption for FDE, faces some formidable challenges. This is another grave problem for FDE in addition to the ones already presented in chapter 4 and appendix A, above. It has been shown, I think, that instead of being among the stronger defenses of God's existence against the Argument from Evil, the Free-will Defense is actually among the weakest.

Notes

1. Gen. 6:6, 22:1,12; Deut. 8:2, 13:3; Jer. 3:7.

2. See, for example, Robert Merrihew Adams, "Middle Knowledge and the Problem of Evil," *American Philosophical Quarterly* 14 (1977): 109–17, reprinted in Adams and Adams, eds., *The Problem of Evil*, pp. 110–25. See also William Hasker, "A Refutation of Middle Knowledge," *Nous* 20 (1986): 545–57; and chapters 2 and 10 of Hasker's book *God, Time, and Knowledge* (Ithaca, N.Y.: Cornell University Press, 1989). There have, of course, been defenses of divine middle knowledge against these objections. It is an ongoing debate.

3. Alvin Plantinga, *The Nature of Necessity* (Oxford: Clarendon Press, 1974), chapter 9, reprinted in Adams and Adams, eds., *The Problem of Evil*. See, in particular, pp. 90–91 of the latter work.

Appendix C

Nonbelief and the Will

C.1. Voluntarism vs. Involuntarism

In chapter 5, not only was FDN's premise (P1) attacked, but an attempt was made to show the irrelevance to ANB of all considerations pertaining to free will. The premise in question, it may be recalled, reads as follows:

(P1) For God to have caused people to believe the gospel message would necessarily have interfered with their free will.

It was argued that (P1) is just plain false. God could certainly show people things or help missionaries to show them things that would cause them to believe the gospel message and that need not at all interfere with their free will. Thus, the whole matter of free will is irrelevant to the problem of ANB and people's nonbelief in the gospel message. In addition to the arguments of chapter 5, there is another approach by which one might try to derive the same result. One might argue that free will relates only to actions whereas ANB pertains only to the acquisition of beliefs; but the acquisition of a belief is not an action; therefore, free will is irrelevant to ANB. It also follows that (P1), above, is false, which makes FDN unsound. The critical step here is the proposition that the acquisition of a belief is not an action. To assess this step, we need to inquire how beliefs are formed and to what extent a person's will is involved in that process. Some philosophers and theologians have claimed that belief is directly subject to the will while others have denied it. These positions may be termed "doxastic voluntarism" and "doxastic involuntarism." To save space, I shall shorten the labels to simply "voluntarism" and "involuntarism."

329

Voluntarism has some linguistic support. In ordinary language, people often say such things as "he chose (or refused) to believe it" and "I find it hard (or easy) to believe." It is a common saying that "people believe whatever they want to believe." These expressions suggest the idea that belief (or the acquisition of belief) is an action and hence a matter of choice and directly subject to the will. That implies that people at least sometimes self-induce their beliefs independently of evidence. Voluntarists claim that people (at least sometimes) choose or self-induce their beliefs by direct acts of will on the basis of how appealing the beliefs are.

In contrast, involuntarists maintain that belief is always involuntary in the way that seeing is involuntary. People have control over whether or not to open their eyes and take a look. But once they do take the look, they cannot control what they see. In an analogous way, people have control over the direction they take with regard to the acquisition of evidence. But once the evidence has been acquired and understood, people do not then have any further control over what they come to believe. Rather, that is totally determined by the evidence itself. One cannot believe contrary to the evidence, or in the total absence of evidence, any more than one can see something that is contrary to what is presented to one's eyes, or in the total absence of light. As for the alleged linguistic support for voluntarism, involuntarists would say that it is insufficient. When people say such things as "he chose to believe it" or "he refused to believe it," that may be just an elliptical or metaphorical way of saying "he came to believe it" or "he came not to believe it" (or "he came to deny it"). And when they say "that is easy (or hard) to believe," they may simply mean "the evidence supports (or is contrary to) that." Alternatively, such statements may be just flat-out false, as is the generalization "people believe whatever they want to believe." Certainly they are false if taken literally, according to involuntarists.

Some involuntarists have gone so far as to claim that it is logically impossible for people to control their beliefs. They have argued as follows. Suppose X were to self-induce belief B by a direct act of will. Then X would know that B was formed in that way. But beliefs formed in that way need not correspond with reality. (If they do correspond, it would be sheer coincidence.) Thus, X would know that B may not correspond with reality and there is no good reason for thinking that it actually does so. But that is the same as knowing both that B may not be true and that there is no good reason for regarding it to be true. Anyone who knows that a proposition may not be true and that there is no good reason to regard it to be true must be at most epistemically neutral regarding the proposition: such a person cannot believe it to be true. Hence, the initial supposition that B is a belief which X has successfully self-induced must be false, and it follows that people cannot possibly form beliefs by a direct act of will. Richard Swinburne puts the point as follows:

> If I choose at will to believe that I now see a table, then I would realize that this belief originated from my will and so had no connection with whether or not there was a table there, and so I would know that I had no reason for trusting my belief, and so I would not really believe.[1]

I find the given argument unconvincing because it assumes that everyone knows the truth of the various steps in it, which is not so. For example, the argument assumes that everyone knows that self-induced beliefs need not correspond with reality, but on the contrary, maybe not everyone knows that. Some people may think that in the process of self-inducing a belief they somehow make the given proposition true. I would certainly agree that that is a wildly irrational notion, yet there may be people out there who think that way, though they may not have said so. Extreme epistemological relativists, who go around saying things like "we carry around our own separate realities within our minds," might be inclined to think along those lines. Furthermore, perhaps in the very process of self-inducing a belief by an act of will, one could erase from one's mind the realization that the process by which the belief was acquired was that of self-inducement. That, too, would prevent the involuntarist's conclusion from being derived. It follows that the given attempt to show that direct voluntary control over belief is impossible is a failure. It may always be irrational for people to exercise such control, but such control is possible, and in fact, from my observation of other people and discussions with them, it does seem to me to actually happen on occasion. Furthermore, the claim that it happens is often made and widely accepted within the general population.

Thus, I accept voluntarism. Although I find myself totally unable to control my beliefs by direct acts of will, I think that there are people who can actually do such a thing. In a similar way, some people may be able to blush at will, though there would be very few like that, if any. And some people no doubt have more control over their emotions than others, for example, make themselves angry or afraid or make themselves love their neighbors (as the Bible commands). Perhaps it is possible to train oneself to gain such control over one's own states, somewhat like the way that yogis have managed to gain control over such bodily factors as pulse rate and blood pressure. Maybe biofeedback equipment could be used for such training. All of these things are at least logically possible. I would say they are psychologically possible as well, and actually happen, though only rarely. I put the willful self-inducement of belief into the same category.

I think a good case could be made for saying that the Bible presupposes voluntarism, and that therefore evangelical Christianity must accept it and advocate it. In Rom. 1:18, St. Paul refers to "men who suppress the truth by their wickedness" and in Eph. 4:18 he mentions "the ignorance that is in them due to the hardening of their hearts." Both of those passages imply that people have direct control over their beliefs. In addition, according to 1 John 3:23, God has commanded people "to believe in the name of his son Jesus Christ." Certainly that presupposes that belief is directly subject to the will, for it makes no sense to command people to do something that is not under their direct control. Also, in many passages it is implied that to disbelieve and to disobey are equivalent (e.g., Heb. 3:18–19) or that all nonbelievers are automatically sinners (Heb. 3:12; Rev. 21:8), which is a common biblical theme, and which again seems to presuppose voluntarism.

There is also reason to take the story of Adam and Eve as presupposing voluntarism. According to the story, God told them one thing and the serpent contradicted it. Then Eve came to believe what the serpent said (that for them to eat the fruit would not be fatal but would instead make them wise like God). However, the serpent presented no evidence, so why did Eve believe what the serpent said? I take the Christian interpretation to be that she willfully chose to believe it, and therein lay her sin. It seems that in order for God's punishment of Eve to be just, considering that she was presented with conflicting messages regarding the fruit, it is necessary that her coming to believe the serpent's message was an act of will on her part. But that presupposes voluntarism. So, on the assumption that it was just for God to punish Eve, voluntarism must be true.

Furthermore, the whole biblical doctrine of "salvation by faith" seems to presuppose that belief is directly subject to the will. In the Great Commission, when a missionary has preached the gospel message to people, "whoever believes and is baptized will be saved, but whoever does not believe will be condemned" (Mark 16:16). That implies that it is a matter of choice whether or not to believe. For God to justly condemn people for their nonbelief requires that they be culpable either for the nonbelief itself or for whatever actions or omissions of theirs led to the nonbelief, and that, in turn, it might be argued, requires that belief and nonbelief be directly subject to the will. Billy Graham, the great evangelist, has often said in his sermons and newspaper columns: "There is only one thing that will send you into eternity separated from God, and that is your refusal to accept God's truth." His monthly publication is entitled *Decision*, and he has spoken repeatedly of a "decision for Christ," which is taken to be a decision to do certain things, including believing the gospel message. Such claims, which are based on the Bible, seem clearly to presuppose voluntarism.

We could, in the abstract, divide people into two groups, those who are able to directly control their own beliefs by means of their wills and those who are not. It would be an open question whether or not the first group is empty. Assuming it is not empty, people within it could be arranged in a spectrum according to how easy it is for them to directly control their own beliefs and how often they do it. Perhaps there are people who do it easily and frequently and others who are totally unable to do it at all, with still others falling between these two extremes. The extreme positions on the spectrum could be called the "voluntaristic end" and the "involuntaristic end." It would then be an empirical question whether there are people at the voluntaristic end, and if so, how many. My own encounters with students and others have led me to the hypothesis that there do indeed exist people who are able to directly control their beliefs and that they are arranged all along the described spectrum. I would say, then, that some people are more or less able to control their own beliefs by direct acts of will, while others, myself included, totally lack that ability. Just what the various numbers might be, I cannot say for sure. However, I would venture the guess that at least 10 percent of people can directly control their beliefs, at least on some occasions and to a slight extent.

It might be maintained that belief is subject to the will but not immediately, only over an extended period of time. H. H. Price held such a view:

> Can one make oneself believe something, or make oneself go on believing it, just by an effort of will? . . . It seems to me pretty clear that one cannot do it directly, by just making a voluntary effort here and now. . . . Indirectly, though not directly, and over a period of time, though not instantaneously, one *can* voluntarily control one's beliefs—at least up to a point. . . . Pascal recommends somewhere that if a man's religious faith is weak, he should "Use holy water and order masses be said."
>
> By such methods—by dwelling upon a proposition continually and repeatedly, by considering again and again what it would be like if it were true and imagining in detail what it would be like (if you can), by acting as if the proposition were true on all occasions to which its truth or falsity is relevant, and by increasing the number of these occasions wherever possible—by such means you will gradually get into a state of believing the proposition. You will wake up one fine day and find that you do believe it. . . . Of course the state you have got into is one of nonreasonable belief, just because it is independent of the evidence. . . . But the point at present is that it *is* a state of belief, and of very firm belief too; and that it is brought into existence by your own voluntary efforts. . . . Everyone admits, of course, that such a state can be produced in us *in*voluntarily, by what is called "Social Conditioning" (the process which Hume in the *Treatise* calls "education"). But it was worthwhile to point out that it can be produced voluntarily too, though only with considerable effort and trouble, continued over a long period of time.[2]

I would call this view also a form of voluntarism, though it is not as robust a form as that which proclaims it possible to control one's beliefs not only over an extended time but also immediately.

Voluntarism can be thought of as a series of views ranging from strong to weak, where the strong form maintains two theses. The first thesis is that direct and immediate self-inducement of belief is very common, and so

should be considered (statistically) "normal." It is the way beliefs are usually formed. The basic principle of strong voluntarism is: "People usually
believe whatever they want to believe." If evidence plays any role at all, it
is merely an advisory one, influencing the will but not in any way determining it. The second thesis is that direct self-inducement of belief is psychologically normal, or healthy, and in no way pathological. At the other
end of the spectrum is weak voluntarism, which grants only that some
people sometimes form beliefs through direct acts of the will, but it is very
rare and not "normal" in any sense. Perhaps it can be done at all only over
an extended period of time, as Price maintains. Evidence still dominates
the belief-formation process in almost all cases. Price would be classified
as a weak voluntarist, and I would put myself in that category as well. However, I would differ with Price on the issue whether people ever self-induce
beliefs by immediate acts of will. He denies that it ever happens, but I think
it does, on occasion. Price and I would both be weak rather than strong voluntarists because we would both regard belief acquisition through self-
inducement to be rare and abnormal. The usual way by which people form
beliefs is through an assessment of the evidence presented to them, that
assessment being an automatic process which does not involve the will.

I have three main objections to strong voluntarism. One is simply an
appeal to observation. I have talked to many people about the matter and at
least 90 percent of them claim not to have much, if any, control over their
beliefs. The majority are like me, claiming to have no such control whatever. I assume that if they did indeed have control then they themselves
would be aware of it. Since so many people deny ever (or often) self-
inducing belief by a direct act of will, I conclude that the strong voluntarist's claim that it is very common and is the usual mode of belief acquisition is, as a matter of empirical fact, simply false.

My second objection is that if self-inducement of belief by a direct act
of will should ever occur, it would be an *irrational* mode of belief acquisition. It would be symptomatic of insanity, at least to a slight degree. Thus,
the strong voluntarist's claim that direct self-inducement of belief would be
psychologically healthy is erroneous. More will be said in support of this
point in section C.3.

My third objection proceeds out of the second one. Suppose I am right
about the irrationality and insanity of direct self-inducement of belief.
Probably, if most people were irrational or insane, then society could not
function adequately. And since society does (thus far) function adequately,
it is highly likely that most people are not irrational or insane. Hence, the
strong voluntarist's claim that self-inducement of belief by a direct act of
will is the usual mode of belief acquisition is probably false. My first and
third objections attack the statistical normality of direct self-inducement of
belief, and my second objection attacks its psychological normality.

My own view on the topic is, again, that of weak voluntarism. I grant that some people sometimes self-induce beliefs by direct acts of will. However, I deny strong voluntarism's claim that such occurrences are common and its claim that they are usually rational. On the contrary, such cases seem to me to be almost always abnormal both in the sense of being uncommon and in the sense of being psychologically unhealthy or pathological. Strong voluntarism is incorrect, and for that reason all views and arguments which presuppose strong voluntarism are also incorrect. It is simply not the case that all (or most) people believe whatever they want to believe and that to do so is rational.

The question may be raised which views and which arguments presuppose strong voluntarism. I would say that the Bible presupposes it, for (as indicated above) the Bible commands people to believe in God's son and equates disbelief with disobedience. That assumes that people *commonly* have direct control over their beliefs, which is strong voluntarism. Thus, evangelical Christianity, which accepts the Bible as inerrant, must also presuppose strong voluntarism. A closely related point is that strong voluntarism is assumed by the Great-Commission Reply (discussed in section 5.5), according to which God wants missionaries to proclaim the gospel message to all nations and "whoever does not believe will be condemned." Certainly Christian exclusivism must assume that strong voluntarism is true. Otherwise, God's condemnation of nonbelievers would be unjust. Hence, since strong voluntarism is an incorrect theory, all of those views (the Bible, evangelical Christianity, the Great-Commission Reply, and Christian exclusivism) must be false as well.

As for *arguments* that presuppose strong voluntarism, the most obvious one is TDN (the Testing Defense applied to ANB), at least the version of it that was discussed in chapter 7. It proclaims that God is testing people to locate those who willfully reject the gospel message. Since the argument takes the group in question to include all non-Christians (a group comprising two-thirds of the earth's population), it must assume that a great many people have direct control over their beliefs, which is strong voluntarism. Thus, in addition to the objections raised against TDN in section 7.2, we can add this "Strong-voluntarism Objection." Another argument that might be thought to presuppose strong voluntarism is FDN. However, I do not take it as making that assumption. This issue will be discussed in section C.4.

C.2. Indirect Belief Formation

Even if the will were never to play any direct role in the process of belief formation, even over an extended period of time, it might play an *indirect* role. I am here using the term "indirect" somewhat differently from Price, for he apparently regarded any instance of belief formation over an extended time to be indirect, whereas I do not. I would still call it "direct," even if it occurs over an extended time, provided that it is just a single individual trying to come to believe something on his own solely through a use of the will. Price's terminology has the drawback of having to draw a temporal distinction between direct and indirect. That is, on his view, how many seconds or minutes must one spend on the self-inducement of a belief before it becomes an "indirect" self-inducement? My terminology avoids such a puzzle because I would call it direct no matter how long it takes, so long as just one individual is involved. However, I do think it possible for the will to play an indirect role in belief formation, and that might come about in two different ways. These ways are captured by what I shall call the "outside-aid model" and the "investigation model."

The outside-aid model applies when someone who does not have a particular belief wants to have it for some reason other than knowing the truth, but is unable to self-induce the belief directly, i.e., on his own, even over an extended period of time. The person may then undertake a program of voluntary "brainwashing" by others in an attempt to acquire the given belief. For example, suppose that a man wants to give up smoking. He knows that if he were to believe that his next cigarette would kill him instantly, then that would certainly cause him to give up smoking. So, the man may then hire a hypnotist to instill in his mind the false belief that his next cigarette would kill him instantly. If he is successful, then through the use of an outside aid, namely, the hypnotist, the person will have indirectly self-induced a particular belief.

Another example is where a man desires a certain set of religious beliefs, say, because he thinks they will bring him happiness and peace of mind. Although he is unable to self-induce the given beliefs directly, i.e., on his own, even over an extended period of time, he may join a religious cult that he knows will make great efforts to instill in him the given beliefs. Over a period of time, after frequently performing the cult's rituals and proclaiming the given beliefs in the presence of other members, with their encouragement, such a person may actually come to acquire the beliefs. Again, through the use of an outside aid, he would have indirectly self-induced one or more desired beliefs. This is the "Pascal-type" example that Price mentions. It is important to note here, though, that the motivation for acquiring beliefs in accord with the outside-aid model is something other than knowing the truth.

The investigation model applies whenever we make choices regarding which propositions to consider and to try to verify or falsify, and how strenuously such attempts are to be pursued. Such choices indirectly affect what beliefs we end up with. Even the simple act of choosing to open or close one's eyes affects one's subsequent beliefs. So it is clear that even if the will is not used directly to form beliefs, it is involved in the belief-formation process in an indirect way. Suppose, for example, that because of time constraints I have to choose between reading one book or another book, and cannot read both. I am aware that both books contain good evidence or persuasive arguments. So if I pick one book to read, then I would acquire a certain set of new beliefs. But if I pick the other book, then I would acquire a different (though not conflicting) set of new beliefs. By an act of will, I choose which book to read, and I thereby indirectly bring about my own future beliefs. So, in effect, I have indirectly caused beliefs in myself through an act of will.

In addition to choosing the book, my will could be involved as I acquire beliefs during the reading. For example, I may choose to pay very close attention to the reading by eliminating distractions, taking caffeine for alertness, reading slowly, and concentrating on it very hard. I could willfully use such techniques as underlining important passages or writing notes as I go along. I could think hard (perhaps even using symbolic logic) to try to work out the logical entailments of what is written and I could willfully dwell upon the connections between those entailments and my own prior beliefs. There are many choices to be made in such a process and they do have an effect on what beliefs I end up with. Thus, in an indirect way, my acts of will are part of the process by which I acquire beliefs.

In the outside-aid model, evidence plays no significant role, but the investigation model has the will working together with evidence to form beliefs. Also, unlike the outside-aid model, the investigation model always has coming to know the truth as at least part of one's motivation for acquiring beliefs. However, one might have additional reasons for trying to acquire one set of true beliefs rather than another in a situation where it is not possible to acquire both sets (e.g., deciding which book to read). The additional reasons usually appeal to one's prior beliefs regarding which set of beliefs will be more useful or valuable in terms of one's overall goals. And those prior beliefs may have been acquired in normal ways, on the basis of evidence, and not in a way that conforms to the investigation model. Ultimately, the chain of beliefs began with evidence and is based upon that.

It is clear, I think, that people do often indirectly control their own beliefs in the way indicated by the investigation model. The indirect control of beliefs by the method indicated by the outside-aid model is much less common, but still possible. More will be said about it later. This position regarding beliefs (that they could be brought about indirectly by acts of will) is compatible with involuntarism. The voluntarism-involuntarism issue only concerns direct acts of will, whether performed over a short span of time or a long one.

There are a number of questions that arise in connection with the two methods described. One of them is the extent to which they are practiced. As mentioned above, I think that the indirect control of beliefs in accord with the investigation model is quite common. Every day we make decisions about what to read (or hear on the radio or view on TV), where to go, what to do, and how hard to concentrate on any incoming data, and those decisions affect what beliefs we come to acquire. But the other form of indirect control, in accord with the outside-aid model, seems to me to be considerably less common. I would judge that it is even less common than the direct control of belief (whether performed immediately or over an extended period of time). Of all instances of belief formation that occur daily, I would estimate that fewer than 1 percent are either indirect self-inducements in accord with the outside-aid model or direct self-inducements by the will. More than 99 percent are induced by evidence, not by the will, except perhaps indirectly (with the will working together with the evidence) in accord with the investigation model. (Although at least 10 percent of people are able to directly control their beliefs and do so at least occasionally, most of them employ that ability only very rarely.)

Another question is whether either of the indirect forms of belief control mentioned above is sufficient for assigning culpability with regard to nonbelief. For example, suppose person X lacks a certain belief in proposition P but could have acquired it by one of the methods described (outside aid or investigation). We are supposing that X made some choices in the past which eventually led to X's nonbelief in P, where, if X had chosen differently, then a belief in P would have been acquired. Does it follow from that alone that X is culpable either for the nonbelief itself or for the past actions or omissions which led to that nonbelief? We will consider that question and related issues in section C.5.

C.3. The Rationality Issue

People can be divided into the following three groups:

Type A: those who have direct control over their beliefs and sometimes self-induce belief or nonbelief by a direct act of will, either immediately or over an extended period of time.

Type B: those who have no direct control over their own beliefs, but who sometimes indirectly affect their beliefs by an act of will in accord with the outside-aid model.

Type C: those who are not of type A or B but who at least sometimes indirectly affect their own beliefs by an act of will in accord with the investigation model.

It is an empirical question how many people fall into each group. My own view is that each group has members, but type-C people are in the vast majority. I would be very surprised if the total class of type-A people and type-B people combined should turn out to comprise more than 20 percent of the population.

I want to propose that there is a kind of irrationality inherent in groups A and B, i.e., in either directly controlling one's own beliefs or indirectly bringing them about in accord with the outside-aid model. In that regard, I agree with Price's comment about the matter in the quotation above. ("The state you have got into is one of nonreasonable belief.") I would say that beliefs are like "a road map through the pathways of life," where the more closely the map matches the actual roads, the better. To interject one's will into the process of belief formation, where the goal is anything other than coming to know the truth, would go counter to that function of belief, for it would be interjecting something additional to experience, thereby preventing the belief from representing reality exactly as experienced. It would be like capriciously inserting new lines on a road map. Obviously a map will be less useful if it contains lines that do not correspond to actual roads. It seems more reasonable to relegate the will to its proper role, the performance of actions, and keep it as far away as possible from the process of belief formation. I think there do exist type-A and type-B people, but they are to some extent irrational and tend to "lose touch with reality." Normal people (i.e., type-C people), who are motivated in the belief-formation process solely by the desire to acquire useful knowledge, do not do that.

An objection might be raised here. People have various goals other than coming to know the truth. Why couldn't one of those goals be adequate rational justification for self-inducing belief? For example, if I want to give up smoking and I know that my coming to believe a certain probably false proposition would cause me to do so, then why would it not be rational for me to self-induce belief in that proposition, either directly (if I could accomplish that) or indirectly, say, with the aid of a hypnotist? It may not be rational in an epistemological sense, but why not say that it is rational in a prudential or practical sense? Another example is that of optimism, which may be defined as belief that good things will happen in the future, where the belief goes beyond the available evidence and so would need to be somehow self-induced by an act of will. Health professionals have pointed out that optimists are healthier people and live longer. Wouldn't that make it rational in a prudential sense to become an optimist, assuming it is in one's power to do so?

I am willing to concede the prudential rationality of self-inducement of belief in special cases. However, I also want to maintain the epistemic irrationality of it. Belief that does not fit the available evidence is always epistemically irrational, by definition. Furthermore, the alleged prudential rationality of self-induced belief must be examined with care. After all, it is a form of self-deception. I suspect that despite the alleged health-related evidence in favor of optimism, there may be drawbacks to it which have not been fully explored. And the same would apply to the hypnosis example. One obvious drawback would be the risk of shock should it be discovered that one's belief is false. ("What a bummer!") Of course, anyone who believes anything at all risks such shock, but those who willfully believe beyond what is warranted by the evidence run the greater risk. Another drawback would be that of falling into bad epistemic habits. Even if a particular case of self-inducement of belief were to have some practical benefits, such action might set a precedent and incline a person toward further willful self-inducement of belief that would have negative effects later on. For example, a person who initially had misgivings about willfully self-inducing a belief would tend to lose those misgivings the more often such actions were performed. Overall, beliefs not based on the available evidence tend to distort one's view of reality, which in turn would probably have harmful practical effects down the road. People who are "out of touch with reality" do not normally lead happy lives.

Another point that needs to be made here is that in some cases a person's beliefs are caused, not solely by an act of will but by a combination of will and evidence. The evidence might warrant belief of a certain degree, D1, but the person's will is used to induce belief to some other degree, D2, where D2 is greater (or less) than D1. I would say that such belief is epistemically irrational to the extent that its degree, D2, deviates from D1 (the degree of belief warranted by the evidence), which may be only a very slight amount. Of course, the act of self-inducing the belief to degree D2 might be prudentially rational, given certain special circumstances surrounding it, as discussed above, and in that way the person in question might be said to be prudentially rational in performing such an act. But I am somewhat doubtful about such cases for the reasons stated (the risks of shock and of falling into bad epistemic habits). For that reason, I would be reluctant to praise people for their alleged prudential rationality if what they did was willfully to self-induce belief to a degree unwarranted by the evidence. I would always be more inclined to view such people as being psychologically abnormal.

So if voluntarism were taken to imply that it is normal or rational, and even sometimes recommended, for people to directly self-induce belief, then I would not count myself as a voluntarist, even a weak one. But if all that the view implies is that some people sometimes directly self-induce belief (which is how I take it), then I do go along with the view, but only the weak form of it, as explained above.

C.4. The Interference Issue

In the debate over FDN, the question arises how causing beliefs in others might interfere with their free will, and whether it makes a difference whether or not the people in whom the beliefs are caused are of type A. The argument that I wish to consider in this section goes as follows. If God were to show things to people who are of type A, then possibly he might interfere with their free will, for the wills of type-A people are involved in belief formation. They go around choosing their beliefs, but here is God causing beliefs in them, thus possibly disrupting their belief-formation process and thereby interfering with their free will. However, if God were instead to cause beliefs only in people who are not of type A, i.e., in normal people, then he could not be interfering with their free will for the simple reason that the wills of such people are not directly involved in belief formation. Wills that are not directly involved cannot be interfered with: a rather simple idea. But almost all of the billions of non-Christians in the world *are* normal people, i.e., not of type A. Hence, FDN is a great failure with regard to *them*. God could certainly show things to such people without interfering with their free will. Thus, there is no conflict between God bringing about situation S (which only requires that *almost all* people believe the gospel message) and people having maximal free will. Let us call this attack on FDN the "Normality Objection." The idea of it is that, since almost all non-Christians are *normal* people, who do not go around self-inducing beliefs by direct acts of will, God could bring about situation S by selectively causing beliefs only in them, without thereby interfering with anyone's free will. That would refute the first half of FDN.

One response that might be made to the Normality Objection is that people's free will can be interfered with by causing beliefs in them even if they are not of type A and do not directly use their wills to form beliefs. Our free will is an expression of our desires plus beliefs. Whenever I choose to perform act A1 rather than act A2, it is because I desire result R1 more than result R2 and I believe that A1 would lead to R1 while A2 would lead to R2. I do act A1 of my own free will provided that my desires and beliefs are not deliberately modified by external forces. But if someone were to do something to cause me to give up my belief that A1 would lead to R1, then that would probably cause me not to choose to perform act A1. Hence, even if people are normal in that they do not directly use their wills to form beliefs, their freedom of will is closely connected with their beliefs. So, any external force that causes their beliefs to be altered would necessarily interfere with their free will.

The main objection to this response is that it confuses having free will with performing given actions. It is true that to alter people's beliefs may cause them to perform different actions. But that does not entail any interference with their free will. People would certainly object to having their free will interfered with, but they usually have no objection to having their beliefs altered, even where that leads to a change in their behavior, so long as true beliefs are being put in place of false beliefs. There are exceptions to that. In some circumstances, people say, "Don't tell me; I don't want to know." But those circumstances are almost always ones in which the undesired knowledge is of little importance or would carry with it some sort of undesired responsibilities. For example, if you are my friend and want to tell me of some misdeed that you have committed, I might say, "I don't want to know," because I do not want to be caused to dislike you or be placed in a position in which I have an obligation to harm you because of your misdeed. Such exceptions are few and far between. Almost always, people would welcome having their erroneous beliefs corrected. Almost always, then, they would not regard such correction to be in any way an interference with their free will.

What we need to address at this point is whether the specific case in question (the one related to ANB) is one of the exceptions. The specific case is that of God causing non-Christians to become Christians by some means or other. Let us say that it is by skywriting passages from the New Testament in a spectacular fashion. The non-Christians would read the messages in the sky, realize that their religious beliefs are erroneous, and come to believe in Christianity. Is that a situation in which the given people did not want to know the truth, so the truth would in effect be foisted upon them? If so, then perhaps such an action on God's part would interfere with the people's free will. But if the people were to welcome having their beliefs corrected, then it would not interfere with their free will. So, which is it? Would non-Christians resent having their beliefs corrected or would they welcome it? It seems clear to me that if they were to view it in retrospect they would welcome it. We need only examine cases where people convert from one religion or belief system to another. Such people hardly ever come to resent the conversion. They say things like, "It was the best thing that ever happened to me." If some particular person was instrumental in bringing about the conversion, then that person would be praised and sometimes even revered. No one would say of him, "He interfered with my free will." Thus, I reject the given response which draws the conclusion that altering people's beliefs interferes with their free will simply from the fact that altering people's beliefs affects their actions.

It may be that some people would resent having their basic outlook on reality altered. They may prefer retaining their old beliefs even if those beliefs should be false. We might say of them that they prefer to "stick with their illusions." Perhaps for God to show things to such people and thereby get them to change their basic outlook on reality would indeed interfere with their free will. But how many people are there like that? In my opinion, not many. But of course this is an empirical matter. Let us divide people into two groups: those who want to "stick with their illusions," which we can call the "illusion" people, and those who want to know what reality is like even if it should call for a radical change in their outlook, which we can call the "reality" people. This division would cut right across our earlier categories of types A, B, and C. In my opinion, "reality" people are in the vast majority, and are "normal," whereas "illusion" people are (like type-A people) in an "abnormal" minority.

According to the Normality Objection, if God were to show things to normal non-Christians then he would not be interfering with their free will, for they would be people who base belief on evidence, not on acts of will. The argument could be altered slightly to refer just to those non-Christians who are not of type A and who are also "reality" people. For God to show things to them would not interfere with their free will. Such people are normal and yearn to find out the truth about reality. I think that the revised version of the Normality Objection is still acceptable. It maintains that in order for God to interfere with a target person's free will simply by altering that person's beliefs, it is necessary that the target person be of type A or else be an "illusion" person (as described above). But there are very few such people, if any. Thus, causing beliefs in people would not usually by itself interfere with their free will. And in the particular case of God causing non-Christians to become Christians, say, by showing them things, that would not in any way interfere with their free will so long as they are of the right type. And almost all non-Christians, in my view at least, are of the right type (i.e., "reality" people who are not of type A). Thus, FDN's premise (P1) is false and the whole first half of FDN, leading to step (C2), is unsound.

One reply that FDNers might make to the Normality Objection is that I have my facts wrong and just about everyone really is either a type-A person or an "illusion" person. The objection concedes that for God to cause beliefs in such people would indeed interfere with their free will. Thus, since just about all non-Christians are in that category, God could not bring about situation S, after all, without interfering with people's free will, which he wants to avoid. This shows the Normality Objection to be a great failure. Let us call this the "Self-deception Reply." I have two quite different rejoinders to it.

The first is that the Self-deception Reply is simply false. The empirical data are as I claim, not as it claims. In fact, the reply may even involve an appeal to strong voluntarism, which I reject for reasons given previously. If it includes the idea that type-A people are very common, then it would be open to that criticism. As initially formulated, FDN does not presuppose strong voluntarism, for the hypothetical interference with free will that it appeals to is not usually viewed as a kind of conflict between God's actions and people's "will to believe what they want." Of course, if that is indeed how FDNers view the situation, then the Strong-voluntarism Objection would apply. It is simply an empirical fact about people that very few of them, if any, have a "will to believe what they want," as argued above in section C.1. Thus, if FDN presupposes strong voluntarism, then it is false for that reason alone.

On the other hand, the Self-deception Reply may not be emphasizing the type-A people, but rather the "illusion" people. In that case it need not be presupposing strong voluntarism, for "illusion" people need not be of type A: they need not ever willfully self-induce beliefs. However, if the reply is mainly appealing to the idea that "illusion" people are very common, then it could still be attacked on the grounds that what it says is just not so. People generally want to know how things are in reality rather than sticking with their illusions. So, the first objection to the Self-deception Reply is simply that it is wrong about the facts. Almost everyone is a "reality" person who is not of type A. To go to the opposite extreme and claim that almost everyone is either of type A or an "illusion" person is to be mistaken about the way things are.

My second rejoinder to the Self-deception Reply is that even if it were true that almost everyone is either of type A or an "illusion" person, it would still be possible for God to bring about situation S without interfering with people's free will. Take, first of all, type-A people. They go around self-inducing beliefs in themselves by direct acts of will (whether it be done quickly or slowly). Suppose God were to arrange the world to be just the way that would cause type-A people to self-induce a belief in the gospel message. The exact procedure by which he might accomplish that is somewhat unclear. Presumably, he would need to make the gospel message seem appealing to them. It may be that for different people, God would need to make the world appear in different ways. But since God is supposedly omnipotent and omniscient, there should be no problem about him accomplishing the given task. The question becomes that of whether such action on his part would necessarily interfere with people's free will. I would say no. The people need not be aware of God's actions; he could be working "behind the scenes." People would still go around self-inducing beliefs, just as before. So I see no interference with free will here.

Now consider "illusion" people. They do not wish to be enlightened about the nature of reality but just wish to stick with their illusions. Would *their* free will have to be interfered with if God were to somehow cause them to believe the gospel message? Again I would say no. People acquire new beliefs every day, and that is just as true of "illusion" people as "reality" people. So long as they do not sense any sort of coercion, people have no objection to the acquisition of new beliefs. Well, since God is omnipotent and omniscient, he could certainly cause "illusion" people to come to believe the gospel message in a way which would be unobjectionable to them. He could again be working "behind the scenes" to bring about situation S. Maybe such people would come to feel that the gospel message is part of their "illusion" regarding the way things are. But that is all right. They would still be believing it, which is what God wants. So, again, I see no interference with free will here.

This second rejoinder to the Self-deception Reply is actually a departure from the Normality Objection, for it is in effect saying that the normal-abnormal distinction is irrelevant. It makes no difference whether non-Christians self-induce their beliefs or not. Even if they do, God could still cause them to believe the gospel message without interfering with their free will. This would revert to the sort of objection to FDN's premise (P1) that was raised above in section 5.1. It is a kind of "fallback" rejoinder. I put forward the Normality Objection based on certain empirical claims about the way people acquire their beliefs. If I have my facts right, then the first rejoinder would adequately defend the Normality Objection against the Self-deception Reply. On the other hand, if my empirical claims are wrong, then I would give up the Normality Objection and simply attack FDN in the way presented in chapter 5. Either way, FDN is refuted.

C.5. The Culpability Issue

At various places in the book we have addressed the question whether or not nonbelievers are culpable. Let us call the claim that they are culpable either for their nonbelief itself or for their actions or omissions that led to the nonbelief the "Culpability Thesis." This issue was discussed in section 5.5 in connection with the Great-Commission Reply to the Irrationality Objection to FDN. The objection was that God would be irrational for wanting people to (irrationally) believe the gospel message with insufficient evidence. The Great-Commission Reply maintains that God wants the message spread by human missionaries and that they do have sufficient evidence to back it up. (Usually that evidence is taken to be the Argument from the Bible, which will be discussed in appendix D.) Almost all advocates of the Great-Commission Reply go on to infer that since there is sufficient evidence, the many people who are presented with the gospel message but come not to believe it must be willfully refusing to believe it, for which they are culpable. We can see, then, that both strong voluntarism and the Culpability Thesis are usually part of the Great-Commission Reply.

The culpability issue was also discussed in section 7.23 in connection with the Unfairness Objection to TDN. The version of TDN that we considered maintains that God is testing non-Christians to try to ascertain who among them would willfully refuse to believe the gospel message when it is presented

to them. TDN itself presupposes strong voluntarism (in virtue of its description
of the test being conducted) and almost all TDNers would go on to maintain
that such people as described in the test are culpable for their refusal to
believe. Thus, the Culpability Thesis is usually part of TDN. According to the
Unfairness Objection, such a test would be unfair, because, first, non-Christians are not people who are "refusing to believe" the gospel message, and,
second, even if they were, they would not be culpable for doing so. The culpability issue was also discussed in section 14.21 in connection with Schellenberg's distinction between "culpable nonbelief" and "inculpable nonbelief," which I found to be somewhat obscure. Let us explore the issue further.

There are two initial questions that need to be raised. One of them is
that of the precise formulation of the Culpability Thesis. What is it, exactly,
that nonbelievers are supposed to be culpable for? Presumably it is not for
the nonbelief itself but for actions or omissions that led to the nonbelief.
But which of those two is it? Are nonbelievers culpable for things they did
or for things that they neglected to do, or might it be both? The second initial question is that of whether the Culpability Thesis entails or presupposes strong voluntarism. That is, in order for nonbelievers to be culpable,
is it necessary that people usually (and rationally) self-induce their beliefs
by direct acts of will?

Let us assume that people are only culpable for the actions they perform or fail to perform, that being the prevailing view, so the Culpability
Thesis may be expressed as follows:

> If non-Christians hear the gospel message from a missionary but fail to
> believe it, then that is always because of certain actions which they
> performed (such as willfully "tuning out" the missionary's message or
> self-inducing the belief that it is false) or because of certain willful
> nonactions on their part (such as refusing to investigate further the evi-
> dence that the missionary claimed to have for the truth of his message),
> or for a combination of such factors. All such non-Christians are *cul-
> pable* for such actions or (willful) nonactions.

As worded here, it is not immediately clear whether or not the Culpability
Thesis entails strong voluntarism, for the actions or omissions for which
non-Christians are culpable need not be willful self-inducements of belief
or refusals to believe, but prior actions or omissions of the sort appealed to
in the Investigation Model, described above. We need to inquire why non-
Christians would "tune out" a missionary and refuse to investigate his
claims any further. It seems that in almost all cases they have a prior belief
that the missionary's message is false. But how did they acquire that prior
belief? If it was totally a matter of the assessment of evidence, then voluntarism need not enter the picture. But if the Culpability Thesis were to
include the idea that such prior beliefs are never supported by any good

evidence and must always have been willfully self-induced, then it seems it would entail or presuppose strong voluntarism. That is, since there are so many non-Christians in the world who have heard the gospel message but rejected it, if that is always due to some willful self-inducement of belief or nonbelief on their part, then such an action must be a common phenomenon, which is the view of strong voluntarism. I believe that is a plausible way to interpret the thesis. From my observations, almost all advocates of the Culpability Thesis are also strong voluntarists.

Certainly if the Culpability Thesis entails or presupposes strong voluntarism, then it could be attacked by the objections to that view formulated above at the end of section C.1. And I do indeed regard the thesis as including that view, which makes it subject to the given objections. However, let us disregard this point and consider other objections to the thesis. For the sake of argument, we could assume that the Culpability Thesis does not entail or presuppose strong voluntarism.

In section A.6, I indicated that I lean toward the view that no one is ever culpable for any action whatever. There would be different ways to support such a claim, but one way would be through a restricted form of determinism, with which I tend to agree. As explained in A.6, one could adopt a consequentialist morality without any need to appeal to the idea of culpability. For example, the death penalty may be argued to be a good thing, merely for consequentialist (rather than retributivist) reasons. From that point of view, the Culpability Thesis would be false. However, I shall not further pursue that line of argument in this book.

In appendix B it was argued that the idea of free will is incompatible with the doctrines of divine foreknowledge and predestination (or quasi-predestination), which are supported by Scripture and held by many Christians. I would also argue that the idea of culpability is incompatible with those doctrines. People cannot be culpable for actions that God knew ahead of time they would perform or that were in some way divinely predestined to occur. That would be another objection to the Culpability Thesis within the context of evangelical Christianity, for most evangelical Christians agree with at least one of those doctrines. However, let us not pursue that line of thought here. We did enough with it in appendix B.

How, then, might the Culpability Thesis be refuted, given that it does not entail strong voluntarism, and assuming for the sake of argument that people are sometimes culpable for their actions? I would say that a person, X, is culpable for an action, A, only if all of the following conditions obtain:

(1) X is sane.
(2) A leads to harm for one or more persons other than X.
(3) X was aware of the given harm but performed A anyway, for a selfish reason.

A voluntaristic example of someone who would satisfy all three conditions would be a mother who has some evidence that her children are ill but who wants them not to be ill because she does not want to devote time and money to them. Suppose she willfully self-induces nonbelief in the proposition that her children are ill. She knows that the action (self-inducing such nonbelief) would harm her children but she performs it anyway, because it provides her with comfort. If such a woman could be regarded to be sane, then all three conditions would be satisfied and she would be culpable for her self-inducement of nonbelief. To make the example less voluntaristic, we could eliminate the belief aspect and merely suppose that the mother refuses to seek medical treatment for her children in order to devote her time and money to selfish pursuits. Again, all three conditions would be satisfied.

The question then becomes that of whether these conditions can all be satisfied in the case of some non-Christian, Mr. X, who hears the gospel message but comes not to believe it. Let us assume that Mr. X is sane, so condition (1) is satisfied. How might condition (2) be satisfied? That is, who might be the persons harmed by Mr. X's nonbelief? Let us say that Mr. X is a role model for his children and the children are subsequently harmed in some way by his nonbelief. (We need not elaborate how.) That would take care of condition (2). But what about condition (3)? I cannot see how condition (3) might be satisfied. If Mr. X rejects the missionary's message, then he cannot be aware of any harm that his nonbelief might have on his children. But satisfaction of condition (3) is crucial for culpability. Since it is not satisfied, it turns out that non-Christians are not culpable for any actions or omissions that lead to their nonbelief. That, then, would be another objection to the Culpability Thesis. It fails to explain how non-Christians are aware of harm that their nonbelief causes to others. It therefore fails to explain how they might be in any way culpable for their nonbelief.

It might be objected that condition (2) is too narrow and should be changed to:

(2) X leads to harm either for X or for one or more persons other than X.

This revised concept of culpability is one that would apply to people who harm no one but themselves. An example would be smokers who suffer ill effects from their smoking. The idea is that they were warned about such effects and therefore are culpable for incurring them. I shall refrain from considering whether or not such a change in condition (2) is warranted.

Even with the given change, I still fail to see how condition (3) might be satisfied in the case of non-Christians who reject the missionary's message. How could they be aware of harm that their nonbelief would cause to themselves? To be aware of that is to be aware of the truth of the message itself, but we are assuming that they do not believe the message. Furthermore, even if non-Christians were to be aware of harm that might befall them as a consequence of their nonbelief, how could they perform actions or omissions that lead to such nonbelief for selfish reasons? That makes no sense. If people do things for selfish reasons, then it is because they expect some benefit to follow, not harm. The Culpability Thesis claims that non-Christians are culpable for actions or omissions that brought about their nonbelief because they were aware of the harm that such nonbelief would eventually cause them and went ahead and brought about the nonbelief anyway, for selfish reasons. Such a claim strikes me as utterly absurd.

I conclude, then, that even if the Culpability Thesis were taken in a way that does not entail strong voluntarism, and even if we grant that some people are culpable for their actions, and even if we disregard possible conflicts with the doctrines of divine foreknowledge or predestination (or quasi-predestination), which were discussed in appendix B, the thesis can still be refuted. We can put forward a reasonable definition of "culpable" and argue that the sorts of nonbelievers referred to in ANB do not satisfy the definition. But if they are not in any way culpable for their nonbelief, then what are we to make of the fact that no divine actions have occurred to prevent such nonbelief? It seems that the very best explanation for that fact is the hypothesis that the God of evangelical Christianity does not exist. That is ANB in a nutshell.

Notes

1. Swinburne, *Faith and Reason*, p. 25.

2. H. H. Price, "Belief and Will," *Proceedings of the Aristotelian Society, Supplementary Volume* 28 (1954): 1–26; reprinted in Stuart Hampshire, ed., *Philosophy of Mind* (New York: Harper & Row, 1966), the quotations taken from pp. 106 and 110; also reprinted in Robert R. Ammerman and Marcus G. Singer, eds., *Belief, Knowledge, and Truth* (New York: Charles Scribner's Sons, 1970), the quotations on pp. 68 and 71–72.

Appendix D

The Argument from the Bible

Almost all evangelical Christians believe that the writing of the Bible was divinely inspired and represents God's main revelation to humanity. They also believe that the Bible contains special features which constitute evidence of its divine inspiration. This would be a use of the Bible to prove God's existence within natural theology rather than within revealed theology, since the book's features are supposed to be evident even to (openminded) skeptics. Furthermore, since a divinely inspired work must be true, those features are thereby also evidence of the Bible's truth, and thus can be used in support of Christianity as the one true religion. When expressed that way, the reasoning can be construed as an argument for the truth of the gospel message from the alleged special features of the Bible. We may refer to it as "the Argument from the Bible."

The Argument from the Bible can be used in various places to defend the existence of the God of evangelical Christianity against ANB. One place is in the Great-Commission Reply to the Irrationality Objection to FDN. According to FDN, God preserves epistemic distance between himself and humanity because he wants to avoid interfering with human free will. The Irrationality Objection maintains that such a divine policy seems tantamount to wanting people to choose Christianity as their religion (and to come to believe the gospel message) in the total absence of any good evidence, which would be irrational. According to the Great-Commission Reply, the method by which God wants humans to form a belief in Christianity is by hearing the gospel message from missionaries (who are directed by the Bible's Great Commission) and coming to accept that message. But then the issue comes down to whether such acceptance would be irrational. Certainly it would be irrational for people to believe everything they hear from strangers. They cannot be expected to do that. There is where the Argument from the Bible comes in. If the missionaries could point out features of the Bible that show it to be divinely inspired and hence true, then it would be quite *rational* for their listeners to accept the (gospel) message contained in the Bible. Furthermore, God's epistemic distance would be preserved since his revelation would be presented by humans. That would refute the Irrationality Objection, which in turn would reinstate FDN as a strong attack on ANB.

Another place where the Argument from the Bible can come in is in defense of the Testing Defense (TDN) against the Lack-of-evidence Objection. According to TDN, there is good evidence for the truth of the gospel message, so if people fail to believe that message then it can only be because they have willfully rejected it, for which they are culpable. The idea is that God is testing people with regard to their belief-formation processes in order to separate those who are open to the gospel message from those who willfully shut it out despite the good evidence in its favor. The Lack-of-evidence Objection attacks TDN's claim that there is good evidence for the gospel message. There is where the Argument from the Bible comes in. Since the gospel message is not supported by general revelation (or the design in nature), the only evidence there could be for it (barring new miracles) would be the Bible itself. And, according to the argument, the Bible does indeed provide such evidence. Even if some evangelical Christians do not agree with TDN and the "testing" idea, most of them would at least regard the Argument from the Bible as a refutation of the Lack-of-evidence Objection.

Another place where the Argument from the Bible is highly relevant is in response to the Burden-of-proof Objection applied to both UDE and UDN (in chapters 10 and 11). Evangelical Christians who appeal to the Unknown-purpose Defense want to maintain that God has some purpose for permitting so much suffering and so much nonbelief in the world, but then they are challenged by a burden to prove that such a purpose exists. If an argument could be put forward for the existence of the God of evangelical Christianity, then it would satisfy that burden of proof (thereby strongly refuting the Burden-of-proof Objection). And the Argument from the Bible would fill that role very nicely. In fact, it is the only argument that might possibly do so.

Still another place where the Argument from the Bible may be relevant is in the context of UDN and the opposition between the two worldviews labeled ANH and UNH. UNH consists of a large conjunction of propositions, and ANH consists mostly of a disjunction of the negations of them. If there is no evidence whatever for the truth of the given propositions, then it might be argued that ANH, merely by virtue of its logical form (a large disjunction vs. a large conjunction), has a higher a priori probability than UNH. The only way to try to refute this directly would be to try to show that there *is* some support for several of UNH's individual conjuncts, which would overcome the disadvantage inflicted on UNH by its logical form. And the Argument from the Bible might be brought in to confer that support on those propositions. Viewing the matter more generally, it is evident that the argument is needed by evangelical Christians who appeal to UNH, since they are in effect saying that no one has as yet thought of a purpose for God's permission of so much nonbelief in the gospel message and so God must have some unknown purpose for it. But that inference would be rational only if there were some independent reason to believe in the God of evangelical Christianity, and only the Argument from the Bible could provide such a reason.

Although the Argument from the Bible is useful to Christians and although almost all evangelical Christians agree with it at least to some extent, it is an argument that is for the most part ignored by professional philosophers of religion. One explanation for such neglect is that the argument can be easily refuted. In this appendix, I shall try to sketch how such a refutation might be formulated, though I am sure many will feel that I am attacking a strawman. The appendix is put into the book mainly for the benefit of those who think that the Argument from the Bible might have some merit. Those who do not think that way are encouraged to skip it.

D.1. The Argument Formulated

The Argument from the Bible is usually regarded as a kind of "cumulative-case" argument. It may be formulated as follows:

(1) The Bible contains a large number of prophecies of future events which have been remarkably fulfilled.

(2) The Bible does not contain any unfulfilled prophecies.

(3) The only reasonable explanation for the above facts is that God used his foreknowledge to make the prophecies and inspired the authors of the Bible to record them.

(4) The Bible contains a convincing eyewitness account of the resurrection and subsequent appearances of Jesus of Nazareth.

(5) The only reasonable explanation for the above fact is that Jesus was and is a divine being, which shows the truth of the Bible and its gospel message.

(6) The Bible contains no contradictions.

(7) The Bible contains amazing facts about the planet earth, compatible with modern science, which were unknown in ancient times. Also, the Bible contains no conflicts with modern science or errors of a factual nature.

(8) The Bible contains a perfect morality, and no ethical defects.

(9) The only reasonable explanation for facts (6)–(8), above, is that the ultimate author of the Bible is God himself.

(10) Putting together results (3), (5), and (9), above, we may infer that the Bible is not a purely manmade work, but divinely inspired, which establishes the truth of Christianity and its gospel message.

Other premises are sometimes appealed to in the formulation of the argument. For example, Henry M. Morris places much emphasis on the alleged uniqueness of the Bible.[1] He also mentions what he takes to be remarkable numerical designs in it.[2] But for our purposes, the given formulation should suffice. It includes what are regarded to be the main factors within the Argument from the Bible.

Premises (3), (5), and (9) might be challenged by suggesting alternate explanations for the given data. An appeal might be made, for example, to the possibility of ESP or precognition on the part of some humans in the case of (3), or the phenomenon of spontaneous remissions and resurrections of some humans in the case of (5), or simply the exceedingly high intelligence of the biblical authors and editors in the case of (9). But for our purposes here I shall ignore such challenges and simply focus on the argument's basic premises, which are its premises (1), (2), (4), and (6)–(8). If those steps are erroneous and do not express facts, then premises (3), (5), and (9) can be attacked on the grounds that what they call "facts" are not that but errors instead. What I put forward is merely a sketch. Details to fill out the sketch are provided elsewhere.[3]

D.2. Alleged Fulfilled Prophecies

There are hundreds of alleged prophecies in the Bible, most of them in the Old Testament, which are supposed to have been remarkably fulfilled, thereby showing the divine inspiration of Scripture. I shall here look at just one group of them, the alleged messianic prophecies contained within the description of the "suffering servant" of Isaiah 53.

Among the alleged prophecies contained within Isaiah 53 that are claimed to have been fulfilled by Jesus are the following (with their respective verse numbers indicated):

(1) that the Messiah's message would not be believed, supposedly fulfilled by Jesus at John 12:37-38;

(3) that the Messiah would be despised and rejected, supposedly fulfilled by Jesus in that his own people did not believe in him, according to John 1:11, 7:5;

(5) that the Messiah would be wounded, supposedly fulfilled by the scourging of Jesus at Matt. 27:26;

(7) that the Messiah would be silent before his accusers, supposedly fulfilled by Jesus at Matt. 27:12 (and Acts 8:32–35);

(9) that the Messiah would have a grave provided for him by a rich man, supposedly fulfilled for Jesus by Joseph of Arimathea at Matt. 27:57–60;

(12) that the Messiah would be arrested as a criminal (which is perhaps Jesus' own interpretation at Luke 22:37) or perhaps that the Messiah would be crucified with criminals, supposedly fulfilled by Jesus at Matt. 27:38 and Mark 15:27 (with Mark 15:28 inserted later) and Luke 23:32;

(12) that the Messiah would make intercession for his persecutors, supposedly fulfilled by Jesus at Luke 23:34.

But there are many problems with taking Isaiah 53 in such a way, among which are the following:

(1) According to Isa. 53:3 in the *Tanakh*, the suffering servant was "despised [and] shunned by men." It seems doubtful that that is fulfilled by Jesus simply by virtue of the fact that his own people did not accept him, for he apparently was widely accepted by the common people elsewhere. According to Luke 4:15, he taught in the synagogue and everyone praised him. And later, huge crowds supposedly followed him, and he was described as making a "Triumphal Entry" into Jerusalem (Matt. 21:8–11; John 12:12–13,17–19).

(2) Verse 3 in the *Tanakh* also declares that the suffering servant was "familiar with disease," and verse 4 says that he was "stricken by God," where the Hebrew word for "stricken" is one that is used in the Hebrew Scriptures to stand only for leprosy (as at Lev. 13:3,9,20 and 2 Kings 15:5). But Jesus is not known to have suffered from leprosy or any other disease, so those verses are not applicable to him. It may even be part of some forms of Christian doctrine that Jesus needed to be perfectly healthy in order to play adequately the role of "sacrificial lamb" (which by law needed to be "without blemish"). It is clear that the suffering servant of Isaiah 53 could not adequately play such a role.

(3) As for Jesus being silent before his accusers (thereby satisfying verse 7), that seems not to work either. Verse 7 says (twice): "He did not open his mouth." But according to John 18:33–37, 19:11, Jesus said *much* to Pontius Pilate. In each of the four gospels Jesus opened his mouth and said something before his accusers. Hence, Jesus did not actually fulfill that part of the prophecy.

(4) In verse 9 it says of the suffering servant "his grave was set among the wicked, and with the rich, in his death." It is unclear how that applies to Jesus, for there were no other bodies in the tomb in which Jesus' body was placed. The verse definitely does not say that the servant would have a grave provided for him by a rich man, so that part of the alleged prophecy is sheer invention.

(5) According to verse 10, "the Lord chose to crush him by disease, that if he made himself an offering for guilt, he might see offspring and have long life. . . ." That seems totally inapplicable to Jesus, for Jesus was not crushed by disease, nor did he see any offspring, nor did he have a long life.

(6) Isaiah 53 does not actually mention the Messiah. In fact, when we look closely at the chapter, it is hard to find anything in it that *is* applicable to either the (Jewish) Messiah or to Jesus. Verse 1 does not actually say that the servant's message would not be believed, but merely asks, "Who can believe what we have heard?" There seems to be no prophecy there at all. Nor is there any indication that the servant would be arrested as a criminal or scourged or crucified with criminals or make intercession for his persecutors. None of that is in there. Verse 6 does say, "the Lord visited upon him the guilt of us all," but there are other interpretations of that than the Christian one.

(7) There is a Judaic interpretation of Isaiah 53 that seems plausible. The suffering servant is the nation of Israel which is represented by King Uzziah, who was its king in Isaiah's time and who died of leprosy. According to Shmuel Golding, Isaiah's message may have been: "Here is your leprous king, who is in type suffering under God's hand for you the backslidden servant nation of Israel" (which explains verse 6).[4] Uzziah was taken away from the royal palace because of his affliction as a leper and spent his remaining years in isolation, which fits verse 8. Golding says the following:

> Israel is portrayed as a suffering servant on account of its anointed leader being stricken with leprosy. Israel, like the leper, is a suffering servant of God. Both have suffered humiliation at the hand of their fellowmen: the leper because of his unsightly appearance; Israel through its defeat at the hands of the Babylonians. The gist of the message is that Israel like the leper has suffered, but nevertheless will retain its identity in the form of the exiled Jewish people and that they will prosper in this form.[5]

This interpretation of Isaiah 53 seems preferable to the Christian one because it does not suffer from drawbacks (1)–(6) mentioned above. It would also better explain the many changes of tense that occur in the chapter. And Israel is indeed referred to as "God's servant" (e.g., at Isa. 49:3). However, the given interpretation does not make the chapter into a prophecy so much as an explanation of Israel's situation at around the time of Isaiah. At the very least, it shows, I think, that Isaiah 53 is not a clear example of a fulfilled prophecy (or set of fulfilled prophecies) in the Bible. So it is not any good support for premise (1) of the Argument from the Bible.

In a similar way, all the other alleged fulfilled prophecies of the Bible can be attacked. None of them is what its advocates maintain. Indeed, many of them are not prophecies at all. Of the ones that are prophecies, almost all remain unfulfilled. And the few that are fulfilled prophecies are not remarkable, for one reason or another. Therefore, premise (1) of the Argument from the Bible has not been adequately supported and may reasonably be doubted.

D.3. Unfulfilled Prophecies

According to premise (2) of the argument, there are no unfulfilled prophecies in the Bible. Dozens of counterexamples have been put forward but I will here just mention one of them. Many verses[6] prophesy that Christ's second coming would occur soon. Some of them specifically say that it would be within his listeners' lifetime, i.e., before *that* generation (there with Jesus) passes away. But in truth more than nineteen centuries have elapsed since then and the event still has not occurred. Of all the examples of unfulfilled prophecies, this one strikes me as the clearest and most powerful.

This counterexample shows that premise (2) of the Argument from the Bible is false. It might be suggested that the argument dispense with that premise, but it serves an important purpose. With many unfulfilled prophecies in the Bible, even if there had been some fulfilled ones, they would, in effect, have gotten "canceled out." The law of probabilities would allow some prophecies to come true, just as a matter of coincidence, provided that many of them do not come true. Thus, it is important for the advocate of the Argument from the Bible to insert premise (2). As it turns out, since in fact none of the alleged remarkable fulfilled biblical prophecies really turns out to be that, all of the many unfulfilled ones are a kind of "overkill." They could have been used for "canceling-out" purposes, but are not needed for that after all.

D.4. The Resurrection

According to premise (4) of the argument, the Bible contains a convincing eyewitness account of the resurrection and subsequent appearances of Jesus of Nazareth. The gospels do describe Jesus' execution and subsequent burial in a tomb, and they do claim that the tomb was later found to be empty and that Jesus appeared to his followers in bodily form. One main reason for calling them "eyewitness accounts" is that in Luke 1:2 it says, "they were handed down to us by those who from the first were eyewitnesses." There are, however, several problems.

First, it is generally conceded that the accounts of the resurrection were not actually written down until more than thirty years after the alleged event had occurred and that, prior to being written down, they were, in effect, rumors or stories which had been spread orally throughout the region. It is easy for such rumors to become embellished over time. As is well known, changes tend to occur in oral messages, even when their conveyers make every effort to pass them on accurately. So even if the resurrection accounts are based on what are said to be eyewitness reports, there is much room for doubt regarding them. An analogy would be the report of some event in history, such as the explosion and burning of the *Hindenburg Zeppelin* over Lakehurst, New Jersey, in 1937. If the very earliest written account of that event were published in, say, 1967, then historians would be reasonably suspicious as to whether it really did occur, even if the account is based on alleged eyewitness reports.

Second, the event in question is supernatural or miraculous in character. That in itself makes it an event which calls for something more in support than just reports by a handful of alleged eyewitnesses. By analogy, if the explosion and burning of the *Hindenburg* were claimed to be followed by its miraculous reappearance out of nowhere the next day, then historians would need far more than just some alleged eyewitness reports before they would include such an event (as an actual event, not merely a reported one) in their history books. Even if the alleged eyewitnesses were to show their complete sincerity, say, by passing lie-detector tests, that would still not sway historians. The event could still be some sort of mass hallucination or the product of the power of suggestion (as has been suggested in the case of the astronomical miracle at Fatima, Portugal, in 1917).

Third, those who wrote the accounts of Jesus' resurrection were not reporters or historians. They were all motivated to win converts to their new religion, which was at that time a kind of Judaic cult. Even Luke, who says, "I myself have carefully investigated everything from the beginning" (1:3), was not a neutral investigative reporter, but a proselytizer for Christianity (mainly to the Gentiles). That is another fact about the writings which tends to cast doubt upon their objectivity and accuracy.

Fourth, the alleged resurrection appearances were only to Jesus' followers, not to his opponents. If the whole purpose of the resurrection had been for God to convey to the world the truth of the gospel message, as suggested in Matt. 12:38–40, or at least the information that there is such a state as an afterlife, as suggested by St. Paul in 1 Cor. 15:12–19, then the event was very badly staged. More people should have witnessed the crucifixion and certified that Jesus was really dead.[7] And certainly many more people than just a handful of his followers should have witnessed his return from the dead. This is a point made previously in the present book in connection with ANB.

Fifth, the biblical accounts of the resurrection are not consistent and that tends to cast doubt on them. They contradict one another regarding such matters as how many women went to the tomb; whether it was still dark out; whether Mary Magdalene later told people about the empty tomb, whether she went back to it with them, whether there was just one angel there or two; whether the angels were inside or outside the tomb; whether they got there before the women and disciples, and what they looked like; whether there were guards at the tomb; whether Peter went there alone; whether Jesus appeared first to him (1 Cor. 15:3–5); whether he appeared at all to Mary Magdalene; whether he appeared to her at the tomb; whether she was then alone; whether she recognized him immediately, and whether it was after the disciples were told; whether Peter went to the tomb before or after the others were told and whether he was alone; whether Jesus appeared specially to two disciples; whether they recognized him immediately; whether he later appeared to the others as the two were speaking or afterward; whether he scolded the others for not believing the two; whether he appeared to the disciples just once or three times; whether the first appearance was in Galilee; whether they all recognized him immediately; whether he ascended to heaven right afterward; whether he ascended from Jerusalem (Mark), Bethany (Luke), or Mt. Olivet (Acts); and whether he appeared to the Twelve, to over five hundred, and then specially to James (1 Cor. 15:5–7).

It is to be granted that biblical inerrantists have tried to harmonize all of the various accounts of Jesus' post-mortem appearances in a way that would avoid the apparent inconsistencies. But the general consensus, I think, is that all such attempts have been failures. The topic of biblical contradictions is of course complicated. Some apparent inconsistencies might be capable of being explained away by appeal to special interpretations. For example, Acts 26:23 seems to say that Jesus was the first to rise from the dead. (See also Rev. 1:5.) Yet we know there were many prior resurrections described in Scripture,[8] which implies an inconsistency. Perhaps the verse in question could be interpreted to mean merely that Jesus is the first to be resurrected following the atonement for mankind's sin, or something akin to that. It may be that some of the alleged contradictions listed above can be dealt with in some such fashion. But it seems unreasonable to think that all of them can. I, for one, have never seen it done. As for premise (4) of the Argument from the Bible regarding a convincing eyewitness account of the resurrection, we have seen that there are many reasons of various sorts to doubt the accuracy of that claim.

D.5. More Contradictions

According to premise (6) of the argument, the Bible contains no contradictions. We have already seen above how that claim might be challenged. It might be objected that the alleged contradictions only concern trivial matters. However, there are also inconsistencies regarding the important matter of salvation,[9] so not all of them are over trivial matters. Furthermore, even the trivial contradictions are important in the present context. The fact that the Bible contradicts itself at all, whatever the matter may be, does make a lot of difference. It shows that God was not the author (or inspirer) of all of the Bible, which refutes the claim on the part of evangelical Christians (and Orthodox Jews) that he was. Without the Argument from the Bible to fall back on, evangelical Christian theology is in a great deal of trouble with regard to many issues, as mentioned in the beginning of this appendix.

The importance of biblical inerrancy to evangelical Christianity is borne out by the fact that the translators of the NIV translation of the Bible, all of whom are certified evangelicals, go through a lot of trouble to try to evade contradictions. For example, although all Hebrew manuscripts containing 2 Chron. 22:2 cite Ahaziah's age when he began his reign to be forty-two, the NIV translation of that verse gives the age as twenty-two, to bring it into conformity with 2 Kings 8:26. They justify this on the grounds that the Septuagint and some Syriac manuscripts give the figure as twenty-two. But in just about all other cases they rely on the Hebrew manuscripts. It seems to be a departure from the task of translating from the Hebrew into English (which presumably is the translators' task) to engage in such juggling of the texts.

D.6. Factual Errors

According to premise (7) of the argument, the Bible contains amazing facts about the planet earth, compatible with modern science, which were unknown in ancient times. One verse that is often cited in this regard is Job 26:7, which says that the earth is suspended upon nothing. That is indeed a remarkable insight, coming from an ancient writer. One wonders, however, what to make of it, since the same writer refers to "the pillars of the earth" (9:6, 38:6) and "the pillars of the heavens" (26:11). The idea that the earth rests on a foundation or pillars is also expressed at 1 Sam. 2:8 and Ps. 75:3, 104:5. In addition, premise (7) of the argument declares that the Bible contains no conflicts with modern science or errors of a factual nature. We have already seen biblical errors in the form of unfulfilled prophecies and contradictions. But the claim can also be challenged by appeal to dozens of other examples. Here are just three:

(1) The Bible (1 Chron. 16:30; Ps. 93:1, 96:10, 104:5) declares that the earth does not move, whereas we know for a fact that the earth does move.

(2) The age of the earth according to the Bible (computed from Gen. 1, 5, and 11 and Luke 3:23–38) cannot be much over six thousand years, yet

scientists have determined that the earth is 4.6 billion years old. The evidence that it is *far* over six thousand years old comes from many different fields and is overwhelming.

(3) According to Gen. 1:20–25, birds were in existence before reptiles and insects (things which "creep upon the earth"). But science has established that there were reptiles on the earth 150 million years before there were any birds and that insects go back another 100 million years before reptiles.

Dozens of other examples of the above sort could be cited. It seems quite clear that premise (7) of the Argument from the Bible, according to which the Bible contains no conflicts with modern science and no errors of a factual nature, has been refuted.

D.7. Ethical Defects

According to premise (8) of the argument, the Bible contains a perfect morality and no ethical defects. But that claim seems incompatible with the fact that God is described in the Bible as killing people for no good reason. We have already mentioned the many children killed in the Great Flood, in Sodom and Gomorrah, and in the ten plagues on Egypt (especially the last). Here are some additional examples of people whom God killed:

1. a man who refused to impregnate his brother's widow (Gen. 38:7–10).

2. two men who offered God incense that he had not authorized (Lev. 10:1–2).

3. a group of about 300 people who opposed Moses politically (Num. 16:1–35).

4. another group of 14,700 who sympathized with the first group (Num. 16:49).

5. more people who complained about the food and other matters (Num. 21:4–6).

6. another 24,000 because of some who worshiped Baal (Num. 25:3,9).

7. the Amorites who besieged Gibeon (Josh. 10:10–11).

8. seventy men who looked into a box (1 Sam. 6:19).

9. another man who, with good intention, touched the box (2 Sam. 6:6–7).

10. a man who refused to use his weapon against another man (1 Kings 20:35–36).

11. forty-two children who called Elisha "baldy" (2 Kings 2:23–24).

12. one hundred and eighty-five thousand Assyrian soldiers (2 Kings 19:35).

God also killed all of Pharaoh's horsemen in the Red Sea (Exod. 14:26–28). He could instead have simply made their horses lame, which would have been far more effective than removing the wheels from the chariots so that the horses had to drag the chariots slowly along the ground (Exod. 14:25). That would have also spared the horsemen.

In addition to killing people directly, God also ordered several people killed (despite his commandment not to kill). Here are some examples of people who died by God's order (and in some cases with God's help):

1. three thousand of the Levites' brothers, friends, and neighbors, who had become unruly (Exod. 32:27–28).

2. all the men, women, and children in all seven of the tribes who were the Israelites' neighbors (Deut. 2:34, 3:6, 7:1–2,16, 20:16–17). Some biblical verses imply that the Israelites numbered 2–3 million, which would make the total population of their neighbors more than 14 million. What God was here ordering, then, if we could go by those verses, was a kind of Holocaust.

3. all the men, women, and children of the cities of Jericho, Ai, and dozens more cities and towns (Josh. 6:21, 8:24–26, 10:26–42, 11:10–23, 21:44).

4. all the Amalekites, including children, and even animals (1 Sam. 15:3,18), where Saul was severely punished for sparing some of them.

5. all the members of the house of Ahab and ministers of Baal within Israel, the latter accomplished through deception (2 Kings 10:11–25), though approved by God (10:30).

6. all the citizens of Jerusalem, including children, who did not grieve and lament over sins committed in it (Ezek. 9:4–6).

It seems quite unethical for God to order the execution of so many people, whatever their offense might have been, especially in the case of the children, who were presumably innocent.

Closely related to the above is the extravagant use of capital punishment among God's chosen people. God ordered people put to death for such minor offenses as the following:

1. consulting a witch (Lev. 20:6; Deut. 18:11).

2. blasphemy or merely having a different religion (Exod. 22:20; Lev. 24:10–23; Deut. 13:1–15, 17:2–5, 18:20; Josh. 23:7,16; 2 Kings 18:40).

3. gathering sticks or kindling a fire on the Sabbath (Exod. 31:14–15, 35:2–3; Num. 15:32–36).

4. eating the wrong food (Exod. 12:15,19; Lev. 3:16–17, 7:22,25–27, 17:10–16).

5. being a disrespectful or disobedient child (Lev. 20:9; Deut. 21:18–21).

It seems unethical to have laws that harsh. The laws of the ancient Israelites are hardly the model of morality that advocates of Dominion Theology (or Reconstructionism) make them out to be.

It would have been impressive if the Bible had gone against the prevailing cultural norms and had forbidden slavery and the oppression of women. But it did not do that. The Bible condones slavery.[10] It also contains many rules that are discriminatory against women.[11] It is hard to find much in the Bible that stands out as ethically noble.

Even biblical doctrines are unethical. A good case could be made that Adam and Eve were victims of entrapment and did not deserve their punishment. It was also unethical for Jesus, who was innocent, to be sacrificed for humanity. If people deserve a certain punishment, then they ought to receive it. That is what justice is. To knowingly punish the innocent is always morally repugnant. Also, the exclusivist threat of "accept Christ or else be damned" is unethical. We have already applied the Unfairness Objection to evangelical Christianity. It applies equally well to the Bible itself. But probably the most unethical biblical doctrine of all is that of eternal damnation.[12] It is hard to understand how anyone who interprets the Bible to say that God keeps people alive for purposes of eternal torment, instead of simply annihilating them, could also suggest premise (8) of the Argument from the Bible. And yet there are such.

This sketch of how the argument might be attacked is admittedly in need of filling out, and that is something done elsewhere, as mentioned above. But from the little that has been presented, I hope that the reader has become convinced of the total bankruptcy of the Argument from the Bible.

Notes

1. Henry M. Morris, *Many Infallible Proofs*, rev. ed. (Green Forest, Ariz.: Master Books, 1996), chapters 2 and 5.

2. Ibid., appendix A.

3. There are dozens of excellent sources for the purpose. Two recent titles are: C. Dennis McKinsey, *The Encyclopedia of Biblical Errancy* (Amherst, N.Y.: Prometheus Books, 1995), and A. J. Mattill Jr., *The Seven Mighty Blows to Traditional Beliefs*, 2d ed. (Gordo, Ala.: The Flatwoods Free Press, 1995). See also my Web article "The Argument from the Bible," which is presently (in 1998) at the following address: http://www.infidels.org/library/modern/theodore_drange/bible.html.

4. Shmuel Golding, *The Light of Reason*, vol. 2 (Jerusalem: The Jerusalem Institute of Biblical Polemics, 1989), p. 36.

5. Ibid., p. 36.

6. Matt. 4:17, 10:23, 16:28, 24:34; Mark 9:1,13,30; Luke 9:27, 21:32; John 5:25; 1 Thess. 4:15,17; Rev. 3:11, 22:6,7,10,12,20.

7. The theory that Jesus was not really dead when he was taken down from the cross has been prevalent. See, e.g., Hugh J. Schonfield, *The Passover Plot* (New York: Bantam Books, 1966). It should also be noted that Muslims deny that Jesus

was crucified, mainly on the basis of a passage in the Qur'an (Surah IV: 157). They usually conjecture that someone else was crucified in his place.

8. 1 Kings 17:21–22; 2 Kings 4:32–35, 13:21; Matt. 9:18–25; Luke 7:12–15; John 11:43–44.

9. See Theodore M. Drange, "Biblical Contradictions Regarding Salvation," *Free Inquiry* 14 (Summer 1994): 56–57.

10. Gen. 9:25; Exod. 21:2–6,20–21; Lev. 25:44–46; Deut. 15:12,17, 28:68; Jer. 27:8,12; Joel 3:8; Eph. 6:5–7; Col. 3:22; 1 Tim. 6:1; Titus 2:9; 1 Pet. 2:18–21.

11. 1 Cor. 11:5–6, 14:34–35; Eph. 5:22–23; 1 Tim. 2:9–14; Titus 2:5; 1 Pet. 3:1.

12. See Isa. 33:14; Matt. 13:40–42,49–50, 25:41,46; Mark 9:43–48; Jude 6–7; Rev. 14:10–11.

Appendix E

The Very Concept of an Afterlife

In chapter 9, various objections to the Afterlife Defense were raised. But the most fundamental objection to it, whether the defense is applied to AE or to ANB, is that the very concept of an afterlife is in one way or another incoherent or inconceivable. In other words, it is an idea which cannot even be entertained in thought and it is in a certain sense meaningless to speak of people surviving their own death. In this appendix I shall consider some reasons for making such a claim. However, my result (as in some previous appendices) will be to some extent inconclusive, and that is one reason I did not include it in the main body of the text. Another reason is that there are other objections to the Afterlife Defense that are less controversial than the one to be discussed here, and those are the ones I focused on in chapter 9.

E.1. The Life-after-life Objection

First of all, there is an argument that is clearly too simple-minded. It says that an afterlife is life after death and that death is the end of life. Therefore, an afterlife is life after life has ended. But it is logically impossible for there to be life after life has ended, since a thing can't still be there after it is no longer there. Thus, an afterlife is logically impossible.

There are at least two ways to attack this argument. One way is to declare that when death ends life, it is only a *temporary* end. This could be called the "gap theory": after a temporal gap, the dead come back to life and are dead no more, at least for the time being. One biblical example of that is when Jesus raised Lazarus from the dead. Lazarus really was dead. His sister Martha even told Jesus, "Lord, by this time he stinks: for he has been dead four days" (John 11:39). But then Jesus brought Lazarus back to life and he was alive, not dead. Still later, he was dead again, a second time. Perhaps Lazarus will come back to life again even after that. (If so, then it might be thought to be, for him, a second afterlife.) In any case, death and life are regarded as mutually exclusive, but just temporary. When one ends, the other begins, and there could, in principle, be recurrent cycles of them, as maintained in some religions. So the step to reject in the Life-after-life Objection is the one which says, "it is logically impossible for there to be life after life has ended." On the contrary, there *could* be life after life has ended simply because it ended only temporarily, not permanently. Just as a song could be sung again and again, with temporal gaps in between, so also a person could live again and again, with temporal gaps in between.

I have two main responses to this. First, I don't want to call the Lazarus example an "afterlife" in the most important sense. Let us draw a distinction between two concepts of death: call them "technical death" and "reducible death." Technical death occurs when the person satisfies all the medical criteria for death but the body is not yet destroyed. The circulation and respiration have ceased. The brain is totally inactive. The body may even have begun to rot. Presumably Lazarus met all these criteria and so was "technically dead." The other concept, reducible death, applies only to the case where the body and brain are totally destroyed. For example, if the body of Lazarus had been cremated and the ashes scattered over the River Jordan, then he would have been "reducibly dead." (If that had been done, then it would have been harder for Jesus to bring him back: Jesus presumably would then have had to create a completely new body for Lazarus.) Using this distinction between "technical death" and "reducible death," I want to define an "afterlife" as the life of a person after he or she has undergone reducible death, in which the body and brain have been totally and irreversibly destroyed.

Note that "reducible death" does *not* mean "death without an afterlife." To define it that way would be question-begging, for it would make the term "afterlife" self-contradictory. I am only narrowing the concept slightly, requiring of an afterlife that it occur only after a person's body and brain have been totally destroyed. I feel it is legitimate to define "afterlife" in this narrower way because I think most people regard it in such terms, and the Afterlife Defense could be interpreted as making reference only to the narrower concept. Certainly if there were any true believers in an afterlife, then they would indeed be taking it as I take it: life that follows reducible death. It is this narrower concept of an afterlife that is appealed to in the present book.

I readily grant that for a person to come back to life after having been just technically dead, though perhaps empirically impossible, is nevertheless conceivable. The ancient pharaohs of Egypt had such an event in mind when they had tombs prepared for themselves. And wealthy people who pay to have their bodies frozen after they die, in the hope of later being revived, also have in mind this notion of coming back to life after having been technically dead. However, if that should ever actually take place, then I suspect that some people would declare that those who are revived were not "really dead" in the first place. They would be seen to be more like the zombies who are revived from apparent death in Haiti or the legendary Rip Van Winkle who slept for twenty years. When it is said here that such beings who come back are not really dead, perhaps the concept of "reducible death" is being appealed to. That is, to be "really dead," according to that line of thought, one would need to be "reducibly dead" in my sense: one's body and brain would need to be totally destroyed. Since that is what actually happens to just about everybody after death, we could, for simplicity, take that to be what is meant in the Afterlife Defense when it says that everyone will have an afterlife.

My definition (or redefinition) of the term "afterlife" as life following reducible death does not in itself refute the gap theory. People could still have an afterlife, so far as that theory is concerned, because they could come back to life again in a *new* body, or at least so it might be claimed. Thus, even if the old body were to be totally and irreversibly destroyed, the same person might still be around, having received a new body. My point here, however, is that the model for the afterlife cannot be that of the raising of Lazarus as described in the Bible. Some other model is needed.

A more important objection to the gap theory is that the very idea of a gap is unclear. Is a person the sort of thing that could cease to exist for a while and then come back into existence later on? I want to say no, but let us postpone this issue, as it will be relevant to our discussion below in section E.3. I shall also want to object to the analogy made in the gap theory between a person and a song. Is a person like a song that can be sung again and again? If persons are unique and not pluralizable, then that may destroy the song analogy. These are matters I shall take up later.

There is another way to try to escape the alleged contradiction of "life after life" and that is by distinguishing two different kinds of life: physical life and mental life. Mental life could still exist, or so it might be argued, even after physical life has ended. The step in the Life-after-life Objection that says "an afterlife is life after life has ended" might imply that an afterlife is mental life that continues to exist after physical life has ended. But then there would be nothing logically impossible about an afterlife, for there is no contradiction in *that* concept of "life after life."

One objection to this idea is that if "mental life following physical life" involves the existence of a mind without a brain, then it would be empirically impossible. In other words, the situation of mental life going on without any physical basis for it would violate fundamental laws of nature. Let us postpone consideration of such empirical issues to a later section.

Another objection has to do with *identifying* the so-called "mental life" which continues on after physical life has ended. If there is no body or brain to appeal to, then how could such identification be made? We will consider this issue in the next section. If identification of a disembodied person is impossible, then perhaps the very idea of "mental life following physical life" would turn out to be inconceivable, and perhaps logically impossible as well. So far as the Life-after-life Objection is concerned, we may for the time being dismiss it as too simple in itself. But it leads to complex issues, and within them there may be more formidable objections to the conceivability of "life after life."

E.2. A Disembodied Afterlife

Given our understanding of an afterlife as being a *personal* one, it seems clear that in order for an afterlife to be conceptually possible, there must be some way for the identity of the person having that afterlife to be established (either by someone else or by the person himself). If there were no way whatsoever to establish a person's identity, then there would be no way to connect him or her with anyone in a former life, and thus no way to conceive of that particular person as presently being in an afterlife.

However, in a totally disembodied afterlife, i.e., one in which there is no body of any sort, it seems that people would have to be blind, deaf, numb, paralyzed, and incommunicado: such people could not see, hear, or feel anything by touch, or perform any physical action, or communicate with anyone else, since there would be no body by means of which any of these things could be done. Therefore, there would be no way for such people to be identified by anyone else. Furthermore, if such people were to have any thoughts or ideas about who they are, then, without any bodies by which they could perform actions, they would have no way to determine for sure that the thoughts or ideas are (genuine) memories, as opposed to mere figments of imagination. So, such people would have no way to establish their own identities either. Hence, there would be no way for the identities of such people to be established either by someone else or by they themselves. It follows that a totally disembodied afterlife is not conceptually possible. This may be referred to as the "Identification Objection."

The soundness or unsoundness of the objection depends in large part on whether there can occur perceptions without sense organs. Is that at all conceivable? Some people have reported having so-called "out-of-the-body" experiences. Such experiences would presumably be like those of a disembodied afterlife. In one biblical verse (2 Cor. 5:8), St. Paul spoke of his desire to be "absent from the body and present with the Lord." Presumably people who say such things claim to have had, or to be able to conceive of, experiences that occur apart from any body of any sort.

However, I am not one who has ever had such an experience, and I am skeptical about it all. For one thing, I don't understand what seeing without eyes, or even a head, could come to. If there is no head to block one's vision, then does one see in all directions simultaneously? Also, does one see from a certain location? If so, what exactly is it that is located there to do the seeing? Presumably there are no eyes to do the seeing, so what is it that is there in that exact spot that is doing it? Similarly with hearing and the other senses. How can real hearing, as opposed to hallucinatory hearing, occur in the total absence of a physical body? And how can communication occur in such a circumstance? Is it by mental telepathy? If so, then what exactly is that and how does it work? For example, how does the receiver of the telepathic message know who the sender is (or even that it is a message at all)? These are not merely matters of detail, but fundamental conceptual issues. There are many such puzzles which arise, and for which the people who report "out-of-the-body" experiences have not as yet, so far as I know, provided solutions. Maybe such people are simply hallucinating or dreaming and then misdescribing their experience as being an actual perception rather than a hallucination or dream. So far as I can see, the challenge of the Identification Objection, that of describing how someone in a totally disembodied afterlife might possibly be identified, has not been met.

I am not aware of any studies that have established that those who report "out-of-the-body" experiences could not have been merely hallucinating or dreaming. For example, such people should be able to provide information about objects in remote places (that they witnessed while "out of the body"). But none of them, so far as I know, has demonstrated possession of such abilities. Until such studies come along, I am inclined simply to dismiss the various reports of experiences that occur apart from a body. Those reports do not prove anything to those of us who have never had any such experiences, even regarding the very possibility of the experience itself. For the time being, until we ourselves have actually had the experience, we are forced to classify the idea of a disembodied afterlife as something incoherent or inconceivable.

This topic connects with the issue (considered in chapter 3) whether it makes sense to speak of God as a disembodied being. God is usually thought of as a being who knows about what is going on and who performs physical actions. He is supposed to have created the universe, flooded the earth, destroyed cities, brought his people out of Egypt (Exod. 13:14), and to have played an active role in the affairs of nations. The coming "kingdom of God" is to be an active reign. The question might be raised how God can do such things if he has no body. I have no conception of how that might occur. Perhaps even theists who say, "God has no body," really do think of him as having a body anyway. (It may be analogous to the situation of those who say, "God is perfectly loving," but who think of him as behaving in a very unloving way.) On the other hand, I remain open to the possibility that some sense could be made of the idea of experiences occurring apart from a body. If I should in the future come to grasp that notion, then perhaps I shall then be able to comprehend the idea of a bodiless deity as well.

E.3. An Embodied Afterlife: the Problem of Identification

An embodied afterlife, that is, one in which the person receives a new body, would seem to have more hope of at least being comprehensible, especially to those of us who have never had an "out-of-the-body" experience. But there are at least two objections that might be raised against the idea of an embodied afterlife. I shall take up one of them in this section and another in the next section.

The same point should be raised as in section E.2: in order for any sort of afterlife to be conceptually possible, there must be some way for the identity of the person having that afterlife to be established, either by someone else or by the person in question. Now, in an embodied afterlife, we can say, using our concept of an afterlife as life following reducible death, that a person must receive a *new* body (i.e., a numerically different body from the one that the person had before dying). If there is to be any physical resemblance between the new body and the old, then the new body would need to be some sort of *replica* of the former body. But there is no way for the identity of a person to be established (either by someone else or by the person in question) by appeal to, or through the use of, a replica of a former body. There would be no way to know that this is the person in question rather than some sort of replacement or substitute for the person. Hence, there would be no way for a person's identity in an embodied afterlife to be established (either by someone else or by the person in question). It follows that an embodied afterlife is not conceptually possible. This is the Identification Objection (of section E.2) applied to an embodied afterlife.

The step in the argument that most people would reject, I think, would be the premise that there would be no way to identify a person with a new body. It might be argued that even if Lazarus's body had been cremated and Jesus had created a completely new body for him, the person then created or recreated could have looked like the old Lazarus and could have had all of his mental characteristics, including memories. Lazarus's sister Martha and others in his family would then have had no trouble recognizing him. He would speak to them in just the way that Lazarus would have. And then they would know for sure that this person was indeed Lazarus and not some other being who had been conjured up to replace him. Thus, the given premise of the Identification Objection turns out to be false. In effect, this defense against the Identification Objection appeals to what I referred to previously as the "gap theory." It is the idea that people can have gaps in their existence. Their bodies and brains can be destroyed and they can even go out of existence for a brief spell only to be recreated again later on in a new body and with a new brain.

What I most dislike about the given defense is its claim that the family and friends of Lazarus would know for sure that this being created by Jesus was indeed Lazarus. How could those who cremated the body of Lazarus now know for sure that this new being was Lazarus? Isn't it more likely that they would take him to be some sort of substitute or stand-in? How can people have gaps in their existence? They are not like shadows that can go out of existence at one moment and come back into existence in the next. We really have no good way to deal with or even comprehend such notions. Our concept of a person seems not to leave room for the possibility of a person popping into and out of existence. Such a thing would not appear to us to be a person but a phantom.

Another problem has to do with the *form* of the new body. What does the doctrine of resurrection have to say about this? Suppose a man dies at the age of ninety-five, crippled, frail, wrinkled, and so on. What sort of body will he have in the resurrection? Will it be a body similar to the one he had at age twenty-five? Who will recognize it? And what about those who were deformed or handicapped all through life? What sort of resurrection body might they receive? Could they still be the *same* people they were if they received a body very unlike the one they had before? Then there are special cases like people who were very obese at one time and very thin at another time or who had undertaken some sort of body-altering operation, such as an amputation or radical plastic surgery or a sex-change operation. What type of body will they get in the resurrection? And who is to decide?

Another special case is that of fetuses and infants who die very young. Will they receive adult bodies in the resurrection? If so, then what is to be made of the "gap" in their lives and how could such people possibly be identified? They would lack a childhood and an adolescence. What could bridge such a large gap in a way that would make the adult the very same person as the infant?

According to Frank B. Dilley, we should leave all such identification problems up to God:

> Surely if the religious view that God created selves to begin with is accepted as possibly true, one should not cavil at the further claim that God is able to recreate that self, this time out of imperishable substance, and be able to certify that He has created the same self again. . . . Doubts as to whether I am *really* a reconstituted me would be ridiculous in heaven. However, should the tempter succeed in raising such doubts, I

could always, as I have noted, ask God whether what he recreated was really me. (Original italics)[1]

In effect, Dilley is saying, "Not to worry: God will solve all these problems." But that won't do at all, for these are not merely practical matters. They are conceptual difficulties that cast doubt on the very possibility of framing an intelligible theory of the resurrection. Omnipotent beings cannot perform inconceivable acts. They can only solve practical problems, not conceptual ones. It would be like defining the resurrection as "a state in which people draw four-sided triangles" and then answering the question "how is that possible?" with "Not to worry: God will show them how to do it." When the issue is a conceptual one, it does not help to "leave it to God." As another example, one cannot refute a valid proof simply by declaring that God can make the premises true and the conclusion false. Without some solution to the conceptual problems, the resurrection theorist must concede that his theory is simply absurd.

What is needed is a statement of both necessary and sufficient conditions for personal identity through time that would permit a person to survive (reducible) death. Apart from failing to solve the conceptual problem, Dilley's appeal to God (if it were to work) would only supply a sufficient condition, not a necessary condition. So it suffers from incompleteness as well as obscurity.

As a last resort, someone might introduce the term "soul." It might be said that each of us possesses a soul and it is not the body but the soul that individuates us and makes us unique. The main problem with this is that it is unclear just what a soul is supposed to be. What are its properties or constituents, if any? How might it be appealed to in order to identify a person? What is one to look for? What test might be performed to ascertain that person A, who exists at a certain time, and person B, who exists at a later time, have the *same* soul? Such fundamental conceptual issues have never been adequately addressed, and until they are, the "Soul Theory" will be of no use in solving the identification problem or defending the Afterlife Defense against the Identification Objection.

To go back to the example of Lazarus where the body had been cremated, suppose Jesus had created *two* new bodies, both of them looking and behaving just like Lazarus. Would Martha and the others have accepted *both* of them to be Lazarus returned from the dead? Probably the two new persons would be taken to be Lazarus-substitutes rather than Lazarus himself. Anyone who goes along with my view here ought to accept the claim that there would be no way to identify someone if the person's body is no longer available. It might be objected that the identification would be possible if there were definitely only one new body. But that will not work. Even if Martha and the others were presented with only one being who resembles Lazarus and behaves like him, isn't there at least the possibility that there is another such being over there behind the hill or that Jesus will create a second one five minutes from now? Given these possibilities, how could they "know for sure" that this being standing in front of them really is Lazarus? Even if he claims to be Lazarus, there is always the possibility that he is wrong. If there were two of them both claiming to be Lazarus, then surely at least one of them would have to be mistaken about who he is, and there would be no way to tell which one it is. We will do more with the pluralization issue in the next section.

The upshot of all this is that there would be no way to definitely identify Jesus' creature as Lazarus, either by others or by himself. And this same situation would exist whenever someone's body and brain were totally destroyed. If there suddenly appears a being who looks and behaves like the departed one, then there really would be no way for anyone (including the being himself, whoever he is) to know for sure who he actually is. I lean toward the view that the Identification Objection is sound and that it establishes the inconceivability of an embodied afterlife.

E.4. An Embodied Afterlife:
the Problem of Pluralizability

Here is another closely related argument against the conceivability of an embodied afterlife. We have seen that the identification of a person in an afterlife cannot be by the body (which is necessarily something "new"). It must be by something mental, or at least nonphysical. But everything in that category is pluralizable, i.e., of a sort such that it would be possible for there to be two or more of them. Thus, if it were conceptually possible for a person to have an afterlife, then that person would need to be the sort of thing that is pluralizable, i.e., rendered plural. In other words, a person would need to be capable of becoming two or more (not copies, but "originals"). For example, Lazarus would need to be capable of becoming two or more ("original") Lazaruses. But every person is necessarily unique: it is not possible that there should be two or more ("originals") of a person. Hence, it is not conceptually possible for a person to have an embodied afterlife. Let us call this the "Pluralization Objection."

There is much to recommend this argument. Since we have defined an "afterlife" as life following reducible death, it seems clear that such a life could always be plural. There is no longer any original body or original brain to appeal to in order to establish identity, so that in itself seems to make pluralization possible. If a new body has to be created, then there could always just as easily be two (or more) of them as for there to be only one. It is only the existence of "an essential original" that (conceptually) prevents pluralization.

One might object that God is benevolent and would not pluralize anyone. But that misses the point of the argument. The issue is not "*Would* God do it?" but "*Could* God do it?" I have gone by the assumption that, though God is omnipotent, he is still restricted by conceptual requirements: he can do anything except that which is conceptually impossible. (To *not* make this assumption would lead to intolerable difficulties both in one's theodicy and one's theology generally.) Thus, if the pluralization of a person is conceptually impossible, then not even an omnipotent being could do it. Yet, if there were such a state as an afterlife (as we have defined it), then God would need to be able to pluralize a person in that state, as argued above in the case of Lazarus. It follows that if the pluralization of a person is conceptually impossible, then an afterlife as we have defined it is also conceptually impossible. That is the Pluralization Objection in a nutshell.

One might again introduce the idea of a "soul" as something possessed by each person and which is necessarily unique and nonpluralizable. Then it might be maintained that the pluralization of a person in an afterlife is impossible simply because an afterlife is the survival of death by a person's soul and souls are necessarily unique. Thus, even though pluralization of a person is inconceivable, an afterlife would be conceivable, because to have an afterlife would not entail pluralizability. But, again, this won't do. We do not know what a soul is supposed to be. No information is given about how to perceive or recognize souls. And it would be vacuous to define a soul as simply that, whatever it may be, which identifies and individuates a person. In everyday discourse, persons are identified and individuated by their physical and behavioral characteristics. If souls are, by definition, nonphysical, then they cannot be identifying or individuating principles, so far as our ordinary concept of a person is concerned. In the end, the Soul Theory is rejected because it has not been given any operational meaning. Since no criterion has been supplied for identifying or individuating souls, whatever they may be, soul-talk must be regarded as cognitively meaningless.

Taking a quite different course, one might argue that pluralization *is* conceivable after all. There *could* be two, or ten, Lazaruses. In that case, even if an afterlife does require pluralizability, the Pluralization Objection would still fail because its claim that pluralization is inconceivable is to be rejected. On that view, people *are* like songs, after all. Being nothing more than minds, or sets of mental characteristics, they are universals rather than particulars. Dilley seems to take this sort of position when he says, "There is no reason . . . to deny that there can be multiple versions of me."[2] Presumably he would liken himself to a computer program which is capable of being put on many different disks or tapes. Just as all the disks and tapes would have on them the very same program, so also it is possible for many different bodies to be the bodies of the very same person. Dilley would say, then, that the pluralization of a person is indeed possible.

But I have a quite different concept of a person. To me, a person is a particular, a unique individual. It makes no sense to speak of "Lazaruses," or Lazarus pluralized. As I think about myself, who and what I am, there is no way for pluralization to fit into the picture. I ask you: can you imagine yourself pluralized? Does that notion make sense to you? Think of it in terms of a future afterlife. Can you imagine yourself becoming ten people in heaven or becoming resurrected as ten different bodies? Into which body would you anticipate going? Or would you somehow anticipate going into all ten of them simultaneously? If you agree with me that such a notion is unintelligible, then you presumably share my concept of a person and should agree with that part of the Pluralization Objection. On the other hand, I must concede that Dilley and others who have the idea of a person as a kind of abstraction (like a computer program) can get around the Pluralization Objection.

In the end, it is not totally clear whether an afterlife has been proven to be inconceivable. It depends on the outcome of various unresolved issues, such as: (1) the issue of whether or not "out-of-the-body" experiences are conceivable, (2) whether or not a theory of personal identity through time can be formulated which would permit a person to survive (reducible) death, (3) whether or not the term "soul" can be intelligibly and usefully defined, and (4) the issue of whether or not a person can be thought of as an abstraction, like a computer program. My own present view is negative on all of these, but I want to retain an open mind on them, too.

E.5. Empirical Considerations

It will be useful to divide this section of appendix E into three different sub-sections, each dealing with a different type of empirical consideration related to the afterlife.

E.51. The Belief Argument

Since billions of people claim to believe in a personal afterlife, it might be argued that such an afterlife must at least be conceivable, for it is impossible to believe in the existence of something that cannot be conceived. Belief is not merely a disposition to assert and assent to some sentence, but requires that there be some mental object of belief. Thus, the very act of coming to believe a proposition P requires thinking P or entertaining P in thought. So if people really are believing the proposition that there is an afterlife, then they must be conceiving it; therefore it must be conceivable. We can call this the "Belief Argument." I include it as an "empirical consideration" because whether or not people actually do believe something seems to be an empirical issue, but that may not be the best way to construe the matter.

The Belief Argument is inconclusive, for there remains the possibility that when people *say* they believe in an afterlife, they really don't. They may be mistaken or confused about their own beliefs and are really believing in something else, something other than an afterlife. Maybe, instead, they are in some sort of "state of denial" and have the suppressed idea that death does not occur and that life simply goes on and on. One cannot assume that people really believe something simply because they say they believe it, for their verbal report could be just the result of some sort of conditioning process. It could be that children are simply trained from very a young age to recite religious slogans and to say of themselves that they believe those slogans. (This was referred to in section 3.3 as the "mumbo-jumbo theory" of some forms of religious language.) Perhaps *that* is the source of the widespread claim by people that they believe in an afterlife. Note that people could just as well claim to believe in time travel, or four-sided triangles for that matter, but that in itself would not make time travel or four-sided triangles conceivable. The verbal report could be merely the result of conceptual confusion brought about by misleading experiences. In the end, it may not be an empirical matter at all.

E.52. Brain Correlations

Consider the following argument (call it the "Brain-correlations Argument"):

(1) Studies have established such a strong correlation between brain events and mental events that it would be legitimate to declare the latter empirically impossible without the former.

(2) But, in an afterlife, there necessarily occur mental events without brain events.

(3) Hence, an afterlife is empirically impossible.

Is this argument sound? To say of a situation that it is empirically impossible is not to say that it is inconceivable, only that it is a violation of some known law(s) of nature. Although premise (1) of the Brain-correlations Argument is by no means clearly true, I shall not question it here. Scientists have determined that certain types of brain damage are always followed by a loss of mental function, which implies that total destruction of the brain results in total annihilation of the mind. And other correlations between brain and mind have been discovered, in addition to the brain-damage connection. But whether or not any of them are lawlike relationships is a complex topic which I shall here bypass.

It might be argued that premise (2) of the argument, which denies that all mental events in an afterlife could occur within brains, is just flat-out false. Since the whole Christian doctrine of resurrection involves an *embodied* afterlife, that doctrine could easily accommodate the idea that all mental events that ever take place in an afterlife occur within the resurrection and hence within brains.

In response to this, it should be pointed out that many people, even Christians, think of the afterlife as a mind without a body. They talk of the soul going to heaven, and such. Well, in that sort of afterlife, there are no brain events at all, so the argument clearly does apply to it. Even Christians who advocate the resurrection doctrine often regard the person as existing and as being conscious in some sort of intermediate state while waiting for the resurrection to occur. So again there would be the idea of mental events without brain events. The point of the Brain-correlations Argument is that science has established physiological laws to the effect that mental life ceases when brain processes cease. For there to be any conscious life at all following brain death, no matter how temporary, it would have to be a violation of such laws. It would have to be a miracle. It is clear that this point does have relevance to the common description of the afterlife as (at least at some stage) involving a mind without a body. So the given argument does indeed apply there.

This brings us to the conclusion of the argument. Even if it were true, one could ask, "So what?" To say of an event that it is empirically impossible is only to say that it conflicts with some law(s) of nature. Despite the conflict, religious people have no trouble believing in such events. They believe that Jesus of Nazareth created loaves of bread out of nothing, that he walked on water, and that he came back to life again on earth after having died. They say things like: "Jesus showed that an afterlife is possible." How can people believe that such events actually occurred when the events violate known laws of nature and are therefore empirically impossible? The studies referred to in the Brain-correlations Argument only impress scientifically minded people. They do not impress all religious people, or even most of them. Those who are not scientifically minded say, "There is a whole other world out there, a spiritual reality that is beyond scientific investigation. It is a world that includes miracles. Scientists only provide a part of the truth, not the whole truth." We can see from this that the conclusion of the argument is not forceful enough for many people. They have no trouble simply accepting it as true and yet continuing to believe in a disembodied afterlife. What is needed to debate such people is an argument to show not only that a disembodied afterlife is empirically impossible, but that it is *conceptually* impossible, that is, that the very idea of it is inconceivable or unintelligible. I am not claiming that the Brain-correlations Argument is unsound or defective in any way, only that it will not impress people who believe in miracles. The really important philosophical issues do not arise with that argument but with the ones considered in sections E.2–E.4.

E.53. Alleged Evidence for an Afterlife

Some think that empirical evidence has been found that supports the existence of an afterlife. They may point to reports of near-death experiences or reincarnations or ghosts summoned by mediums. But as I see it, all this is misguided. Near-death experiences are not relevant to the concept of an afterlife as we have defined it, for the situation does not even involve technical death, let alone the complete destruction of body and brain. With alleged reincarnations, the main issue has to do with *identifying* the person as someone who had died, that is, with showing how the challenge of the Identification Objection might be met. So far as I know, this has never been accomplished satisfactorily in any of the cases studied. And alleged ghosts summoned by mediums have been shown to be hoaxes in many cases. It is possible that they are all hoaxes or in some other way explainable naturalistically. It doesn't make sense to try to find evidence for a proposition before one has rendered intelligible what that proposition is supposed to be. Before one can even make sense of the evidential problem (i.e., the problem of whether or not there is any evidence for an afterlife), one first needs to solve the conceptual problem, which is the problem of what the term "afterlife" might mean in operational terms, or what an afterlife could possibly be like if there were such a state.

My conclusion is that the conceptual problem of the afterlife has not as yet been satisfactorily solved. Maybe some people can make sense of the idea, for example, people who have had "out-of-the-body" experiences or who have the concept of a person as an abstraction rather than as a particular. But those of us who are excluded from these select groups must simply find "afterlife-talk" to be unintelligible. For us, the Afterlife Defense (whether applied to AE or to ANB) cannot get off the ground. But since I did not wish to base my rejection of the Afterlife Defense on that consideration alone, I presented other objections to it in chapter 9.

Notes

1. Dilley, "Fool-Proof Proofs of God?" pp. 26–27.
2. Ibid, p. 27.

Appendix F

The Fine-Tuning Argument

When AE and ANB are fully formulated, including all support for all premises, they are inductive arguments, whichever concept of deity they are applied against. But a full assessment of inductive arguments calls for a consideration of the total evidence available. Therefore, a full assessment of the overall strength of AE and ANB would call for a consideration of all arguments which aim at the negation of their conclusion, which is the proposition that God exists. Although (in appendix D) I hope to have refuted the main (if not the only) argument for the existence of the God of evangelical Christianity, I have not attempted to refute arguments for the existence of God in general. Hence, I do not consider this book to contain a full assessment of the strength of AE and ANB as applied to God in general, since it does not include a consideration of all (or even many) arguments for God's existence. Such a consideration is omitted because it would be too long, and it has already been done reasonably well elsewhere (e.g., in the previously mentioned books by Michael Martin and J. L. Mackie).

It is my view, however, that none of the arguments for God's existence that have ever been put forward in the public arena is any good. Using the scale that I appealed to in chapters 12–15, I would give them all a score of zero. I do not mean to include here appeals to private religious experiences, for I have no way to assess those. If someone claims to have experienced God directly, then that person may have some reason to believe that God exists, but such a situation has no relevance for me or anyone else, so far as I can see. Not having had anything like the alleged experience, I have little or no idea what such a person might be talking about. There would not in that situation be any objective evidence or argument that is relevant to the assessment of AE and ANB, both of which are arguments put forward in the public arena.

There are at least three places in this book where my view regarding the lack of success of theistic arguments would be relevant. One of them is section 7.21, where the Lack-of-evidence Objection to TDN is used to argue that there is no good evidence for any of the propositions of the gospel message, even the first one which simply states in effect that God exists. Another place is in section 9.2 where a certain version of ADN claims that part of what gains people an opportunity for salvation in the afterlife is their rational response to general revelation. I would argue that there is no such thing as general revelation, where that is taken to be good evidence of God's handiwork in nature. Finally, another place is chapter 14, where the Probability Objection is used to attack UDE and UDN as applied to God in general. Those versions of UDE and UDN appeal to hypotheses or worldviews (UEH and UNH) which are large conjunctions of propositions. In order for the hypotheses to have a probability at least as great as the ones in opposition to them (AEH and ANH), it is necessary that there be good evidence for all the individual conjuncts that comprise them, including the one which proclaims the existence of God. But the Probability Objection maintains that there is no good evidence for any of those conjuncts, even the one about God's existence. Hence, there is good reason to declare that the hypotheses in question do not have a probability at least as great as that of the hypotheses which are in opposition to them.

But the main connection between the project of this book and my claim that no theistic arguments succeed lies in my assessment of AE and ANB as strong arguments, even within the context of theism in general. It is clear that such an assessment very much depends on the given claim. Nevertheless, the claim has not been adequately supported. In this appendix I hope to partially rectify that in the hope that it will point the way toward a fuller treatment elsewhere.

F.1. The Argument Formulated

In order to sketch out my position regarding (public) arguments for God's existence, I shall pick one to consider. Much of what I say about that one could be applied to others. The argument that I would like to consider here is that version of the Argument from Design which appeals to the so-called "fine-tuning" of the physical constants of the universe. Let us call it "the Fine-tuning Argument." One advocate of it is George Schlesinger, who says:

> In the last few decades a tantalizingly great number of exceedingly rare coincidences, vital for the existence of a minimally stable universe and without which no form of life could exist anywhere, have been discovered.
> . . . [G]iven any one of infinitely many universes, some conjunction or

other of physical magnitudes will have to obtain. However, the prevailing conjunction is not merely one of indefinitely many; it is also an instance of a virtually infinitesimally rare *kind* of universe: the kind capable of sustaining life. The hypothesis that it was produced by a Being interested in sentient organic systems adequately explains this otherwise inexplicably astonishing fact.[1]

A more precise formulation of the argument is the following, with premises indicated by "P" and conclusions by "C":

(P1)   The combination of physical constants that we observe in our universe is the only one capable of sustaining life as we know it.

(P2)   Other combinations of physical constants are conceivable.

(C3)   Therefore, some explanation is needed why our actual combination of physical constants exists rather than a different one.

(P4)   The very best explanation of the given fact is that our universe, with the particular combination of physical constants that it has, was created out of nothing by a single being who is omnipotent, omniscient, all-loving, eternal, and interested in sentient organic systems, and that he "fine-tuned" those constants in a way which would lead to the evolution of such systems.

(P5)   But such a being as described in (P4) is what people mean by "God."

(C6)   Hence [from (P4) & (P5)], there is good evidence that God exists.

Various objections might be raised against this argument. For the sake of brevity, I shall just consider two objections to its premise (P4). They may be labeled "The Inadequacy Objection" and the "Alternate-explanations Objection."

F.2. The Inadequacy Objection

The explanation described in (P4) can be called "the God Hypothesis," or just "G" for short. I do not find that G is a good explanation, or even adequate, for the fact to be explained. First, it does not supply any information about *how* God is supposed to have created anything or *how* he is supposed to have "fine-tuned" the physical constants of the universe. It fails to address what Paul Edwards calls the "*modus operandi* problem."[2] For that reason, it is an explanation that is grossly incomplete. And not only is creation out of nothing not described within G, but it is an idea that conflicts with the conservation laws of modern physics. It is also an idea which is hard to understand. We have no experience on the basis of which we might understand it. None of the acts of creation with which we are acquainted (such as by artists) involves creation out of nothing. Not only is G incomplete, but it is incomprehensible as well.

Second, we need some understanding of the properties ascribed to the being in G, but they are very hard to comprehend. What, exactly, does it mean to say of some being that it is omnipotent, omniscient, all-loving, and eternal? Each of these properties is in need of clarification, especially as they might be applied to a being that exists prior to the existence of a physical universe. How could such a being, which, on the basis of premise (P5), I shall refer to as "God," possess the given property with no physical universe in existence? For example, what sorts of actions did he (as an omnipotent being) perform and what sorts of things did he (as an all-loving being) love? Advocates of G usually declare it to be simply a "great mystery," but that is unsatisfactory in an explanation. We started out with a mystery (why the physical constants are what they are). How has anything been adequately explained or illuminated if we end up with a still greater mystery (the nature of God and his activities)? G is too obscure to be regarded as an adequate explanation of anything.

Third, according to G, God had an interest in sentient organic systems. Why, then, did he take so long to bring them about? And why did he confine his efforts to the planet earth? Science tells us that more than ten billion years passed from the Big Bang to the origin of sentient organic systems on the planet earth. Why did God allow the process to take so long? As an omnipotent and omniscient being, why didn't he simply create the sort of systems in which he had an interest right from the start? And why didn't he create them all over the universe rather than just in one insignificant section? It seems unreasonable to think that a being with the properties ascribed to God in G would have done the thing that G says he did. G is a poor explanation because it is unreasonable and counterintuitive. It certainly cannot be said to *adequately* explain anything.

Finally, even assuming that God was willing to wait a long time and to confine his interest to just a small bit of space, there is the question why he didn't do a better job with evolution. He is supposed to be all-loving. Why, then, didn't he set up evolution in a way would cause less suffering to the organisms involved in it? One thing he could have done would have been to increase the proportion of beneficial mutations within the total set of mutations. Instead of having only about one out of a thousand mutations turn out beneficial to the organism and the species, why not have it, say, one out of five? That would certainly have speeded up the evolutionary process and eliminated much unnecessary suffering along the way. It is an additional bit of ""fine-tuning" that one would expect from the sort of being described in G.

Furthermore, God could have arranged things so that the initial conditions on the planet earth were more stable and more conducive to the well-being of the sentient organic systems in which he is said to have an interest. For example, there could be fewer storms, earthquakes, volcanic eruptions, and droughts, as well as a more favorable balance between the power of germs and the immune systems of the more advanced organic systems on the planet. G is incomplete and anomalous in failing to explain why God, who is claimed to love those more advanced systems, did not arrange things in the ways described.

For all of these reasons, G can be seen to be a very poor explanation for the fact to be explained. It is incomplete, incomprehensible, obscure, unreasonable, anomalous, and counterintuitive. It also appeals to still greater mysteries than the fact to be explained, so it hardly qualifies as an adequate explanation. It fails to illuminate anything or to enlarge our understanding. This may be called the Inadequacy Objection. To be "the very best" among competitors, an explanation needs to be at least minimally adequate, but G does not qualify in that respect. Hence, (P4) of the Fine-tuning Argument is a false premise.

F.3. The Alternate-explanations Objection

Another way to attack premise (P4) is to bring up explanations for the given phenomenon (the fact that our universe has the particular physical constants that it has) other than G. First, as a preliminary point, it strikes me as possible that there should be some *physical* explanation for why our universe *had to* have the particular combination that it has. It may be that scientists of the future will discover such an explanation. If they were to come up with some sort of "theory of everything," then it would presumably show why other combinations of constants (though conceivable) are not physically possible. If any physicist has proven that no such explanation could ever be given, no matter how far the science of physics advances, then I am not aware of that. Schlesinger made no reference to any such proof. Of course, he could say that premise (P4) in the Fine-tuning Argument only appeals to actual explanations, not merely to possible ones. The suggestion about a "theory of everything" is akin to the "Unknown-purpose Defense" in that it only says there may be an explanation without actually providing one. Schlesinger may insist that we confine our attention to *actual* explanations and claim simply that the God hypothesis, or G, is the best explanation of all those that might be put forward today.

The Alternate-explanations Objection is that there are other explanations for the given fact that might be put forward today and which are at least as good as G. One of them is that the combination of physical constants that we observe in our universe is sheer coincidence, meaning that it just is the way it happens to be and has no explanation beyond it being simply a brute fact. This could be called the "Brute-fact Hypothesis," or B, for short. One advantage of B over G is that it does not have the defects mentioned in section F.2. Another advantage is that B does not multiply entities beyond necessity. Schlesinger would probably say that B is deficient in that it fails to account for the fact that our universe is "one of a kind." But that is not so. Whatever combination of physical constants may obtain, it would be one of a kind.

Schlesinger would insist that our universe is a special kind (one capable of sustaining life as we know it) and that none of the other kinds would be special. But I see no reason to believe that. Assuming that other combinations of physical constants are physically possible, I see no reason to believe that all of them would result in a universe with less variety and complexity than our universe. For all anyone knows, maybe one or more of those alternate universes would have a lot more variety and complexity than does ours. There may not be life as we know it, but there may be other things going on in them that would be at least as interesting to us (if we could somehow peek in without being destroyed and comprehend what was going on) as the things which go on in our universe. The problem is that no one has much of an idea what sorts of things might emerge over time in universes having physical constants different from ours. There is no way for our science, at its present stage, to extrapolate that sort of information from what we know.

One point that should be made is that although we may be able to show that life as we know it could not possibly exist in one of the alternate universes, there is no proof that mind or intelligence could not exist. In fact, theists themselves believe that since God existed prior to our universe, it is thus possible for mind or intelligence to exist apart from the physical constants of our particular universe. Therefore, they should concede the possibility that some other combination of physical constants could, over time, produce a universe that contains mind or intelligence, even if it is in a form quite different from any life that exists on our planet. Schlesinger's claim that only the particular combination of physical constants in our universe is of a *special kind* is totally unsupported. There is no reason whatever to believe it.

There is another way to defend B against the charge that it fails to explain why our universe has the particular features that it has. It may be that there are regions of space-time that are completely outside our observational field and in many of those regions the laws and physical constants that obtain are *different* from the ones in our region. Thus, it would be illegitimate to assume that the only laws and physical constants that exist at all are the ones that we have observed. If there were to exist such other regions of space-time, then there would be nothing remarkable in the fact that we observe the particular physical constants that we do. It could simply be chalked up to coincidence.

Consider an analogy. Suppose sets of dice are being rolled in various parts of the universe. Each set contains one hundred dice. If one hundred sixes should suddenly come up on a single roll, the dice become conscious; otherwise, they remain unconscious. Given a sufficient number of rolls, it could be highly likely that one hundred sixes should come up somewhere. Wherever they would then happen to come up, they would become conscious and raise the question "Why did we come about here?" The answer is that it is simply a coincidence that one hundred sixes should come about *there*, but it is not puzzling that the event should happen at all *somewhere*, given the number of rolls that have occurred. It could be like that with the physical constants. In other parts of the universe, other physical constants obtain, but in our particular section, our constants obtain. If our constants had come about elsewhere, then in that place the resulting beings would ask, "Why here?" And the correct answer would be the same there as it is here and that is that it is simply sheer coincidence, which is another way of expressing the Brute-fact Hypothesis.

I conclude from this that the criticism of B in question, that it fails to explain the fact that only our particular universe is a special kind of universe, is an invalid criticism. First, since there is no reason whatever to believe the given alleged fact, it is illegitimate to refer to it as a "fact." Hence, there is no fact there that B fails to explain. And second, B does explain why the particular physical constants that we observe are as they are: it is simply sheer coincidence, and there need be nothing puzzling about that. I know of no advantages of G over B, but I do know of advantages of B over G (which were mentioned previously). I conclude that B is a better explanation of the given phenomenon than is G, which makes premise (P4) of the Fine-tuning Argument a false premise.

Of all the possible explanations for the fact that we observe certain physical constants in our universe, I regard B (the Brute-fact Hypothesis) to be the very best of the bunch. But there are still other explanations, different from both B and G, that are at least as good as G. One such explanation is that there exists a group of beings (let us call them "the fine-tuners") who go around and make occasional adjustments to the physical constants of our universe. The fine-tuners are beings who are very powerful but not omnipotent, highly intelligent but not omniscient, and generally good-natured but not all-loving. Like God, they are eternal, but they may not have created our present universe out of nothing. I shall set aside the question regarding the origin of our universe, since the issue before us is a different one: why our universe presently has the particular combination of physical constants that it has. The explanation under consideration is that the fine-tuners did it, having had the power and motivation to make it that way. Let us say that they had an interest in the evolution of ants, especially as it occurs when confronted by nuisances such as anteaters and humans. The fine-tuners made just those adjustments to the physical constants that they foresaw would lead to the eventual extinction of anteaters and humans (the latter bringing about their own extinction through overpopulation, pollution, and the exhaustion of resources), which would produce just the sort of world that the fine-tuners were interested in: one in which the ants take over the world. We could call this "the Fine-tuners Hypothesis," or "F" for short.

I think that B is a better explanation than F for many reasons. One of them is that F contains the unclear (perhaps even incomprehensible) notion of beings who are eternal. Another is that F does not explain *how* the fine-tuners do their work. The whole idea of a being or beings changing the physical constants of the universe is exceedingly obscure. F also seems to have the defect of introducing still greater mysteries. B, on the other hand, does not contain any such defects.

I think that although F is not as good an explanation for the physical constants of our universe as is B, it is not as bad as G. First of all, G has all the defects of F mentioned above. Further, F does not have any of the obscurity that surrounds G regarding the properties of being omnipotent, omniscient, and all-loving, because the fine-tuners lack those properties. Nor is F affected by the obscurity and incomprehensibility of creation out of nothing, for it does not appeal to that notion. Nor is there any problem for F about the long time that it took for ants to evolve or the fact that it is (presumably) only here on earth that such evolution occurred. The fine-tuners would have liked it to occur faster and in more locations, but they lacked the power and knowledge needed to bring that about. And finally, the enormous suffering that has occurred on earth through the centuries is not a problem for F. Either they did not feel bad about all that suffering (not being all-loving) or else they lacked the power and knowledge needed to prevent it. Thus, although G and F share several defects, there are still many other defects possessed only by G and not F. Furthermore, there are no defects possessed by F that are not possessed by G, so far as I can tell. For all of these reasons, G is a *worse* explanation than F, which again shows the falsity of premise (P4) of the Fine-tuning Argument. By appeal to alternate explanations for the facts in question, that premise is refuted, and thereby the argument itself is refuted.

I have not here considered other arguments for God's existence, but most of them are, like the Fine-tuning Argument, an appeal to the God Hypothesis as the "very best explanation" for something or other. I would attack all such arguments in the same way as indicated above: by means of the Inadequacy Objection and the Alternate-explanations Objection. I think they can all be refuted by one or both of such objections. There are other arguments of a different sort, such as the Ontological Argument, which would need to be dealt with in a different way. But I leave that project for another occasion. Although I have not here come close to establishing or very strongly supporting my claim in chapter 14 that there are no good arguments for God's existence, I hope to have sketched out one main way in which such support might be put together.

Notes

1. Schlesinger, *New Perspectives on Old-time Religion*, pp. 130, 133.
2. Paul Edwards, *Reincarnation: a Critical Examination* (Amherst, N.Y.: Prometheus Books, 1996), pp. 301–303.

Appendix G

Some Applications

G.1. Professional

There are at least three sorts of application that my results might have, which I shall label "professional," "personal," and "social-political." By professional applications I mean to refer to discussions in the philosophical literature pertaining to atheological arguments. I hope to have made some contribution to those discussions, despite the fact that the bulk of the book has been focused rather narrowly on AE and ANB as applied to evangelical Christianity. There are various ways that might have been accomplished. First, the issue regarding evangelical Christians is of interest in itself. In the United States and elsewhere, there are very many people in that category, including some professional philosophers. We would certainly want to know of it if all those people are in some way mistaken. Second, the issue has analogues with other viewpoints. For example, FDE as applied to a defense of the God of evangelical Christianity against AE has an analogue in the form of an argument (also called "the Free-will Defense") that defends God in general against AE. I have not explored such analogues in the book at great length, but what I have said provides some suggestions that might be of use in that regard. Finally, AE and ANB are applied to other conceptions of God in chapters 12–14. If there should be any professional philosophers of religion who lack an interest in evangelical Christianity, they should nevertheless find some challenging arguments and connections with their own work in those chapters, and perhaps also in one or more of the above appendices.

The main value of my work may not lie so much in the specific arguments addressed as in certain innovations of approach and methodology. Some examples of those innovations are the following. First, there is the treatment of ANB as a completely separate argument from AE (rather than a "species" of it), as argued in chapter 1. Not even J. L. Schellenberg, who devoted an entire book to a certain version of ANB, viewed it in that way. Although ANB is separate from AE, the two arguments are analogous to one another and might be given parallel treatments. This book serves to illustrate that point.

Second, there is the emphasis on applying AE and ANB to various concepts of God, not just to the God of classical theism. The Basingers are right about the matter: in the problem of evil each separate concept of God should receive its own separate treatment. I would add that the same consideration applies to the problem of nonbelief as well.

Third, my formulation of AE is an innovation. One main difference between it and previous formulations is its distinction between premise (A2) and premise (A3). One benefit derived therefrom is that it makes it easy to say that there is something, X, that God wants but does not bring about because he wants something else even more that conflicts with X. Earlier writers on the subject should have emphasized the idea that God has a conflict of desires, but they lacked a simple conceptual apparatus for bringing that out. The formulation of AE in this book provides such an apparatus. Another benefit is the isolation of premise (A3) as the pivotal issue in the problem of evil. Earlier atheologians who put forward versions of AE (such as J. L. Mackie and H. J. McCloskey) should have expressed something like premise (A3) as one of their assumptions. Had they done so, it would have provided a simpler way to show the futility of maintaining AE as a conclusive proof than some of the other ways that have been used. In any case, it would have made the debate clearer and better focused.

Fourth, the benefits mentioned above also apply to my formulation of ANB, but there the formulation is not so much a revision of previous formulations as a totally new atheological argument. It is true that Schellenberg's book contains an excellent treatment of what might be considered a version of ANB, but it is a version sufficiently different from mine to warrant saying that the two are quite separate arguments. I do not believe that the argument which I have labeled "ANB" in this book appeared previously (apart from my 1993 essay in *Religious Studies*). Perhaps its introduction into the literature of philosophy of religion is my main innovation.

Fifth, my treatment of various defenses against AE is new. I cite, in particular, my treatment of FDE, TDE, the Punishment Defense, ADE, and especially UDE. In fact, there are too many new issues introduced in this book for them to be easily summarized. Philosophers who have done a lot of work on the problem of evil should appreciate the innovations. The various defenses against ANB are also new. Schellenberg does discuss something like FDN in his chapter 5, but his approach to the issues involved is quite different from mine. In any case, my discussions of TDN, ADN, and especially UDN are something new in the literature.

There are other innovations as well, but the above citations should show how the subject matter of the present book has applications to work being done by contemporary philosophers of religion. I regard those applications to be among the most important ones. Although I hope the book will be used as a text in philosophy courses and have appeal to general readers, the way I view the matter, its main value lies in the above-mentioned professional applications.

G.2. Personal

I would say that the book also has personal applications, by which I mean the effects of my arguments on the reader's own life. The subject of atheological arguments is not as dry and dispassionate as some other philosophical issues. It should have some impact on individual attitudes and behavior. Theists who become persuaded by an atheological argument may subsequently give up or reduce their church attendance and support, and may spend less time in prayer. Possibly they may feel less guilt about past actions, which could lead to an improvement in psychological health. That would be especially true regarding transgressions of the first four of the ten commandments, as opposed to transgressions of the latter six. Such people may also experience less apprehension regarding the afterlife, which would also be healthful, both physically and psychologically. But the most important change, as I see it, is in their attitude toward "nonbelievers," i.e., people with a different viewpoint on matters pertaining to God, religion, or life. If those people should be loved ones, then it would be a relief, to say the least, to become rid of an exclusivist outlook regarding them. Many exclusivists feel anguish over loved ones who are nonbelievers and whom they thereby believe are headed for damnation. But even if the nonbelievers are strangers, a change in attitude on the part of theists who come to accept my arguments would be called for and would be important. One long-range purpose of the book is to get theists with a particular religious outlook to be more tolerant of strangers who have a different outlook. I regard that as a generally beneficial effect, should it ever come about.

It may seem that my main target is Christian exclusivism. Certainly that would be the outlook furthest from my own. But even inclusivists could become more tolerant of people with a different religion or philosophy of life if they were to become persuaded of the cogency or strength of some atheological argument(s). Instead of viewing such people as "saved, though misguided," the inclusivists (or former inclusivists) may come to view them as "not so clearly misguided, after all." The whole idea of salvation in the afterlife may even be given up, which to my way of thinking would be progress.

It is possible to construe my atheological arguments (especially ANB) as directed against the God of the Bible, and to be in that respect an attack on Scripture itself. Obviously, if the God of the Bible does not exist, then Scripture is not the "word of God" but only a human creation, and mostly fiction at that. In appendix D, there are additional arguments that aim at the conclusion that the Bible is only a manmade work. Such "Bible-bashing," as it is sometimes called, does have the same sort of aim as mentioned above, in particular, to get evangelical Christians to be more tolerant of those who reject Scripture. Even if the Bible itself is not discarded, there may come to be a clearer understanding of why it is not universally accepted. Just to be able to say, "I disagree with your (errantist) interpretation of those verses, but I can readily understand how you arrived at it" would be progress for some of the more intolerant Bible believers. In any case, ANB (as applied to the God of evangelical Christianity) and the "Bible-bashing" arguments (of appendix D) do have a common aim: greater tolerance among evangelical Christians for people with a quite different worldview.

My treatment of AE and ANB in chapters 12–14 is partly aimed at getting people in certain other groups (Orthodox Jews, liberal Christians, and theists in general) to think about their basic theistic assumptions and perhaps to reevaluate them. It might be objected that it is a bad idea to do anything to incline people toward giving up their religious beliefs, since it may cause them to become immoral. That strikes me as highly unlikely for two reasons. First, the connection between people's religious beliefs and their morality is so very tenuous that for them to give up the former should have no effect on the latter. Some secular humanists would even claim that the effect would go the other way: for people to give up their religious beliefs would actually make them more moral than they were before. I see some merit in such a claim, though I shall not address the issue here. It is enough to point out something well known and that is that many religious people have exhibited immoral (even scandalous) behavior, whereas some of our most morally upright citizens are not religious at all. The second reason is that morality is an expression of concern for others. People who are not sociopaths may have such concern just as a natural part of their mental makeup. Morality may be genetic. It is a feature of many animal species, and obviously has survival value for the group. It is at least in the interest of both society and its members that people cooperate with each other and thereby help foster a general spirit of cooperation within society. That in itself provides sufficient motivation for moral behavior and for the instilling of morality in children. Religious beliefs are not needed. Thus, I have no concern about corrupting my readers. The personal applications of the arguments in this book, as I see them, are all beneficial, at least in the long run. The reasons given above for such an assessment (such as those regarding tolerance of others) are only a few of the many that might be given.

G.3. Social-Political

Closely related to the personal applications of the present book are what I call the social-political applications. They could occur worldwide, but I shall just consider them here from the standpoint of the United States. If the assessments of AE and ANB which I made in chapter 15 were to become generally accepted within the United States, then I would expect that to have certain social effects. Some of the events which would probably occur are the following:

1. less religion-based opposition to
    (a) birth control, abortion, euthanasia, and assisted suicide;
    (b) homosexuality;
    (c) the idea of rights for women, children, and animals;
    (d) divorce;
    (e) sex outside of marriage;
    (f) "adult" literature and media materials;
    (g) sex education in the public schools;
    (h) ideas (including scientific theories) that are incompatible with a literal interpretation of the Bible;
    (i) the principle of separation of church and state;
    (j) secular humanism and other naturalistic ethical systems.
2. less religion-based support for
    (a) the Republican Party and political conservatism generally;
    (b) amending the U.S. Constitution so as to bring it into greater conformity with Christian ideas and ideals;
    (c) laws that help or favor Christianity, such as Sunday "blue" laws;
    (d) overt prayer in the public schools and at public gatherings;
    (e) the Ten Commandments;
    (f) public displays of religious (particularly Christian) symbols;
    (g) censorship of reading material in the public schools;
    (h) the use of tax dollars for educating students in private schools.

Most of these events and situations, I think, would be beneficial for the country. In that way, this book could have beneficial social applications. American society would be improved if my various conclusions were to be generally accepted. The likelihood of that happening in the near future is admittedly low, and so this talk of "social-political applications" is admittedly quite premature. However, I think it worthwhile to acknowledge connections with the world outside academia. Not only do the conclusions of this book have "relevance" (in the 1960s sense), but they have a great potential as well, and that is something worth mentioning.

Bibliography

Adams, Marilyn McCord. "Redemptive Suffering: A Christian Solution to the Problem of Evil." In Robert Audi and William J. Wainwright, eds., *Rationality, Religious Belief, and Moral Commitment*. Ithaca, N.Y.: Cornell University Press, 1986.

———. "Horrendous Evils and the Goodness of God." *Proceedings of the Aristotelian Society, Supplementary Volume* 63 (1989).

Adams, Marilyn McCord, and Robert M. Adams, eds. *The Problem of Evil*. Oxford: Oxford University Press, 1990.

Adams, Robert M. "Must God Create the Best?" *Philosophical Review* 81 (1972).

———. "Middle Knowledge and the Problem of Evil." *American Philosophical Quarterly* 14 (1977).

Alston, William P. "Religious Diversity and Perceptual Knowledge of God." *Faith and Philosophy* 5 (1988).

———. *Divine Nature and Human Language*. Ithaca, N.Y.: Cornell University Press, 1989.

———. "The Inductive Argument from Evil and the Human Cognitive Condition." In Tomberlin, ed., *Philosophical Perspectives*, 5.

Basinger, David. "Evil as Evidence against God's Existence." *The Modern Schoolman* 58 (March 1981).

Basinger, David and Randall. "The Problem with the 'Problem of Evil.'" *Religious Studies* 30 (1994).

Brown, Patterson. "Religious Morality." *Mind* 72 (1963).

Christlieb, Terry. "Which Theisms Face an Evidential Problem of Evil?" *Faith and Philosophy* 9 (1992).

Craig, William Lane. "'No Other Name': A Middle Knowledge Perspective on the Exclusivity of Salvation through Christ." *Faith and Philosophy* 6 (1989).

Crittenden, Charles. "The Argument from Perfection to Existence." *Religious Studies* 4 (1968).

Dilley, Frank B. "Fool-Proof Proofs of God?" *International Journal for Philosophy of Religion* 8 (1977).

Drabkin, Douglas. "The Moralist's Fear of Knowledge of God." *Faith and Philosophy* 11 (1994).

Drange, Theodore M. *Type Crossings*. The Hague: Mouton & Co., 1966.

———. "The Argument from Non-belief." *Religious Studies* 29 (1993).

———. "Biblical Contradictions Regarding Salvation." *Free Inquiry* 14 (Summer 1994).

Edwards, Paul. *Reincarnation: A Critical Examination*. Amherst, N.Y.: Prometheus Books, 1996.

Ewing, A. C. "Meaninglessness." *Mind* 46 (1937).

Fales, Evan. "Should God Not Have Created Adam?" *Faith and Philosophy* 9 (1992).

Gale, Richard M. *On the Nature and Existence of God*. Cambridge: Cambridge University Press, 1991.

Golding, Shmuel. *The Light of Reason*. Vol. 2. Jerusalem: The Jerusalem Institute of Biblical Polemics, 1989.

Hasker, William. "A Refutation of Middle Knowledge." *Nous* 20 (1986).

———. *God, Time, and Knowledge*. Ithaca, N.Y.: Cornell University Press, 1989.

Hepburn, R. W. "From World to God." *Mind* 72 (1963).

Hick, John. *Evil and the God of Love*. New York: Harper & Row, 1966.

———. *An Interpretation of Religion*. New Haven, Conn.: Yale University Press, 1989.

———. *Philosophy of Religion*. 4th ed. Englewood Cliffs, N.J.: Prentice Hall, 1990.

Howard-Snyder, Daniel. "The Argument from Divine Hiddenness." *Canadian Journal of Philosophy* 26 (1996).

———. "The Argument from Inscrutable Evil." In his anthology *The Evidential Argument from Evil*.

———. Review of Schellenberg's *Divine Hiddenness and Human Reason*. *Mind* 104 (1995).

Howard-Snyder, Daniel, ed. *The Evidential Argument from Evil*. Bloomington and Indianapolis: Indiana University Press, 1996.

Keller, James A. "The Hiddenness of God and the Problem of Evil." *International Journal for Philosophy of Religion* 37 (1995).

La Croix, Richard R. *What Is God?* Essays edited by Kenneth G. Lucey. Amherst, N.Y.: Prometheus Books, 1993.

Mackie, J. L. *The Miracle of Theism*. Oxford: Oxford University Press, 1982.

McKim, Robert. "The Hiddenness of God." *Religious Studies* 26 (1990).

———. Review of Schellenberg's *Divine Hiddenness and Human Reason*. *Faith and Philosophy* 12 (1995).

McKinsey, C. Dennis. *The Encyclopedia of Biblical Errancy*. Amherst, N.Y.: Prometheus Books, 1995.

Madden, Edward H., and Peter H. Hare. *Evil and the Concept of God*. Springfield, Ill.: Thomas, 1968.

Martin, Michael. *Atheism: A Philosophical Justification*. Philadelphia: Temple University Press, 1990.

Mattill, A. J., Jr. *The Seven Mighty Blows to Traditional Beliefs.* 2d ed. Gordo, Ala.: The Flatwoods Free Press, 1995.

Mitchell, Basil, ed. *The Philosophy of Religion.* Oxford: Oxford University Press, 1971.

Morris, Henry M. *Many Infallible Proofs.* Rev. ed. Green Forest, Ark.: Master Books, 1996.

Morris, Thomas V. "The Hidden God." *Philosophical Topics* 16 (1988).

————. *Making Sense of It All.* Grand Rapids, Mich.: Eerdmans, 1992.

Nelson, Mark T. "Naturalistic Ethics and the Argument from Evil." *Faith and Philosophy* 8 (1991).

Nielsen, Kai. *An Introduction to the Philosophy of Religion.* New York: St. Martin's Press, 1982.

Penelhum, Terence. *God and Skepticism.* Dordrecht: Reidel, 1983.

————. *Reason and Religious Faith.* Boulder, Col.: Westview Press, 1995.

Peterson, Michael L., ed. *The Problem of Evil: Selected Readings.* Notre Dame, Ind.: University of Notre Dame Press, 1992.

Pinnock, Clark H. "Acts 4:12—No Other Name under Heaven." In William V. Crockett and James G. Sigountos, eds. *Through No Fault of Their Own? The Fate of Those Who Have Never Heard.* Grand Rapids, Mich.: Baker Book House, 1991.

Plantinga, Alvin. *God, Freedom, and Evil.* New York: Harper & Row, 1974.

————. *The Nature of Necessity.* Oxford: Clarendon Press, 1974.

————. "Reason and Belief in God." In Alvin Plantinga and Nicholas Wolterstorff, eds., *Faith and Rationality.* Notre Dame, Ind.: University of Notre Dame Press, 1983.

————. "Self-Profile." In James E. Tomberlin and Peter van Inwagen, eds., *Profiles: Alvin Plantinga.* Boston, Dordrecht, and Lancaster, Pa.: Reidel, 1985.

————. "A Defense of Religious Exclusivism." In Louis J. Pojman, ed., *Philosophy of Religion: An Anthology.* 2d ed. Belmont, Calif.: Wadsworth Publishing Co., 1994.

Price, H. H. "Belief and Will." *Proceedings of the Aristotelian Society, Supplementary Volume* 28 (1954).

Prior, A. N. "Entities." *The Australasian Journal of Philosophy* 32 (1954).

Puccetti, Roland. "The Loving God: Some Observations on Hick's Theodicy." *Religious Studies* 2 (1967).

Reichenbach, Bruce R. *Evil and a Good God.* New York: Fordham University Press, 1982.

Rowe, William L. "The Problem of Evil and Some Varieties of Atheism." *American Philosophical Quarterly* 16 (1979).

————. "Evil and the Theistic Hypothesis: A Response to Wykstra." *International Journal for Philosophy of Religion* 16 (1984).

Russell, Bruce. "Defenseless." In Howard-Snyder, ed., *The Evidential Argument from Evil.*

Sanders, John. *No Other Name: An Investigation into the Destiny of the Unevangelized.* Grand Rapids, Mich.: Eerdmans, 1992.

Schellenberg, J. L. *Divine Hiddenness and Human Reason.* Ithaca, N.Y.: Cornell University Press, 1993.

Schellenberg, J. L. "Response to Howard-Snyder." *Canadian Journal of Philosophy* 26 (1996).

Schlesinger, George. *Religion and Scientific Method.* Dordrecht: Reidel, 1977.

———. *New Perspectives on Old-time Religion.* Oxford: Oxford University Press, 1988.

Sproul, R. C. *If There's a God, Why Are There Atheists?* Wheaton, Ill.: Tyndale House Publishers, 1988.

Stump, Eleonore. "Knowledge, Freedom, and the Problem of Evil." In Peterson, ed., *The Problem of Evil: Selected Readings.*

Swinburne, Richard. *Faith and Reason.* Oxford: Oxford University Press, 1981.

———. *The Existence of God.* Rev. ed. Oxford: Oxford University Press, 1991.

Talbott, Thomas. "The Doctrine of Everlasting Punishment." *Faith and Philosophy* 7 (1990).

———. "Three Pictures of God in Western Theology." *Faith and Philosophy* 12 (1995).

Tomberlin, James E., ed., *Philosophical Perspectives, 5, Philosophy of Religion.* Atascadero, Calif.: Ridgeview Publishing Co., 1991.

Van Inwagen, Peter. "The Problem of Evil, the Problem of Air, and the Problem of Silence." In Tomberlin, ed., *Philosophical Perspectives, 5.*

———. "Reflections on the Chapters by Draper, Russell, and Gale." In Howard-Snyder, ed., *The Evidential Argument from Evil.*

Wainwright, William J. *Philosophy of Religion.* Belmont, Calif.: Wadsworth, 1988.

Wykstra, Stephen J. "The Humean Obstacle to Evidential Arguments from Suffering: On Avoiding the Evils of 'Appearance.'" *International Journal for the Philosophy of Religion* 16 (1984).

———. "Rowe's Noseeum Arguments from Evil." In Howard-Snyder, ed., *The Evidential Argument from Evil.*

Index